The Aspen Kid:

Growing Up In Aspen, Colorado in the Fifties and Sixties

by Terry Morse

To Danny: I know
Hope you enjoy these "
vignettes of The "old days"
in Aspen
Terry Morse

ISBN: 978-0-9910293-1-0

Dexter A. Morse
PO Box 367
Moab, UT 84532
theaspenkid@gmail.com

Cover Design by eBook Cover Designs
eBook-coverdesigns.com

Cover Photo by Franz Berko
Terry and Wendy 1949

Dedication

These remembered vignettes are for Anne Vitte, the love of my life, Sine, Natasha and Hesse, our global children, and for their children here and to come - Mia, Max and Zayne. And of course for my extended family who made it all happen...

ACKNOWLEDGEMENTS

Having this much fun remembering "the good old days" could never have happened without the quiet patience of my wife, Anne Vitte. Her encouragement and forbearance gave me the room needed to record these vignettes some semblance of understandable order.

Many others of you have helped me in numerous ways, some profoundly. You know who you are and I am indebted for you guidance, suggestions and critique.

Kudos to daughter Natasha, Ann-Toy Broughton, and Kathy Grossman who did the first complete read through, helped with the final edits and followed up with their input. More kudos to the Moab Poets and Writers group who suffered through my reading of some of the earlier chapters of the book. A hearty thanks to Ann Gordon who helped me through the maze of putting the book in a format for publishing.

Thanks to Tony Vagneur and Cherie Gerbaz Oates who provided me with background material that helped fill in some of the events and names forgotten or misplaced.

Finally, my appreciation to all the Aspen folks of the Fifties and Sixties who endured me as "one of those Morse boys." In one way or another we all are inevitably a large part of the environment we grew up in. What we do with that in the end is up to us.

The Aspen Kid

...(the star-child) waited, marshaling
His thoughts and brooding over his still untested
powers.
For though he was a master of the world, he was not
quite sure what to do next.
But he would think of something.
~ Arthur C. Clarke

Prologue

This is the story of a boy who grew from infancy to
adolescence in a little mining town in the Colorado Rockies.
That boy was me. I tell this story in that voice - and the voice
I grew into. I write from the memories that linger in my
mind.

We moved to Aspen, Colorado in early March of 1946,
when I had reached the tender age of six months. I, in my
mother's arms, was accompanied by my father and two older
brothers who shared the early days with me. My parents left
the comforts and predictability of a life on the East Coast for
a life of adventure and misadventure in the post-War West.

What follows are vignettes of my growing up in the
hardscrabble '50s as Aspen turned from penniless to pricey,
from a ghost-filled mining town to one of the world's most
glamour-filled ski resorts.

Late summer 1949

I am running for my life. I am not quite four years old,
and I have just done something wrong, something very bad

which, in my panic, I cannot remember. I only know that my life is in very real peril. My mother is coming after me in a fit of anger. I feel the hollowness of impending doom. I am in flight-or-fight mode before I have ever learned that term. Flight now. Perhaps fight later.

I feel my legs pumping, my heartbeats resounding in my ears, and my fear making my skin cold even in the autumn heat. Normally my mother relies on my dad to dole out the day's punishment when he comes home at sunset. Today is different. I have crossed some indefinable line and my mother is in a fury I have never seen upon her before. She is heavy with my baby sister who will be born into this godforsaken dangerous life in four or five more months. Little does baby sister know the trials that await her.

As young as I am, I have managed to stay ahead of the rage pursuing me. Around the west side of the house. Past the huge cottonwood tree. Around the corner to the south side of the house, past the gardens of shasta daisies and the clothesline. Only a few steps to the far southeast corner of the house. Another cottonwood tree looms there. I can feel the brush of the shasta daises on my arm as I pass them. Even in my panic, they feel soft. The daisies reach out and touch the length of my arm as if to tell me everything will work out. But I know it won't.

As I bound along the length of the house like a spooked deer, I remember myself and why I am running. I have killed one of the chickens. Even though an unintentional act, it is a serious one because we need the eggs, the chickens, and all the luck and good fortune we can get. But my mother is not chasing me for the murder. She is chasing me because I have left the evidence of my crime on her newly washed sheets hanging on the clothesline.

~~~

This particular disaster began when I was on the roof of the garage by myself. I'd been hunting for metal washers and nuts to throw. I didn't find enough, so the next best thing I could find were the river rocks dug from the cobble on the hillside for the garage foundation. I managed to lug a handful of roundish rocks up on the roof and was throwing them down toward the log shack, judging my performance by how high they hit on the shack's roof. I was about to move on to other more interesting projects when I decided to throw one final round.

I had climbed down off the roof and wandered toward the chicken coop, gathering up three or four of the largest rocks that would fit in my pockets. I started chucking them at the coop hoping to land one over the wire and into the chicken yard. The first rock performed well. It hit the wire fence about a foot below the top; the next two did as well. The fourth rock was charmed. It sailed upward in a great arc. A fencepost made from ragged old wood my dad had scavenged stood between me and the coop. The fourth rock slammed into the fencepost, took a mighty jump, bounced high into the air and fell toward the ground. I congratulated myself. The rock was going to clear the fence and land in the chicken yard.

Then horror filled me. I saw the stone was headed for the middle of the chickens that were clucking cheerfully and pecking at some leftover feed. My missile scored a direct hit on the head of a large white hen named Minnie. She fell to the ground on her side. Blood seeped from her head.

I scrambled to the coop gate, opened it, and scurried inside. Minnie was bleeding from her mouth and from the head wound. There was no movement in her limp body, no last flickers of life to give me some indication I had not killed her. No, she was as still as a stone. I picked her up, hoping against hope. To no avail. She was warm and very dead – and bleeding all over my hand and arm.

I gazed around in panic. What could I do? I knew that all hell was going to break loose in a few hours when my dad got home. I'd heard one of my dad's friends say once that desperate times call for desperate acts. I wasn't completely sure what it meant, but I knew I felt desperate. I knew I'd have to rise to the occasion. My plan evolved: Place Minnie next to the fence on the west side where the coyotes have been digging under the fence. Escape from the coop. Make sure to close the gate. Then run for it. Get as far away as possible.

I finished Phase One of the plan. On to Phase Two. What was I to do with all the evidence of blood on my hands? The wash had just been hung out and was still wet enough for me to clean up on one of the bed sheets hanging there. Evidence staged, evidence erased, the perfect crime. Maybe it would be okay.

It was time for other distractions. How about a trip to my fort, slaying a few Indians or perhaps outlaws, on my way to deliver a secret message from headquarters? I sauntered off to the front of the house, intending to amble up toward the oak brush on the hillside to my fort. I wasn't far away from the clothesline when my mom burst out the front door yowling like a fiend. There had been a witness! My mother had seen me from her bedroom window, wiping my hand on the newly washed sheets.

I shifted into flight mode and headed back the way I came. My strategy gave me a tiny head start.

"You little turd! If I catch you I'll kill you," I hear behind me. "Don't you know I'm pregnant? I'll lose the baby if I have to chase your little ass around this house. You just wait until your father gets home!"

Uh oh, I tell myself. *This could really be trouble.*

Rounding the corner on the east side of the house, and sliding between it and the lilac tree, I enter the small grass corridor separating the two, and a flash of realization explodes in my mind. In that instant the knowledge that I must take care of myself overwhelms me. No one is going to take care of me, not even my mom who is now going to kill me if she catches me. My survival in this world will be up to me. It is a choice I must make. Only I can do it, that is, live my life. Rounding this corner has set me free from the wrath of my fearsome pursuer for the moment and free from the notion that others control my survival forever.

I have outrun her. Impending punishment will not come for a long time in the future. It is still early in the day. I slow to a walk and drop over the bank bordering our house, heading down toward the river to ponder new realizations about myself, my life and my future. For this moment I am independent and free.

Chapter 1

Easton, Connecticut

Early October 1946

Edward Wendell Morse III is sitting behind his desk at work. It is afternoon and on top of the mass of shuffled paperwork on his desk sits the model of a clipper ship. Balsa wood, razor blades, and thread are scattered haphazardly around the hull of the vessel. "Wendy," as he is known, is absorbed in his work and does not hear the gentle knock on the doorframe of his office.

"Wendy?" a voice says.

My dad looks up, flushes red, and says, "Oh, hello sir. I was just taking a late lunch and am finishing up on this lower spar."

The model tools disappear into the desk drawer. The model finds a place on a bookshelf where it will later be made to reappear the instant there is privacy in the office.

"Wendy," the president of the Bridgeport Trust Company says, "I have been watching your progress as a mortgage loan officer here at the bank and am wondering if perhaps you should take a few months off and decide if banking is really the career you want to pursue. I appreciate your service to the country in the Pacific on the battleship USS New Jersey, but the War is over now, and it's time for the country to get back on its feet. This means we all have to use our talents in the best way we can. If you had time to think…"

"Well, as a matter of fact, I was just going to talk to you about that," my dad cuts in. "I've been thinking maybe Rudy and I should take a trip out West and see what opportunities are there before we get too far down the road here. I would appreciate the opportunity for a short sabbatical to take a look."

"Why don't you do that. I'll hold your job for three months. If you decide you want to continue with the Trust Company, you'll be welcome, if not, then no hard feelings."

"Thanks. Would it be inconvenient if I started tomorrow?"

Both men laugh, and the arrangement is in place.

Later that day, my dad returns home and as he crosses the threshold of their Easton Connecticut home, he shouts, "Rudy!"

Ruth Ann Bryant comes from the kitchen where she is trying to figure out how to use a new MixMaster that her father, Waldo Gerald Bryant, or Popeye as he is called, has given her.

"Hi," she says. "Aren't you home a little early?"

"Yep. Pack your bags, we're headed West to see if we can find a ranch!"

"But, Wendy," she says, "I have to finish cooking dinner. Can it wait until after?"

Several days later they leave me, barely out of the womb, and my two brothers, with our mom's parents, Popeye Bryant and his wife Syl, and set out on their search for a homestead suitable to bring up a young family. Their travels take them to the Roaring Fork Valley and a little defunct mining town named Aspen, in the heart of the White River National Forest in Central Colorado.

Aspen, Colorado

Early October 1946

My dad had an adventurer's heart and brain from the time he'd been a kid. His family had been devastated by the

Great Depression. Through the quick wit and hard work of my grandmother, my dad, at the age of thirteen, ended up as a scholarship student at the Fenn School, a boy's prep school in Concord, Massachusetts, just outside of Boston. When summer came around after his second year at Fenn, he was invited by one of the masters to work on a dude ranch in San Cristobal, New Mexico. My dad had already reached his full 6' 2" with the weight to match.

He arrived at the ranch in mid June with eight other youngsters and worked all summer with the schoolmaster and his gang of the kids. In the fall it was back to Fenn for the school year. The following summer he returned to San Cristobal. By then my dad was almost sixteen and more mature than most of his Eastern peers. Hard days of ranch work, the southwest sun, and the New Mexican señoritas had tempered him—often blissfully—into a young adult. That fall of 1937, his return trip east to Fenn took him through the Roaring Fork Valley.

He drove from New Mexico to Colorado over Colbank, Molass, and Red Mountain passes to find himself overnighting in Delta, Colorado. He then decided to go off route and drive from Delta to Glenwood Springs, then to Aspen, over the 12,000-foot Independence Pass to Leadville and on in to Denver from there. While passing through Aspen, he fell in love with the magic of the Colorado Rockies and the most beautiful valley he had ever seen. He promised himself to return.

~~~

Now, almost ten years later, he and my mom are in the Roaring Fork Valley looking for a ranch to buy. It has been a disappointing four or five days. Because the War is over, optimism has set in and all the ranchers are looking forward to better times. They have spoken to all the ranching families—the Vagneurs, the Trentaz clan, the Marolts, the Cerices—no one wants to sell. Disappointed, he and mom are driving back toward Glenwood Springs and are crossing the Maroon Creek Bridge about two miles out of Aspen. The bridge was an old railroad trestle for the Midland Railroad back in the mining days and has been refurbished with a 4" x 10" timber road surface that rattles as they drive over it. My dad drives up behind a youth on a horse-driven hay wagon. At the end of the bridge my dad pulls him over.

"Hey, Sonny," my dad says, "Do you know anyone who wants to sell their ranch?"

The teen glares down at my dad. "Hell, I don't know, Mister, but I heard my old man say this morning that for two bits he would sell the whole goddamned spread."

"Really," my dad says, "and where would that spread be?"

"It's the Lazy Chair Ranch. Right up that dirt road about a half a mile or so."

"I think I'll go up and talk to him," my dad says half to himself.

"Suit yourself," the teen says and slaps the reins on the horses to get them moving up the road.

My dad and mom drive their old Dodge up the road which borders Maroon Creek some two hundred feet below them, around a bend, past a ramshackled ranch house, and out into the barnyard where they find Art Roberts swearing up a blue streak at a recalcitrant mare he is trying to head into the corral. "Goddamsumavabitchin no good motherofaturd, get your sorry ass in there before I take you to the glue factory! And what the hell do you want, Mister?"

"Like to buy your spread," my dad says.

"How much you willing to pay?" old man Roberts snaps.

"How much you want?"

Not more than fifteen minutes later they have a handshake deal. Art Roberts has a one hundred dollar bill in his left hand as earnest money. My Dad has a grin on his face.

My mom looks a little stunned. They drove East knowing they'd be back to this eight-hundred-acre spread. To start a new life.

~ ~ ~

Six months later they pull into the spread with inspiration, energy, a dream, and three rambunctious young boys. Almost immediately they begin patching up the old ranch house, repairing the outbuildings, and generally cleaning the place up so it can be run as a productive eight-hundred-acre ranch.

One of the first things they do is add another bedroom to the house on the east ground floor level of the house. This serves as their master bedroom. Along with this addition they put in a septic tank and leach field to bring the plumbing indoors and get rid of the "one holer" that commands obverse prominence in the front yard. Once the house is livable, they turn their attention to the barn and the outbuildings. Over time, they tear down some of the dilapidated buildings and repair others. They leave the barn, which is in good condition as it is.

By the summer of 1950 they are ready to build a garage that will never be used as a garage. It is built on the hillside next to the chicken coop. Actually, it is built into the hillside because old Adair Rippy, the Cat skinner from down in Newcastle, came up with his Cat and dug out a hole in the hillside for the backside of the garage to sit in. They poured concrete walls coming out from the hill. The back of the roof to the north was only a foot or two above the ground where it ran into the hillside, making it easy for us kids to climb on. Aunt Mary Leigh, dad's sister, who was visiting us that summer, had finished shingling the roof and was going home to Concord Massachusetts, not long after. Me and my brothers had some great times rolling left-over nuts and washers down the roof and watching them skip and bounce off the roof's edge.

Next to the garage are two log buildings: the old log shack closest to the garage is a place where Art Roberts stored a bunch of junk, and the one to the west is used as a chicken coop. It has a high wire fence surrounding it so the chickens cannot fly out.

It was this very chicken coop that is the scene of the crime I am now running from.

Chapter 2

Lazy Chair Ranch 1947

My first memory in this life is when I am somewhere around six months old. Later in life I will come to wonder who can say how much of memory is ours and how much our minds fill in from oral history related by friends and loved ones to make up the story that is our lives, perhaps recreating our past to fit our present? I am certain of this much: I am in my mother's arms, one of my few memories of her holding or hugging me. She is carrying me into the kitchen of our ranch house. There is a presence on the kitchen counter that I later will have learned to call a chicken. The "chicken" flies off the counter and onto the floor. Mother is making noises, and the chicken is running.

Winter 1948

It is the winter of 1948. Our house has a small stoop with a shed roof attached to it that covers the front door. This shed roof is shallow. The rooflines on the rest of the house are very steep. Under the stoop, the front door leads to the kitchen, a small and dark room with only one window to the north and one to the west. Adjacent to the kitchen is a small living room, a bedroom, and a set of stairs going up to two small bedrooms. There is a screened porch running the length of the west side of the small structure.

I share one of the upstairs bedrooms with my brother Teddy who is two years older. He—as I would learn later in my tender life—is an instigator, and my mom's favorite of us three boys. Mom has put us down for an afternoon nap. It has become our routine: an afternoon nap for an hour and a half whether we are tired or not. It is apparent that the nap is not for us kids, rather for my mother who, by noon each day, is feeling the effects of three rambunctious boys born two years apart. At this point in my life I am learning to love my solitude. Naps are not a problem for me. If rest is not needed, my travels in fantasyland fill the time wonderfully.

This particular afternoon I am eighteen months old, and my brother is three and a half. We are in our bedroom upstairs and are not in the mood for sleeping. My brother Teddy has begun mastering the art of speech. Using what he still remembers of his baby language, adult language, and sign language, he makes me understand that there is trouble to be made.

He points to the framed picture of Mickey Mouse above my crib. By some child-weird communication, he entreats me to regard the lithograph with a new appreciation of what can be done if one were to use his creativity. Once my attention is drawn to the picture, I (an apt student and quick learner) take it from there. I stand on my tippy-toes and, with one hand on the side of my crib and the other flailing in the air, manage to neatly knock the picture off its mount. It crashes most satisfactorily down on the corner post of the crib with a noise that excites my young impressionable mind.

My brother grins his goofy grin. I look at him for direction and see he is giving me that "your ass is in deep shit for knocking the picture off the wall and breaking glass all over the sheets of your crib" look. He's no help. He just stands on the side of his bed with that stupid grin on his face. Getting nothing but the grin and a few "uh-oh's you're in trouble now" looks, I turn to other pursuits.

About that time I realize that my "ass is in deep shit" in more than one way. My diaper is filled with the real thing. The smell of it has captivated my imagination and it is time to investigate. The diaper is loose, so is not hard to get off.

Once I have removed myself from its restrictions and have spilled its contents out onto the crib sheets, I begin my exploration. I have no tools to poke it, so I take up a piece of the broken glass and begin stabbing at the smelly pile. Soon the brown is changing to red and my hand is beginning to hurt. I smell the distinct scent of blood mixed with the stench of the feces and deduce that something is most definitely out of order. Here I am taking a nap and because of my prodding and instigating brother, my senseless curiosity and my refusal to go to sleep, my whole afternoon has literally turned to shit. I begin to cry. Sobbing and letting out a long wail I bring my hands to my face to rub my tears away. Now tears, blood, and feces are spread all over the bedding, my undershirt, and my face.

More trouble to my already shitty afternoon arrives immediately. Between my heaving sobs and through copious tears, I see my mom rushing into the room. Her voice hurts my ears. I feel myself being whisked out of the crib and plopped on the floor. I don't need a big vocabulary to know she is furious.

At first I feel proud of my explorations, then almost immediately I feel abandoned. I am sitting here on the floor, my brother feigning sleep, and my mother is more interested in changing the bed linens than she is in extracting the fecal matter from my nose, mouth, and hands. I think hard. I suddenly realize that it is my choice to actually nap at naptime, not the whim of my mother. Mickey Mouse has taught me the world is a place of great possibilities but one that will demand great creativity. I also realize I do not like being dependent on my mother to clean my face and hands and want badly to do it myself.

Summer 1949

I am almost three years old. It is morning and I am walking across the barnyard with a basket, headed out to the chicken coop. It is a long walk for me. The barnyard is a big space of dirt on the west side of our house between the hitching post where we tie up our horses and the barn. The barn is a beautiful old two-story building of sun-beaten wood, magnificent with rich browns, reddish browns, tinges of grays and yellows. The chicken coop is a dumpy little brown-and-grey sun-dried log structure with few redeeming features. The best part of it is probably the chicken wire fence surrounding the chicken yard.

I'm walking toward the barn and on my left-hand side there is our pond with fish and salamanders and things. On my right-hand side is the chicken coop between the house and the barn at the base of the "hill," a small knoll to the north of the house that borders the length of the barnyard and then drops down to the lower fields. The hill is high enough to block the view of the ranches across the valley on McLain Flats and Woody Creek. On the south side where it borders our house and the barnyard, it is covered with low-lying sage, grasses, wildflowers, and some gambrel oak bushes. The garage has not been built on the hill yet, but my dad is talking about building it next summer.

I have chores to do on the ranch. Collecting eggs from the chicken coop is one of them. The chickens sometimes frighten me, but most of the time I feel okay around them. The roosters are the bad ones. Our three sheep dogs are with me: Peter, Pan, and Wendy. We call Peter "Dirty Peter Morse" because he is always getting into hay and mud and all sorts of stuff. They sometimes come along to see if one of the chickens will spring free when the low gate is opened. Carefully I open the coop gate and shut it behind me so the dogs won't get in. They watch me as I collect the eggs and count each one as it is laid in my basket. There are fourteen of them, one for each hen. No one knows I can count. It is one of the many things I keep safe within myself.

The barnyard dirt is red and rocky. The stones are flat or round and sometimes there are washers and an occasional nail to be found. Today there is nothing of interest. I take the eggs back to the house and give them to my mom.

"This afternoon, after your father gets home, you and your brothers are going to help us rake the hay," she says to me as she takes the basket.

I do not say anything but head outside to spend my day wandering around the ranch with Peter, Pan, and Wendy. They are Border Collies and my friends. All three are black and white. Peter has a little brown fur just next to his nose. Peter and Pan are married and Wendy is their son. We do lots of things together on the ranch. They like to come with me whenever I go wandering unless they are hungry, then they hang around the house because they know it's about mealtime, usually early morning and at night.

It is early afternoon when I return from somewhere, dogs following, to get something to fill my empty belly. My dad has just returned home and is getting ready to hook up the old hay rake to the Jeep. He has driven the Jeep out into the barnyard where my two brothers are standing. I watch a few minutes, then I head for the house and find my mom getting ready to go out to the barnyard. I convince her to get me something to eat. She slaps together a peanut-butter-and-jam sandwich on Wonder Bread. We walk across the barnyard, me munching my sandwich as we go. Dad has finished hooking up the hay rake, and we all get in the Jeep. My dad boosts me into the back over the tailgate and sits me next to my middle brother, Teddy. There is no top on the Jeep, and there are two back seats facing each other, running from the driver and passenger seats to back to the tail end of the Jeep. We are seated in on one of these seats, me next to the tailgate.

The Jeep bounces down the road headed for the "bottom field" on the north side of the ranch, next to

Highway 82, where my dad and my oldest brother, Gerry, have laid down a large area of hay. The cut hay has dried for a week and is ready to rake and bale. We drive to the lower side of the field, and my dad gets out to work the mechanism on the huge steel hay harrow, which drops the large C-shaped steel rods. It makes the machine appear to have teeth. There is a seat on the machine that someone is supposed to sit on if it is being pulled by horses. Since we are pulling it with the Jeep no one has to sit there.

My dad gets back in the Jeep and begins to bounce around the field with the rake. I notice the hay is flat. When the rake has gone over it, the hay ends up in piles that form rows. This is interesting to me for some time. Finally I tire from trying to figure out how the machine works. The rocking of the Jeep and hum of the motor is relaxing. I stick my thumb in my mouth and nod off to sleep. I feel myself falling and awake with a thump and pain. Lots of pain. I cannot move. I can smell the hay around me. I open my eyes and see the steel beast above me. I hear my mother screaming.

"Wendy! Wendy!" she screams.

My lungs are on fire. I can no longer smell the hay. My head feels like it is going to burst. Everything is blackness.

I wake in my bed. My neck and back are very sore. I see it is dark out as I look out the window. I can smell dinner. I hear my mom coming upstairs, my dad behind her. I know the sound of their feet. Mom comes into the room with a tray.

"How are you feeling?" she says. "I brought you some dinner in case you're hungry."

My dad puts his hand on my forehead. "He doesn't have a fever," he says to my mom. "I think he'll be all right."

I look at them. I'm not hungry, so I close my eyes and go back to sleep.

It will be five years before I can piece together the whole story. I had fallen asleep in the back of the Jeep and fallen out. My mother screamed as she saw me fall. My dad stopped the Jeep. The wheel of the huge machine was resting across my neck, cutting off my air. I had turned purple and did not seem to be breathing. My dad jumped from the Jeep and ran to the hay rake. In one huge thrust of adrenaline, muscle, and fury, he lifted the wheel from my neck and with one foot kicked me out from under the hay rake. Gerry told me later my dad tried to lift the wheel of the hay rake sometime he ran over me and could not get it off the ground.

~ ~ ~

It's been awhile since I fell out of the Jeep. There are some men coming to the house every day to help dad do something with the house. They drive up the road every morning in two beat-up old trucks. They come from Aspen down Highway 82 for a couple of miles and turn up our road which follows the edge of the steep embankment dropping down into Maroon Creek. Our road is pretty long, maybe more than half a mile. When they get to our house and park out in front of it, they say, "Damn if that road isn't the bumpiest, dustiest road in the valley."

They are building another room on the east side of the house where mom and dad will sleep when the baby is born. Right now they sleep in the room downstairs, and us three boys sleep upstairs. Gerry has his room, and Ted and I sleep in the same room. This is the second time they are adding on to the house. The first time I don't remember because it was right when we got here.

Dad is helping the workmen. Right now the plumbers and electricians are putting pipes and wires in the walls. I am having lots and lots of fun watching them. It's not time for lunch yet, but I'm hungry. I know where I can get some food because, for the last couple of days I have been hungry before lunch and have gotten some food out of the lunch boxes that the workmen leave under the cottonwood tree where they sit to eat. I have found a peanut butter sandwich in one, some cookies in another, and some crackers in another one.

I head around to the south side of the house to find the lunchboxes. I'll just have a little snack. As I reach the tree I see them there, just waiting for me to explore them. I go for the black one first. That's where I've been finding the peanut butter sandwiches. I kneel down in the grass and open the box. Just as I am about to take the sandwich out of the waxed paper I hear, "Goddamn it you little shit! What the hell are you doing eating my lunch!"

Uh oh, I think. *Here we go.*

I stand up and start to run away around the side of the house. Before I have gone two steps, a strong hand grabs me by the arm and nearly pulls me over.

"Whaddya think you're doin'?" the burly Dean Gordier says.

"Nothin'."

"We'll just see about that."

He grabs me by the arm and walks me around to the other side of the house where the workmen are with my dad.

"Wendy," Dean Gordier says. "I like working for you, but this has gotta stop."

"What's that?" my dad asks.

"For the last two or three days I haven't had any lunch because this little hellion has been eating it."

"So that's where my cookies have been going," says Kenny Broughton, the electrician.

I can see there is no way out of this one. There's going to be hell to pay.

"You been eating their lunches?" dad says sternly.

"Yes, Sir."

"Well, that has to stop."

"Yes, Sir."

"I'm going to deal with you later. Now go into the house and get your mom to fix you lunch. It's almost lunchtime anyway."

I can tell he is mad. I head inside and find mom. I ask her to make me a sandwich. She does. After I have finished eating I head back outside and find Dirty Peter Morse home for a change. I decide we should go out to the barnyard where, if by some strange circumstance we get in trouble, there won't be anyone around to see it. On the way to the barn, I stop to throw some rocks in the pond and watch the ripples go out in concentric circles across the still water.

In a short while the pond is too full of ripples to track the ones from the rock just thrown, so I wander up to the chicken coop to see what is going on there. Dirty Peter follows me, his long pink tongue flopping out the side of his mouth. We stop in front of the fence. Peter sits on his haunches and scratches his ear with one paw, then sits there panting. I look in at the chickens. They are all scratching around for something to eat, sometimes finding a grain seed or something and sometimes pecking at each other. This soon becomes boring so we head back to the house to see what the workmen are doing. I can hear them banging nails as I get closer and am a bit curious about that because I've only heard them drilling holes all morning.

I round the big rock by the driveway and head over to the east side of the house. I see they have built something that looks like a big square box. I move closer until I am up next to it and ask Kenny Broughton, "What is that?"

"It's a cage," he says.

"A cage?" I ask him, now curious.

"Yep."

"We've made a special cage to catch a special kind of animal."

About that time Dean Gordier comes up and nails a board on the side of the cage that had some words painted on it. I can tell the paint is still wet because it smells and shines in the sun.

"What kind of animal?" I ask.

"You." Dean Gordier says. He picks me up and puts me inside the box and plops the roof on top. I'm standing in the middle looking out through the bars, stunned.

"Now maybe you'll stay out of my lunch box," he says.

Kenny Broughton is laughing.

"That's a good place for the little rascal. What did you put on the sign?"

"Lion's Den," says Dean.

I am silent. I'm so surprised to be trapped in the cage, barred on all sides and the top I don't know whether to cry or holler or what.

My dad comes around the corner with a large 2 x 4 on his shoulder.

"What's this?" he says to the workmen. "It looks like a cage, and..." he looks at the sign on the outside "it looks like you caught the lion. That's probably a good place for him."

He looks at me and says, "Well, Terr-Ass, guess you won't be eating the men's lunches anymore." Then he walks over to the sawhorse, picks up the handsaw, and begins work like nothing has happened. It is late in the afternoon when I am released from my bondage. Dad walks by the cage and lifts the top off.

"Guess you can come out of there now. It's quittin' time. You might be smart to keep your distance unless you want to spend more time in the cage."

"Yep," I say, even though I know that would never be possible. I face it: I would have to both run for my freedom or be caged up if I am to satisfy my curiosity as to how all of these things go together to make a room on a house.

Chapter 3

Early Winter 1949

My mom is putting some clothes and boxes in the closet next to her room. She is packing up the important things in the house because we are going to live in Aspen for the winter. She is now big in the belly with my little sister, much bigger than in the summer or fall. The closet is small and is filled with the old brick chimney that goes through it up to the roof. The only other closets downstairs are my parents bedroom closet and the broom closet in the hallway by the screened-in porch.

Mom is singing to the music she is playing on an old phonograph she has brought from the East. I hear her singing,

"I'm as corny as Kansas in August

High as a kite on the Fourth of July

If you'll excuse the expression I use

I'm in love, I'm in love,

I'm in love, I'm in love

With a wonderful guy!"

I know this song is from a play or something back East because she has told me so.

"Why are you moving your dresses out of your closet?" I ask.

She looks down at me and says, "Because we are not going to be living in the house this winter, and I need to put my clothes away so the renters can have a closet for their clothes."

This does not sound good to me.

"What are renters?"

"They are people who are paying us to use our house for the winter. We will be moving into town so they can have our house," she explains.

"Where are they going to sleep?" I ask.

"They will sleep in our bedrooms," she replies.

I don't say anything because it is hard to understand how anyone is going to live in our bedrooms with us. They are already so small. I am sleeping in the same room with my brother. It does not seem like they can fit anyone else in the room with us.

"There's not enough space in our room for more people," I say.

"Of course there is. You and Teddy are not going to be sleeping there. You will be sleeping in the house we are using in town," she explains. "It will be fun. You will get to play in town and see more of Aspen. Besides I need to be closer to town when this baby is born so I can go to the hospital," she continues.

I look at her belly. It is definitely much larger. I decide she really is going to have a baby. Being in town may be fun if there is enough snow. I let it drop.

February 1950

I am supposed to be taking a nap. We are at the Hume's house in Aspen. The Humes have let us borrow the house for the winter while my mom has her baby. We have rented our house on the ranch to some people. I hate my borrowed room. It has wallpaper on the walls. The wallpaper is blue. There are patterns that remind me of gigantic spiders. I am counting them. I can count to twenty but that is as far as I want to go. I know what is after twenty. Thirty. Then forty.

It is afternoon. The sun is shining through the white curtains. They are made of a material that tears easily. I know this because I have already poked my finger through one of them. On the windowsill is a blue bottle. It is the color of the bottle that Kayopectate comes in. When I had diarrhea last summer, my dad gave me a spoonful of the nasty-tasting stuff, and it was in a blue bottle. This bottle is really blue. I get off the bed and put my face close up to the bottle to see if I can see through it. The sun is behind the bottle when I am looking at it, so all I can see is blue. I love blue. It is a beautiful color that makes me feel peaceful. I like blue glass too. I wonder who put the empty bottle on the windowsill. There is snow outside on the ground. It comes almost up to the window.

I am finished looking through the bottle. I open the door to my room and go quietly into the living room and over to the bedroom door of my mom and dad's room. It is slightly open, and my mom is on the bed holding something. I push the door open a bit more to see if I can tell what she is holding. The door makes a squeak, and the floor creaks as I move forward.

"Terry, is that you?" I hear the voice but do not answer, hoping I will not be discovered out of my room before naptime is over.

"Terry, is that you? Open the door so I can see you. Now!" she demands.

Slowly I open the door and walk forward.

"What are you doing?" I say to take her attention from me as I edge closer to take a look at what is going on. But I know what is going on. Her breast is bare and she is nursing my baby sister.

She sees me staring and says in a voice too hard and flat for me to take it as endearment, "I'm feeding the baby. Now you get out of here and back to your room. Out. Out, damn it! You'll give her colic!"

I turn to leave. I was supposed to be a girl. Even before I was born she bought me pink baby clothes. She bought me a pink baby book. She has her girl now, and I know that there will be tectonic shifts in the world of Terry. I take one last look. My sister at the breast, the white, wrinkled bed covers over my mom's feet, her hair just so, and her eyes looking down in a way I have never seen her look at me. I do not care, but I do notice it. Somehow deep within me I know I have never been nursed as my sister has.

"Humpf," I think.

Chapter 4

Summer 1950

I'm kicking rocks across the barnyard, counting the number of times it takes to kick a rock from the hitching post by the house clear across the barnyard to the steps that lead up into the shop. The shop smells of horseshit, oil, and metal filings. I'm sad because I can't help build the garage. I'm trying not to pay much attention to the garage as it is being built into the side of the hill, now with Mary Leigh and my mom putting shingles on the roof. Of course Teddy gets to help. Who knows where Gerry is. Jennifer is sleeping in the baby carriage inside the garage.

The hole cut in the hillside for the garage was dug some time ago. Adair Rippy was up there with his dig-dig getting the sides just so and the ground leveled for the floor. Then the concrete floor was poured. When the walls were formed, they had the smell of oil that was painted on the wood before they were set in place and braced, ready for the concrete. On top of the concrete walls they framed the half walls and built them up to the roof ledger where the rafters would sit. I saw my dad and a couple of guys putting up the rafters, one up on the ridgeline nailing, and one down on the ledger nailing, while a third held the long plank of wood in place so it did not slide down into the dirt. I was continually shooed away from the project because I was too small or "a pain in the ass always getting into things" or it was too dangerous. Same with today.

"Go do something and stay out of the way," my mom said.

Okay, never mind. Today I am kicking rocks, and they can build the goddamned garage. I wonder what goddamned really means. It is a swear word just like pain in the ass, shit and sumofabitch, but I'm not sure what the words really mean. I know what shit is. Everyone knows that. But goddamned and sumofabitch, I just know they are bad. I hear them around the house enough, but when I say them, I catch hell for it. Oh yeah, that's another one. Hell. Somehow it does not seem so serious as shit or sumofabitch. There must be some way to rank swear words from bad to really, really bad. I suppose I should ask about it, but I know that my mom will have a hissy fit if I do, because I have to use the swear words to ask about which cuss word is ranked higher.

So here I am kicking rocks across the barnyard, going back and forth. Mary Leigh, our aunt from "Massoftwoshits" as Gerry calls it, is up on the garage roof nailing on shingles with my mom. My mom has a bandana on her hair so the dust doesn't wreck her hair-do, and Mary Leigh just has her hair tied back with a rubber band. She has very red cheeks and a pretty big butt. Supposedly they are going to finish the roof today, and the garage will be ready to use. Dad is down in Aspen building a house with Dick Wright.

I give a great boot to the rock I am kicking and it flies up but somehow veers off to the left and lands just in the water of the pond. It's a made pond. About a year after we moved onto the ranch, Adair Rippy came up here with his Cat and moved a bunch of dirt around to make a pond on the south side of the barnyard. It is a pretty big pond and has small fish in it because they put some in. It covered over an area that was marshy because somewhere there is an underground spring. Anyway, the whole pond filled up from the snow and the spring water, so now we have green algae, frogs, salamanders, and some fish in the pond.

I go over and look in from the edge to see if I can see my rock. I can. I wade in and fish it out. As I do, a fat salamander moves just a bit away from me. It is long and has four feet with toes sticking out. It is a greenish-brown color like the color of the bottom of the pond. It would be real hard to see except that it is moving slowly across the bottom of the pond. I want to reach down and grab it. Gerry has told me not to touch salamanders because they can sting you. I don't believe him. He is only trying to scare me. I put my hand down over the salamander to pick it up but it slithers off, leaving a whirlpool of pond dirt drifting up around my hand like a dust devil. I track it with my eye and watch it go out into the pond further and bury itself in the mud. If I take my eye off the spot for only a moment I'll not be able to find it.

I step further out into the pond. Pond dirt swirls up around my feet. My shoes and socks are wet. A huge blue dragonfly flies up to my face and looks at me. I see two huge eyes staring at me. It is like each eye has a thousand eyes inside it. It is one of the huge dragonflies, not the little ones we call "blue bottles." Dragonflies are really pretty creatures. They come in blue and brown at the pond. This one is blue. Sometimes I watch them when they land on the edge of the pond or on a small rock in the water. They have invisible wings that you can see right through except for the veins in them. The dragonfly is buzzing its wings looking at me for a long time. I reach up to see if I can catch it, but it flies away quickly. It would be neat to have a dragonfly for a pet.

Looking back to where I saw the salamander bury itself, I cannot make out the place where it is, so I give up and wade out of the pond. Nothing is happening today. Nothing is going to happen either unless...

"Lunch!" I hear my mom yell. I can hear her all the way out to the pond and don't realize so much time has passed since I have been playing in the water. I'm hungry so run back to the house. I sit down at the picnic table. Teddy is there and who knows where Gerry is. I look down at the peanut-butter-and-jelly sandwich. White Wonder Bread. Glass of milk. Okay. This will do.

The milk comes from Hoagland's diary at the base of the ski mountain. The owner's name is Marvin Hoagland. I've been to his dairy. We have two milk cows and a bunch of other ones that we do not milk. We milk our cows and take the milk into town to Marvin Hoagland. We get milk in bottles back from him. It tastes good. There is a layer of cream on top of the milk, so we have to shake up the bottle before we drink it. In the winter when dad leaves the milk out in the Jeep because he forgets to bring it in, the milk freezes and comes out of the bottle with the cap balanced on the cream, which is a round plug that looks like a white icicle.

Mary Leigh is sitting next to me on the bench at the picnic table. She ruffles my hair and asks me, "What have you been up to all morning?"

"Nothing," I mumble and look down at the paper plate in front of me. Mary Leigh does not hear me.

"Rudy," she is saying, "it looks like we will finish the roof this afternoon".

"That would be great," my mom replies. "You will be on your own for awhile because I have to feed Jennifer after these boys finish. I have her food on the stove. The boys are supposed to take a nap, but I suppose it will do no good to try to make them. They just raise hell in the room, or they sneak out and raise hell outside somewhere."

"Okay," I say to myself. "Finally...victory."

I'm not sad at all to know I won't have to take naps anymore.

~ ~ ~

It is night, and my dad is cooking dinner. My mom is in bed. She doesn't feel well. My dad has set a tray to take into her in bed. She is going to eat in bed. Teddy and I have set the table. The table is big enough for all of us to sit around. My grandfather Popeye made it.

He visited us this summer while Mary Leigh was here helping us build the garage. He drove all the way from Connecticut in a new car. He told me it was a 1950 Ford. It has wood on the sides and is long. It has a door on the back. Popeye has a camera and takes lots of pictures. He goes home and sends us the pictures he takes. Some of them are of me. He sent one of me on my dad's shoulders when I was two years old. We were riding Geronimo, one of our horses. The others are named Smokey, Paint, and Laddie, and some others that are boarded at our ranch like Whoa Boy. I ride Smokey when I get to ride.

Popeye also made two benches for the table. One for each side. The kitchen is small, and the table fits in between the sink and the cabinets. I always sit on the side where the cabinets are, next to Gerry. My dad sits at the end, and my mom and Teddy sit on the side by the sink. The table is too high for me when I sit down, so most of the time I sit on a book or something so I can scrape the food off my plate into my mouth.

Lots of times I am "farting around" (that's what my dad calls it) at the table and fall back and hit my head on the knob on the cabinet door. I fell backwards last night because I fell asleep at the table and my head has a big scab where it bled all over the cabinet and on the floor. It still hurts, and I think I will not be farting around at the table tonight because I don't want to fall off the bench again. My head seems to be sore all of the time from falling off the bench and hitting it on the knob on the cabinet door.

We have set the table, and I am watching my dad cook. I see he is doing it like my mom does. He has a pot for the vegetables and a pot for potatoes. He is frying something in the frying pan-I think is venison- but maybe not, because my mom doesn't really like venison. But that is mostly what we eat, so it probably is. The venison gives us pinworms and our butts itch all the time. My mom says, "Quit scratching your butt."

Then, "Wendy, the kids have worms again. You need to stop by Dr. Lewis's and pick up some medicine on your way home tomorrow."

He does, and we have to take the stuff and the worms go away for a while. But they always come back because we eat so much venison. The worms are these little white skinny things not very long that squirm around when they are in the light. I know this because my dad has to look at our butts to make sure there are worms in there. I saw the worms in Teddy's butt. If one of us has worms, we all have to take the medicine because we can give each other worms somehow.

I am watching him cook the venison and wondering if I will get more worms from eating it, but don't care because I'm hungry. He is singing like he always does in the kitchen.

"I ride an old paint, I lead an old dan
I'm goin' to Montana to throw the hoolihan
They feed in the coulees, they water in the draw
Their tails are all matted, their backs are all raw
Ride around little doggies, ride around them slow
For the Fiery and Snuffy are rarin' to go."

My dad loves cowboy songs. He sings them while he is in the kitchen when he cooks now and then, but mostly when he sometimes helps Gerry with the dishes. I love cowboy songs, too. I sing them to myself when I am outside and no one can hear me.

My dad is finishing cooking the meat, and he puts it on a plate with a fork. It smells good. Suddenly there is an explosion, and the frying pan is on fire. He takes the frying pan over to the sink and sets it in the sink and turns on the water. There are curtains above the sink covering the window, and they are on fire. I scream. My dad rips the curtains down and throws them in the sink all burning and flaming. He is swearing.

"Goddamnedsumbitch. Hell. Shit."

He runs the water over the flaming curtains and slowly the flames die out, and the smell of fat and curtains and charred wood fills the kitchen.

"Don't tell your mother!" he says to Gerry, Teddy, and me who are all looking on in wonder.

"She doesn't feel well!"

Of course we know that because she is not in the kitchen cooking. I wonder if the sink will ever be the same with all the charred gunk in the bottom of it. Lucky it is deep so all the mess fits and so the water is deep enough to put out the curtains and the frying pan. That sink used to be deep enough for all us to bathe in at the same time. Lots of times my dad would come home from work and throw Gerry, Teddy, and me in the sink and wash us down before dinner. He doesn't do that anymore because we are all too big now.

The kitchen smells like burnt meat and is full of smoke. My dad is in the bedroom talking to my mom. He comes out to the kitchen and tells us to sit down at the table so he can get us our meal. Then he puts the food on our plates and sets them on the table after he opens the door and the window above the sink to let the smoke out. Sure enough it is venison. My dad has a burn on his hand where he pulled down the curtains.

"I love the West," he says and tucks into the venison on his plate.

Chapter 5

Winter 1950–51

It is a sunny day. I'm outside with my cousins, goddamned Johnny and Kenny. I'm wondering if I can survive until they leave and go back home. They don't like to play outside and are strangers to the West and our western way of life. Uncle Dexter is getting divorced from "Little Syl." Little Syl is my grandmother's daughter. Only my grandmother Sylvia is not my real grandmother because my mom told me her mother, Ruth McCaskey Bryant, died when mom was sixteen, and then Popeye got re-married to Sylvia. Uncle Dexter is Popeye's son with mom's real mom. I'm not sure what it all means except that it means that goddamned Johnny and Kenny have come to live with us for the winter. My older brothers, Gerry and Teddy, call them goddamned Johnny and Kenny, so that is what I call them. But never in front of my mom or dad. They are a "royal pain in the butt" as my dad says when my mom can't hear him. My mom makes me play with them because they are about my age.

"Wouldn't it be nice if you boys all got along?" she said. "Now go outside and play in the snow. And don't forget your mittens and hats."

That's all I need on a nice cold sunny day. I can see my breath in the air. It is like the steam that comes off the pond some fall mornings when I go out to the chicken coop to collect the eggs. Goddamned Johnny and Kenny are on our sled and are shouting at me to pull them across the walkway out onto the driveway so they can slide down the road and around the corner where the sled will stop when it reaches the flats. I don't want to do this, but they are shouting at me so loud I'm afraid they will bring my mom out and she will begin shouting at me too. "Just get along, damnit," she'll say.

And I will have to hear about it tonight at the dinner table when my dad comes home from teaching skiing on the big mountain in Aspen.

Right now the sled is stuck on the boardwalk. It won't slide because the runners aren't slippery enough. Goddamned Kenny is shouting, "Pull the sled! Pull the sled!"

"Be quiet," I say. "I can't pull it. It's stuck. You'll have to get off so I can get it out on the driveway."

"I'm not getting off," goddamned Kenny says.

"You'll have to if you want to sled," I say.

Neither one of them moves. What a pain in the ass. Suddenly I have an idea. I remember my dad telling Gerry that we should wax the runners of the sled so the sled will go faster and won't stick to the boardwalk between the house and the driveway.

"Wait a minute!!" I shout at them. They look at me like I am stupid, but I have shouted loud enough so they shut up.

Snot is drooling down from goddamned Johnny's nose. He smears it all over his face with his mittens, which have gobs of snow clinging to them. This will make his face colder, but I don't say anything because I hope he will have to go inside to get warmed up.

"Wait a minute!" I yell again, this time not so loud. "You guys have to get off the sled so I can wax the runners."

"I'm not getting off," says goddamned Kenny.

"Fine," I say. "You sit there until I get some paraffin from my mom."

"What do you have to do that for?" goddamned Kenny asks me.

Goddamned Johnny is still smearing the snot all over his face and looks ready to cry.

"Just sit here!" I say as I stomp around the sled in the deep snow so I can get to the kitchen door and shout at my mom for some paraffin.

Mom uses paraffin when she cans the vegetables from our garden.

"Mom!" I holler. "Maaaaaahhmmm!" this time louder. She comes to the kitchen door. "I need some paraffin. The sled won't slide with goddamned Johnny and Kenny on it. They're too heavy," I say.

"Don't you use that language!" she glares at me.

"Why not? That's what Gerry and Dad say."

"Well, just don't. You wait here, and I'll get you a little wax. And you play nicely with them." She goes back into the house to fetch the paraffin and hands it to me. I go back outside to the sled.

"Okay," I say to goddamned Johnny and Kenny, "get off now, and we can turn the sled over and wax the runners so it will slide on the walkway."

They look at me holding up the wax, beginning to understand what I am talking about, and get off the sled. Together we turn it over. I slide the paraffin bar up and down the runners like I have seen my dad and brothers do. After I'm finished, I set the paraffin on the front stoop, we turn the sled over and I say, "Okay, I have to test it out, so you stay here."

I go behind the sled, take a few running steps, jump on the sled and slide off the boardwalk on to the driveway to the point where the road starts going downhill. This has been a slick trick, because now I don't have to pull them across the boardwalk and onto the driveway.

"Okay, you guys get on the sled," I say.

"We want you to pull us," whines goddamned Kenny.

"Just get on the sled so I can push you. You can take a ride down to the flats. And you have to bring the sled back up after you stop. That's the rule. Otherwise you can't have another ride down. Who is going to steer?" I say.

I think this is going to be a problem. As it turns out, it isn't, because goddamned Johnny is now trying to pick the snowballs off his woolen mittens which he has gotten wet with all his snot. Goddamned Kenny jumps on the front of the sled and puts his feet up on the steering bars. He grabs the rope and says, "Come on snot nose, get on so we can leave the station."

"Don't call me that," goddamned Johnny says and sits down on the back of the sled.

"Kenny, put your feet on the foot brace so you can steer,"

He manages to follow directions. I get behind goddamned Johnny and give them a running push down the driveway. The sled takes off on the plowed surface. The goddamned twosome are shouting and laughing. I figure it will be some time before they get back up the road with the sled. I have time to myself.

I go around to the west side of the house. I want to see if I can find the coyote my dad says has been running through the yard between the house and the hitching post. I am plowing through the deep snow. It is over my head and I have to push my way through the white fluffy stuff with my arms. Soon I give up going farther because it is just too deep.

I look at the snow closely and see the sun reflecting off each little crystal. It is like a desert of crystals, all silver and white. As I move my eyes across the surface of the snow, the crystals change from silver to blue to white and to gold, and shimmer in the light. When the sun hits them just right, I can see all the colors of the rainbow. It is very beautiful. I stay there a long time looking at the crystals and the sparkling landscape of snow.

The light seems to dance as I move my head. The flakes of snow are really big. They are still light enough so that when I blow on them, my breath lifts them off the surface of the snow as though my breath is a little wind. I watch them twirling in the light and eventually come to rest not far away.

I remember that I am looking for the coyote. I know the coyote can't be here because I can't see it. Besides I think the snow is too deep here for anything to be out in it without getting buried. I'm almost buried. I don't know what the coyote looks like, only that it is like a dog and it eats chickens. I know my dad saw one. I give up and turn around to head back in my own steps. It is easier for me to get back to the driveway side of the house because I have stomped out a path.

"Terrrrrry!" It's my mom.

What now? I think. I shout back, "Whaaaaat!"

"Come around here so I don't have to shout." Reluctantly I do what she asks, knowing what the next question will be.

"Where are Johnny and Kenny?"

"They took the sled down the road."

"I thought I told you to stay with them!" she snaps.

"There isn't enough room on the sled for three. Besides, they wanted to go by themselves." I say.

"Well, you will just have to go find them because we have to go into town."

"Right now?"

"Yes, soon," she says. "Now go find Johnny and Kenny and get them ready to head into town."

I look down the road to the corner in hopes that goddamned Johnny and Kenny will be coming up with the sled but do not see them, so I start walking down toward the corner to find them. Dirty Peter Morse comes off the front porch and joins me. He has not paid much attention to us this morning, probably because he is tired from loping into town yesterday. Lately he has been taking off in the morning and not coming back until night. My dad says Guido and

Kuster told him that Dirty Peter Morse has been by their restaurants looking for handouts. "Good for him," I say. We don't have Pan and Wendy anymore because last fall Cerise put strychnine poison out to kill the coyotes over on his ranch. Pan and Wendy ate it and came home with convulsions. They got all stiff and died.

I walk down the road almost to the corner, Dirty Peter Morse brushing up against me, and I see goddamned Johnny and Kenny coming up the road without the sled. I'm already mad at them, and I just get madder. The rule is that we always have to bring the sled back. Goddamned Johnny and Kenny think the rules around here don't apply to them.

"Where's the damn sled?" I shout at them.

They don't answer. It is like they don't hear me. Then I hear goddamned Johnny sniveling. What a baby.

"Where's the sled?" I say again as they come closer.

Goddamned Kenny says, "It's too heavy to drag back up."

"You always have to bring the sled up, that's the rule," I say.

"Well I'm not going to."

"Come on, we have to get ready to go into town," I say.

Since they didn't bring the sled back up the hill, I'll figure out how to make life hell for them later. One way or the other they will have to get the sled, even if I have to sick Gerry or Teddy on them. We walk up the rest of the driveway to the house.

My mom has her coat on and is almost ready to get into the car, our new 1950 Ford station wagon that Popeye left with us last summer. He thought my mom and dad needed a better car to replace our old broken-down Dodge. Mom uses the Ford to haul us kids around when she goes shopping. My dad uses our old Army surplus Jeep for his car. It doesn't have any canopy, so is really cold when we ride into town. We go into town with dad and amuse ourselves skiing or fooling around at the base of Little Nell where the T-bar ski lift, while my dad spends the day teaching skiing. That's where Teddy and Gerry have gone today. Not me, though. I have to stay home with goddamned Johnny and Kenny. *Well, at least I will get to ride in the Ford*, I think as we walk up the road.

When we get to the top of the road and on our driveway, I see my mom is already outside putting Jennifer in the car.

"Come on, kids. Get in," Mom says. "And, Johnny, brush the snow off yourself before you climb in."

Good luck, I think. *He is just one ball of snow and snot.* But I don't say it because I know my mom will give me hell if I do.

My mom carries a big cardboard box of frozen beef wrapped in butcher paper and puts it in the back of the Ford. Dad butchered a steer last fall when the weather turned cold and left the meat hanging in the barn to age for a week where the coyotes wouldn't get it.

We get in the car, and mom slams the door. We're in the back seat because the three of us fit better than having mom and all of us in the front. Jennifer is in the front with Mom and is wrapped in a bunch of blankets. She is a year old now. We go down the road about a half a mile and then turn right and cross the Maroon Creek Bridge, which is really high and has wooden railings on each side so the cars won't drive off and fall into the river. It's an old railroad trestle. Then we drive a couple more miles and go across the Castle Creek Bridge, which is another old railroad trestle, but with metal railings on each side because they were put there when they built the railroad bridge. Then we are in town.

"Where are we going?" I ask.

"We have to go to Sardy's, Beck and Bishop's, and get the mail. Then I have to take Jennifer by Dr. Lewis's house so she can get her check up," Mom says.

Whatever that is, I think.

We go to Sardy's first. Then we leave Main Street and turn up the street by the Hotel Jerome and go toward the ski mountain. This is the way you get to Sardy's. All of the sudden my mom stops in the middle of the road. We are at the cross street where the Isis movie theater is.

I look over at the theater and think, *I haven't seen a movie yet. I had to stay home when they all went to see* Cinderella. *That was when Teddy and I were playing up in our room and I kicked a hole through the wall. It tore the wallpaper and I was in trouble, so I couldn't go to the movies. Dad stayed home with me, and Mom took Gerry and Teddy.*

Then I hear mom talking to me.

"Terry," she says. "Get out, and go see if there are any cars coming across the intersection."

"What's an innersession?" I ask.

"Intersection," she says. "It means the place where two roads come together and cross each other."

I mull this over for an instant too long. "Just go out and look down the cross street both ways and see if anything is coming. If there's nothing coming, wave and I'll drive across the intersection."

I get out of the car and walk out into the middle of the street and look to the left and then look to the right. I sort of get why she wanted me to be a lookout. Snow is piled up past the first floor of the buildings. My mom can't see around the corner to know if another car is coming, so she has me looking down the street to see if there are any cars.

Nothing coming. No cars are moving. There are a few cars all covered where the snowplow has plowed snow over them. They don't count because they're not moving. I still wonder why my mom doesn't do it because she has to get out of the car to let me out of the backseat. She could have looked at the same time. I think maybe it is because if there is a car coming she doesn't want to be the one who gets run over. I go back to the car.

"Nothing coming," I say. Mom lets me in, eases out into the intersection and crosses it with no problem. We do the same for the next block. Then she pulls the car close over to the snow bank and stops. We can't open the door because we are almost in the snow bank. She has to park this way so, if another car is coming from the other direction, it can get by. There is lots and lots of snow piled up.

"You kids stay in the car while I'm at Sardy's," Mom says. "And don't wake up Jennifer." I look over the seat and see that Jennifer has fallen asleep on the way into town.

Sardy's is the hardware store. Tom Sardy owns it, and he owns the lumberyard where you can buy wood of all kinds and lengths. He also runs the mortuary and fixes people up before they are buried like he did Bill Anderson when he died. My mom has to buy something at Sardy's. Goddamned Johnny and Kenny aren't saying much. I figure they're pooped from walking up the road. They are from the East and do not run around much like we do on the ranch. Just as well, because I am tired of playing with them anyway. My mom comes back to the car after a bit and looks in on Jennifer who is still sleeping. She then goes to the back of the car and takes out the meat she is taking into Beck and Bishop's. Beck and Bishop's is our grocery store, and luckily it is right across the street from Sardy's. My mom carries the box of meat across the street and goes through a tunnel in the snow to get in the door. She comes back later with another box, which she puts in the back.

"What's in the box?" I ask.

"Vegetables," she says.

"What about the meat?"

"We traded the meat for the vegetables."

This gives me something to think about while we stop at the post office, Dr. Lewis's, and on the drive home. It is difficult for me to understand how you can trade meat for vegetables. *Is it done by how much each weighs? Or is it how much will fit in the box? How do you know how much meat equals how many vegetables?* I realize during that ride that I need more information to figure this problem out. I know when I trade things with my brothers, we have to argue a lot about it and generally size wins. By that I mean, if Gerry wants it, he just takes it, and that is that.

I come out of my thoughts as we go up the driveway. My mother stops the car by the sled in the snow bank on the side of the road.

Hah! I think. *She's going to make goddamned Johnny and Kenny walk home with the sled! What great news.*

I am filled with glee until my mom puts on the brakes, gets out of the car, and opens the back. My glee turns to glum as I watch her pull the sled out of the snow bank and throw it in the back with the vegetables. Then she gets back into her seat, takes the brake off, and begins driving up the driveway.

"Goddamn you!" I say to her. "You're not fair! The rule is that whoever rides the sled down has to bring it up. Those guys should have to bring it up!"

It slips out of my mouth before I can catch it. *Shit,* I think. *There I go again.* Suddenly my day has taken a turn for the worse. I see goddamned Kenny smirking in the seat next to me, and now I'm really mad. I hit him on the arm.

"What?" my mom shouts, turning around in her seat and shooting daggers at me from her eyes. Goddamned Kenny is whimpering. Why, I don't know, because he has too many clothes on for my feeble blow to have hurt him. He's just making a show so I will get in more Dutch.

"What did you say? You don't talk to me that way!" her voice is shrill and she is screaming. "You wait until your father gets home!"

She goes dead silent. I know she is so mad that she can't speak. If she wasn't driving the car I know she would kill me. This is the first time I have sworn at her. Sometimes I talk back, but I have never sworn at her before. I know I'm in trouble now. She's going right to the "wait until your 'father'" line. Not even "wait until your 'dad' gets home." There is a big difference. "Dad" means she'll forget about it before too long. "Father" means she won't. Ever since I killed that chicken last summer and she chased me around the house trying to catch me and kill me, she gives me more room to roam, but always calls on Dad when I get in trouble. And there he is with the belt.

Mom stops the car in our driveway. I jump out as fast as I can get the door open and take off for the barnyard. I know she has too many things to do to chase me: Jennifer in the front seat crying because Mom's shouting has woken her, goddamned Johnny and Kenny, and all the vegetables still in the car. And me, with hell from my dad awaiting me.

Chapter 6

Early Spring 1951

It is morning, and I've finished breakfast. I'm on a chair looking out the kitchen window at the hillside. The seasons are changing. I notice the snow is slowly melting. It has been a long winter with lots of big snowstorms. I see a black shape out in the snow over by the big rock between the house and the barnyard. Maybe it is the coyote. I remind myself that I need to go take a look at it when I get outside. I have been looking for the coyote since goddamned Johnny and Kenny left and haven't seen it. I still don't know exactly what makes a coyote look different from a dog, and it occurs to me to ask my dad about it before he goes to work. Then I remember that today I have to go to work with him and spend the day on Little Nell with my brothers. Gerry is coming today so it must be the weekend, otherwise he and Teddy would be in school. I start school in the fall. Sometimes now I go to work with my dad and on some days my mom takes me to Mrs. Prectle's, my nursery school. I have been going to work with my dad for a long time, ever since I was three. I would much rather go to work than to Mrs. Prectles. I like being outside more than being inside all day. I am thinking of how it will go this morning as we head into town.

It's like this when we go to work with my dad. We load our skis and poles in the back of the Jeep and climb in to wait for him. We still have the same old Army Jeep we had when I fell out and the hay rake ran over me. At first Dad had to set me in the back because the Jeep was too high for me to climb in. Now I can do it by myself. So we climb in, and we sit there and wait. Pretty soon my dad comes out and gets in the Jeep. He tries to start the Jeep by stepping on the starter button on the floor. The motor goes uuuuh, uuuuh, uuuuuuuuuuuuh but doesn't turn over. My dad gets out of the Jeep and pushes it across the driveway until it is rolling down the hill. He always parks the Jeep backwards after work so it's heading downhill. He pushes the Jeep, and it begins rolling. He runs and jumps in. He shifts the gear stick, and "pops" the clutch. That's what Gerry calls it, "pops the clutch." The motor catches and begins to cough and belch like a farting old cow. The Jeep hiccups down the road for a while, whipping us back and forth in our seats and then the engine smoothes out. My dad puts down the snowplow and rams some of the snowdrifts to push the snow further off the road.

When we hit the bottom of the road, my dad pulls off his right glove and fumbles in his parka pocket for his pack of Lucky Strikes. He shakes the package with his hand until one of the smokes pops up, puts the package to his mouth, and grabs the cigarette out with his teeth. The package disappears back in his parka pocket and out comes a Zippo lighter. He shakes the Zippo lighter a few times, holds the steering wheel between his knees and uses his left hand to shield the cigarette from the wind while he lights it with his right hand. Then the Zippo lighter disappears back into his parka pocket. He takes a long puff and says, "Aaaahhhhhh."

He puts the cigarette in his mouth and with his right hand he gets the glove he has set between the two front seats and puts it in his left hand. He holds the steering wheel with his left wrist while he uses his left hand to help his right hand get back into the right glove, and finally his hands are back on the steering wheel. By now his eyes are all scrunched up because he has smoke in them. Finally, with his left hand he takes the cigarette out of his mouth, grabs it between his first and second fingers, holds on to the steering wheel with the cigarette glowing red, and, with his right hand, he rubs at the frost on the windshield to create a peephole so he can see the road before he drives too far across Maroon Creek Bridge. It seems like he never scrapes the windshield before we take off down the road, and I can't figure out why. I think he just likes it the way he does it.

I watch the smoke and his frosty breath rise to just over his head and disappear in the wind blowing into the open Jeep. In the back, my brother Teddy and I huddle together "freezing our asses off" as Gerry says. Gerry gets to sit in the front seat so he stays warmer. That's how it goes when we have to go to work, which we are going to do today.

~~~

I am jolted out of my reverie about how it will be driving into town when my dad touches my shoulder and says, "Look up there on the hillside. Do you see it?"

I look up on the hillside above the barn. I don't see anything except the melting snow, some grassy spots, aspen trees, scrub oak and a few of the straggling cows and horses coming down toward the barn where my dad has just finished putting out the hay.

"No," I say, "I don't see anything."

"Just above the spring box to the left of the willows," my dad says.

I shift my eyes over to the spring box in the clump of willows on the hillside. There is something moving slowly, stopping, grazing on the exposed grass around the spring box, and every once in awhile looking up and around.

"Oh, yeah! I see it now!" I say. "It's a deer!"

"Yes," my dad says, "and it's a big buck."

"Rudy," he calls to my mom. "How're we fixed for meat?"

My mom shouts back from somewhere, "We are out of beef and are about out of venison."

My dad turns and looks at the clock on the kitchen wall. I can see his mind working over the time problem. He is wondering if he has enough time to shoot the buck, gut it, bring it down and hang it, and still get to work for the ski school meeting at nine o'clock.

We've gotten up at 5:30. We're early risers on our ranch because we have lots to do. Dad is fast, but I am not sure if he can get it all done. He muddles it for only a moment longer. Then he says quietly, almost to himself, "We'll have to hope he is back tomorrow. I don't have to be at work until ten tomorrow for a private lesson."

I look up on the hillside again, and the buck is still there eating lazily and pawing through the snow for whatever grasses he can find. I stand on the chair and watch the buck while it forages diagonally across the hillside and up into the aspens above the irrigation ditch. I decide I love looking at the deer, the snow, the trees, and the blue sky. It is all very beautiful.

~~~

It's later the same morning, and we are in the Jeep. My dad has finished lighting his cigarette and is driving us into town. We take the same way as always. It is just like I imagined it would be when I was thinking about it earlier this morning. Down our road, dad lighting his cigarette his special way, across the Maroon Creek Bridge, past Marolt's Ranch, across Castle Creek Bridge, past Waterman's store, down Main Street to the Court House, right turn towards the ski mountain and presto, he pulls the Jeep up at the base of Little Nell.

He jumps out of the Jeep and tells us to get out. All three of us scramble onto the street while he grabs our skis and poles and sticks them in the snow bank. It is cold out now but it is going to be a nice day and warm up some. Winter is starting to move into spring. I watch my dad go into the ticket shack at the base of the T-bar. I know he is going to tell Frank and Luds Loushin he is leaving us at Little

Nell for the day while he teaches skiing, and would they mind "keeping an eye" on us.

My dad walks out the door of the shack with Luds behind him. Luds has a broken hand. I think he got it caught in the T-bar and got his thumb ripped off. I hear him saying to my dad, "Gol darned it, Wendy, this has to stop. Those kids are terrors. They take the bead chains and string them together, they fish nickels out of the Coke machine, and they're into the oil and grease in the shop when Frank is lubing the T's. They terrify the skiers riding up the T-bar when they ski slalom down between them going like bats out of hell."

My dad grins. "Yeah, that's what I understand. Just kick the shit out of them if they get in any real trouble."

I think to myself, *Yeah he will have to catch me if he is going to kick the shit out of me.*

Luds is a slow mover. But, of course there is always Frank, who is not.

My dad throws Luds his pack of Lucky Strikes.

"You kids behave yourselves!" He heads toward the Jeep to drive over to the Hotel Jerome where the tourists meet to get their instructors for their classes or private lessons.

"Do you have your lunches?"

"No," we say in unison. "They're in the Jeep."

My dad grabs them and gives them to Gerry who immediately opens all three bags and looks in.

"Peanut butter and jelly on Wonder Bread," he says.

He then folds up one bag and stuffs it in his jacket pocket and gives the other two to Teddy and me.

"I'm going skiing," Gerry says.

Gerry is eight and knows how to ride the chair lift and how to get over to the base of Aspen Mountain from Little Nell. From there he can take Lifts One and Two clear up to the Sundeck on the top of the mountain. Teddy and I have to stay on the T-bar at Little Nell because we don't know how to get over to the big mountain yet. Gerry takes his skis and poles out of the snow bank, sets them on the snow by the T-bar gate, puts them on, and slides over to the lift to wait for Frank Loushin to grab a T and pull it down. Gerry can have the T on his butt because he is big and heavy enough so the T won't lift him into the air. If the T lifts you in the air in some of the dips on the lift line, you fall off if you have the T on your butt. I have to hold on to the T with my arms wrapped around in front so I can't hold onto my ski poles. That's why I don't ski with ski poles. If you have your arms around the T like I do, when you get lifted off the snow all you do is spin around and hope your skis are pointing uphill when you come down. Otherwise you have to fall, to let go of the T, ski down to the bottom, and start all over again. Then Frank or Luds says, "Got a stiff one that time, eh, Morsie?" Or sometimes they say, "Too bad you don't have tips on both ends of your skis, Terror."

Sometimes they call me Terry the Terrible or Terry the Terror. I'm not too sure why.

After Gerry leaves, Teddy and I are left at the bottom of Little Nell to figure out what to do for the day. Teddy sets his lunch bag down by his skis and wanders off toward the Coke machine to see if he can fish any nickels out or find a quarter someone has dropped between the two by fours on the wooden deck. I see his lunch sitting there and know that it will get eaten by a dog if he is not careful. I don't say anything because he is always getting mad if I catch him goofing up.

"Hey, Morsie!" Luds Loushin shouts at me. "Come 'ere."

"What for?" I'm leery of Luds. He plays a lot of tricks on me.

"Just come 'ere, damn it. I've got something for you to do." Luds tells me.

I walk over to the ticket booth. Luds opens the door and motions me in.

He closes the door behind me and says, "Here, this is the chain you and your brothers screwed with last weekend. I want you to take it apart. Make sure you don't bend any of the chains."

Damn, I think. *This could take me all day.*

I don't say anything because I am locked in the ticket shack, and Luds is standing in front of the door. No escape. He motions to the stool next to the one he sits in and says with a grin, "Get up there on that stool because this could take you awhile."

The ticket shack is built by the T-bar and has a wooden counter in front of a glass window where people line up to buy their tickets. Luds or Frank take their money and put it in a drawer under the counter inside. Then they take out a yellow ticket that has a hole in it at the top. They set it on the counter and take a rubber stamp and you hear a "SLAM, SLAM" as they stamp today's date on both sides of the ticket. They then pass the ticket out the window, and the tourist takes it. On the right side of the counter on the outside of the ticket booth, there is a big box of bead chains. The tourists are supposed to take one bead chain and attach their ticket to their parkas with it, so the mountain ski patrol can see they have paid to ride the lifts.

Last week Gerry, Teddy, and I took the whole box of bead chains and snapped them all together making one long chain. There must have been a thousand of them because it was really, really long. We put the box back and watched as the tourists had to figure out how to unhook one small chain from the whole big chain so they could fasten their ticket to their parka. Luds had a shit fit when he saw what we had done. I thought fire would come out of his ears while he was swearing up a blue streak at us. Of course, we didn't know what he was so mad about. We didn't have anything to do with it.

Now here I am with no escape, trapped on my stool, unsnapping each one of these little chains and putting them back in the box. Teddy has managed to avoid this job like he always does. He seems to get out of making it right after the trouble is done. His luck runs that way. Luds sits by the door selling tickets and talking to the tourists, so he is blocking any hope of flight. After what seems like hours and probably is, I finish the job and decide to go skiing. Luds sets me free from jail, and I go out to get my skis. Teddy is wandering around and comes up to me.

"Did you take my sandwich?" he says.

"Where have you been?" I say. "I had to untangle all those bead chains."

"Too bad for you," he smirks. "Have you seen my sandwich?"

"You always sneak off when there is work," I complain.

"You just have to be smarter than you are," he says. "Did you take my sandwich?" he asks me again.

"No," I say, "You set it down over there by your skis."

We walk over to our skis and see one or two pieces of paper bag on the snow.

"There's your sandwich," I say. "Maybe Mambo came by and slurped it up."

Mambo is Fred Islen's St. Bernard dog. He is about as big as a horse and slobbers like a pig at the trough.

"Damn it," Teddy says. "Where is yours?" I see him eyeing my parka pocket. "Come on, give it to me," he says. "Can I have it?"

I have already had enough of this and know where it is headed, which is where I am not going.

"Nope, already ate it," I lie. "I'm going up the T-bar," I say as I pick up my skis and head over to the lift line.

As I'm walking over it occurs to me that I have told the first intentional lie I am aware of. It is a real lie, not just a story I make up which I know no one will believe anyway so it doesn't count for a lie. It gives me a sense of power over my world, but somehow it scares me and doesn't feel right. I don't like how I feel in my body. I know what Dad and Mom have taught us about lying, cheating, and stealing.

~ ~ ~

It is the next morning, and I am once again standing on a chair in the kitchen looking out the window trying to see the coyote. There is nothing moving across the expanse of snow between the window and the hitching post. I look up on the hillside near the spring box to see if the buck has returned today. He has. I see him paw the snow by the edge of the spring box to get at some of the tender grasses that grow there.

I wonder if I should tell my dad, or if I should just stand here on this chair and watch the buck until he moves across the hillside and up into the trees again. I know if I tell my dad, he will go outside with his thirty-aught-six, kneel in the snow and, using the hitching post to steady the rifle, he will shoot the buck. It makes me sad to think about. But I know we need the meat because we gave the last of the cow to Beck and Bishop's, and we don't have any cow meat left. We have a little venison like my mom told my dad yesterday. I finally decide to tell my dad about the buck. I know we will be hungry if we don't have the meat to eat. I get down from the chair and wander off to search for him.

I find him over by the screen porch where he is bringing in some wood for the fireplace. We don't burn much wood. Mostly oil in the furnace down in the basement where there are spiders and other creepy crawlers.

"Dad, the buck is back by the spring box," I tell him.

"Thanks, son," he says as he puts the last of the kindling into the wood box. He closes the lid and walks into the house.

"What are you going to do?" I ask him, already knowing the answer.

"Well, son," he says, "I'm gonna get some meat."

"You mean you're gonna shoot him?" I say.

"Yep. Now you stay here inside so you don't scare him away."

He puts on his big sheepskin coat and walks toward the door stuffing bullets into the thirty-aught-six. He takes his gloves and hat in the hand that has the loaded gun now tucked under his arm and over his elbow. In his other hand he has a cigarette. I watch him go out the door and then go stand on the chair by the kitchen window to look from there. Soon I see my dad walking out to the hitching post. He has his gloves and hat on now, and his big sheepskin coat is open and flaps a little when he moves. The coat is dirty and smells like horses. He stamps down the snow in front of the hitching post and gets down on one knee. He rests the thirty-aught-six on the hitching rail and leans his head on the stock so he can see down the sights of the rifle. The buck is still pawing at the snow, chewing and lifting his head up from time to time to sniff the air and look around. My dad takes his right glove off, the cigarette out of his mouth and drops both in the snow. Just about this time the buck lifts his head.

He's gonna run, I think.

But he doesn't. He looks toward the house for a minute and just as he is putting his head down to eat more I hear a loud bang. I glance back at my dad and see the smoke coming from the barrel of the rifle as the hot air turns to frost. Then I look back up to where the buck was standing. He is still standing, then, all at once, his front legs fold under him, and he falls in the snow. I don't need to be told he is dead. My dad's a good shot.

"What did he shoot? What did he shoot?" Gerry's come up behind me.

"The buck," I say.

"Wow," Gerry says "Guess that means we won't be going to Sunday school today. Good," he says.

He knows what is in store for him, and I do too.

My dad is walking back toward the house with the thirty-aught-six, bolt open, tucked under his arm. He is putting his glove on, and the cigarette he has picked up is hanging from his mouth, the red ash visible against the white of the snow behind him. He turns his head once more to look back up the hillside to see if the buck has moved, but he knows it hasn't.

I am still on my chair looking up at the buck. There is a dark patch on the snow below his head now. I hear my dad stamp his boots on the front stoop and open the door. He sees me and says, "Terry, go get Gerry and Teddy down here. I'll need some help getting the buck down off the hillside." Gerry has left my side and has gone upstairs to get his clothes on because he knows that he will have to help Dad pull the buck down to the barn.

'Okay," I say and leave my perch on the chair. I walk out of the kitchen and shout as loud as I can, "Gerry and Teddy, Dad wants you!"

Gerry comes right away. Teddy is slower getting ready. He finally shows up.

"Come on, boys," my dad shouts. "Get yourself dressed, and let's get going. We have to get the buck off the hillside while it's still warm." He stands in the door between the porch and the kitchen, lighting a new cigarette.

Gerry and Teddy come downstairs dressed in their work clothes. They go to the closet and get their coats, hats, gloves, and boots, put them on and walk out the door without saying a word. My dad follows them.

I turn back to the window and watch as they make their way across the barnyard, over the corral fence, over the fence on the far side of the corral, where they stop. Dad is kicking the snow away from the corral gate so he can open it to bring the buck through when they get it off the hillside. When he has the gate open, they trudge slowly up to the buck. My dad takes the buck's back legs and moves him slightly away from the spring box. I can tell the deer is heavy because my dad is struggling to move its body in the snow.

He takes his hunting knife from the sheath strapped to his belt and cuts the animal's throat. More black on the snow. He ties a rope around the hind legs and I watch the three of them pull the buck away from the spring box and down the hillside. About midway down, they stop. My dad takes out his knife and begins cutting on the buck. Soon I see him reach his hands inside the buck and pull out all the guts and gizzards. He throws them out on the snow so they are not in a large clump but spread around. I am going to ask him why he does that, but I figure out that it must be so the animals won't fight over them. They can just sneak up, grab some, and run off. I see magpies are in the air already. A little while later, Dad and the boys pull the buck into the corral. I jump down off my chair and get into my coat, hat, mittens, and boots and head out to the barn.

By the time I get there, Gerry, Teddy and my dad have the deer in the barn. They are getting ready to hang it by its back legs from the rafters where it can cure for a week before my dad saws it into pieces. My dad has tied a rope to an old wooden part of a plow horse tack thing-am-a-jig that he uses to hang the deer. It is a long round piece of wood with hooks on each end that he sticks through the skin on the back legs. It holds them apart so skinning the deer is easier. I think the rig is called a whippletree, at least that's what my dad calls it. Once my dad has the whippletree in place, he ties the rope to an O-ring in the center of the rig and throws the rope over one of the barn rafters. Then he gives the rope end to Gerry and Teddy and tells them to hang onto it so they can all pull hard until the buck is hanging head down with his hind legs up in the rafters.

Then my dad gets his sharp knife and starts cutting the skin off the buck from the back legs down. He makes a few cuts between the skin and the meat, then pulls really hard on the skin and it moves down off the buck a few inches at a time. We are watching him, and I think maybe Gerry is right: we will be skipping Sunday school next weekend. We will have to help my dad cut the buck into smaller pieces and wrap the deer meat in the paper Albert Bishop gave him. Since it's early spring, it is cold enough to leave the deer hanging in the barn for a week.

"It'll be finer if it ages," my dad says. "The meat'll taste better. We'll butcher it next weekend."

When it is aged, we can cut it up with a carving knife my dad uses. He will saw the bones with a hacksaw. Dad will cut different parts of the meat off the buck, wrap them in Albert Bishop's paper, and write on the paper just what part of the buck it is. I wonder if it will all fit in the freezer. It is a big buck. I count five points on each antler. You have to look at its teeth to see how old it is. My dad told me this. "When are you going to butcher it?" I ask my dad.

"Probably next Sunday after it has cured for awhile," he replies.

Yes, I think. *I was right about Sunday school.*

I look at the skinless corpse that was once a large buck, hanging dead from the rafters of the barn, and feel sadness for it. There is nothing I can do about it, so I leave the barn and walk outdoors. I wonder about killing animals, death, and all the mess that goes with it. I know we have to have the buck for its meat. Still, I have a hollow feeling in my stomach. And I don't look forward to having an itchy butt all spring from the worms we will probably get from it.

~ ~ ~

Today is Sunday, I am thinking as I walk back across the barnyard toward the house leaving my dad, Gerry, and Teddy to figure out the rest of the deer. Tomorrow I have to go to Mrs. Prectle's nursery school again. I have had to start going back there since goddamned Johnny and Kenny left. Last time I was there was a pain.

I was lying on the floor looking at a book that had trains in it. Mrs. Prectle was making everyone lie down to take a nap. I told her I didn't take naps.

"You do while you're here," she snapped. "So lie down and get quiet. You tell me every day at nap time that you don't take naps."

I lay down on my back and thought, *if I tell her enough times, maybe she will get the idea I don't take naps. Naps are for adults so they have time away from the kids and can get some rest. Instead, they make us nap so they can do something else. If I close my eyes, maybe she will think I am going to nap and will move out of the room so I can start fiddling around.*

But she didn't leave. Instead she clomped over to Dinah Smith and put a blanket on her. Then she walked back my way climbing over the kids one by one. As she came closer, I realize she was going to pass over me, too. She was on her way to the shelves for another blanket for someone. As she stepped over me, I looked up and saw her foot. Then I looked right up her skirt and saw her underwear! I had to bite my lip to keep from laughing. It didn't work, so I tried to muffle my laughter by faking a coughing fit. That didn't work either. Mrs. Prectle looked down at me and said, "What are you laughing about? Are you up to no good again? Now settle down and get quiet."

I did the best I could to control the laughter. I was laughing because her underwear looked so funny with frilly bottoms. They looked like the underwear I had seen in magazines where ladies are dancing and lifting their skirts up.

When I asked my mom why the dancers were showing off their underwear, she said they are called bloomers not underwear. I know that modern-day women don't wear bloomers (except Mrs. Prectle) because of something that happened last fall.

~ ~ ~

Gerry and I were playing in the house because it was raining out. We played a game of hide-and-seek. I knew he must be bored because he doesn't play with me much anymore. He said he is getting too old to fool around with kids. I found a great place to hide in the clothes hamper in mom's bathroom. It is a big green thing and is woven with fake straw. It has a top on it. I climbed in and pulled the lid down so Gerry couldn't see me. I could see out between the straws through the holes in the sides, so I knew if he was coming to find me. It took Gerry a long time to find me even though he is older than me. I even had to cough once or twice. He opened the lid and said, "There you are, I found you!"

'Yeah," I said "but I had to cough so you could. I could see you the whole time I was hiding inside."

"You could?" he said.

"Yep."

"Here, let me see," he said as he helped me out and climbed in.

"Wow," he said. "What a great hiding place!"

Then he got the idea we should hide in the hamper when it's time for my mom to take her bath, which was pretty soon because the sun was going down. So we climbed—more like stuffed ourselves—in the hamper because there was hardly any room for two people. Pretty soon my mom came into the bathroom and began to undress for her bath. I saw she wasn't wearing bloomers; she was wearing modern-day underwear. About the time she started taking off her garters and stockings, I started sneezing from the hay dust Gerry had on his clothes. Gerry elbowed me and I cried out, "Ouch, don't hit me!"

My mom was already shouting and swearing at us with some words I hadn't heard her say before, and probably shouldn't repeat. She opened the lid and, about the time she did, Gerry pushed on me, and the hamper turned over on the floor. Somehow I managed to scramble out first and run out of the bathroom in a flash. Gerry wasn't so lucky. He ended up with some scratches from my mom. Then my dad walked in the door and Gerry caught real hell. I stayed upstairs out of the line of fire and got off free because mom and dad knew I was too young to conjure up such a dirty trick. And that's why I was laughing at Mrs. Prectle's nursery school, because I remembered the clothes hamper incident last fall.

There it all is in my mind. A dead buck hanging in the barn, bloomers, a clothes hamper, and knowing its time to have breakfast. I wonder how my thoughts can change in my head so quickly, one leading to another. I decide to think about it some more later. I go into the house to have breakfast and get ready to go to the ski mountain when Dad takes us to work with him.

Chapter 7

June 1951

I'm going to be five years old in September. It is June right now, and I have a really long time to wait, all summer. I'm sitting on the ripped driver's seat of the old Army surplus Dodge truck we have on the ranch to haul heavy stuff around. It has a big steering wheel and metal pedals on the floorboards I can't reach. It is painted a dull green and has a flat bed on the back with boards on it so it can hold hay bales and machinery. There is a starter on the floor my dad presses with his foot to get the engine going. The windshield is cracked, and the doors don't close too well. That's why I'm in the driver's seat now, because my dad didn't shut the door when he got out yesterday.

The truck was left parked in the barnyard by the pond last evening before dinner after dad swore up, down, and sideways at the spring on the hillside and told me to come to the house with him. I didn't say anything as we walked across the barnyard because I knew he was mad. He usually swears up a blue streak when he is mad. I look up on the hillside where the spring box used to be and see the big cistern next to it. This is what happened to lead up to my dad's swearing fit yesterday. I watched the whole thing.

~~~

Earlier in the spring after the snow was off the ranch, Adair Rippy came up with his big Caterpillar machine and dug out a hole on the hillside a little below and sort of next to the spring box. The spring box collects our water before it runs down to our house in the pipe Old Art Roberts buried years ago. Adair Rippy is a weather-beaten, leathery man who is shorter than my dad but who has gorilla arms. He wears coveralls like the ones I wear in the summer. His are all stained with dirt, oil, and hydraulic fluid. He is nice to me and once let me sit in the seat of the big Cat when the engine was shut off.

Adair Rippy and my dad dug a flat place on the hillside for the bottom of the cistern. When the flat place was done Adair Rippy left, and a cement truck came from down to pour concrete for the floor. The truck groaned and creaked as it worked to make it up the hillside. After it finished pouring the cement, it went back down the hill easily banging and rattling the whole way as it went. My dad and some other man I do not remember spent the rest of the afternoon smoothing out the slab. It stayed there drying for a week.

"How's that thing going to hold water?" I asked my dad one day.

"Well," he said "now that you ask, tomorrow we are going to build the forms for the walls and when they are done, we will pour the concrete in them."

"What are forms?" I asked him.

"They are called forms because they hold the concrete in place when we pour it to make the cistern walls. The forms make the shape of the wall."

"Oh," I said.

The next day my dad and the other man built the forms and tied them all together with lots of wood braces and wires. The forms sat there for another few days until the concrete truck could come groaning and struggling back up the hill to pour more concrete. When they had finished pouring the walls, the truck once again rattled back down the hillside and was gone. The cement stood drying in the forms another week. Then my dad came to get me and said, "It's time to pop those forms off the walls. Adair Rippy is going to be back up here tomorrow to backfill the cistern on the uphill side so we can divert the water from the spring box into it and have a better water supply. You want to help me out today?"

It seemed like the only time that I got to spend with my dad was "helping him out," which meant work. But I said "Yes" for lack of better things to do. So we drove the old Dodge truck up the hillside and my dad started taking the forms off the concrete. He took his hammer and, with the claw side, twisted off the wires holding them together. It looked like he had to be pretty strong to do it because the wires were made out of iron or steel. My job was to pick up all the wire pieces he broke off and put them in a box so they wouldn't stay at the bottom of the cistern and rust when it was filled with water. It didn't take Dad too long to dismantle the forms and put the big sheets of oily plywood on the bed of the truck. Just about the time he was finished, I felt the ground vibrating, and heard the clank, clank, clanking of the Cat tracks as Adair Rippy drove the Cat up the hillside toward us.

"Good timing," my dad said as Adair Rippy parked the idling Cat and got down off the high seat. "I'm just finishing up with the forms right now. You're a day early. Here, grab this," my dad said.

Adair Rippy just grunted. Then my dad lifted me up above his head and set me on my butt on the top of the wall. Adair Rippy grabbed me and set me on the ground. I watched as my dad passed up the box of steel ends I had picked up. Then he climbed up the ladder and out of the cistern. I stood to one side as they loaded the last plywood form on the Dodge and backed it down the hillside so it wouldn't be in the way when Adair Rippy backfilled the cistern. I saw Adair Rippy climb back up on the tracks of the Cat so I walked further up on the hillside and sat down to watch. Adair Rippy fired up his Cat and pushed the dirt in against the upslope wall and down the sides of the cistern until the dirt surrounded the concrete, and the foundation hole was filled up. When he was finished he stopped the Cat and put it in neutral. It idled there on the hillside, shaking everything, as my dad got up on the track, said something to Adair Rippy, and gave him some money. Adair Rippy fired up the Cat and drove it across the hillside below the cistern and spring box to the track he made coming up the hill, then the Cat turned and headed down the hill. As he got farther away, the earth stopped shaking, and the noise subsided.

My dad stood back and watched. He watched Adair Rippy drive his Cat up on to the trailer behind his big dump truck. He watched the truck disappear across the barnyard and out of sight past the house. He watched the sky and the clouds and the barnyard. Then he put his hand on my head and said, "Let's see if this thing will work."

"Okay," I said.

He got a pipe and set it into a hole at the upper corner of the cistern and pointed it up to the pipe coming out of the spring box.

"Hold this pipe here," he said to me.

"Okay." I held the pipe in the hole.

My dad climbed up to the spring box a few yards away to divert the flow of water from it into the pipe I was holding. I watched him as he picked up his end of the cistern pipe and started to connect it to the spring box pipe. All of a sudden he stopped. He shook his head and said, "What the hell?"

He set the cistern pipe back on the ground and took a step up to the spring box and looked in. Then he started swearing. I put my pipe end down and climbed up to see what was the matter. As I stood next to my dad and looked into the spring box, I could see that it was empty. There was no water coming out of the hillside where it always came out.

"Where's the water?" I said.

"Damned if I know."

He stood with his cowboy hat pushed back on his head, his gaze on the empty spring box, and a quizzical expression on his face. He sat down in the dirt thinking.

"The spring has disappeared," he said. "The Cat must have disturbed the ground enough to put it on a different course. Now we don't have water."

"What are we going to do?"

"What can we do?" he said. "We'll just have to figure something out. You walk back down to the house. I'm going to sit here awhile and think."

I started walking down the hillside. As I passed the lower end of the cistern, I stepped in a soft muddy spot that had not been there when I walked up.

"It's all muddy down here," I shouted up to my dad.

"Lemme see," he said and got up to join me. "Sure enough. It is muddy," he said. "Looks like the spring dried up where it was up above the cistern, and now it is coming out down here below it. Well, at least we know where the water is."

I knew he was relieved that we still had water but was mad he had spent time and money building a cistern to collect the spring water, only to have the spring disappear from its outlet on the hillside above the cistern, and to reappear in a new place down below the cistern.

Now the swearing started in earnest. He cussed the cistern, the spring, the waste of money, the waste of time, and about anything else he could think of in the moment. I listened in awe as I learned more new swear words than I had ever heard before. He motioned me toward the Dodge and we drove down the hill.

It was not until dinner, when the cussing had subsided and my dad had explained the day's events to my mom, that I realized what dad was swearing about. The spring water is coming out of the ground below the cistern and can't be collected in it because water doesn't flow uphill. I thought we had to figure out how to get the water up to the cistern and said so to my dad. He said we couldn't do that without pumping the water back up the hill, so all our work was useless. It was then I realized that the cistern is going to sit on the hillside unused forever.

That's why my dad was in a swearing fit yesterday, and that is why I'm sitting in the Dodge right now practicing my new cuss words since I am commander of a regiment of Dodge trucks making sure that the other drivers follow my orders to wherever we are going. It takes a lot of swearing.

Chapter 8

Late Fall 1951

I am watching down the hill for Gerry and Teddy to walk up the road coming home from school. The school bus drops them at the Maroon Creek Bridge every day after school and they have to walk up the road. It is a long walk. More than a half-mile my dad says. Maybe it doesn't seem far to grown-ups, but to us kids it seems to be a really long way.

When you start out from the bridge, the road is flat for a while along the side of the field and the irrigation ditch that's used to take water to the hay. Then, after lots of walking, the road goes uphill. It is steep until it gets flatter at the top. Then the road goes up to our house still climbing but not so steep. It turns right, before our house, wraps around the hill north of the house, and then you are in our driveway. If you keep going, you end up in the barnyard.

I am looking for them to come up the road, but they don't come. I think it must be too early, but it seems like the right time because the sun is getting low. Still, they don't show up. A car drives up the road instead. I watch it as it kicks up a cloud of dust. It climbs the last way up the hill onto the edge of the driveway near the walkway to the front stoop. The car stops, and a tall man gets out. He brushes his pants off with one hand and puts a cowboy hat on his head with the other. He is as tall as my dad but skinnier.

"Hi there," he says.

"Hi," I say back to him, shrinking back toward the front door. He looks like a cowboy with his jeans, cowboy boots, big silver belt buckle, and his hat. He doesn't look like a rancher though because most of the ranchers have lots of machinery oil and dirt on their jeans. And their boots are much more beat up.

"Your dad here?" he says.

"Yep," I say. "He's around back. Come on, I'll show you."

I start off around the back and before I take two steps, he says, "Wait a minute, young fella! I think I ought to know your name."

I turn around and look up at him, a bit afraid, but say to him, "My name is Terry. Freidl calls me Terry the Terrible and my dad calls me Terr-Ass."

Without knowing why it just spills out of my mouth. Freidl is the head of the ski school, and he comes from Austria or Germany or somewhere. His last name is Pfeifer. Someone said he was a Nazi. Whatever that is. I never believe that because my dad told me he was in the Tenth Mountain Division. They were Army skiers. Freidl speaks with an accent. About a year ago, he bought the ranch next to ours.

"I know Freidl," he says. "Why does he call you Terry the Terrible?"

"I don't know," I say. "I think maybe because every time I am over at their ranch playing with Freddie and Ricky, I get in lots of trouble."

"Trouble, eh? Well nothing wrong with that if it's the right kind of trouble. Why does your dad call you Terr-Ass?" he continues.

I look up at him wondering what kind of person this guy is, asking me all these questions. Adults don't talk much like this to kids unless it is in school. Usually all I hear is, "Terry don't do this, Terry don't do that. Terry, have you done your chores?" You know, that sort of thing.

I think about it a moment then say to him, "My dad calls me Terr-Ass because he says that I am always tearing ass around the house, the barnyard, and everywhere."

"That's the sign of a spirited pony if I ever heard of one," he says. "Well Terr-Ass, I think I'll call you that. With that cowlick in your hair and those mischievous blue eyes, you look the part. My name is Gary Cooper. You can call me 'Coop.'"

"Yes, sir, Mr. Coop," I say. Then I walk around the side of the house, Coop close on my heels.

We round the corner and see my dad sitting on a wooden sawhorse with a Pabst Blue Ribbon beer in one hand and a cigarette between the fingers of his other hand. He is looking out over the pond like he is thinking hard about something.

"Dad," I say. "Mr. Coop is here to see you."

My dad turns and looks our way. He stands up and says, "Well damn, Coop, I didn't know you were in town. Come on and have a beer."

"Don't mind if I do," Coop says. "How ya doin', Wendy?"

"Son," my dad instructs me, "Go get Mr. Cooper a beer."

I take off toward the house as I hear my dad asking how're ya doin'? how's the movie business? and, how was your trip? All the preliminaries to an adult talk over a couple of beers. I've seen it quite a bit because my dad and mom are pretty popular, and people are always showing up unexpectedly. Last winter a guy drove up our driveway in a blizzard and got his car stuck. He wandered into the house and slept by the heat register in the kitchen until we found him there in the morning. The guy was still a bit cold, but we fed him breakfast, and my dad pulled his car out, after using the Jeep to plow the road to the guy's rig.

I come back with the beer and give it to Mr. Coop. He says, "Thanks, Terr-Ass."

"You're welcome, Mr. Coop."

Coop starts in. "You know how to ride a horse? I'll bet a young cowboy like you rides pretty well, eh?"

"Yeah," I say, pouring it on some. "I can ride Smokey pretty good if my dad puts me on or if I can get him over by the rock and climb on from there. Someone has to saddle him for me because I'm too short to put the saddle on and cinch it up tight. My brother says the only reason I can ride Smokey is because he is an old nag ready for the glue factory. I don't believe him."

Coop laughs and takes his hat off and stuffs it on my head. It is too big and covers my eyes and ears. He and my dad chuckle.

"Can I have this hat?" I say.

"Tell you what," Coop says. "I think this hat fits your dad better. Let's give it to him."

He takes the hat off my head and plunks it down on my dad's head where it fits perfectly.

"What do ya think?" he says, looking at me seriously. "Since the hat doesn't fit you, I'll give you a horse ride."

He gets down on his hands and knees and says, "Get on!"

I say, "Are you sure?"

"Yep!"

So I climb up on his back. He grabs my legs, stands up, and trots me around the house once. I am laughing and telling him, "Run like the wind, run like the wind!" He is laughing and out of breath. We get back to my dad, and he sets me down.

"One more ride!" I say.

My dad says, "Time for you to do your chores, Terr-Ass. Go on now. We have to talk."

I walk out to the barn to check on the chickens. I get sidetracked before I get to the chicken coop and end up chucking rocks in the pond. After some time, I hear Coop driving away.

Several days later Coop drives back up to the ranch. My dad has taken to wearing the hat Coop gave him because it fits better and is in better shape than his old greasy, broken-down, grey Stetson. Coop doesn't stop at the house, but drives right out to the barnyard where we are messing with the hay sickle replacing some of the blades. My dad is removing the dull or broken blades with a wrench, and replacing them with sharp new blades. I am collecting the blades all neatly in a pile because I am going to save them for skipping across the water of the pond. They are the best because they are completely flat. I have gotten about five skips out of one of them. Gerry has gotten fourteen because he is older and stronger. Teddy is pretty good at skipping too. I think he has done one about ten or twelve.

Anyway, here we are working on the sickle, and Coop drives right out and parks in front of us. The dust collects around him as he gets out of the car carrying a big paper sack.

"Wendy," he says and nods toward my dad.

"How're ya doin', Terr-Ass," he says to me.

"Fine, Mr. Coop" I say.

"Come here, and see what I have for you," Coop grins.

I walk over to him, and he hands me the paper sack. I open it up and look inside. There is an actual double-holstered, six-gun, cap-pistol set with matching silver pistols. I reach in and pull them out. "Wow! Are these for me? They're neat."

"Well, since I had to give my hat to your dad, I thought I'd better get something that fit you and that you could use," Coop says.

I already have them out of the holsters and am loading caps into them. They are genuine Hubley Texan cap guns with triggers that work, and hammers that move back and slam forward on the cap when you pull the trigger. Not only that, they automatically advance the caps. When one is fired and you start to pull the trigger again, the next cap in line on the roll feeds up and is in place just in time for the hammer to hit it. It goes off with a loud bang. I've seen them advertised in a Roy Rogers comic book.

"Wow," I say again. "Thanks a lot, Mr. Coop. These are really cool."

"You're welcome," he says. "Have fun with them."

"I will," I say as I begin shooting bad guys and Indians heading in on us from the other side of the barnyard. I duck down to avoid fire and run to the side of the barn for cover. Soon I am lost to Gary Cooper and my dad.

Chapter 9

Winter 1952

My life is changing. I can feel it. It is winter, and I'm looking out the window at the snow. Gerry has brought the mumps home from school. Now I have them. I've been sick for a long time. Sometimes I'm burning up, and sometimes I'm cold. Mom makes me stay in bed. She says, "You have to get over the mumps before you can go outside again."

Gerry is already over them. Mom says he didn't have as bad a case as I do. Teddy has them, too, and is swollen in the face like I am. To make matters worse, his kidney problems have kicked up because of them. He must feel sicker than I do. We have to stay away from Jennifer so she doesn't get them. She is so small that, if she catches them from us, they will make her really, really sick. We don't talk much, mostly sleep or read magazines and comics. Dad brought home a few Superman and Archie comics. Although I don't read yet, I do know some words, and I can tell what is happening by the pictures.

~~~

In a few days, Teddy is doing better than I am. He has been sick a lot longer than I've been. Dad says to him, "Well, Teddy Old Sock, you look better today. How do you feel?"

"I feel pretty good, " Teddy says.

"One more day, and you can go back to school," Dad says. He looks at me and says, "Terr-Ass you look like hell."

I grunt and turn over. It makes me mad that Teddy gets to go back to school, and I have to stay in bed.

~~~

Some more days have passed, and today is the first day I feel well since I caught the mumps. Mom and Dad both say I have to stay in bed another day or two before I can go outside.

"You gotta shake this thing," Dad says. "Maybe in a couple of days you'll be well enough to go out."

Teddy has been back at school for a while. I wish I could go to school or outside or anywhere but being here in bed. I'm tired of being in my room all the time. Maybe I'll be able to go out tomorrow.

~ ~ ~

Finally, today I'm back outside. I've spent all morning building a snow fort. I made a large hole in the snow with a place for me to hide. Then I made a platform to hold a bunch of snowballs so I have ammo when Gerry and Teddy walk up the road. I can't throw very far, and the snowballs always miss. It's okay because maybe today they won't be paying attention, and I can pelt them. I still don't feel great, but Dr. Lewis says that's because I had a real bad case of the mumps, and it will take me awhile to get my strength back.

"You're on the mend, young man," he said the last time he saw me.

He was right, I think, *because today I'm playing outside in freedom.*

Spring 1952

It's spring now, and the snow is almost melted on the grass on the south side of our house. I'm back in my room sick with the chicken pox. I'm looking out the window again the same as I did when I had the mumps. It seems like I was just locked up here with the mumps, and now I'm locked up all over again with the chicken pox. Teddy brought them home from school, and my dad said, "Well, we might as well let them all get it at once."

Mom and Dad let me stay in my room with Teddy while he was sick and sure enough I got the chicken pox. Now I can't go outside again until they go away. Chicken pox are these small red bumps on my skin that are all itchy. I have a fever and vomit up my dinner a lot. Dr. Lewis says I have a very bad case. He says, "Well, young man, I see you have the chicken pox. They're going around. You just had the mumps, no? Well, you probably didn't get over them totally."

"I guess not," I say.

Now I get to drink lots of ginger ale. That is good. But I have to stay in bed all day. That is bad.

~ ~ ~

The snow is gone on the entire lawn when I finally get to go outside again. Winter has all the way changed to spring. Most of the spring I feel tired and don't feel like doing much. I finally begin to feel better as summer comes. Gerry and Teddy get out of school for the summer soon. I hope they won't bring something else home to make me sick.

Chapter 10

Summer 1952

My parents have gone East for a few weeks. Grandpa Morse has died. Grandpa was my dad's dad. He was a tall man, like my dad, with blue eyes and a bald head. He was very grumpy most of the time and scared me. My brothers and I have to stay here in Aspen. My mom and dad have taken Jennifer with them, or maybe left her somewhere else. They have left me with Old Art Roberts and his family on their spread in Brush Creek. After they sold the ranch to us, the Roberts's moved over to Brush Creek.

Teddy and Gerry get to stay at Werk Cook's ranch. Lucky them. Jeff Cook and Barb Cook are about their ages, so they have some kids to play with. I don't have anyone to play with. Here there are only Anita Roberts, Keith Roberts, and the oldest and meanest Roberts kid whose name is Ray. They are all teenagers and meaner than a pack of badgers. I don't like them. I don't like being here. Shirley Roberts is the mean kids' mom and Art is their dad. Art doesn't talk to me. Shirley calls me "Hey, Morse kid" because she can't remember my name. I keep telling her it is Terry, but she never remembers. Sometimes I think she is a little slow. The Roberts kids all call me "Hey, little Morse shit."

The ranch is on a hillside so everything is at angles. The barnyard isn't flat like it is on our ranch. This ranch is a broken-down place. The barn is tilting, its weather-beaten wood all brown and black. The grey wooden shingles are coming off the roof. The wind has blown big piles of them across the ground so they lie on the edges of the barn.

Art Roberts says, "I'll get to that barn roof someday." But he never does. Next to the barn are two corrals, one on each side. One is for the horses when they come in from the fields for some hay. One is for the damned pigs. They have four pigs. If you stretched one pig out, it would be taller than I am. It would also weigh a bunch more than I do. I have to feed them leftover garbage, one of my several chores. Shirley Roberts makes me take them the slop she collects from the food the Roberts kids and her and Art don't eat. She puts it in a bucket and tells me, "Here, little Morse kid, take this bucket of slop across the barnyard and dump it in the pig trough."

The pigs run at me when I come through the gate to dump the slop. I'm afraid they will eat me instead of the slop. Keith and Anita say the pigs will eat me if they get hungry enough, so I shouldn't go into the corral without the slop bucket. They threaten to throw me to the pigs when they are being mean to me. I don't know whether to believe Keith and Anita but am not willing to take the chance. I don't go into the pig corral without the slop bucket, and, when I do, I get out as fast as I can. Those pigs really are damn pigs.

Now the chickens are another matter. I know how to handle them from all my chores at home on our ranch. I don't have to do anything with pigs at home because we butchered them all a long time ago and didn't get any more. The chickens seem to like me. When I throw them grain and corn from the sacks stored in the tack room, nice and handy for the mice, the chickens come up to me clucking and ruffling. I don't mind them. We have had a good understanding so far.

~~~

"Hey you, Little Morse kid," Shirley Roberts shouts to me one day. "Come over here."

She stands by the hitching post close to the low two-story ranch house. The house has dirty white paint peeling off in great flakes, leaving splotches of grey wood. The green trim has faded and cracked. There is an attached screened-in porch. Down the hill a few steps is the outhouse. The sun has beaten it into the same dingy brown and black color as the barn. I walk over to Shirley. She looks at me and says, "How old are you?"

"I'm almost six."

"Hrumpf," she says. "Old enough. Go out to the hen house and get me that dappled red-and-white hen that has quit laying."

"What for?" I say. "She doesn't like to be away from the other hens."

"Just do what I say," Mrs. Roberts says.

So I walk across the sloping barnyard kicking some rocks here and there, wondering what she wants with the hen. I open the gate to the chicken yard. I use my foot to gently shoo away the hens that are trying to get out so they can roam in the free space of the ranch. Once I'm inside the fence with the gate closed, I look around for the dappled hen. I see her over by the coop. I walk over and snatch her up quickly in my arms, holding her wings down tight so she can't struggle away. In a few seconds, the hen settles down and looks at me. She's quiet as I carry her to the gate, nudge the other hens away with my foot, and leave the yard, closing the gate behind me. I take the hen over to Shirley Roberts.

"Here, give me that bird," she says, kinda mean.

"It's a chicken, not a bird," I say as I hold it out to her.

She reaches under the hen and grabs her legs and holds her upside down. Then as quick as a flash she lays the chicken down on the wooden stump. From behind her skirt, where she has been holding it with her left hand, she swings upward with a hatchet and... SLAM! The hatchet goes down, cuts off the chicken's head, and buries itself into the wood. The hen's head pops off and almost hits me as it sails to the ground. I look on in horror as Shirley lets the chicken go. The hen beats her wings and hits the ground running or tumbling, I don't know which, blood spurting from her neck. She flaps and runs around on the ground helplessly, then suddenly falls to her side frozen in death. By this time the beak on the severed head has stopped moving open and shut and I see both parts of the hen are really quite dead.

"That!" says Shirley Roberts loudly, "IS NOT how you kill a chicken." Then she starts laughing and says, "Go pick it up and set it out back on the table behind the kitchen. You can start pulling the feathers out."

I watch in dumbstruck horror as Mrs. Roberts walks off to the chicken coop. Quick as a blink she comes back with another doomed hen.

"Go on now," she says. "Get to work."

My feet are frozen to the spot where I stand. Mrs. Roberts walks to the cottonwood tree next to the house and hangs the hen up by her feet. She waits a few minutes, then slits the hen's throat and lets the blood run all over the ground. I know this is the right way to slaughter a chicken because that's how we do it at home. You have to hang the chicken upside down and slit its throat. If you don't, the feathers are hard to pull out. I can't figure out all my feelings but know I am really mad at Shirley Roberts for cutting the head off the dappled hen. It will take me the rest of the day to pluck the dead bird because the feathers will be so hard to pull out.

"Go on, get to work," Shirley shouts at me again.

Slowly I go over to the dead hen, pick it up and carry it around back to the low table. I put the hen on the table and begin struggling with the feathers.

Dumb ass, I think. *She did this on purpose so she won't have to look after me for the rest of the day.*

Just about that time she comes around the side of the house with the other hen and puts her on the table.

"This ought to keep you out of trouble for awhile."

I send her one of my I'll-get-even stares and continue with the chickens.

It is late in the afternoon before I take the chickens into the kitchen and give them to Mrs. Roberts. She drops them in the boiling pot she has on the stove. I watch the hens sink into the scalding water, then walk out of the house before she can say anything to me.

~~~

It is night. I am awake, and crying. I have to sleep in the same bed as Anita because there isn't anywhere else in the house for me to sleep. Anita keeps hitting me with her elbow when she tosses and rolls like a boat floating down the Roaring Fork River. I am awake trying to decide what I should do to get even, to make it so hard on these people that they will find another place for me to stay. Better yet, maybe I'll send a letter to my parents asking them to come get me. But I'll have to ask one of the Roberts to write it for me. *As if any of them know how to write.* I think. *Maybe I should just run away.*

It is finally morning and I smell pancakes on the wood stove griddle.

Maybe today will not be as bad, I think.

I go down to the kitchen and Mrs. Roberts says, "Here, sit down. Here's some pancakes."

I sit down, and a plate appears in front of me.

"Thank you."

I dig into the pancakes and quickly finish them off. I finish my glass of milk, still warm from the cow that Old Art Roberts has milked early this morning. The Roberts don't send their milk down to Art Hoagland's dairy to pasteurize it. They drink it straight from the cow. So I have to. I get up from the table, set my plate down somewhere near the sink, and go out to use the one holer before Anita and Keith get up. They are lazy and like to sleep as long as Shirley and Old Man Roberts let them. I know I have some time to do my business.

Afterward I go to the barn, get the feed for the chickens, and get that chore out of the way. Then I start to sneak off up Brush Creek to play for the morning until it is time for me to feed the pigs. As I'm leaving, I get sidetracked. I putter around the barn wondering why everything is such a mess. It must be hard to find tools when you need them. My dad's barn is much more orderly. When I have taken inventory of the mess, I work my way through the barn past the stalls, and head out the back door. I wander around outside the horse corral and notice there are lots of prairie dog holes. Just about that time, I hear Old Art Roberts saying to Shirley, "I'm headed over to the Anderson place to see if I can get Bill to help me with the haying this fall. You tell those kids to get rid of them prairie dogs that are tearing hell out of the outside of the corral. First thing you know, the fence will be falling down." I see him get into his busted-down truck and head up the valley on the old road that hugs the hillside.

Later in the morning, my roaming takes me back to the vicinity of the corral, and I hear Keith and Ray talking about getting rid of the prairie dogs.

"Well, shit," Ray says. "I guess he don't want us to poison them. That takes too long, and besides we may poison the horses. I guess we better shoot them."

"Yeah," says Keith. "I bet he wants us to shoot them. Get rid of them quick."

"I'll get the .22s." Ray walks toward the house.

"What are you doing?" I say to Keith as I approach warily.

"We're about to get rid to the prairie dogs."

"Can I watch?"

"Dunno, have to ask Ray. He's the boss here."

Not too long after, Ray appears with two .22 rifles and two boxes of shells.

Ray loads up the rifles and gives one to Keith.

"You be careful now, damnit," Ray says to Keith, "This is all the ammo we have."

"Can I watch?" I ask Ray. He looks at me like I am from some other planet.

"What are you doin' here, you little Morse shit?" he says.

"I just want to watch."

"Okay. You stand over there out of the way."

I can tell he is thinking something because he looks at me like he does when he is about to slug me or play some dirty trick. I think for a moment it might be a better idea for me to go off and mind my own business. Before I can get to it, the prairie dogs are sticking their heads out of their holes. Keith and Ray are shooting at them and not hitting them.

"Hey, little Morse shit" Ray says after a few minutes of silence while they wait for the prairie dogs to show themselves again. "Why don't you go over there on the left of where we are shooting, and you can tell us if we hit anything. Go on now! Get."

I think about ignoring him for a minute, but he is the meaner of the two, and I know he will slug me if I give him any lip. I look at him for a minute longer, just to let him know I'm not afraid of him, then go over by the fence out of the line of fire. I'm in my position only a short time before the prairie dogs begin sticking their heads out of the holes. I watch them to see if Ray and Keith are going to plug them. I hear the shots but don't see any bullets kick up dust near the prairie dogs. I don't see any of the prairie dogs getting hit either. Then a .22 slug hits the fence behind me. I turn around and see some dust coming up from the ground. I turn and look at Ray. He is aiming right at me! He shoots another shot, and it lands in front of me and the dust puffs up in a ball. I panic and start running and crying all at once. I hear Ray and Keith laughing. I run across the barnyard almost to the house still crying. Then I turn around and shout at them,

"You goddamned shitheads! I'm gonna tell my dad on you, and then there will be hell to pay! Shitheads."

Then I ramble off a whole line of swear words that I have been saving for the right time. Just about when I am finishing up my great cuss, I feel my ear being twisted and my hair pulled. I fall over backwards, and Shirley Roberts is standing over me with her hands on her hips and the wrath of God on her face.

"Don't you talk like that around here, you little shit!" she says.

Little shit? I think. *She is talking like that, why shouldn't I?*

I don't say anything, just keep crying. I feel lonely and very sad. I hate this place and these people.

"I want to go home," I plead.

She stands there for a minute, then turns around and goes into the house. Finally I pick myself up and head down to the creek to lose myself for the rest of the day. I don't give a damn about the pigs or Anita or Ray or Keith or Shirley or Old Man Roberts. Just before dark I wander back to the house. I go into Anita's room and lie down on the bed and fall asleep.

The next morning Old Art Roberts shakes me out of my sleep.

"Come on," he says. "I'm taking you over to Werk Cook's place. This ain't working out for any of us."

He gathers up my clothes and stuffs them in the sack I came with, and I follow him out to the truck. I don't say a word as we drive down Brush Creek Road, every mile a mile closer to freedom and further from hell. They trade me out for Gerry, who can hold his own at the Roberts' place, and the rest of my summer is delightful. I meet Jimmy Green who is my age and is the son of the ranch hand on the Cook ranch. He is the fastest runner I have ever seen. After being on the Roberts' place, and then at the Cooks' place, I know for sure I prefer to have friends and nice people around me.

Chapter 11

Late Summer 1952

My mom and dad are back from the East. Grandpa has been buried, and Mom and Dad have visited all our relatives. They have decided that they're tired of work and need a weekend off. They're going camping up in the Hunter Creek Valley with Lenny Woods, Carl and Tukey Jonas, and some other friends. They have left us at Piss Pot Allen's. I don't know his last name. I don't even know him. I only know he is called Piss Pot Allen. Piss Pot Allen lives in a dump of a hovel in town by the Glory Hole. The Glory Hole is a big hole in the ground where the old Midland Railroad terminus turnstile was, back in the early days. There was a big mine tunnel underneath it, and one day it caved in and made the big hole.

Piss Pot Allen is a bachelor and looks older than my mom and dad. He is real dirty, but then most everyone around here is because of the work they have to do. Still, he is even dirtier and messier. There is junk all around the shack, which is a small two-room log cabin built back in the mining days. The logs are weathered brown and black like the boards on the side of Art Roberts' barn. The roof has warped grey shingles that are split and falling off. In some places, the roof is covered with rusted tin. The door to the house is one of those that opens on the bottom and the top, called a Dutch door. You can have the top open and the bottom can be closed.

Piss Pot has a one holer on the side of the house that smells to high heaven. To get to the one holer, you have to go out the front door, through the chicken yard which is attached to the house and then around to the side of the house. He has running water in the kitchen sink. He has a wood stove that burns wood and coal.

My parents dropped us off here at Piss Pot Allen's after we came into town in the Jeep. We were surprised when we had to walk through the chicken yard to get to the front door of the house. Dad spoke with Piss Pot Allen for a while, then got in the Jeep with Mom and drove off down the street.

Piss Pot Allen looks at the three of us standing outside in the chicken yard.

"You kids can stay out here and play. I'm gonna lock the gate so the chickens don't get out."

He walks over to the gate and puts a chain around it and locks it up tight with a padlock. Then he turns around, walks into his house, closes the bottom half of his front door, and says, "And don't you raise hell with those chickens. They're skinny enough as it is."

I look at the chickens. They are skinny, and a few of them are missing clumps of feathers. They seem to be wandering around kind of listlessly. It doesn't seem right to me.

~~~

We kids have been out in the chicken yard for most of the afternoon. We're tired of playing tag and whatever else we can think of. Finally Gerry says, "I wonder what in hell he's doing in there?"

He goes over and looks in the house over the top of the door. Then he waves us over to the door and says, "Take a look at this. He's drunker than a skunk."

Teddy looks in and shakes his head. I ask Gerry to give me a boost so I can see in. He does. There is Piss Pot Allen sitting in a chair by the stove, a crumpled newspaper in his lap and a whiskey bottle on the floor. Piss Pot Allen is snoring like a mule.

"He sure looks drunk," I say to Gerry.

"He is."

"Maybe we should wake him up," Teddy says.

"No, probably just piss him off," Gerry replies. "Anyway, the last thing we need is him making life miserable for us. Just being at this place is bad enough."

We fart around chasing the chickens and playing games until the sun goes behind Shadow Mountain.

"We better wake him up," Gerry says. "It looks like it might rain."

I look up at the sky and sure enough it is dark with clouds. It will rain, this I know, it is just a matter of how soon it will happen. Gerry walks over to the door and shouts at Piss Pot Allen, "Hey!"

Then louder, "Hey!"

Still no response from inside. Finally Gerry shouts again at the top of his lungs, "HEY, PISS POT ALLEN!"

I hear stirring in the house, and Piss Pot Allen comes to the door. He looks like a tornado ran over him.

"What in hell do you want?" he says to Gerry.

"We want to come inside. It's gonna rain."

Piss Pot Allen looks at him and then sees Teddy and me.

"What're you kids doin' here?" He has forgotten that we are staying with him.

"We're staying here while Mom and Dad are up in Hunter Creek," I say.

Piss Pot Allen looks at me like it's a mystery I can even talk. He rubs his skinny belly and then says to no one in particular, "Oh, yeah. I told Wendy I'd take care of you while he was up in the woods. Well, you better come in then."

He opens the door, and we pile into the house.

"We're hungry," Gerry says. "We haven't had any lunch."

"Well, its about dinner time soon, so you might as well wait till I fix it," Piss Pot says.

Then he says to himself. 'Wendy didn't tell me I'd have to feed these monsters. Wonder what I have around here that I can give them. Should've never taken them on. Don't know why I did.'

Then he mumbles a bunch of other stuff. Finally he takes a pot out of the sink and sets it on the stove. He fires up the stove and after a fashion has it going hot enough to cook something on it if he is lucky. He opens the cupboard, takes out two cans of Boston Baked Beans, opens them, and pours them into the pot. He stirs the beans with his finger, then sits down and picks up his paper.

"You kids amuse yourselves while these here beans cook," he says.

We look around the small cabin for something to amuse ourselves, gazing at all his junk to see what we can find of interest. There isn't much. Lots of times other peoples' junk is interesting. Not Piss Pot Allen's. After some time has passed, I say to Gerry, "I'm really hungry."

"Yeah," Gerry says, "so am I. It's getting dark out."

For the first time, I notice that in fact it is getting dark. I can hardly see my hand in front of my face. We look over at Piss Pot Allen and see he is still drunk and snoring in his chair. We walk over to the stove and see the fire has gone out. There are a few embers from the coals but not enough to heat the beans on top.

Suddenly Piss Pot Allen stirs and moves around like he's going to wake up. Gerry walks over to him and shakes him by the shoulder. Piss Pot comes fully awake and says, "Why don't you kids eat them beans on the stove?"

Gerry looks at him and then walks over to the stove and studies the beans. He finds a spoon and stirs them up a bit.

"These beans are cold and besides they're all burned. The bottom of the pan is blacker than a night in hell. We're not going to eat these. Don't you have anything else?" Gerry says.

Piss Pot looks at Gerry, gets up unsteadily and slams a couple of dishes on the kitchen table. He dishes up the beans and says, "Now set down and eat."

We sit at the table and look at the beans. I wouldn't feed them to Dirty Peter Morse, who will eat anything. Gerry and Teddy refuse to eat them. Piss Pot Allen, when he sees this says, "If you don't eat them, you can just go hungry, you little Morse shits."

I can't figure out why everyone calls us "little Morse shits." We get in trouble sometimes, but we're not shits.

So that's what we do. Go hungry. A little later, Piss Pot Allen makes us get in a dirty old bed and go to sleep for the night. We are all in the same bed and moving and thrashing and bumping each other. Finally we go to sleep.

~ ~ ~

It is about the middle of the morning now, and Gerry, Teddy, and I are out in the chicken yard where Piss Pot Allen has put us. We are glad to be outside because the house is dark and stinks pretty bad. The chicken wire fence is real high, and Piss Pot thinks we will be okay there like we were yesterday. He doesn't want us to be in the house. I think it's because he doesn't want us to see him drinking more whiskey. We don't care if he drinks his whiskey as long as he doesn't get any meaner.

The chickens are all grouped in a corner of the chicken yard. We have scared them out of their tail feathers. We're mad and hungry and bored. Gerry says, "Okay, you guys, we have to make a plan."

Teddy and I move in close to make sure Piss Pot Allen can't hear us.

"I'm not staying here a minute longer," Gerry says. "Piss Pot Allen is an old sumofabitch and meaner than hell.

He didn't feed us last night or give us breakfast. I'm gonna climb over the fence and get out of here."

"You can't go without me," Teddy says.

"Me either," I say. I look up at the fence. It looks real high, and I'm not sure if I can climb over it.

Gerry walks over to the door of the cabin and pokes his nose in. Piss Pot Allen is busy sleeping off his drunk, the newspaper still crumpled up in his lap. Gerry comes back and says, "It looks like he is sleeping it off."

We move over to the side of the house where the gate is locked with the chain. Gerry says, "Just watch where I put my feet, then try to do the same, and you can climb out."

Teddy and I watch him as he puts his foot in the chicken wire and stretches it out some. Then he sets his other foot higher up and takes the next step up to the two-by-four support on the gate, then up on the wire two more steps, and a leg over the top. He shuffles over and climbs down the same way but much faster because he slips on the second-to-last step and lands on his butt on the ground.

"Shit," he says. "That hurt." He gets up and brushes himself off, then looks back at us to see who is going next. Teddy and I start to laugh.

"Shhhhh," Gerry whispers. "You'll get him out here."

Teddy starts up the fence but can't reach as high as Gerry, so has to kick in the wire with his tennis shoe to make a bit of a hole so he can get a foothold. Luckily for us, the chicken wire is the big-hole cheap stuff, not the little-hole stuff, because the little hole stuff is a lot tougher. Teddy manages to hoist himself over the top and also misses the last step but jumps and lands on his feet.

"Didn't even fall over," he grins.

Now it is my turn, and I start up the same way using the dents in the wire Teddy has kicked. I am going over the top when I catch my pants on a nail or something and hear a ripping sound. I look down and see that I have ripped my pants for about two inches just below the crotch, but am happy that I haven't cut myself. I climb down and try to do the tricky dismount Teddy has done but land on my butt in the dust like Gerry. I get up and see that Gerry and Teddy have taken off toward town and run to catch up with them.

"Free at last!" Gerry exclaims. "I really don't like that Piss Pot Allen. He's real mean, his house smells, he smells, and his food is crap."

"Yeah," Teddy says.

"Yeah," I say.

Off we head into Aspen toward the Red Onion Bar about five blocks away. We are also eight or nine blocks away from the Hotel Jerome Bar. We all know where these places are because that's where my dad goes after teaching skiing when he has to have a drink with his clients. Sometimes we have to wait for him until it is dark out and we are freezing our butts off. Then we have to climb in that open Jeep and drive home and really freeze our butts off.

We hit the main road where it goes out of town toward Independence Pass, and walk in the other direction on Cooper Street toward the Red Onion. We are wondering if we will get there before Piss Pot wakes up and starts looking for us. That is, in case he notices we are gone.

Gerry's idea is to go to the Red Onion and see if we can bum a hamburger off of Werner Kuster. Maybe we can buy it on account. That's what Beck and Bishops say to my mom when she buys groceries.

"I'll put it on your account," Albert Bishop says.

We walk down Cooper Street to the Red Onion and into the bar. Bill Marolt is behind the bar wiping a few glasses and talking to Hoofy Sandstrom, the local afternoon drinker. He sees us come in and says right away, "Well, if it isn't the Morse boys. What're you doin' here? Wendy told me you was goin' campin'."

Teddy and I look at Gerry. Gerry says, "Well, they did go camping but must have forgot to tell you that we have to stay over at Piss Pot Allen's for a couple of nights. Last night he got drunk, and tried to feed us cold burnt beans that we couldn't eat. He has locked us in the chicken yard so he doesn't have to look after us. We haven't eaten since yesterday breakfast, and we're wondering if maybe Kuster will give us a hamburger."

"Well, that's a mouthful," says Bill Marolt. "How'd you get out of the chicken yard?"

"Climbed the fence," Gerry says.

"Climbed the fence?" Bill Marolt continues. "How'd you do that? That fence is eight feet high. Must have been a chore." He chuckles. "You Morse kids."

Just then Kuster comes around the corner into the bar.

"Hey, Kuster!" Bill grins. "Guess what these Morse kids just done. They are stayin' over at Piss Pot Allen's place, and they climbed over the fence out of the chicken yard to come get one of your hamburgers."

"Well, this is a good laugh," says Kuster in his heavily accented English. "Piss Pot Allen will piss his pants when he sees they're gone. Goddamn, he'll be scared for his life if he don't find those kids before Wendy gets back. Wendy will be madder than hell."

"Come on, kids, we get you a hamburger, then we will watch the fun with Piss Pot Allen when Wendy gets back."

Kuster takes us back in the kitchen and gets us a hamburger and some of his home-cut greasy fried potatoes. We have sodas on the side and are in heaven. After I have eaten, my brain starts working again, and I say to Gerry, "When Dad and Mom find out that we left Piss Pot's, they are going to be really mad."

Gerry looks at me like I have just stolen his dessert or something. A light goes on in his head, and he says, "Damn, I guess you're right. We'll probably get a whipping for sure."

Teddy is listening to us discuss the number of ways we will be punished and looks white as a sheet. I wonder to myself if he is going to vomit. He doesn't like the belt at all. Gerry and I are used to it. It's only five or six good smacks and doesn't burn too long. We have to cry a lot to put on a good show so Mom thinks Dad is really going to kill us and tells him, "That's enough, Wendy. I should have never said anything."

I could never figure out why she did say anything in the first place if she didn't want us to get the belt. Gerry is getting too big for the belt. I think Dad knows it, and probably has quit. Gerry hasn't been spanked for at least since last spring, and I know he has done a lot of bad stuff. I am musing over this while Gerry and Teddy are finishing their sodas. I hear the thunder crashing outside and look out the window at the rain coming down. I remember that it rained last night too. I woke up and heard the rain on the tin roof of the cabin. I wondered if it was raining in Hunter Creek.

Kuster comes into the kitchen and says, "You kids stay here for the time being while the rain goes through. I'll get you some comics to read." He walks off and gets some old comic books that he has for kids, to keep them quiet while they are at the table with their parents eating. When he comes back with them, I see Gerry isn't too pleased about the idea because we have already bummed from Kuster. Gerry doesn't want to test him. We are already in enough trouble. We have run away from Piss Pot Allen and, almost as bad, have bummed a hamburger from Kuster. Dad will be furious.

~ ~ ~

Sometime later I hear a commotion out in the bar and leave the kitchen to peek around the corner. I shudder at what I see. My dad is in the bar, and he looks fit to kill. He is talking to Bill Marolt, who has set a beer up on the bar.

"So I walk into that tumbled down shack," my dad is saying, "and there's Piss Pot Allen sound asleep with the damned newspaper over his face. I wake him up and ask him where my boys are. He tells me he has locked them out in the chicken yard so he can get some rest. Well, the stupid sumofabitch. I tell him to go look in the chicken yard. He does, and then he comes back and says, 'I can't understand it. The kids were there just a few hours ago.'" My dad takes a sip of beer.

"Then I ask him when he set the boys out there, and he says, 'just after breakfast, which they didn't eat because they were picky and didn't like my cooking.' Then I say 'what did you feed 'em?' and he says, 'beans that they didn't eat last night.' So I walk over to the stove and look at the pot sitting there that's a crusted mess of indefinable gunk I wouldn't feed to a pig. I ask him, 'When did they last eat?' He says, 'I don't know, they are pretty picky.' So they didn't eat anything at his place."

"Then I take him out in the chicken yard and tell him to look around. Pretty soon he sees the fence where they must have pushed it out of shape climbing out, and he starts in on me about how I owe him for the fence because those little shits have wrecked it and on and on. It was all I could do to not let him have it right in the kisser."

My dad takes a long pull on the beer and continues, "I was so damn mad, I could have killed him right there."

"Sounds like you got back early," says Bill.

"Yeah. We got rained out pretty good last night. Then this morning we went fishing, hoping the weather would clear up. It didn't, so we decided to pack up and come home. Now I've gotta figure out where those little monsters might have gone. Somewhere they could get something to eat, I'm sure, because they must be real hungry. They haven't had anything since yesterday breakfast."

"Well," Bill says, "you don't have to look too far, because they must have stopped at the first place on the street, which would have been here. They're here, back in the kitchen. Werner fed them a burger and some fries and fixed them up with some reading material figuring you might be down early because of the weather. I don't know what he had in mind if you decided to stay up there the night."

"Thanks for the beer, Bill" my dad says as he put a quarter down on the bar. "I guess I better get the kids and head home. Rudy's already having a fit. She is over at the Epicure and the Jerome looking around for them."

My dad walks toward me, and I quickly step back in the kitchen and grab a comic book looking absorbed. My dad rounds the corner and says, "Come on, kids, we're going home. That'll be the last time we leave you with anyone when we go camping. You are probably better off by yourselves."

Gerry looks at me. That we are.

Chapter 12

Early Fall 1952

It's the first week in September. School starts today, and I'm going into first grade. Teddy went to first grade two years ago, and had Miss Lumsden who will be my teacher. I'm very excited about going to school today. I am wearing a new shirt and jeans. The shirt is a blue-and-white-plaid flannel my mom bought out of the Monkey Wards catalogue. She usually makes our shirts, but this year she bought us each a new shirt from Monkey Wards. It's too big, but she says I will grow into it before the year is over because I'm "growing like a weed" now. I love blue jeans. They have deeper pockets than my overalls and need a belt to hold them up. I also have new brown leather shoes. I know they will be beat up by the end of the day. I don't mind because shoes need to be beat up to fit right.

"Come on, boys, we're gonna be late," my dad says as we grab our lunches and head for the door.

"We're coming," Gerry says. "I get front seat. You pipsqueaks can sit in the back."

I climb up over the Jeep's tailgate and sit on the bare metal back seat facing Teddy. It's a cold windy ride in the back of the Jeep. We drive down the road toward the highway, my dad's cigarette smoke blowing in my face. We drive across the upper cattle guard, down past the north field, across the lower cattle guard, and out onto the highway. We cross the Maroon Creek Bridge with its big wooden planks now covered with pavement. The old railroad trestle is still supported by its tall steel towers, and still has its wooden side railings. We drive the two miles or so into town, and pass Waterman's Store on our way down Hallam Street to the red brick schoolhouse.

My dad stops the Jeeps and says, "Okay. Pile out. Have a good day at school. And Gerry, you make sure to collect Teddy and Terry and get them on the bus for home before it leaves. Bernard Stapleton isn't going to wait around for you."

"Yeah, Okay." Gerry says.

I'm nervous and don't know where to go. Teddy and Gerry have started to walk across the lawn to the playground. I follow them. Soon a loud bell rings, and all the kids walk and run from the playground out to the sidewalk facing the front of the school building. I follow everyone and watch what they are doing. We line up in a long line facing the school building. A teacher is out on the grass raising the American flag on a tall white flag pole.

"What's going on?" I ask Gerry.

"Shhhh! We're about to say the Pledge of Allegiance."

"What's that?" I say.

"You'll find out, just shut up and listen. We have to say it every day."

I shut my mouth and look at the teacher. He has his hand on his heart and is standing in front of the flagpole waiting for everyone to be quiet. When it is quiet, he signals, and everyone says, "I pledge allegiance to the flag of the United States of America," and a bunch of other stuff that I can't follow. Soon it is over, and everyone starts going in the doors. The schoolhouse is a long red brick building with four doors, one on each end and two in the front of the building. Gerry heads off to one of them, and I start to follow.

"No," he says, "You go over to that door."

"Well, I don't know where to go," I say.

"Just go through that door and go to the end of the hall. First Grade is on the left."

I go through the west door and wander down the hall with all the other little kids, getting shuffled this way and that as they hurry into their classes, pushing and pulling each other. In a moment the hall is empty and I'm alone. I walk down to the end of the hall and enter a room on the left. A lady is shushing kids and whisking them to their seats like trying to shoo flies out an open window.

"Who are you?" she says to me.

"Terry," I say in a little voice. I hate this. I am nervous, shy, and know that all the kids are looking at me. I hear them say, "He's lost." "He must be a first grader." "This is second grade." "Where is first grade?" "It's across the hall this year." They're all giggling and whispering.

The teacher bends over and says to me, "My name is Mrs. Johnson, Terry. Are you supposed to be in first grade with Miss Lumsden?"

"Yes," I whisper.

She grasps my hand, which I am not sure I like, but I let her because I'm frightened. She pulls me across the hall, and into another room, where she brings me up in front of Miss Lumsden.

"This is Terry," Mrs. Johnson says.

"Hi, Terry," Miss Lumsden says, "I'm Miss Lumsden. Why don't you sit over there?"

I shuffle over to the desk she has pointed to and sit. I look at my feet and notice my shoes are already scuffed up. There are some other kids in the class, maybe ten or twenty, but I don't count them because I'm looking up at the blackboard and the large letters on white cards tacked above it. Each letter is written in capitals and in small letters like my brothers have told me about. There is one big letter and one small letter for every letter in the alphabet. I count them. Twenty-six. I know lots of numbers, clear up to a hundred now, and know some letters but not all of them. My brothers have told me that you need to learn them to know how to read. I look at them and pick out the ones I know. A-D-E-G-H-I-M-O-R-S-T-W-Y-Z. Miss Lumsden is talking and talking. I'm not listening. I want to start learning the letters I don't know so I can learn to read. Soon I notice the classroom is quiet. Then there are hushed giggles and Miss Lumsden says, "Terry? Are you with us?"

I feel my face getting red.

"Yes, ma'am," I say.

"Please pay attention," Miss Lumsden says. "I'm telling you about how our days will be here, and you need to listen."

"Yes, ma'am," I say, now embarrassed because I know everyone is looking at me.

~~~

It is later, and I am on the bus with Gerry and Teddy heading home.

"How do you like school?" Gerry says.

"It's okay," I say. "Some of it's stupid. I don't need to learn how to cut and glue colored paper. I can already do that. I want to read. I don't much like the writing because I'm not real good at making the letters. We had to practice making A and B over and over until it looked like the ones above the blackboard. Mine never looked like that."

"It'll get easier once you get the hang of it," Teddy said.

I looked out the bus window as we passed over Castle Creek to Maroon Creek and headed for our stop at the bottom of our road. As I thought about it, I figured school would probably be okay as long as we did stuff that was as fun as playing around the ranch, although I didn't like spending most of the day indoors.

~~~

We've been in school a few weeks now, and things are settling in pretty well. I have some friends, Tony Vagneur, Richard Sabbatini, Chris Grove, John Autrey (his dad is a teacher in the high school), and Jimmy Green. There are a couple of other boys who do not talk to me much: Cecil

Lowderback, Dennis LaPlant, Paul Coble, and maybe one other, but I don't remember his name.

We have lots of girls in our class. Janie Johnson, her mom teaches second grade; Kathleen Herwick, her dad is the sheriff; Marilyn Durox, and Diane Stapleton, her dad drives the school bus. There are others like Catherine Bargsten, Nancy Lewis (her dad is a teacher too), Katie Benninghof, Pam Bishop, Betsy Patterson, Norma Just, and Gay Gann.

We get out of school for an hour at lunch, and all the big kids get to go into town after they eat their lunches if they want to. Some go into town or home to eat. They have to be back at school by one o'clock. We're supposed to stay on the playground. Richard and I have finished our lunches, and put our lunch pails in the hall under the coat hooks where we hang our coats. I have my jean jacket hanging there. We go back outside, and I say to Richard, "Let's go into town like the older kids do at lunch."

Richard looks at me. I start walking down the street by the Glidden's house. He is wondering if he should follow me, then decides to, and runs to catch up with me. We walk past a vacant lot, two houses, and then by the Beck's house and across the street by the fence surrounding the swimming pool beside the Hotel Jerome. The streets are still dusty and rocky because they haven't put oil on them for a long time. They oil the dirt streets to keep the dust down from the car traffic. We walk across the little alley next to Matthews' Drug Store and into the store. This is all new to us, but I'm excited about it because I feel like a big kid getting my lunch in town.

There are a bunch of big kids sitting at the soda fountain laughing and talking. I can smell the tuna salad sandwiches Walt Matthews has toasted up for them. To the right of the door as we walk in I spot a comic book rack. I pick up one of the comic books and begin looking at the pictures. I can't read many of the words but can recognize some small ones. One of the big kids walks by and smacks me on the top of the head.

"Aren't you one of the Morse kids?" he asks.

I look up at him but don't know him. I look down and say, "Yes."

"You look like one. You all look the same. What are you doing off the school yard?"

"Nothing," I say.

Seeing he is not going to get any more information from me, he walks over to the soda fountain and begins talking with some of the other big guys. I put the comic book back and wander over to a display shelf at the end of the soda fountain where there are bags of candy. Jellybeans, lemon drops, jawbreakers, cinnamon drops, and the like. I ask Richard, "Do you have a dime?"

"No," he says.

"I sure would like to have a bag of jelly beans," I say. The jelly beans are shining through the cellophane wrapping.

Without thinking about it further, I pick up a bag of jellybeans and a bag of lemon drops and stuff them in my shirt. Richard sees me and does the same. We head for the door and on the way out Richard takes a comic book off the rack and stuffs that in his shirt as well. We walk around the corner and back toward school the way we came. We're by the Beck's house and feel pretty good about getting free stuff at the drug store. I'm thinking it is a pretty good way to spend the lunch hour, when suddenly I feel a hand on my shoulder and hear, "Okay, boys, the fun is over. Time to come back to the store. You don't steal from Matthews' Drug Store."

I turn and see an angry Walt Matthews looking down at us. Immediately my stomach begins to churn. He marches us back to the store. I am dreading the outcome of this situation. I have the feeling we have done something really truly wrong and in the back of my mind I know what it is. Richard begins to cry, and I'm feeling the whimpers come over me as well.

"What are your names?" Mr. Matthews asks.

"Terry," I say. I can hardly hear my own voice.

"Oh, I recognize you. You're one of those Morse kids. But who are you?" he says, looking at Richard.

"Richard."

"Richard who?"

"Richard Sabbatini," Richard almost whispers.

I can see Richard is as frightened as I am. We both know we didn't pay for the candy, and that must be why doom is upon us. We enter the drug store, and Walt Matthews says to us, "You two stand here and don't move. But first, empty your shirts and pockets."

We unload our treasure and lastly Richard takes the comic book from his shirt. We set it all on the candy display on top of the comic book. Walt Matthews goes behind the soda fountain and picks up the phone. Somehow he must know the number because he doesn't have to look it up or anything, he just dials.

"Elbie," he says, "I've got one of those Morse kids down here and a Richard Sabbatini. They've taken some candy and a comic book from the store without paying for it."

After a really long minute, he says, "Yep, okay." He hangs up the phone and says, "You two are to walk right back to school and see Mr. Gann in his office as soon as you get there. And don't fool around on the way."

I know this is big trouble. The principal's office - and not even in school for a month. Dad is going to kill me.

We take our time walking back to school, both afraid of what is in store for us. We don't say much while walking. My mind keeps repeating, *There's gonna be hell to pay now*, something I've heard numerous times from Ed Ticoucih who sometimes helps out on the ranch. When I do something wrong, Ed looks at me and says, "There's gonna be hell to pay now."

"There's gonna be hell to pay now," I say out loud to Richard.

Richard says, "It's all your fault. It was your idea."

"Yeah, but you didn't have to come with me."

We go back and forth trying to figure out if one or the other of us can get off by blaming it on the other. We finally fall silent as we enter the school and walk down the hall to the principal's office.

We edge into the office and Mrs. Twinning, the school secretary, looks at us over the top of her glasses and shakes her head.

"Just a minute," she says. "You two sit down over there." She points to a couple of chairs up against the wall.

We sit down waiting for what will happen next. In a moment we are startled by the deep booming voice of Mr. Gann. "You two, come in here!"

We shuffle into his office and stand nervously in front of his desk.

"What do you think you are doing trying to steal candy from Matthews' Drug Store? Don't you know he has eyes in the back of his head? Don't you know stealing is a sin and a crime? People go to jail for that. And worse!"

Hell to pay, I think.

He says a bunch of other stuff I am not paying attention to until I hear, "I'm going to have to tell your parents about this. And I'm going to use you as an example to the rest of the kids in this school. I'm taking lunch privileges away from the whole school for a week. Everyone will have to eat their lunches here at the school, no more going to town. No more Matthews' Drug Store, no more going off the school grounds for the whole week."

"*Wow*," I think. "That's not bad. I just have to deal with a whipping at home and can't go into town for a week." I'm feeling pretty good about the whole thing without really knowing exactly what kind of hell we have brought down on ourselves.

Richard looks pale and scared. I wonder why.

"You boys get back to your class," I hear Mr. Gann saying.

We turn and walk out the door heading down the hall to Mrs. Lumsden's room.

"Well, that's not bad," I say to Richard. "I'll probably get a whipping when I get home but other than that…."

"I don't want a whipping," Richard says. "Besides, my dad won't give me a whipping. He will just make me stay in my room after school and for all weekend for a long time."

"I would rather have a whipping," I say. "At least I can go outside afterwards. It only burns for a little while."

~~~

School is out. I'm walking from the classroom outside to climb on the bus for home. One of the big kids comes up behind me to get on the bus and says, "Here's the little Morse kid who lost us our in-town privileges! Thanks a lot, you little thief."

I turn to look at him but don't know who he is. I'm embarrassed and angry to hear him say this. I get on the bus and see two girls together on the seat behind the driver. They look up at me and then put their heads together and start whispering, still looking at me as I walk past. I sit down in a seat toward the back next to another kid. He punches my arm when I sit down.

"So here he is, the famous little Morse brat who lost us our lunch hour!" he spits. "Thanks a bunch!"

I can feel tears in my eyes and am determined not to cry. I cannot stop them from running down my cheeks.

"Oh, now he's crying like a little baby," the boy says.

I move away from him, sliding into another seat closer to the girls. My stomach is turning upside down and my tears are running like a river, but I keep my mouth shut.

It is a horrible ride home. By the time I get out at the bottom of our road, everyone in the bus has teased me or thumped me or called me names. Stepping out and beginning my walk up the road is a relief. Gerry and Teddy haven't said a word to me the whole ride home. And they sure didn't stand up for me. It's the worst day of my life. I start walking up the road and as I walk over the first cattle guard, Gerry says to me, "Damn, Terry, you've got the whole school mad at you. You're in for a bad time for the next week. What the hell were you doing stealing from Matthews' Drug Store? Everyone knows he's a hawkeye. You're lucky he sent you back to Mr. Gann's office instead of calling Dirty Herwick to come and arrest you."

"Well, it wasn't planned, it just happened," I reply. "And I don't care if the whole school is mad at me. Everyone in that stupid school has probably stolen something from Matthews' Drug Store. I must have gotten the idea from somewhere."

"Well, I wouldn't want to be you," he says.

I'm silent the rest of the way home. I walk in dread of my future: what Dad will say, the licking I am going to get, what will happen in school for the next week. It all seems like a bad dream.

By the time I get home, I am well behind my two brothers. I walk into the house and hear my mom say, "I understand you had some trouble at school today. Your dad will be home soon."

I am mortified by what I have done. I know I have stolen from Matthews' Drugs, and I know stealing is one of the big three. My dad says, "You don't lie, cheat, or steal." This is the first time in a long time that I am truly frightened about being punished.

I set my lunch box on the kitchen counter after I have taken out the waxed paper my sandwich was wrapped in and thrown it away. Everything seems like a bad dream. I walk back outside and head out toward the barnyard. Time passes quickly as I chuck stones into the pond and watch the ripples make their way shoreward.

"Dinner! Teerrrry diiiinnnnerrr" I hear Teddy shout.

I make my way back to the house knowing Dad is home and probably ready to give me what for. Once in the house and seated at the table, I am relieved to know that my whipping will have to wait until after I've eaten. We'll finish dinner first. Everyone is at the table and eating when my dad says to me, "Hear you had a little trouble in town today, Terr-Ass."

"Yes." My mouse voice has returned.

"Want to tell me what happened?"

"Not really," I say. I know he already knows what happened.

"Well, suppose you go over it for me," he says.

I know there is no way out. "Well," I say, trying to buy a little time. "Richard and I went to Matthews' Drug Store on our lunch hour. I guess we sort of took some candy and didn't have the money to pay for it, so we just put it in our pockets and went back to school."

My dad looks at me sternly. His eyes are like ice. "Yeah," he says, "that's about the story I heard from both Walt Matthews and Elbie Gann. I gather you caused the whole school to lose lunch privileges for a full week."

"I guess so," I mumble.

"Well, I don't ever want to hear that you have stolen anything again. Do you understand me? Stealing is against the law, and you can go to jail for it. I won't have it. Now sit up like a man and finish your dinner."

"Wendy," my mom intervenes. "Aren't you going to punish him? This is a horrible thing. Everyone in town's going to know about it. It is so embarrassing."

My dad looks down at me and then over to my mom. "I guess he will learn his lesson from the punishment he'll get at school.

I look up at him and begin to understand that I'm not going to get a whipping and that my next week in school promises to be a living hell.

Chapter 13

October 1952

Dad, Gerry, Teddy, and I are in the Jeep driving out to Woody Creek. It's early on a Saturday morning, and it's time to pick potatoes at Clifford Vagneur's place. He is my friend Tony's dad. It's seven or eight miles over to the Vagneurs' spread. It hasn't frozen solid yet, but it is freezing some nights because it's fall. The long trip, the cold, and wind whistling through the Jeep make our ears, noses, and hands red. It seems like a long ride this morning.

We pull into the Vagneur's place. Everyone piles out of the Jeep, and we walk over to the potato cellar. There are a bunch of grown-ups and a bunch of kids hanging around waiting for something to happen. Pretty soon Mr. Vagneur says, "Okay, we'll start on the east end of the field and work our way towards the house and the cellar here. That way we'll have less of a distance to move the potatoes as the weekend goes on and we get more tired. You little kids, I'm paying you seven cents a hundred-pound sack for the potatoes you pick. So keep at it and you'll be rich by Sunday night. Grab a sack or two and off you go. We'll have more sacks over at the field after you fill the ones you have."

We all grab a sack or two and head out to the field. Tony, a couple of other Vagneur cousins, and some kids from the neighboring ranches are going out to the field with us. We reach the potatoes and line up at the end of the rows, one person to a row. Then we pick the potatoes from the plowed earth and put them into a gunnysacks. We drag the sack along as we move down our line. There are thousands of potatoes. I can see in a minute that this job has the potential to make for one long boring weekend.

We separate the potatoes as we go, putting the really little ones in piles that will be picked up later and used next year as seed potatoes. We put the large ones in the sacks.

I work my way up the row and am going pretty fast, because I'm cold, and working fast is a good way to get warm. After about a half hour, the sun comes up over the ridgeline, and the day begins to warm up ever so slightly. I pick and pick and pick. Finally I have filled the bag with so many potatoes I can no longer drag it behind me. I move forward, collect more potatoes, and bring them back to the sack which I have left it in my row. When I decide I have to walk too far back and forth, I get another sack and begin filling it.

~ ~ ~

It must be mid-morning because the sun is high in the sky. My back hurts, I'm thirsty, my hands and face are filthy. I stop picking and head over to the water jug for a drink. After I'm satisfied and can drink no more, I head back to the row I'm working on. I've finished two rows and am on the third. Tony is ahead of me on the row next to me, and my brother Teddy is two rows over. I take a small potato from the pile I'm making and chuck it over at Teddy. It bounces off his back. He looks around but can't figure out who threw the potato because both Tony and I are busily picking. When I see Teddy go back to work, I toss another spud over his way. This one bounces in front of him. Now he knows it's probably me, so he grabs one of his small potatoes and chucks it back at me. The potato nearly hits Tony on the way by and lands just short of where I'm picking.

Tony looks up. He doesn't want to be caught in the crossfire and at the same time doesn't want to miss out on the beginnings of a spud war. He casually picks up one of his small potatoes and lobs it over toward Teddy. He is a little strong, and the potato misses Teddy and hits Calvin Vagneur smack in the middle of the back. Just as I'm ready to launch another missile at Teddy, Calvin turns around and sees me throwing. He thinks I'm the one who has hit him, so he sends a salvo over my way.

Potato hell breaks loose. With four kids now involved in the melee, it takes no longer than fifteen seconds for a full-scale potato war to develop. Almost immediately there are potatoes flying all over the field, some of them scoring hits, some falling as duds.

I'm having fun now. Suddenly picking potatoes doesn't seem so boring. That is until one of the misfired potatoes, launched by who knows who, whacks one of the adults in the side of the head. In an instant, Clifford Vagneur is there. "Damn it, it's hard enough getting these potatoes picked without you kids throwing them all over Pitkin County. Now cut the horse play, and get back at it."

Truce is declared. Not by our choice, but we're all laughing and having much more fun with the job.

By Sunday we have tallied up three more wars, one black eye, numerous welts and bruises, and I don't know how many tons of potatoes picked for transport. We all walk back to the root cellar at the end of the day for the count. Clifford Vagneur has added up the number of one-hundred-pound bags we each have picked. When he reads off my total, I'm surprised to find I've picked thirty bags of potatoes. Mr. Vagneur gives me two dollars and ten cents and says, "Thanks for your hard work."

"You're welcome," I say.

I take the two dollars and ten cents and feel like the richest man on earth. It is the first time I have ever been paid for doing ranch work. It feels good to work and realize that my work has value.

Chapter 14

December 1952

It is coming up on Christmas. Only twenty more days to go. There is snow on the ground, and the sky is cloudy. I'm outside playing with a bow and arrow I cobbled together last summer with some advice from my dad. He said that a long willow branch would probably work best for a bow, and I should try to find some straight old dead branches for arrows. So that's what I did.

I shoot the arrows up in the air to see if they can reach as high as the cottonwood tree on the west side of the house. I stand out in the driveway away from the tree so the arrows won't get caught in it as they come back to earth. So far the two arrows I've shot haven't gone very high. The next arrow I shoot goes higher and lands in the tree but doesn't come down. I'll have to wait for the wind to blow it down because it is too far out in the small branches for me to climb to.

I take my last arrow and shoot it. It lands on the roof over the kitchen. This is upsetting because it's my one. It's up on the roof, a black mark on the snow like a pencil line on white paper. This requires action. The next thing I know, I'm making my way out the upstairs window and onto the roof. It is very steep and slippery.

I know I shouldn't be here. I can feel in my stomach that something is not right. I'm not afraid of being up on the roof, nor am I afraid to make my way down the roof a small ways to fetch my arrow. I just have this feeling in my stomach that something bad is about to happen. I think, *What could happen? I've been up here before. Nothing bad has happened before. I know I can do this*. My mind says its okay, but my stomach says it isn't. Finally my mind wins out, and I begin climbing down the roof.

The snow holds me as I make my way down toward the arrow. Just as I am about to reach out and grab it, the snow gives way in a huge wooosh and I feel myself falling through the air. I know in that instant I should have listened to my stomach and not my mind. But this knowing passes in a flash, and I think, *Oh, shit!*

When I land face first on a metal dish we use to feed the dog, I know I am hurt. My head hurts, my face hurts, and there is blood everywhere. I can't breath. I lie in the cold snow for a few moments trying to find my breath and try to move my arms and legs. They move okay. There are no tears, no sounds of crying or moaning. Wondering if my ears don't work, I listen for sounds. From inside the house I hear the usual kitchen sounds of my mom making lunch. I listen some more and realize I am not crying, just hurting. Slowly I pick myself up off the snow and stand up.

Okay, I think. *I guess I'm okay, but my mouth hurts a lot. And my head hurts too.*

I walk into the house and take off my boots on the porch bench. In the kitchen my mom is making a couple of sandwiches. Wonder Bread over peanut butter and strawberry jam.

"What'ths for lunch" I say. I suspect I'm not thinking clearly.

My mom turns to look at me and screams. She scares me so much I start crying.

"What happened to you?" she says. "Come here and let me see your face."

I walk over to her. She holds her finger under my chin and looks at me closely. I'm bleeding all over my coat and now her hand.

"Oh, Jesus, Terry what's happened?" she says.

"I fell offss sssa rrroooffsss," I mumble.

"You fell off the roof?"

"Yefff, offss ssa rrrooffsss."

"Dear god, what were you doing on the roof?" she says.

"Getting my arrow."

She is already taking stock of the damage.

"Oh, my God!" she says to the air above my head. "You've lost both your front teeth and you have a big cut on your scalp. It's a wonder you weren't killed. The roof is at least twelve feet off the ground at the eaves. Come here and let me get you cleaned up. I wonder if you will need stitches. I better look at it. Are you dizzy? You probably landed on your head by the looks of it. I wonder if you have a concussion. Jesus, I better have Doc Lewis look at you. Doesn't feel like anything is broken. What am I going to do with you? You are constantly being banged and bumped and cut and broken. You boys are going to be the death of me. Well, luckily it's only your baby teeth not your permanent teeth."

I listen without saying anything. My tears have dried up. My mom cleans me up. It's not my favorite thing. My mouth hurts where my teeth were knocked out. My head aches and the cut burns where she has put iodine on it. Without my front teeth and with my mouth hurting so much, it is hard for me to eat, so she makes me a bowl of Campbell's soup.

~ ~ ~

It is a couple of days later, and I am back at school. We have been practicing for the Christmas play we will put on at the Wheeler Opera House like they do every year. Miss Lumsden tells me that I have a special part in the play that I have to practice. Everyone will sing some song, and at the end of it I have to step forward and say really loud, "All I want for Christhmath is my two fromt teeth."

Winter 1953

I walk in the house from outside. The house is "warm and comfy" as Mom says. The Christmas play is over, and my head is all healed up. I don't have any stitches. It just bled a lot, and I have a big lump. Doc Lewis told me, "You were a very lucky boy."

I don't know how I can be lucky if I fell off the roof and landed on my head.

We have lots of snow around the house and I'm inside for lunch. Mom is making me my favorite sandwich. Yep. Peanut butter and strawberry jam on Wonder Bread. I wander into the little red living room and sit at the desk where Mom pays the bills. Dad is too busy to pay the bills, so Mom does it. She has her pen and ink out. The ink comes in a bottle, and you have to put the tip of the pen in the bottle and suck some ink into it so the pen will write.

I take the top off the pen and scribble something on the green blotter. The pen doesn't write so it must be out of ink. I look at the bottle of ink and get the idea that I should fill the pen up for my mom. I've seen her do it a hundred times, so it can't be that hard. The glass jar of ink is sitting right here on the desk. I pick it up and take the top off. The ink is a deep blue color like the color of the Milk of Magnesia bottle I saw at the Hume's house. I look deep into the jar and can see the light come through the bottom and sides which makes the ink turn from dark blue in the center to light blue on the sides. I sniff the bottle and the ink smells like the nails from a box in the barn my dad uses to fix stuff around the ranch. It is a metal smell. I smell it some more and wonder what it would taste like. I'm thirsty so it's a good time to taste the ink. I put the bottle to my lips and drink down the whole bottle like a glass of water. It doesn't taste very good, but it is not bad either. Maybe a little salty, but more like the taste of sucking on a penny.

I wipe my mouth with the back of my hand and it turns blue from the ink. My stomach doesn't feel quite right. I stand up from the chair and hear my mom calling me. "Teerrrryyyy, luuunnnnccchhh!"

"Okay, I'm coming," I say. I walk out in the kitchen. Mom says, "What's that on your face?"

"Ink. I wanted to see what it tastes like."

"You what?" Her eyes get big. She dashes into the living room and finds the empty ink bottle.

More trouble, I think. I realize I'm now truly not feeling so well.

She returns to the kitchen with the ink bottle in her hand. With the other hand she grabs the telephone and dials Doc Lewis's number, which by now she knows by heart.

"Go get on your coat and boots," she says to me as she turns back to the phone.

I know she's in some sort of tizzy and I don't feel well enough to argue, so I go out to the porch and find my coat and boots. Moments later she rushes out. She has her purse in one hand and the car keys in the other. She scoots me along the walkway and shoves me into the car. I'm beginning to feel bad, and say, "I don't feel so well."

"I shouldn't wonder," she says. "We have to go get your stomach pumped out!"

"What's that?"

"You'll soon see," she says.

I feel worried. I don't like it when I don't know what's going to happen, unless it's something probably fun.

~~~

Its evening and I am in bed. I'm not sure how I got there. I have a sore throat. I get out of bed and head downstairs where I find everyone just finishing dinner.

"Well, there he is," my dad says. "How're ya feeling?"

"My throat hurts."

113

"Yeah, that's from the tube they put down your throat when you had your stomach pumped out. You swallowed a lot of ink, and Doc Lewis said that it was a good thing he was around to get it out of you. You'll be fine. Are you hungry? Your mom says you didn't get any lunch."

I sit down and eat a few bites of the venison, mashed potatoes, and garden peas. I can't get rid of the taste of a penny in my mouth even after I finish my dinner.

Chapter 15

Spring 1953

I'm at school playing marbles during afternoon recess. Nick Garrish has taught me how to play. Nick is in the class ahead of me, third grade, with Miss Helmcamp. I will have her next year. Nick Garrish is a good marbles player.

We are playing Cat's Eye. It's a game where you make a shape in the dirt that looks like the gold part inside a cat's eye. Each of the players puts three or four marbles in the Cat's Eye. Then we walk away twenty steps and draw another line called the lag line. We take our laggers - laggers being bigger than shooters - and roll the lagger toward the Cat's Eye. Whoever gets the closest gets to take the first shot at knocking the marbles out of the Cat's Eye.

Nick has won the lag and knocked two of my marbles out of the pot. Luckily he missed the third, because the two marbles I have left in the pot are good ones. They are blue clearies, and not so easy to come by in Aspen. Mostly we get cat's eyes, which really do look like cat's eyes except for being lots of different colors. I also have some ades and swirlies. Some of the guys have steely laggers, but usually we don't allow them to be used. They are just ball bearings and you can get them at the car body shop if you are lucky. We don't allow them because if you lag them higher in the air they come down with a plop and don't roll. The idea of lagging is to see who can roll their lagger closest to the edge of the Cat's Eye. Agates are the hardest to get. They're made out of real rock, not glass, and are heavier than glass shooters, so when they knock out a marble they usually stop fast and stay in the pot, if you are playing Pot. That means you get another shot.

Anyway it's my turn, and I'm too far from the Cat's Eye to knock anything out, unless I am lucky or my aim is dead on. So I aim and shoot. Sure enough, I hit one of my clearies. It was a long shot and I'm happy about it. I take another shot and miss my other clearie. I don't want to shoot at Nick's cat eye marbles because I have quite a few of them and not so many clearies. It's Nick's turn, and he aims at my clearie and smashes it out. He has an agate shooter, so it stays close in. Then he cleans out the rest of the Cat's Eye. He has a stubby thumb, so the marble fits neatly between the tip of his index finger and his thumb knuckle. It's a good way to shoot, which I will have to practice because I can see it is more accurate than letting the marble lie on the second joint of my index finger and sort of rolling off my finger when I flick my thumb. Nick's method makes the shooter sail much faster and harder. No wonder I get cleaned out most of the time I play him.

I don't mind because I love playing marbles. I love the feel of the round shooter in my hand. I love the smell of the dirt on the road after the snow has melted, before they put down all that messy oil to keep the dust down. The color of the dirt is mostly brown with some yellow tints from sand. I love the smell and the feel of spring in the morning air. The cold crispness of the early mornings that gives way to a softer warmth as the sun lays itself over our mountain town.

The bell rings and I go back into class to learn something or the other. I'm not paying much attention because I think I already know it. Pretty soon the bell rings again and school is over. I go out in the hall, grab my jean jacket and my lunch box and head for the orange bus.

Mr. Lewis is driving today. He isn't as strict as Mr. Stapleton and lots of times doesn't pay attention to what we are doing behind him. He just drives along in his own world probably thinking up science experiments since he is the science teacher. I take a seat next to Teddy and see that Barbie Lewis is on the bus. Barbie is in the class Teddy was in before he got kidney problems and had to stay back a grade. Pretty soon some of the Stapletons and some of the other kids who live west of town out in Brush Creek get on. Catherine Bargsten gets on and sits next to me. She lives out just past our road. Her brother's name is Tommy. She is pretty cute and once in a while my brother and I walk down the lower field and head across the highway over to their house to see what they are doing and to goof around. I look around some more and ask Barbie Lewis, "What are you doing on the bus?"

"I'm just going along for the ride today. My dad said I could."

"You are going all the way out to Brush Creek and then back to town?"

"Yes," she says.

This gives me an idea. It would be neat if we could ride the bus past our road, out to the end of the bus route in Brush Creek, and back to be dropped off at our road as the bus is headed back into town. I see Gerry get on the bus. He sits across from me next to Sandra Stapleton. I say to him, "Hey, Gerry, I have an idea."

"You have an idea? That's rare."

He says that a lot to me now when he thinks I don't know how to think.

So I lower my voice and say to him, "Why don't you ask Mr. Lewis if we can ride out to Brush Creek with the bus and get dropped off when he goes back past our road?"

Gerry looks at me like I am crazy. Then, when he realizes that it might be fun to take a trip out to the end of the bus line, and put off some of our chores for awhile longer, he nods, "Hmmm, not a bad idea."

So he asks Mr. Lewis. Mr. Lewis is turning the bus around and heading out toward Main Street when Gerry says, "Mr. Lewis, do you think me and my brothers could ride out to Brush Creek, and you drop us off on the way back to town?"

Mr. Lewis turns his head and looks over his shoulder at Gerry.

"First of all, it's 'my brothers and I.' You should know that. And as far as going all the way out to Brush Creek, don't you have chores to do on the ranch?"

I can see Gerry is now engaged in a battle of wits that he is not about to lose willingly.

"Well, as a matter of fact we do," Gerry starts in. "But, since it was such a nice warm morning, and since we all woke up early, we got most of the work stuff done before school. Now all we have to do is tend to the animals a bit and we're done. That doesn't take too long."

I have to bite my cheek. Gerry getting up early is a laugh. He doesn't get out of bed until the school bus is about to leave our stop. Then he sprints down the road. Or if Dad is driving us to school, he doesn't get up until he hears my dad starting to get really impatient. Not just impatient, *really* impatient. But I hold my tongue and look over at Teddy to see if he gets the joke, but he's making eyes at Barbie who is smiling at him.

Mr. Lewis says, "Well, if you are sure you can get all your chores done, I guess it's fine with me."

"Thanks," Gerry says.

By now we are up Main Street and halfway across the Castle Creek Bridge. With our mission accomplished, we pitch in with the other kids, goofing off and generally making noise, laughing, and having fun. I'm excited to be heading up to Brush Creek from this direction. We take the road past Owl Creek, past the Christensen ranch, over the Owl Creek Divide, and down into Brush Creek. The other way to get there is by driving down Highway 82 toward Glenwood Springs. You then turn and go up Brush Creek Road past the Roberts' place, the Gallun ranch, and finally get to the Anderson Ranch and the Faraway Ranch.

The Owl Creek route takes us through a beautiful valley. This afternoon the sun is low and poking its light through the first green of the aspen trees on the hillside. There is a little yellow in the green leaves, so it seems as though the air itself is green, as well as the trees.

We drive past the Christensen place, the Sinclair place, and the Anderson place. The Juricks live somewhere up here. The Juricks are an old couple who have taken care of us once in awhile. One time I stayed with them here in Brush Creek for a week. His name is John Jurick. She is just called Jerky. She cooks oatmeal for John to eat in the morning, letting it simmer on the stove all night. Mr. Jurick eats it when he gets up. He likes it cooked overnight because he says it tastes way better to have some time behind it.

Mr. Lewis turns the bus around, and we head back to town with only Gerry, Teddy, Barbie Lewis, and me left in the bus. Mr. Lewis is humming to himself looking down the road, and as usual lost in thought somewhere. Gerry sees this and says to Barbie, "Aren't you hot with that sweater on?"

Barbie looks at Gerry and then at Teddy and then at me. Gerry is in his shirtsleeves. He has a tee shirt on and has his school shirt in his lunch box like he does sometimes. Teddy has just a long-sleeved shirt on, and I still have my jean jacket on because I am too lazy to take it off even if it is warm. Barbie finally says, "I guess so."

"Why don't you take it off?" Gerry says.

"Okay." Barbie takes off her sweater and puts it on the seat. Somehow we have all scooted to the back of the bus where we are out of earshot or Mr. Lewis' vision, if he bothered to look. The western sun is pouring in through the back window, and it is actually heating up quite a bit. I take off my jean jacket.

Barbie says, "Wow, it is a bit warm in here."

Gerry, says, "It sure is. Why don't you take off that dress and get comfortable?"

Strangely, Barbie does. Not much further down the road with several more comments on the heat in the bus and the necessity to stay comfortable, Barbie is completely naked. She is standing in the back of the bus totally bare assed with her little butt toward the windows. I glance forward to see what is going on with Mr. Lewis. He is still looking down the road, humming to himself.

Gerry says to Barbie, "You should turn around so you don't get sunburned on your back."

Barbie looks at him and thinks this is a good idea, so begins slowly turning around like a chicken on a spit. We are treated to several full turnarounds before she almost stumbles and falls into the seat. Luckily she reaches out and grabs my shoulder and Gerry's arm before she does. Then she is standing right in front of Teddy and me, face to face on with no clothes on. Of course we both have seen naked girls before. My sister was naked when Mom changed her or gave her a bath. But this is different because it is someone our age. I am taking my time looking at her from top to toe. I want to reach out and touch her, but restrain myself, because somehow I know it would break the spell into a million pieces.

I look at Gerry and can see he thinks the whole thing is funny. He is enjoying himself. After some time of Barbie turning around and around and us boys with the tinglies, we begin to come to our senses.

By now we have travelled almost back to the highway with Barbie bare naked, and the Morse boys getting all their female anatomical questions answered. Suddenly Gerry realizes that in a very short while we will be at the bottom of our road. He knows that Mr. Lewis will look up in his mirror just before he slows the bus to make sure we are sitting down before he comes to a halt. Gerry panics and says, "You better get your clothes on quickly. We're gonna stop soon and your dad will see you naked for sure."

Barbie, now for the first time realizing that she is totally naked in front of three boys, blushes and puts her shirt, skirt, shoes, and sweater back on like nothing has happened. Just as we are about to stop, I see Barbie's underpants on the floor and silently point to them as I stand up to get off the bus. She bends over in the seat and snatches them up and hides them in her skirt, probably to be replaced on her cute little butt on the way back into town.

Once off the bus Gerry, Teddy, and I head up our road laughing and talking about the bus ride from heaven. It seems like we darned near float up the road to home.

Chapter 16

Early Summer 1953

It's a beautiful June mountain morning. School has been out a few days, and I'm farting around in the barnyard looking for flat stones to skip across the pond. I haven't been in much trouble since I swallowed the bottle of ink last winter other than a few things at school. Dad comes out of the shop in the barn and says, "Since you don't seem to have anything better to do, how'd ya like to go into town with me?"

"Sure," I say. "Where are we going?"

"I have to go over to Stillwater Ranch to see Roger Dixon."

"Okay."

We let Mom know what we're up to, pile into the Jeep, and head for town. I just love riding in the old Army Jeep. The wind is blowing around the foot wells, kicking dust up in my face, until we reach the highway where there is no dust, and the air finally clears. I look down at the floorboards. The paint has worn off, and the metal is shiny from boots and shoes rubbing on it a million times. The seats both have small tears in the upholstery, and the springs are beginning to peek out in places where they have no business. The brake and clutch pedals are so worn down that the shaped, stamped metal is almost flat, the diamond pattern barely discernible on the polished silver surfaces. The Jeep is as faithful as an old horse: dents, scratches, faded paint, bald tires, and all. She's still willing to start up and carry the load for the distance, relying on her "four banger" engine, as my dad calls it, to get us there and back. She's never broken down on us and always starts even when we have to push her down the hill in the dead of winter and January temperatures are below zero.

We bounce down the road and across the Maroon Creek Bridge, past the Marolt places, across the Castle Creek Bridge, past Waterman's store, down Main Street, and into town. All the streets in town are still dirt except Main Street, which is really Highway 82. Highway 82 comes up valley from Glenwood Springs, through town and out toward Independence Pass about a mile, where it turns from pavement to dirt again.

We pass right by Matthews Drug, the Hotel Jerome and the Catholic Church around the corner on Original Street, and head out of town on the east side. We take the dirt back streets that will lead us to the Ute Cemetery and onto the dirt road that goes to the Stillwater Ranch, Roger Dixon's spread, about a mile or two down the road. When we pull up to the ranch house, I can tell it is no longer a working ranch. There is no old machinery lying around. There are no cows or chickens or pigs, just an old dog that comes up to the Jeep and sticks his head over the sideboard and licks at my blue jeans.

Roger Dixon comes out of the house to greet us. "Hello, Wendy. How y'all doing on this fine day?"

By now my dad is out of the Jeep and is walking up to Mr. Dixon to shake his hand.

"Hi, Roger," he says. "It sure enough is a fine day."

Mr. Dixon waves us into his house, through the kitchen, living room, and out onto a back patio made from great slabs of red sandstone, laid far enough apart to allow narrow veins of grass to grow between them. From the patio, we see the lawn dipping gently downhill to a split rail fence, beyond which is a stretch of tall grasses: hay, alfalfa, clover, and dandelions interspersed with a lone stand of sage here and there. The grasses fold down to the edge of the Roaring Fork River, slowly meandering its way through the property in a big S. The water is clear and smooth as glass. I can understand why the ranch is named Stillwater Ranch.

I look over to Mr. Dixon and ask him, "Mr. Dixon, are there any fish in the river?"

He says, "Call me Roger, son. Why don't you go down and have a look for yourself while your dad and I share a few words?"

"Okay, Roger," I say and walk down the lawn toward the fence.

When I get to the river, I see that it is not totally calm. There are small riffles in places I couldn't see from the patio of the house. The water seems shallow now that I'm closer to it. I walk along the shore watching the river for movement. I know it is the best way to see fish: to look for the movement. At first I don't see anything but the bottom. I am mesmerized by the flow of the water and the gentle breeze that touches my face, then my side, and around to my back. The soft puffs of air working their way around me seem as if they are looking at me from all sides to see who I am, wondering if I belong here.

The river bottom is covered with yellow sand, a few big rocks dotting it here and there. The water moves slowly and lazily by me. Suddenly I see movement and a fish. Then another. And another. I begin sizing them in my mind to determine how large they are and which is the largest I have seen. I know from playing in our pond at the ranch, the size and location of the fish is distorted by the water, so I can only guess at their size. My best guess is ten to twelve inches.

I walk east on the riverbank, upstream to the S bend, and into a small grove of pines growing near at the base of the S. I stop here and wade into the river where I can stay in the light, which allows me to see the river bottom and any movement of fish.

The current is stronger than I imagined it would be, so I'm forced to turn around and walk downstream with the current for a few yards until the river becomes shallow. Already I am wet up to mid-thigh but do not notice it. I see a big rock in the river peeking its head out of the water and make my way toward it. The flow of water around the rock has created a still pool on the downstream side. I look through the clear water. There is movement. My eyes adjust to see a large rainbow trout lazily moving tail and fins to maintain its position in the current behind the rock. It looks huge, maybe twice as big as any of the other fish I have seen.

I move forward quietly, excited by what I am seeing and not paying attention. I stub my foot on a small rock, lose my balance, and fall into the river. Panic overwhelms me. I don't know how to swim. Not really. I can dog paddle a bit in a pool but usually sink, so I am not allowed to go in the deep end. I have no idea how to stay afloat in deep water; I have never fallen in a river so don't know what to do.

Before I can think, the current rolls me over and tugs me across the bottom where the water is once again shallow. Somehow in an instant I am standing again, soaking wet, and shaking with cold and fright. I'm coughing and sputtering from the water I've swallowed. I stand in the river assessing the situation and try to understand how I'm on my feet.

It happened so fast, yet here I am standing, looking at the pool behind the rock. I realize I'm lucky the current pushed me into shallower waters. Presently I remember the fish and instantly forget I am soaking wet and half-drowned. I inch my way back upstream toward the pool looking for the fish I'm sure will not be there because of the ruckus I've created by falling into the river. Sure enough, I am right. The fish is gone.

The sun is high in the sky and, although I've warmed up some, I know I need to move around to stay warm. I climb out of the river; my feet are in fact cold, really cold, so I head back to the house.

I come up on the patio.

"What the heck happened to you?" my dad says.

Roger Dixon laughs gently. He already knows.

"I fell in the river. I saw this huge fish in a pool by the pines, and it was by far bigger than any of the other fish I've seen. I tried to sneak closer to the fish to see how big it really was and tripped on a rock and fell into the water. I was washed up on the shallow part, so I stood up right away and I'm fine. Just wet," I say.

They can see I am no worse for wear and both laugh.

My dad says, "Looks like it is about time for you to learn to swim."

Roger Dixon looks at me and says, "You know how to fly fish, young fella?"

"No," I say.

"Would you like to learn? Maybe you could get good enough to catch that fish. I know I've been trying for a long time but haven't been able to do it."

"Sure. That would be fun. When can I start?"

"Wendy and I will have to figure out when he is next going to be in town. Maybe he can drop you out here for a morning or an afternoon, and we can work on some of the basics," Roger says. "What da y'all say, Wendy? Think we can work that out?"

"I don't see why not. As long as Terr-Ass takes care of his chores on the ranch and doesn't fall in the river again."

"When can I come?" I say.

"Let's ask your dad when he is coming into town next," says Roger.

"For sure I have to come in the day after tomorrow because I have a meeting at the bank about this Tiehack lift thing."

"Let's do it then," says Roger.

"Great, I say. "Thanks really a lot."

My dad looks at me. "I guess I better get this wet fish home before he begins to freeze. Thanks for your time, Roger."

"No problem. I'll see you both day after tomorrow?"

"Count on it," my dad says and nods to me.

"Thanks, Roger. I can't wait," I say.

We trace our steps back out through the house and climb into the Jeep to return to the ranch.

"Where did Roger come from?" I ask my dad. "I really like him and can't wait to go fishing."

"That's a long story. But the short version is this. He's called 'The Cotton King' of Alabama. He has made a fortune growing cotton in the South and has bought the Stillwater Ranch to have some peace and quiet up here away from the business. He has a wife named Hazel, who I am sure you will meet next time. She was in town today."

I mull this over a bit and then say, "What's the Tiehack thing?"

My dad looks over at me and says, "I'm thinking of putting a ski lift up on the Tiehack ridgeline so we can make some money with a little ski area. I'm trying to get financing for the project, and that's why I was talking to Roger. He doesn't think he wants to put any money in it at the moment because he has other things going on in his life. But we'll see."

"A ski area?" I say. "In our backyard? Won't that mean that there will be a bunch of people hanging around?"

"We'll see," my dad says.

He always says that when he doesn't really want to answer a question. "We'll see," he says, and then we almost never do. I mull over the Tiehack idea the rest of the way home, and while we are driving up our road I say, "I don't think it's a good idea. There'll be too many people stomping around all over the ranch. And besides, how are they going to get all the way out here from town? If they come in their cars, there won't be any place for them to park. We need the barnyard for barnyard stuff."

"We'll see," my dad says, "We'll see."

~ ~ ~

I've been going over to Roger Dixon's every time I can get a ride into town with my dad or mom and can talk them into dropping me off while they do their business. I've decided that being on the river and fishing is about the best thing I can do in life.

Soon I'm going to have to stop going to Stillwater Ranch because we are driving back East. Aunt Mary Leigh is getting married. We are all driving in our 1950 Ford Woody and camping along the way. The car will be crowded. Dad, Mom, and Jennifer will sit up front. Teddy, Gerry, and I will sit in the middle seat. But I don't care. I'm really excited. I've never been East before. All our luggage and camping stuff will go in the back. I think we won't be bringing the big tent but will be sleeping in the car sometimes or on the ground. Luckily we won't be gone all summer because I want to get back to fish on the Roaring Fork River. But still, this big adventure lies ahead of me!

Chapter 17

Summer 1953

We are in the East staying at Granny's - the Leigh House. Her home is a two-hundred-year-old sea captain's house located on Cape Cod in South Yarmouth, Massachusetts, one block from the Bass River. Granny and Grandpa bought the property sometime after the war, re-named it the Leigh House after one of Granny's ancestors, and ran it as a "guest house." They took in boarders to make ends meet.

The Leigh House is a spooky place. It has twenty-one rooms, not counting the screened in porches, of which there are two.

I have always felt a little scared in this house that has so many stories to tell. At night before falling asleep I can imagine many of them. Old sea captains on the high seas hunting for whales. Their wives pining away in their long absences until the women give in and meet another man. There is one story of a captain who returned from whaling, murdered his wife, and entombed her body in one of the walls of the great structure.

Many of these early homes have a widow's walk, a flat platform that is accessed by a trap door on the very top of the roof. Granny told me the sea captains' wives used to go up on widow's walks every day early in the morning and just as the sun was setting, to see if their husbands were coming back from the whale hunts.

The sea captains' wives used the widow's walk as a means to warn each other from house to house when a whaler was entering the waters of Bass River. The women would then know who was coming home in case there happened to be another man in the house. With the warning, the wife could hustle the man out before the captain got home.

~ ~ ~

Today I'm up in the attic on my way to the widow's walk. I get sidetracked looking at some of the things stored there. Old furniture. Chests and baskets. Old pictures and books tied with twine and stacked carelessly in piles. Finally I climb a narrow set of stairs up to a trapdoor in the roof. I open the trapdoor. A salt breeze hits my face. Once on the platform, I look down. The ground seems miles away and I'm glad there are rails around the sides of the platform. I stay on the widow's walk for a long time thinking about the old sea captains sailing their whalers out into the ocean and harpooning whales. I think how hard it must have been to catch a whale, cut it up in pieces, and bring it all onto the boat.

I leave the widow's walk to explore other parts of the house. I'm happy to be out of the attic with its cobwebs, forgotten things, and the ghosts of old memories. I go down the attic stairs and into a hallway across from one of the two bathrooms on the upper floor. I walk down the hall past the Blue Room, past the second bathroom, the Flower Room, the Apple Room, and the Yellow Room. Then I walk down the back stairs into another hallway. In one direction I can walk back to the kitchen, the other to the workshop that separates the main house from the maid's quarters.

The workshop is a long narrow room with a workbench that stretches from the door entering the shop to the back door that takes you out to the gardens. It has lots of tools that Grandpa uses to "keep the place shipshape." I used the workbench a few days ago when Granny let me varnish the seashells I collected on the beach.

On the far side of the shop there is a set of stairs that leads up to a single room. This is the maid's room. Granny calls it the "turret room." Gerry and Teddy say that the rich people who used to own the Leigh House lost everything in the Depression like Granny and Grandpa did. They became real poor. They had to sell the Leigh House because the husband went crazy after the stock market crash, whatever that was. He killed the maid in the turret room. Then he nailed the door shut with the dead maid rotting in the walls. No one could get in. When Granny and Grandpa bought the house just after the war, they opened up the turret room door and found her skeleton behind one of the walls.

Of course, I don't believe them. But as I am sitting in a wicker chair in the room, I get the creeps, imagining the maid's skeleton stashed behind one of the walls. Even though there are other spooky stories, it's the only room in the house that gives me the creeps.

~~~

All around the outside of the house there is a huge lawn, vegetable garden, and a garden shed. There are trees and bushes around the edge of the yard between the street and the house, so it is hard to see to the street. On the lawn you can play badminton or croquet, which are both stupid games or darn near, football if you want. I guess if you were going to play football, you'd have to get rid of the vegetable gardens.

I love Granny. She has blue eyes that twinkle whenever she looks at me. She is tall like my dad and has grey curly hair that looks frizzy all the time. She has skinny legs and bony fingers because of her arthritis. She jokes with me and calls me funny names that she makes up whenever she feels like it. She calls me names like "Hey, Turnip" or "Hey, Pea Pod," when she wants me to do some gardening, or "Good Morning, Wheat Germ" when I'm eating breakfast.

~~~

Granny knows how much I like fishing, so we're going for a little fishing adventure of our own on Bass River. It's early morning, everyone is sleeping, and we're headed down to the pier to row out on the mile-long estuary that empties out into the Nantucket Sound.

The tide is almost turning. Granny rows us down river until we feel it's the right spot. This is the spot where we will fish. When the tide turns and comes back in, we will stop fishing and head for home, the tide taking us back to the pier with easy rowing.

Granny says, "Okay, Ahab, drop the anchor."

"Who's Ahab?"

"You are. Just throw the anchor off the side and watch out that you don't get your feet caught in the rope."

I throw the anchor overboard and watch it drop out of sight to the bottom. The boat begins to drift and Granny says, "Wrap the anchor line around the cleat on the side of the boat in a figure eight."

I do this.

"Now put a half hitch on top of it on the cleat so it will hold."

She watches me struggle to tie off the anchor rope, and we feel the boat pull up against the gentle current and know the anchor is set on the bottom. We are ready to fish.

The sun is a red ball on the horizon, and the wind is still. The water floats by the boat carrying seaweed, a jellyfish or two, and some old driftwood. I bait my hook with quahog bits we have cut from two quahogs we bought from a baitman at the pier yesterday. I test the knot on the sinker and look at the one on the hook. Everything looks good. I drop the whole rig into the water, letting out line until I feel the sinker hitting the bottom. Then I sit and wait.

Granny and I begin talking about how things are going out West and what it's like here in the East. I keep up a non-stop stream of questions about Cape Cod, the river, the ocean, and everything I can imagine. Granny answers all my questions patiently and asks a few of her own.

Suddenly I have a strike on the line. I pull it quickly, just a little jolt like Roger has taught me, to set the hook if the fish has taken the bait. It has, and I can feel the fish swimming upstream trying to take the line from me. Since it's a hand line and not a fishing rod, I can't give the fish much line because I can't get it out fast enough. I know it may throw the hook out of its mouth before it gets too tired, and I pull it in. In an instant the fish is landed, its shiny body flashing and flopping about the bottom of the boat. I've never seen anything like it. It's a beautiful silver with very distinct scales; nothing like the trout I catch in the Roaring Fork River. The scales reflect gleaming blue in the early morning light. I am ecstatic. It is my first salt water fish.

"What is it?" I ask Granny.

"It's a scup," she says. "They're darn fine eating, Ahab. You can have it for breakfast."

"Wow! This is really great. Maybe I can catch a few more and everyone can have one for breakfast."

"Well, you better get after it," Granny says.

I bait the hook once again and plunge the rig over the side. Immediately I get another bite. I set the hook once again. The fish on the other end fights harder than the first one. As I bring it over to the side of the boat, I see it's another scup. It is bigger than the first and I'm delighted. I throw my line in again, and we catch three more scup in short order. Then no fish for a long while. Granny says, "I think the school has passed by. Maybe it's time to head for home. The tide has turned, and the family will probably be getting up soon."

As I pull in the line, I get a huge strike and jerk the line hard. Whatever fish is on the hook is strong and a good fighter. I can feel it trying to swim, hauling Granny, the boat, and me.

"Darn," I say looking at Granny, "I've caught something real big!"

"Well, see if you can get it in."

I struggle with the line for a few minutes and finally get the fish alongside the boat. I look over the side and discover it's not a fish at all.

"Whoa!" I say. "It looks like a giant worm!"

"Pull it into the boat and let's see what it is," Granny says.

I get the sea creature into the boat. It squirms, twists, and gets tangled up in the anchor rope.

"Good God!" Granny says, "It's a huge eel. I've never seen one that big!"

"What do we do with it?"

"They're very good eating but very hard to skin. We may as well take it home. We'll have to have one of the men help you skin it."

I give up on trying to get the eel off the hook. It is squirming too much.

"It looks like a snake the way it twists itself all up," I say.

"Yes, it does rather," Granny says as she takes up the oars. "Guess we'll ride the tide back to the pier."

We row back up Bass River on the tide with five fish and an eel in the hold. Not a bad day for the first time on salt water. I am excited about having caught the fish, about our visit to Granny's, about the day on the water, and about everything I can think of at the moment.

~~~

We left the Cape early this morning after saying goodbye to everyone and drove to Popeye's house in Connecticut. We've been in Popeye's house for about an hour. I've been exploring, and now I'm pretty bored. There isn't really anything to do here, so we can't get in much trouble. The house has no workshop or spooky rooms.

Nothing to do but wait for the adults to finish talking. Gerry gets to stay with the adults and talk. Jennifer gets to stay with Mom because she's little. Teddy and I are on our own.

Eventually we wander outdoors to see if there is something to do outside. I don't know if we're going to stay here for the night or not. I think maybe we are, because it's getting to be late in the afternoon. I get back in the car to see if there is a comic book I haven't read. Teddy doesn't have anything to do, so he gets in the car with me. There's nothing to read, so we climb in the way back where the suitcases are. I move them around a bit and make a little space for myself.

Teddy says, "Hey, I've got an idea. Let's play a game."

"What game?" I look up at him from my hole in the suitcases and see he has Dad's hunting knife in his hand.

"Where'd you get that?" I say.

"I found it under the front seat."

"Well, you better put it back before you get in trouble."

"No," he says, "We have to use it in our game."

"What game?" I say again.

"It's called Statues. Let's pretend that you're a statue. You have to stay real still like a statue. Then I pretend to stab you with this knife, and you die. Only you don't really die because you're a statue and this is a game so you can't die."

"No, that's a stupid game," I start to say.

Before I can finish the sentence I see he is serious. He is swinging his arm back getting ready to stab me. I don't believe what I'm seeing and literally freeze as solid and still as a statue. He slashes the knife downward toward me. As he does, he has misjudged the height of the car ceiling and the span of his arm. The knife hits the roof upholstery on its downward arc toward my body and rips a large gash in the material before catching on a metal strut in the roof. In that instant I realize he really intends to stab me.

"You stupid ass!! What do you think you are doing?" I scream.

I climb over the back seat and push him over toward the door. While he is off balance, I open the other side door and jump out. I run into the house and sit in Popeye's kitchen catching my breath. Teddy comes in and says, "Don't tell Mommy and Daddy."

"Why not? You tried to kill me."

"No, I didn't," Teddy says. " It was just a game."

"If it was just a game, why did you try to stab me?"

"It was part of the game," he says.

"Well, you're gonna catch hell for it," I say.

About that time Mom and Dad come walking through the kitchen with Gerry, followed by Popeye and Momeye.

"Let's go, kids," Dad says. "We've gotta try to get some miles behind us before it gets too late. Say goodbye and pile into the car."

We say goodbye to Popeye and Momeye, go out to the car, and hop in the back seat. I make sure to try to sit next to a window with Gerry between Teddy and me. Gerry refuses. He doesn't want to sit in the middle where the transmission hump is. I end up sitting in the middle between Teddy and Gerry, just where I don't want to sit. As Dad gets into the car he sees his hunting knife. Teddy has left it on the front seat.

"What's this doing here?" He looks at Teddy and me.

Teddy hems and haws a bit. I jump in and tell Dad the whole story. He looks at the hole in the upholstery and is madder than hell. He gets out of the car and is getting ready to give Teddy a whipping. Teddy is crying and saying it was only a game. It was a mistake. It was Terry's fault. He makes up all the excuses he can think of. All the time I am shouting, "He tried to kill me, he tried to kill me!"

Mom finally says, "Wendy, just get in the car, and let's get going. I'm sure it was just a game, and Teddy had no intention of hurting Terry."

My dad calms down and gets back into the car. He looks back at us and says, "I don't want to hear a peep out of you two."

It was a long, silent five-day trip back across the country to home.

Chapter 18

Fall 1953

It's fall. I love the fall. Actually I love all the seasons. They're all so different, and they all have things I love about them. But today I love fall. It's a school day, and we're all piled into the Jeep getting ready to head into town. My dad comes out of the house with the coveralls and a heavy grey wool sweater he wears before it's cold enough for him to put on his winter sheepskin coat. We're on the way to school, and Dad is on the way to his carpentry job on Red Mountain. The Jeep starts and we take off down the road, a rooster tail of dust following us all the way. We get to the bottom of the road, and I can tell from all the sheep shit on the highway and the road that La Minque has moved his sheep back down valley.

La Minque is a sheepherder who works for a rancher, or maybe more than one rancher, down valley. He takes care of their sheep. Every year in the spring La Minque drives the sheep up Aspen Mountain or up into Hunter Creek, for summering in the high mountain pastures. He herds them up Highway 82 right into town, down Hallam or Bleeker Street, past the school, and on up to Aspen Mountain or Hunter Creek depending on where he's going. Mostly it's Hunter Creek nowadays because they are working on the ski area lots in the summer. When La Minque brings his sheep up valley, they leave a trail of sheep shit that could use to fertilize forty acres if someone picked it up.

Early last summer, my dad let La Minque put his sheepherder's wagon on our lower forty by the highway for a few days, while he was getting ready to drive the sheep up valley. We had the hay baled and nothing was happening on the lower fields. One afternoon Gerry and I went down to La Minque's wagon. We were curious about him.

~~~

We walk across the field to where the wagon sits on its wheels. Gerry climbs up the steps to the door and knocks. La Minque opens the door and says, "What're you kids doin' here?" with a heavy accent.

"We wanted to see who was living in the wagon, so we're here to find out," Gerry says.

La Minque, a short dark-haired, dark-skinned man with kind brown eyes says, "Come inside. You boys Wendy's boys, no?"

"Yes," we both say and step into the wagon.

"Sit down, sit down." La Minque gestures to the floor in front of the sheepherder's stove, which is still warm from breakfast.

"Do you live here?" I ask.

La Minque looks at me for a moment, then says, "Yes, this is my home while I am tending to the sheep. When I am not tending the sheep, I live in a small house."

"Where do you come from," I ask him, curious about his accent and his dark skin.

"I am from the high mountains in Spain. My people are called Basque."

He looks at us and says, "You like some bread?" He doesn't wait for an answer but cuts two slices off a fresh loaf sitting on a shelf near the stove. Then he looks at Gerry and says, "You like some whiskey?" Again, he doesn't wait for an answer. He pours a small glass of whiskey and hands it to Gerry.

"You, young fella," La Minque says looking at me. 'You're too young for this stuff. But your brother is old enough, I think."

"How old are you anyway, son?" he asks Gerry.

"Twelve,"

"See, I was right," says La Minque. "He is old enough."

We talk about sheep herding, Spain, and a bunch of other stuff. Soon he gives Gerry another slug of whiskey. We've finished our bread and are getting ready to leave when he offers us another slice. He merrily drinks a huge gulp of whiskey and passes another cup to Gerry, who is now grinning like Dirty Peter Morse when he gets some good table scraps.

It must be an hour later when we finish a whole loaf of bread, and I tell Gerry it's time to go. La Minque is now singing some song in a language I can't understand. I know he has had a little too much whiskey. Gerry looks at me and says, "Yeah, we probably should be getting back."

We climb down out of La Minque's wagon and begin our walk home. Gerry is unsteady and weaves back and forth up the road.

"I think you are drunk," I say.

"Naw," Gerry says, "just a little tipsy. Don't you say anything to Mom and Dad."

I don't.

~~~

As we drive across the Maroon Creek Bridge, I am remembering that day we visited La Minque in his sheepherder's wagon. We cross the bridge and are just off it when I see a lone sheep on the side of the road grazing in the grass and weeds. It is obviously a stray. My dad sees the sheep too and slams on the brakes of the Jeep hard enough to darn near send Teddy and me through the front windshield. The Jeep skids to a halt. Almost before the motor quits running, Dad is out of the Jeep, and has come to the back. He pushes stuff around on the floor, rooting around for something.

"Move your big feet!" he tells Teddy and me.

We shuffle our feet around, and finally Dad finds what he is looking for, grabs hold of it, and walks off toward the sheep. He has a tire iron in his hand. Before I can figure out what he is doing, he whacks the sheep on the head hard enough to kill a moose. In one swift motion he reaches over, grabs the sheep under his arm, and heads to the Jeep. He throws the dead animal on the floor where Teddy and I still trying to move our feet out of the way. Then he gets into the Jeep, does a U-turn back onto the highway, and heads back across the bridge toward home.

"No school today, kids," he says. "Lucky we found that stray. He'd have died trying to get down valley by himself." Then he looks at his watch and says to hisself, "Damn, I'll just have to be a little late for work."

He has a big grin as he reaches in his breast pocket for his packet of Lucky Strikes and his Zippo lighter. Dad loves lamb chops.

Late Fall 1953

It is night and we have finished dinner and done our after-dinner chores. Teddy and I are upstairs in our room, and I'm doing a second grade project for Mrs. Johnson. She wants us to cut out a bunch of shapes, paste them on a piece of paper, and write the name of the shape under the pictures we have cut out—shapes like a triangle, a square, an oval— easy ones like that. It's a stupid assignment. Everyone knows what a square and a triangle are. I can even read the words. Cutting out paper is stupid, too. I have other things that would be more fun like seeing what happens when I cut the lamp cord with the scissors.

The more I think about it, the more I wonder just what *will* happen. I know the lamp will go out, because I know the cord has to be connected to the wall socket if it is going to light up. I also know when you put the two ends of the electric wires in the cord together when the cord is plugged in there are lots of sparks, a loud pop, and everything stops working. I watched my dad do it in the barn one day when he was testing to see if there was 'juice' in the line. He calls electricity "juice."

I reach over and place the scissors around the lamp cord and say to Teddy, "Watch this."

He looks at me then down at the scissors and is about to say something when I snap the scissors closed around the light cord. There is a huge pop! and a flash of blue-and-yellow light. The shock knocks me off the chair onto the floor. The room goes dark.

Dad must hear the thump of me hitting the floor because he shouts up the stairs, "What's going on up there?"

"Terry just cut the lamp cord with Mom's good scissors," Teddy says.

I look at Teddy, who luckily can't see me in the dark, because I am sending him my dagger eyes.

He didn't have to say I had Mom's best scissors. *Darn it. Now I'll catch hell for that, too. I just know it*, I think.

"Damn it, Terr-Ass, what the heck are you trying to do? Burn down the house?"

"No," I say, "I was just doing my homework for school. It was an experiment."

"Well, get your ass down here, and help me find a fuse for the fuse box."

I feel my way out of the room and down the stairs to where Dad is standing in the little red living room. He lights his Zippo lighter for a minute so we can see the right direction and pushes me toward the kitchen closet where the fuses are kept.

"Honestly, Terry," I hear my mom say from her bedroom. "What will you do next?"

I don't even try to answer that one.

Dad opens the closet door and pulls over a chair from the kitchen. He tells me to stand on the chair and hold the lighter for him while he fishes around for a fuse. I climb up on the chair and Dad hands me the lighter after he has lit it. The lighter is hot, and my hand is ready to burn by the time he fishes a fuse off the top shelf. Once I see he has one, I flip the lighter off on my pj's like I see him do on his jeans when he lights up a cig.

"Okay," he says. "Get your boots on, and we'll go out and change this thing. You can hold the lighter for me again."

"What about the flashlight?" I say.

"Batteries burned out."

I fumble in the dark, put on my boots, tuck my pj bottoms inside my boots, and we go out around the side of the house to the fuse box. I have Dad light the lighter and give it to me so I can hold it over my head while he replaces the fuse. The lights come on in the house. We head inside and my dad says, "Now quit screwing around and get to bed."

"Okay," I say.

I head upstairs again and find Teddy looking at the scissors he's picked up from the floor. I turn my chair upright, sit down, and say, "Give me the scissors so I can finish my project."

"They're no good," Teddy says.

"What do you mean?"

He holds out the scissors to me, blades first, and I see that there is a sizable chunk of steel burnt out of both blades where I cut the cord.

"Wow," I say. "I wondered what would happen to the scissors if I cut the lamp cord. Now I know."

Then it occurs to me to wonder what is going to happen to me in the morning when my mom sees I have wrecked her best clothing shears. But, I don't wonder too much. I'm tired and ready to hit the hay.

Chapter 19

December 1953

Dad is shaking me and yelling at me to wake up. "Wake up, Terry! Teddy, get up and get some pants on!" he shouts.

I'm groggy and very sleepy. Teddy has stumbled out of bed in the dark and is on the floor. He's landed on his pants by the bed where he left them last night when he went to sleep. My dad grabs the blanket off the bed and wraps me in it. He grabs Teddy under the other arm and moves quickly toward the stairs.

"Gerry, down the stairs!" he yells.

I am having trouble breathing. My eyes sting. The house is filled with smoke. We get down the stairs, and I hear my dad shouting, "Gerry, out into the car!" Gerry is running through the little red living room out into the hallway to the kitchen, headed for the front door.

I can see now and realize light is coming from flames shooting upward near the door to Jennifer's room. Dad puts Teddy and me on our feet and tells us, "Run for the car!"

Teddy and I take off running. It is dark in the hallway. We can barely see by the light from the fire reflecting off the snow, though it's enough light for us to see the front door. We reach the car and jump into the back and see Gerry is already there. I pull the blanket over my pj's. Right away my dad comes out of the house with Jennifer under his arm, holding Mom by her arm. He takes them around the car to the passenger side and puts them in the front seat. Dad gets in the car, starts it, turns around in a rush, and drives us out to the barnyard. He parks the car, gets out, and says to my mom, "Rudy, you stay here with the kids. I'm going to see if we can contain the fire."

By now, there are cars and Jeeps coming up the road, and I hear men shouting. My mom says to no one, "We called the fire department, but they won't come. It's too far out of town. If they have another fire in town and are out here..." Her voice trails off.

I sit in the car watching the flames lick at the blackness of the night. Jennifer is in the front seat crying.

"What happened?" I ask my mom.

"Jennifer set the house on fire."

"Why?"

"Jennifer said she was mad because she wanted to sleep with Teddy. She said she was afraid. We wouldn't let her. After we put her to bed, she snuck out to the kitchen, got a paper shopping bag and some matches. Then she lit the bag on fire under her bed. We smelled the smoke and about the same time Jennifer came into our room and told us her room was on fire. We went into her room, and the canopy bed was in flames," my mom says to the air.

I can tell she is not all here with us. We hear more shouts and yells from the men who are throwing snow on the fire to put it out. I hope no one is going to be hurt. We stay in the car for a long time watching the flames pop and snarl up the roof. Shadows of the men are reflected on the snow. We are not too far away from the fire, so the car warms up even in the winter cold. The flames light up the sky with a strange lonely light. Our two huge cottonwood trees look like monsters with many arms dancing behind the flames on the far side of the house.

Suddenly a man knocks on the window of the car. I don't know him.

"Rudy," he says.

My mom opens the window and says, "Hi."

The man, whose face I can't see, says, "Rudy, you and the kids can come down to our house in Aspen and stay there until things get sorted out. The missus will drive the car for you. Wendy can take the Jeep or catch a ride with the others when they get the fire under control or out."

"Thank you," my mom says, still not all here.

A lady comes to the car window. She opens the door. Mom takes Jennifer, who is still crying, on her lap and schooches over to make room for the woman. She gets in and starts the car. We drive into town, us kids not saying a word. The lady is saying nice things to my mom, and my mom is saying a lot of "thank-yous" and "uh-huhs." Pretty soon we stop out in front of a big old house across the street from the school. I know where I am. Chris Grove lives in this house. He's in my second grade class. We get out of the car, are shuffled into the house, and into a room. Mrs. Grove and Gerry quickly make us some sleeping places with blankets that they set side by side on the floor. The three of us boys lie down, pull blankets over ourselves, and talk about the fire before eventually falling asleep.

The next morning I wake up in a strange house. It takes me awhile to remember I am at the Groves' house. I head downstairs to look for something to eat and am greeted by Chris Grove, who hardly says "Hi" before he starts asking me lots of questions like, "What happened? How did the fire start? Did you save your Christmas presents?"

I can only reply, "I don't know."

As we eat breakfast, I begin to wonder what I'm going to wear. All I have are my pj's. I don't think I want to go to school in my pj's. Chris is dressed and ready to go. My mom comes into the kitchen and says, "You kids will have to stay here today while I go over to the Thrift Shop and find some clothes for you. Then I have to go out to the house and see what's left of it. Your dad had to go to the hospital to be treated for his burns. They just got back into town a couple of hours ago."

I stare at her, wondering if I can go to the ranch with her so I can see what a burned-out house looks like. Finally I ask, "Can I come?"

Mom says, "I'll think about it. First I have to get you some clothes."

It is several hours later when my mom comes home from the Thrift Shop with some things for us to wear. We put them on, and Teddy and Gerry run across the street to school. I think they just want to tell everybody about our place burning down. I don't want to go to school; I want to go out to the ranch and see what has happened.

"Can I go with you?" I say to my mom when I see her getting ready to leave again.

"I suppose so," she says.

We drive the Ford out of town across the bridges and up our road. From the front, the house looks the same. We walk into the kitchen, and I can immediately tell the place is not the same. It is still warm and smells campfire smoky. We wander around to find which parts of our wrecked home are still standing. The back part is completely burned. The fire has taken Jennifer's bedroom, Mom and Dad's bedroom, and everything above. Almost the whole backside is open to the outdoors. What is left of it is nothing more than a burned pile of wood scattered on the ground.

The rest of the place is still standing. The snow has melted around the house and grass is showing. Where it hasn't melted, it has been shoveled away by the men putting out the fire.

Mom won't let me get too close to the parts that have burned. She says, "There may still be hot places where you can be burned."

I content myself with looking around to see if we can use anything in the part of the house still standing.

Everything is covered with a thick grey coat of smoke and ash. I pick up the letter opener from the surface of the charred desk in the red living room. It is grey and the metal is still warm. I don't think it can be polished again. The trunk of the Christmas tree is still standing with its charred branches sticking out like rib bones on a skeleton. There are one or two presents under the tree. The wrappers are burned, black with soot, and the ribbons curled like Kathleen Herwick's hair.

I wander into the kitchen and open a cabinet to see what has survived there. To my delight, I find a round tin of Famous Chocolate Cookies. I open the box and pop one in my mouth. It tastes like smoke. Nothing else, just mealy smoke. I spit it out into the grey ash covering the bottom of the sink. I walk back into the little red living room and find my mother sitting on the floor crying.

"What's the matter?" I say.

She sobs and cries and in between sobs says, "I lost my wedding ring and my engagement ring. I took them off last night before the fire to put cream on my hands. I thought I took them from the table and put them in my pocket when we ran out. They must have fallen out. When we got to the Groves' house, I didn't have them on my finger and they weren't in my pocket. I hoped I might have left them on the bedside table and I would be able to find them still there. They're gone. I'll never find them in this mess."

She continues weeping for her rings, for the burnt house, and for losses I cannot understand at the moment. I wander out to the kitchen, onto the porch, and outside. The sun is shining brightly and it's crispy cold. Just the kind of day I love to play outside. I start out to the driveway. I think I'll head out to the barn and the chicken coop to see how things are there.

As I step off the boardwalk, I notice that the snow all around the house is black with soot from the fire. From the boardwalk I reach the driveway and see a small sparkle in the ash-covered snow. I think it's a snowflake that hasn't been covered by the ashes. I love to see the sun reflecting off the snowflakes making all the different colors. Silver, gold, blue. I put my nose closer to the sparkling snowflake for a closer look to see if the light will split up like it does with a prism. I had a prism. It's lost in the fire now.

My nose is up close to the snow and I see that it is not a snowflake I am looking at metal reflecting the sun. I pick it up with my dirty hand and know instantly it is my mom's wedding ring. Carefully I dig deeper into the snow a bit deeper and find her engagement ring. There they are: a simple round silver ring, and a simple round silver ring with a little sparkling diamond stone in it. I grasp the rings in my fist as I see my mom coming out the door.

"Come on," she says. "We have to head back to Aspen."

"Okay," I say. "Mom, I have something for you."

"What now," she says in her busy voice. She is heading for the car with her behind already in front of me.

"Here," I say.

I hold out my hand and wait, motionless for her to turn around. When she finally turns around, she looks into my hand and begins to cry again.

Chapter 20

January 1954

After the fire, when we could no longer stay with the Groves, we rented a house on Third Street between West Francis and West Smuggler Streets. I'm out exploring the neighborhood in the West End. There are many old Victorian houses built in the mining days. Some of them are in bad shape and falling down. Others are empty. Some are lived in and well cared for. There are a bunch of vacant lots where there are no houses. I have explored all the way over to where the concert tent is set up for the summer Music Festival, and have seen the big indent in the snow where the seats are placed on the slanted concrete.

I don't know who owns many of these houses because I've spent most of the time out at the ranch. In town I'm at school all day so I can't explore places like this. I can't wait until I'm a little older so I can find out who lives where and, learn the names of all the streets. Some of the main ones I know, like Hallam Street and Bleeker Street. Others I don't.

I wander home early because we're celebrating Christmas tonight. Mom has made a Christmas dinner. Not our usual Christmas dinner. Christmas has passed, but it's a good dinner nevertheless. Luckily there are dishes and furniture in the house we are renting. We're home now getting ready for dinner, and we're putting on the nicest Thrift Shop clothes. I can't wait until after dinner because Mom says that Dad has gotten us a surprise for Christmas.

It's a small house, so we eat in the kitchen. After dinner we go into the living room where we have set up a small

Christmas tree. There are a couple of presents underneath it. Maybe one or two for each of us. We sit around and open them up and eventually Dad says, "Well, boys, even though the house burned, Santa Claus still found our chimney here. Come look what he left you."

We follow Dad into another room in the house where he shows us three red Hercules three-speed bicycles!

Wow! My own bike, I think.

"They're all the same," Dad says, "so just pick one and call it yours."

Gerry and Teddy have already claimed theirs by the time I think to move forward and touch the magic-wheeled freedom machine.

Now I can really explore the town of Aspen, winter or not, I think.

I look at my dad and say, "Thank you."

He looks at me, and I can see that he understands.

Chapter 21

Early Spring 1954

In the summer my dad works as a carpenter for Dick Wright building houses in Aspen. In the winter he works for the Aspen Ski Corporation teaching skiing to tourists. In the evenings lots of times he works as a bartender at the Golden Horn, a restaurant owned by Steve Knowlton. Of course, he also runs the ranch. He is a busy man, which is why my brothers and I have lots of chores to do around the house and ranch. We all need to "pitch in" as Dad says.

My dad thinks the ski business may be a good business to start on our land. The land is more gentle than the ski slopes on Aspen Mountain, so it would be easier for beginning skiers. He thinks he can build a T-bar up on the Tiehack ridgeline as the start of a little ski area. If the ski area is successful, then maybe he can earn some more money which would come in handy for us, especially after he lost money building the cistern that doesn't have any water in it.

The summer before last, he cut a straight line up the hill through the scrub oak, aspen trees and pines for a "lift line," where a T-bar can be built. He poured pads for the T-bar towers to stand on. This summer he wants to put up the towers and string the cable for the Ts. Then, all he has to do is hook up a big motor to make the thing run so it can haul skiers up the hill. They can have a fun time skiing down to the bottom and ride back up to do it again.

Dad says he is behind on the construction of the lift because he has to rebuild the house this summer after the fire last December. He has a couple of partners on the Tiehack

ski area who say they are going to give him money to help pay
for the cost of building the lift. They haven't given my dad
much money, and now Dad says the whole operation is
getting iffy. In fact they don't have any more money to put
into the project. Dad is talking to a banker in town and some
other friends to see if he can get them to invest. My dad calls
it "a shoe-string operation held together with bubble gum and
bailing wire." He can buy the cable for the Ts to hang on if
his financing comes through with the bank, or he gets more
partners. Dad says he plans to build the towers out of wood
like the ones on Little Nell.

A few weeks after the snow melts, he is ready to get to
work on the project while at the same time he is rebuilding
the house. I wonder how he will be able to be working on the
house and on the lift at the same time. He says to my mom,
"Mouse (he called her Mouse lots of times), I have to take the
Dodge down to Glenwood Springs to pick up some parts for
the T-bar. First I have to go into Aspen and get the word on
our financing. We have the bill for the cable and I have to pay
for the other parts when I get down to Glenwood. I have the
last of what we have saved but will need the financing money
before I go."

"Okay," Mom says.

I watch my dad, hoping he will suggest that I come
along for the ride, but he doesn't. I like to ride in the old
truck, but Dad says it's dangerous because the door on the
passenger side does not latch right and I could fall out. I
watch him get into the truck and drive off down the road.

Not much time later my dad comes back up the road in
the truck. He stops in front of the house and gets out. I can
see by the look on his face he is upset. I follow him into the
house so I can listen to what he has to say to my mom.

"Mouse," he says. "You're not going to believe this! The
bank won't lend us the money to finish the lift and rebuild

the house both. They're locked up tighter than a frog's ass, and there's no way they are going to lend us anything. I don't know what we're gonna do because we still owe for the cable, and I don't have enough money to pay for it."

"Well, Wendy, that just stinks," my mom says.

I look at both of them wondering what this all means.

"If I can't find anyone who is interested in investing in Tiehack, we'll have to give up on the idea," my dad worries. They keep talking, and I walk outside and get into the Dodge.

I love sitting in the seat of that truck and moving the steering wheel back and forth. I can't see over it through the front window, but I don't care. It is just fun bouncing on the seat. The truck smells like the shop in the barn. Lots of cigarette smoke, oil, and dirt. It is a familiar smell. One that makes me feel safe.

Chapter 22

Late Spring 1954

By now the snow has melted. I have had lots of time to ride my bike all over Aspen while my dad and mom worry about rebuilding the house and how to get out of debt from the Tiehack thing. I'm glad I'm a kid. I feel like an explorer on my bike. I get to know my town more and more. Here's what I have found out.

As near as I can tell, the town starts at the Castle Creek Bridge. If you start at the bridge, and bike on Highway 82 into town, after a while the name of the road changes to Main Street. Just after the bridge on the left side of the road are a couple of old houses from the mining days. One is a small white house that the Skiffs live in. I don't know who lives in the other. It is a yellow house with white trim and is two stories. It has steep roofs, frilly wood shingles on the side near the roof, and decorative supports under the roof. My mom calls it a "Victorian house." A black and rusted iron fence that guards all the weeds in the yard surrounds it.

The last house before turning the corner and heading towards Shadow Mountain belongs to the Forest Service but is used by the Weidenhofs'. Mr. Weidenhof is the Forest Ranger for the White River National Forest. His daughter Carol Weidenhof is in Gerry's class. I think he likes her. He likes a lot of girls. Across from their house is a big vacant lot with nothing on it except some trash and maybe a leftover tire or two.

Just after the Weidenhofs' house, the road turns right, and on the left side of the street is Waterman's Store and

Cabins. Mr. and Mrs. Waterman have a gas station and maybe eight or ten cabins on the property. They run the gas station and store. They rent the cabins to tourists and motorists. They have two kids that I know about, Judy and Bob. They're much older than I am. I always get the flats on my bike fixed at Waterman's because he's such a nice guy about it. He's taught me how to patch and change my tire and always has a few bicycle patches on hand when I roll my bike in with a flat. At first he changed the tire for me. Now I mostly do it myself unless I have trouble getting my tire off the rim.

If you bike past Waterman's toward Shadow Mountain, you go for two blocks and the street turns left. It's a straight line down to the center of town. I think this is where Main Street starts. There are houses on each side of the road. Some of them are lived in and some don't seem to be. There's a large Victorian on the corner just as you turn down Main Street, a couple of miners' cabins, and smaller houses on the left side of the street. The Brauns live in one of them. Across the street is Judge Shaw's house. His house is a large two-story Victorian with a white picket fence. It is brown and has lots of windows. The Lowderbecks live in one of the houses on the left side of Main Street just before you get to the Mesa Store.

The Mesa Store is about four blocks up from the Hotel Jerome and is a big building where you can buy a limited range of groceries, candy, sodas, and sometimes comic books. The Mesa Store isn't as good as Beck and Bishop's in town. Heading on toward downtown Aspen, there are ten or twelve houses left over from the mining days. Some of them are well cared for; others are falling down. I suppose I should name some more of the houses and who lives in them, like the Lowderbecks, the Elishas, the Conners, the Twinings, the McCabes, and so on, and all the buildings like Matthew's Drug, the Aspen Times, the Monarch Building, the Chevron

Station, and so on, but if I start doing that, you may get bored.

All you have to know is, the part of town on the west all the way down to the Hotel Jerome is called "the West End." The West End is made up mostly of old mining houses, some big, some little. Many of them are lived in. Then there are vacant lots and vacant houses that are falling down. The rodeo grounds are out on the west end over towards the Roaring Fork River. All the streets in the West End, well actually all over town, are dirt streets except Main Street.

If you go from the Hotel Jerome down a dirt road toward Red Mountain, you come to the train station. Beyond that you cross the Roaring Fork River and go up a hill to Red Mountain. There are a couple of ranches up there, but mostly it's too steep to build on. There are a few houses at the bottom. If you go south from the Hotel Jerome, you end up at Aspen Mountain where the ski area is. There's really nothing but vacant lots and a couple of old buildings up by the mountain. The Tipple Mine buildings are still standing at the base of the mountain. My dad says he's going to take some of the big beams out of the mine buildings to use on the house when he rebuilds it.

Beyond the Hotel Jerome to the east is "the East End." The East End is a "hodgepodge" (that's what my dad calls it). It is a mix of broken-down mining cabins, a trailer court or two, a few houses, and lots of vacant land. There are also big heaps of mine tailings from the Smuggler Mine on Smuggler Mountain and mines in the Smuggler Mountain area. If you stay on the paved Main Street past the East End, you go out of town and the road turns to dirt again as you travel towards Independence Pass.

There are about fifteen hundred people in the whole Roaring Fork Valley. Everyone pretty much knows everyone else or at least who they are. We have some street names, but not a lot of them, or at least ones that I know of. If you want to give someone directions, you do it by telling them it's two blocks down from the courthouse, then two blocks towards Aspen Mountain on the left. Like that.

There are a bunch of empty buildings and vacant lots scattered all over town. They're fun to explore, but you have to be careful not to get caught. Adults usually get mad if they see you farting around the old buildings. The adults say, "Those buildings aren't safe, so don't go playing around in them."

You have to be real careful riding your bike across any vacant lots because they have lots of nails, broken glass, metal pieces, and the like. Some of them have old mining equipment, a broken down car, or an abandoned something or other. You'll get a flat tire pretty easily if you ride across the vacant lots.

Aspen was called Ute City before it was called Aspen. The train comes to Aspen once a day as near as I can tell. You can ride it to Glenwood, then take the California Zephyr to Denver. There is a great hill just behind the Hotel Jerome where you can zip down and jump your bike. You have to be able to stop before you get to the train tracks or you will take a whopper of a crash. There are lots of mines to explore, but you should never do it without a rope and a light. In the winter, skiing is about the only thing you can do that is fun. The rest of the time you are either shoveling snow or moving it somewhere out of the way so you can get some other work done or drive your car somewhere. It's really pretty, but it's a pain in the butt. On some days, the snow all around town is black from everyone burning coal for their cook stoves and heating furnaces. Then there'll be a storm and the air will clear out, and it'll be nice for a while, with the snow nice and white.

All us kids in Aspen have the whole valley as our playground. We can go pretty much anywhere we want as long as we don't destroy property and don't get ourselves killed. The adults are on the lookout for kids doing stupid things and won't hesitate to give you what for if you are screwing up. It's okay when they do give us hell because you usually learn something from it. Like why something is dangerous or what can happen if you do this or do that. It's nice that we can wander a bit. It makes life more exciting and interesting.

Adults know I'm a Morse kid. We all have blond hair, blue eyes, and fair skin with a few freckles. We all look like Morses, so people know we are. When we get in trouble, we're "those damn Morse kids." I've actually heard some of the adults call us that. I don't understand why. Most of what we do is just having an adventure or exploring things. You need to do that to find out how it all fits together. Most everyone in town is nice to you if you smile at them and are polite. I probably don't do that as much as I should because I'm pretty shy.

My dad says to Mom, "Aspen is a broken-down mining town with the potential to become a World Famous Ski Resort." We'll see about that. Right now it's nothing more than a broken-down mining town.

Chapter 23

Early Summer 1954

It's early in the summer and my dad hasn't found any money for his ski area. He says he may have to go bankrupt. I don't know what that means, so I ask him, "What does going bankrupt mean?"

"Don't worry about it, son, everything will work out in the end."

"Yeah," I try once again, "but what does bankrupt mean?"

"It means you don't have the money to pay your bills, so you have to settle the matter in court so the people you owe money to are happy with the results. Then you have to pay them a certain amount of the money back. I may have to go bankrupt on the Tiehack lift because the bank won't lend me the money to finish the project. Since my two partners left town without paying their share of the bills for the work we have done so far, I have to pay the bills myself. I don't have the money to do that, so I may have to declare bankruptcy. Going bankrupt is not a good thing. You should honor your debts," he says.

With that explanation, I have too much information, but I do understand the concept: it's better not to borrow more money than you can pay back; otherwise, people will be unhappy with you."

"Well, why didn't you just pay the bills so you didn't have to go bankrupt?" I say.

"It's a long story," my dad says.

I know that's the end of our conversation so don't explore it further. It's enough to know being bankrupt is not a good thing, and I decide not to do it when I grow up.

Mom says we will all have to tighten our belts this winter. I think about this for some time and wonder just what that means.

~ ~ ~

That night I'm playing outside, and I overhear my mom and dad talking out on the terrace. They are talking about having to sell the ranch because of the money they owe on the Tiehack lift after Dad's partners ran out on him, leaving him with all the bills. My dad says, "There's no other way. I don't want to declare bankruptcy and with having to rebuild the house, there isn't the time or the money to keep the ranch up. The three little ones do a good job helping out, but they aren't big enough to take care of all the work that needs to be done. I can't do it all."

"Wendy," my mom says, "We've had a fine time with the ranch. It is a lot of work and with the four kids it's just going to get worse. Maybe we should look at selling."

I know I should probably not be hearing this, so I wander off out in the barnyard, saddened by the prospect that we may have to sell the ranch.

Mid-Summer 1954

So far, this summer has been fun. My dad and some workmen are rebuilding the house. They're taking some wood out of the old Tipple Mine for beams in the living room. The beams are 12" x 12" and twenty-five-feet long. I'm learning about carpentry and can read a tape measure. One of the workmen showed me how the tape measure is broken up into eights and sixteenths, so I know about fractions now.

We're getting rid of the screen porch along the side of the house and making it a hallway. On the west side out toward the barnyard, we're building a new living room with an attached dining room. The living room will have a large lichen rock fireplace. The workmen are hauling the lichen rock down off of Burnt Mountain up above Brush Creek. The kitchen will be larger and will have a door in to the dining room. Above the living room, we are building a bunkroom for us boys. We will each have a bed and a desk. There will be closets and a place for some bedside tables and a bureau. Of course we'll have chairs for our desks. Teddy's and my old room before the fire will be a new bathroom. Gerry's old room will be another bedroom above Jennifer's old room that burned down. Her room and all the area around it that got burned will be fixed too. The stairs to the second floor will come down to meet a new hallway rather than coming out in the little red living room.

The workmen and Dad have poured concrete for the foundation, put in the floor supports, and put down the floor underlayment. The next step is to put up the living room walls. Then on top of the walls, they can lay the huge beams from the Tipple Mine. On top of the large ceiling beams in the living room, they put more flooring and more walls up to the roof to make our bedroom. We call it "the boys room."

Dad has some guys come to do plumbing and wiring: Dean Gordier for the plumbing and Kenny Broughton for the electric. Dad does most of the carpentry but has help with the things he can't manage alone and we can't help him with. He works from when the sun comes up until it is too dark to see at night. My mom has to call him to dinner every night so he can eat.

"Wendy," she says, "You're gonna kill yourself if you don't slow down." Or "Wendy, you be careful up on that roof. You're not getting enough rest and it's dangerous up there." Or "Wendy, don't forget your lunch. You will be starving by noon. Here's your lunchbox."

The place is chaos all day long. When I'm not hanging around the house trying to see what everyone is doing and how they're building the addition, I'm out on the ranch wandering around. I have a fort where I go to read books that my mom picks up at the library. Right now I'm reading Grimm's Fairy Tales. Some of the words are hard, but mostly I can get the meaning of those I don't know. Otherwise I'll just ask someone later what the word means and that usually takes care of it.

Some days I stay in Aspen and ride my bike around town by myself or with Richard Sabbatini. Tony Vagneur mostly doesn't come into town because he lives on their ranch out in Woody Creek. A couple of times I have gotten to go out to spend the night with him, which has been fun. He has some potato fields and an orchard around his house. Down at the barn are horses. I think his grandmother or aunt or someone owns the barn.

~ ~ ~

At the moment we're having dinner and my dad is talking about the day.

"Things are going well at the house. We got the chimney finished today and the decking is down for the roof, so we are all closed in. Windows can go in this week and I can start insulating nights," he says to Mom. Then, "I spoke with Art Pfister on the way home, and the deal for the ranch is set. He's agreed to buy everything except our house and an acre of land around it. He wants to close the deal as soon as possible."

Dad drops this into the conversation like it should be there, just another day at the job site, nothing unusual. I look at my brothers in astonishment. It looks like Teddy and Gerry aren't surprised, but I sure am. I've heard them talking about it but never believed it would happen. Now it has.

"You're selling the ranch?" I blurt out, interrupting him. "You can't do that! That's our home. I don't want you to sell it. What will happen to our fort and all the other fun things we have there?" Before I can really wind up, he cuts me off. "Son," he begins.

Damn! I think. *Here's the "son" line. That means it's gonna be worse than I can imagine. It is.*

We're selling the ranch to Art Pfister. He's going to be the new owner before the end of the summer. We'll have to respect his property, so we won't be able to wander all over hell and gone. We won't be able to go into the barn. We won't be able to ride our horses because we won't have any. We won't be able to this and we won't be able to that. He's going to build a house on the other side of the hill and a bunkhouse for a ranch caretaker where the chicken coop is. He's getting rid of the chickens and all the other animals except horses. It's a disaster.

After dinner, I talk with Gerry and Teddy.

"What else could they do?" Gerry says. "They went broke on the Tiehack thing and can't afford to keep the place. They had to sell it."

"There must have been another way," I say. "And I'll darned well tell you I'm not going to stay off the land or out of the barn or anything."

I've worked myself up into an indignant anger about the whole state of affairs and my hackles are up in full force. "You guys can do what you want, but I'm not gonna do it."

We talk more, and I push my case for the freedom to roam, not all these fun things being ended. The days in the shop messing around with the tools. Feeding the animals. Riding the horses. Even baling hay, and doing our chores. Not that I like baling hay that much.

I can see Teddy and Gerry are thinking about my position on the matter. I decide that if this sale of the ranch takes place, it will happen at the expense of an all-out war. I'll try to enlist Teddy and Gerry in my campaign. If they don't want to join, I'll carry on by myself.

August 1954

It's the first part of August. School starts in awhile, and some days I think I can feel fall in the air after a long hot spring and summer this year. The addition on the house is going very quickly now. All the wiring and plumbing are completed, the walls insulated, and the redwood on the exterior of the house is finished. The chimney is done, and Mom is helping to stain the redwood. Inside my dad is doing the finish work: trimming out windows, setting doors, building our desks, building closets, and staining the wood walls.

I've calmed down about selling the ranch, but I'm still determined to wage a war from hell when the time is right. Gerry and Teddy however, to my surprise, have worked themselves into an inferno, burning mad. Yesterday Dad told us, "Tomorrow is the closing on the ranch, boys. After tomorrow, you will have to stay off the rest of the ranch except the property around the house here."

Like hell! I think.

"Pfister has hired Ed Ticoucih to take care of the place until he finds a ranch manager. As you know, Pfister is out of town most of the time, so he'll need someone good. It may take him awhile to find the right person. You be nice to Ed. You know him and you better do what he tells you. Just stay off the rest of the ranch," Dad says. "Am I understood?" Lecture finished.

We all nod our heads, "Uh huh," we say in unison.

~ ~ ~

It's two days later, and the ranch now belongs to Pfister. We've been too busy to think about much because my mom has us helping her get ready to move back home from our rental house in town. We're unpacking a few boxes of Thrift Shop clothing and some other junk we used in Aspen. Mostly pots and pans, dishes, and kitchen utensils we dragged down to Aspen after the fire. I can tell it's been a hard summer for my mom. She's been helping out with the rebuilding of the house, keeping things afloat in Aspen, taking care of Jennifer, and putting up with "all that crap from you boys" as my dad calls it. It looks like she is skinnier and more tired from all the work.

We finish our chores and wander out in the driveway to figure out what to do next while Mom is putting some of the stuff away before she takes us back town. Tomorrow night we get to come home again and start living here. I can't wait. Gerry, Teddy, and I wander out into the barnyard. We see Ed Ticoucih's truck parked there. Ed's not around, and we're wondering where he is. Gerry begins thinking out loud, "If we discourage Ed from coming out to the ranch, then maybe Pfister will get upset and sell the ranch back to us. Or better yet for Dad, just give it back with us in the bargain."

"It might not be a bad idea," I say. "But how are we going to do it?"

"I've got an idea," Gerry says. "Come with me."

He leads us across the barnyard to the barn. We enter the shop and Gerry rummages around in the drawers, while Teddy and I stand guard looking for Ed, who probably wouldn't care if we were in the shop or not. Ed knows we're upset about the ranch sale and has told us so. Finally Gerry comes to the door with a handful of 16-penny nails.

"Okay, here's what we're gonna do," he says as we walk toward Ed's truck. "We're going to put two nails on each side of each of the tires on the truck so Ed won't be able to go backwards or forwards without getting a flat."

"Good idea," I say. "That ought to discourage him from working for Pfister."

"Yeah," says Teddy.

Gerry gives each of us some of the nails and each we kneel down by a tire and place the nails at angles with the points leaning up against the tires. Two nails on each side of the tire. Gerry does the two front tires, and Teddy and I do one back tire each. When we are finished, we stand back and look at our handiwork.

"That should do it," Gerry says.

"Yeah," says Teddy.

I just stand there thinking, *The war has begun.*

We wander over to the pond, throw a few rocks, and eventually head back to the house when we hear my mom calling to us, "Come get in the car, we're heading back to town."

~~~

It isn't until dinner the next night, now that we are out at our house on the ranch and out of Aspen, that we recall our sabotaging of Ed's truck. Dad has just come in from the barnyard after talking to Ed, and we're sitting at the kitchen table waiting for him to wash his hands and sit down. I can tell by the way he rubs his hands together he is mad.

Uh oh, I think, *Here it comes.*

I try to look invisible, because I know this is going to be one volcanic explosion.

"Goddamn it!" he starts.

I know this is not good. Only when he is really, really mad, does he start with the "Goddamn it" lead in.

"Which one of you little monsters put the nails under Ed's truck tires? He had to spend all day going in and out of town getting his flats fixed."

"Wendy," my mom butts in. "That's horrible!"

"You stay out of this, Rudy. One of these little shits blew out all four of Ed's tires. Ed's always been helpful and treated us nicely when we had the ranch, and now this. I won't stand for it. Who is responsible for this?" he says, his voice now raised.

Wow, he's really mad, I think. *I better cut my losses and limit my damages before he blows his top completely.*

I raise my hand and say, "I guess I did," then mumble "some of it."

Gerry stares daggers at me, but I don't think my dad heard me. Teddy intuits the wisdom of my actions and says, "I guess I helped Terry."

My dad looks at Gerry and says, "What about you? I doubt these two could think this up all by themselves!"

Little does he know, I think.

Gerry finally sees it's no use and caves in.

"You're all going to get a whipping for this. And you all are going to damned well go over there and apologize to Ed and pay for his tires," Dad says.

Dinner follows in silence.

Just as we're finishing dinner, the phone rings and Dad answers it. I can tell it is long distance by the way his voice sounds. While he's on the phone, Gerry, Teddy, and I clean up the dishes and the kitchen like we usually do, then head upstairs to our new room. Dad is still on the phone. We spend the rest of the evening talking and farting around until its time to go to bed. We'll be missing any punishment tonight, and we all agree that it's a good thing. The phone call has saved us.

The next morning we're further reprimanded, sent out to apologize to Ed and pay for the fixing of his tires. No one has said a word about where the money will come from, only that we need to pay Ed. Our dad hasn't offered any of his scare funds, neither has Gerry or Teddy mentioned anything about how we're going to pay for Ed's tires.

Finally I say to them, as we are getting ready to march out to the barnyard, "Do you guys have any money to pay Ed for the tires?"

Together they look at me like I am a freak.

"Why would you think we would have any money?" Teddy asks.

"Because you're always sneaking your money away in your little stash spot somewhere," I say.

Gerry laughs. He knows I'm right.

"Well, I don't," says Teddy.

I know he's lying.

"What about you?" I ask Gerry.

He just looks at me and says, "Nope."

I know he's lying too.

"Well," I finally say, "I have a quarter, so I guess that will have to do."

I'm mad at the two of them because they're Scrooges. They won't come up with any money. I only have a quarter and know it's not enough to pay for the tire patches. I decide right then I will make sure Ed knows it's my quarter that is being paid and that my brothers aren't chipping in.

We walk out to the barnyard and find Ed out in the shop sharpening a pair of shears. He looks at us and says, "That was a pretty dirty trick you played the other day. I know you kids are upset that your dad had to sell the ranch, but you got to get used to the fact that life has its ups and downs."

Gerry looks down at his feet where Teddy and I are both looking and says, "We're sorry for putting nails under your tires."

Teddy thinks this is sufficient, as do I, so we don't say anything. Ed says, "You kids gotta walk the line here. This land don't belong to you no more. It's Pfister's ranch now, and you're just gonna have to get used to that fact. So don't be givin' me no more hard times with your dirty tricks."

Gerry looks up at Ed and says, "Well, we're just so damned mad about Dad selling the ranch. Pfister doesn't even live here all the time. He's hiring someone else to live in the guesthouse he is building. When that happens, we really won't be able to roam about."

"That's jest the way life is sometimes," Ed says. "You win some of 'em and you lose some of 'em. But I can tell you that you better walk the straight and narrow from now on. Your pa was fit to kill the lot of you last night."

"Yes, sir," says Gerry.

"Now get," Ed says.

We turn to leave, and I remember I have the quarter in my pocket. I turn back, fish it out of my pocket, and say to Ed, "Here's a quarter to pay for fixing the tires. I know it's not enough, but it's all I got." I hand him the quarter and look up at him. He takes it and says, "Thanks." I see a slight twinkle in his eye and know that I won't raise hell on the ranch as long as he is taking care of it.

Chapter 24

Late Summer 1954

With all the problems my mom and dad are having with paying for the Tiehack venture, having to sell the ranch, and rebuild the house, I find myself with much more freedom to roam than I have had previously in my life. They're busy and don't have time for us kids except Jennifer who is still small. Since we sold our spread, Gerry, Teddy, and I no longer have the ranch chores. It is fortunate we have bicycles because we have the ability to travel to town and around the valley more freely.

Roger Dixon is back in town. Today I've ridden my bike into Aspen and out the road past the Ute Cemetery to the Stillwater Ranch to go fishing. It's a long ride. My dad told me it is three miles to town from the ranch, then maybe another two to Stillwater Ranch. I've been riding my bike there three times a week over the past month, while Roger and Hazel have been visiting. Roger has been teaching me to cast a fly, how to find fish in the water, and other things about fly-fishing. I love fly-fishing. When I am not at Stillwater Ranch, I drop down over the bank behind our house and fish Maroon Creek. If not Maroon Creek, then Castle Creek. I have fished almost every day either in the early morning or in the late afternoon. Those are the best times to fish, with the fish hungry and the bugs out over the water.

Roger is standing out in front of his house with his dog when I arrive. I have carried my fishing rod, a small box of flies, some leader, and one or two other supplies purchased from Magnifico Sports with me on my bike. Mike Magnifico has helped me pick out some good flies that work on the Roaring Fork. A couple each of, the Royal Coachman, Grey Hackle Yellow, Black Captain, and Black Gnat. My rod is an old one Roger has given me for learning. I'm not sure whether he has actually given it to me, or if I am borrowing it. I'll ask him before he goes back to Alabama.

"Good morning, Mr. Morse," Roger says.

"Good morning."

"I see you rode your bike into town today. You must be tired and hungry."

"Yes, sir," I say.

"Let's go in the house and see what Hazel has in the kitchen. She usually has something around as you know."

We walk into the house, through the living room that over looks the river, and into the kitchen. Hazel is sitting at the kitchen table beneath a window with the same pastoral view as the living room.

"Hazel," Roger says, "What do we have to eat for a hungry young man?"

Hazel looks at me kindly and says, "How are you today, Terry?"

"I'm fine, thank you."

I try to be polite around other folks like my mom and dad have taught us. At home I'm not so good at my manners and my swearing.

"This is your lucky day," Hazel says looking at me up and down. "I have some cinnamon rolls over there on the counter which Roger had a taste of this morning for breakfast. Would you like one?"

I sit down at the kitchen table, eat a large cinnamon roll, and drink a glass of milk while I answer their questions about how things are going "out on Maroon Creek" now that we've sold the ranch. I tell them about getting in trouble with Ed Ticoucih and Art Pfister. They laugh, saying that they are sure I'll get it figured out before too long. We talk about fishing and other things. Then Roger tells me, "We're going to be leaving this weekend. Back to Alabama. We won't be back until next year, so y'all have to practice on your own. Y'all are welcome to come down here and fish anytime you want, but you'll have to leave your bike up at the gate because it'll be locked. If anyone tries to run you off, just tell them that I said it was okay and if they have a problem with it they can call me or write me a letter."

"Okay," I say. "Thank you."

"So, how about you and I go down to the river for a spell and you can show me how to cast. We'll have a look at your wrist action and maybe practice a little. Then I'll turn you lose to catch the Big One."

We walk down to the river. I cast my line several times while Roger teaches me how to throw the line out farther and how to aim the cast to where I want the fly to go. I'm not very good but have improved since the beginning of the summer. Presently he turns me loose to fish on my own and walks slowly back up to the house. I thank him as I watch him go. He walks like an old man, yet he seems young when he is talking about fly-fishing. I like Roger Dixon.

I drift upstream, taking my time. The sun is midway up to the top. It probably isn't a great time to be fishing. Catching a few smaller fish and turning them back to the river, I move slowly upstream. The sound of the rippling water is peaceful and comforting. As it flows by the bank, I watch early fall leaves floating on the surface, and the sun reflecting off the water, like a silver glint from some far-off mirror. I love these times. Thoughts drift by me like the leaves on the river. I can choose which ones I would like to pluck out of the stream to study. Or I can leave them all there just peacefully passing by, not needing to think about any of them.

My mind is serene; I hear only the sound of the rippling water, and see only the light bouncing off the riffles. The buzzing of the gnats and mosquitoes are background noise. There is a great stillness in my heart. A stillness I don't understand. A feeling I love and embrace. I am part of the water and of the field grasses and of the pine trees on the river bend and of the water moving slowly by. There is no need for explanation. Only the need to know the feeling of being. Here. Now. Where I belong and want to be. The feeling frightens me. I'm not sure why.

After some time, I begin to move upstream once again, knowing that I will catch a few more fish, cast a few more flies, and my day will be complete without catching "the Big One."

~ ~ ~

Later, I make my way back to the ranch house to tell Roger and Hazel I'll look forward to seeing them next summer. I thank Roger for what he has taught me.

"You've learned a lot this summer, young fella," he says. "Next summer we'll make a real pro out of you."

"Yes, sir," I answer.

"And by the way," he says, "You keep that fishing pole. And stop by the Country Store and get Phil Wright to teach you how to tie flies."

"Thank you."

And I say good-bye to Roger for the last time.

~ ~ ~

I am in the Country Store. I look up at the man facing me. He isn't as tall as my dad and has rosy cheeks. He says, "What can I do for you?"

"Roger Dixon has been helping me learn how to fly fish, and he said that I should come down here to see if I can learn to tie my own flies," I say.

"Aren't you Wendy and Rudy's kid?"

"Yes," I say.

"You look like a Morse."

I can't understand why people always say that to me. I think I look like myself. But I guess I must look like Gerry and Teddy enough, so they think we all look the same.

"What's your name?"

"Terry," I say.

"I'm Phil Wright. What can I do for you?"

"I was hoping you could tell me how to tie my own flies."

"We have a fly-tying kit for beginners that we sell here in the store. I tie my own flies. Not only is it fun, sometimes you come up with a fly that works better than anything you can buy. You just have to look at the bugs on the river and tie something that looks like them."

We walk over to a counter where he has lots and lots of flies displayed. Then he pulls out a box that has a little vise, some feathers, and spools of colored thread. There are some hooks and other assorted things needed for fly tying as well.

"This is a good kit for a beginner," Phil Wright says. "It's got all the basic things you need."

"How much is it?" I ask.

He turns the box over and looks at the price on the bottom.

"$9.95," he says.

"I guess I'll have to wait until I save some more money," I say. "I don't have enough right now."

"Okay," Phil Wright says, "You come back when you do, and I'll show you how this all works."

I take another look at the fly-tying kit, say thanks and leave the Country Store, wondering where I'm going to get the money to buy the kit.

Chapter 25

Late Fall 1954

We've almost finished fixing the house after the fire last winter. Dad is still finishing off a few things up in our room. There's a little scrap lumber lying around here and there, but mostly the room is set to go and we're sleeping there every night. Tonight Mom and Dad have gone to town to have dinner with Carl and Tukey Jonas. Carl is writing a book. Tukey, his wife, laughs a lot and dresses funny. It's snowing lightly out, the first snow of the fall. Halloween was a week ago, so it is the perfect time for it to start snowing. We have a high school girl babysitting us. I think it is Carolyn Slavens, but I'm not too sure because high school girls all look alike with their hair done the same way, the stupid dresses and shoes they wear.

Gerry, Teddy, and I are all upstairs and Carolyn is downstairs doing something. We hear a car come up the road, the car door open and shut, then voices in the kitchen. Then I think I hear the car drive off. We walk down the stairs, along the hall, and peer around the corner into the kitchen and see two boys and another girl in the kitchen with Carolyn. They are talking and laughing. We watch for a while, then we go into the kitchen to see what is happening. Carolyn says to us, "I thought you kids were upstairs."

"We were," says Gerry, "but we heard all this talking down here so figured we would come down and see what's going on."

"Nothing," Carolyn says. "We're having a little visit and talking about things you wouldn't want to hear. Why don't you go back upstairs and get ready for bed?"

"It's way too early for bed," Gerry says.

"Besides, we're not tired," I say.

Carolyn looks at the three of us and says, "Well, don't give me any trouble. Just go upstairs and play."

We move out of the kitchen and head back upstairs.

"I wonder what those other boys are doing here," Gerry says.

Soon we forget about it. Gerry is building a model plane at his desk, and Teddy is drawing. I'm lying on my bed reading at a book. Sometime later we hear it get noisy downstairs. We sneak down and take a look into the living room where the older kids are sitting on the couch and chairs talking and laughing. One of the boys has a beer, and the other three are drinking whiskey out of my dad's Partners Choice Bourbon bottle. I start to say something but, before I can get the words out, Gerry hits me on the arm and signals that we should go upstairs. The older kids aren't paying attention and don't see us.

Back upstairs, Gerry says, "Man, those kids are going to catch hell. They shouldn't be drinking Dad's liquor and beer. He's gonna be real mad when he finds out."

"Yeah," Teddy says.

Gerry is thinking about something. For a minute we are quiet, and suddenly he says, "I think we should make them leave. They shouldn't be here. And for sure not drinking Dad's liquor."

I add, "We don't need a baby-sitter. Every time we have one, we get in a fight with her and she doesn't come back. Except a few of them. We can take care of ourselves just fine. We do it all day on the ranch."

"Yeah," says Teddy. "And besides I don't really like these older kids. They look mean."

"Okay," says Gerry. "Here's what we're going to do. I'm going to sneak downstairs and get the .22 and a knife or something, and then we'll chase them out of here."

"Good," I say.

"Good," Teddy says.

So Gerry sneaks downstairs and is gone a long time. Pretty soon he comes back with the .22 rifle that he and Dad use to shoot at rodents, and Dad's hunting knife. He holds the .22 and gives the knife to Teddy.

"Well, what am I going to use?" I say to Gerry.

"Well, I don't know, find something."

I look around the room, and my eyes settle on a 2 x 4 piece of fir about four feet long. I heft it up onto my shoulder.

"I'm ready," I say.

"What if they get mad?" Teddy says.

"Duh," Gerry says. "Of course, they'll be mad, stupid. We just have to make them believe we mean business and scare the hell out of them. Let's go."

It's clear to me that we are on a dangerous mission. We could get a real licking from the two guys. They're much bigger than us. But we have it in our minds that they have to go, so they have to go. When we get down to the bottom of the stairs, we peek into the living room and see they've moved to the kitchen. We're in luck. One of the guys is over by the refrigerator kissing one of the girls. They don't see us come into the room. By now we're all in the kitchen and the other two see us. They have poured more of Dad's bourbon into the glasses and there are a couple more beer cans on the counter.

Gerry shouts at them, "All right, you get the hell out of here. You aren't gonna get away with drinking my dad's liquor. Now git or I'll shoot your asses!"

He cocks the hammer on the .22. At the sounds of Gerry's shouting, and the rifle hammer cocking, the two kissers break apart and look at us. No one has time to say anything before Teddy says, "Yeah, you get out of here before I stab you with this knife!"

I say, "Yeah and if that doesn't do it, I'll beat the crap out of you with this 2 x 4!"

The words are hardly out of my mouth before I see Teddy lunging at Carolyn with the knife. She runs around the kitchen table with Teddy chasing after her trying to stab her. Then all hell breaks loose. Carolyn is crying, and the boys and the other girl are shouting at Teddy to stop. Gerry is waiving the gun around, telling them to get the hell out of the house. In only a few seconds all four of them have grabbed their coats and are out the door at a run. We chase them outside and watch them running down the road.

"That's funny," Gerry says. "I thought they had a car. Someone must have dropped them off here and gone back to town."

"Probably," says Teddy.

My arms are weak from waiving the 2 x 4 around, so I set it down in the driveway and begin laughing as the heat rushes out of me. "Wow, did you see them run? Guess they won't be back."

"Probably not," says Teddy.

Gerry looks at the two of us and says, "I guess that takes care of things. There weren't even any bullets in the rifle. I wonder how scared they would be if I had real bullets in the rifle."

We wander back inside the house, kicking the new snow off our feet. We look at the messy kitchen and decide to leave it that way until Mom and Dad come home so they can see what happened. That way maybe we won't get in trouble for kicking the baby-sitter out of the house and making her and her friends walk all the way back to town. We go into the living room and goof around for a while. I wake up on the couch when I hear my mom and dad come through the front door. Gerry and Teddy are already in the kitchen. Mom and Dad see the mess in the kitchen and Dad says, "What the hell happened here? Have you kids...?"

But before he can finish, Gerry and Teddy break in at the same time.

"No, it was the baby-sitter," they say.

"And a couple of guys and another girl came after you left, and they started drinking your booze and raising hell," Gerry says. He makes it sound much worse than it really was.

"So we kicked them out and made them go back to Aspen!"

"The heck you did?" Dad says.

"Yep," Gerry says.

"Yup," Teddy says.

"Yeah," I say "and Gerry had the .22 and waved it at them and Teddy had your hunting knife and chased Carolyn or whatever her name is around the kitchen table, and I was going to hit them with the 2 x 4 that I left out in the snow."

Dad looks at Mom and laughs, "Well, Mouse, I guess they don't need a baby-sitter anymore."

Chapter 26

January 1955

Miss Helmcamp, my third grade teacher, makes school interesting for us. She is a great teacher and is also a champion skier. She won the Roch Cup three years ago. The Roch Cup is a famous ski race held on Aspen Mountain every year.

Miss Helmcamp has encouraged us to read by having a contest that lasts all year. For every book a kid reads, she puts a railroad car cutout up high on the wall. Pretty soon there is a train that goes all the way around the room. So far Marilyn Durox and I have the most railroad cars. I think Tony Vagneur is right behind us.

This morning Miss Helmcamp is mad at me because at show-and-tell I slugged Jimmy Green in the face. I think I lost my mind a little. Jimmy Green was making fun of me and what I was telling the class at show-and-tell. I walked over to him sitting in the front row and gave him a slug in the kisser. Miss Helmcamp made me sit down in the back of the room where I have been sitting for most of the day.

All afternoon I've not been paying attention to the lessons. It doesn't matter because it's only learning how to add and subtract, which I already know. Next year we'll be multiplying. I know some of that, too, but only because I've watched Gerry and Teddy doing their arithmetic homework for years.

Finally school is out, and I am ready to scoot out to the bus before Miss Helmcamp can stop me, but she's too quick.

She tells me to stay where I am, then walks over to me and says, "Terry, do you know there's a ski team in Aspen?"

She knows I like to ski because I told her I go skiing every day I'm not in school. I also go skiing for Wednesday afternoon activities. Every Wednesday they let the whole school out at noon, and we can go skiing, play basketball, go ice-skating or do something at school. I always go skiing.

I was thinking she was going to give me hell about hitting Jimmy Green, but she surprises me by not saying a word about it. It takes me a moment to get over my surprise. I must really have been shocked, because I say, "No, where do they ski?" Of course I know there's a ski team because Gerry goes to ski practice most days after school, and rides home with Dad after work.

"They ski on the mountain, of course." She begins to say something else, but I interrupt. "Yes, actually I do know about the ski team because my brother Gerry is on it. He practices after school in the winter."

Miss Helmcamp knows Gerry is on the team. "There is a meeting of the ski team right after school for a few minutes," she says. "Why don't you go see who is there and if it's something you might like to do since you love skiing so much?"

"I can't," I say. "I have to take the bus home."

"I think you can do both if you hurry to the meeting now and hurry to the bus as soon as you finish the meeting," she says.

I think about this a moment. If I go to the meeting and end up missing the bus, I'll be in trouble. But then I think I can always go over to the Hotel Jerome and get a ride home with my dad and Gerry after the ski school meeting is over. It usually gets out somewhere around 4:30, so I should have plenty of time. School gets out at 3:30, and it is only a few minutes to walk over to the Hotel Jerome. Gerry should be at the ski team meeting.

"Okay," I say. "Where do I go?"

"It's in Mr. Lewis' room."

"Okay."

I get my coat and galoshes on and shuffle down to Mr. Lewis' room. As I go, I wonder when the ski team kids get to ski, where they ski, and all the fascinating possibilities. There is no one at Mr. Lewis's room when I get there, so I think I must be in the wrong room. As I'm about to leave, a girl walks in. She looks at me and asks, "You must be one of the Morse kids? You look a lot like Gerry."

"Yes," I say and think, *Here we go again.*

She is tall, has a pretty face, and acts friendly, so I wait to see what happens.

"My name is Sally Moore. Are you coming to our meeting?"

"Yes," I say, "I'm going to be on the ski team."

Pretty soon another girl walks in, and Sally Moore says, "This is Janie, my sister. Janie, this is one of the Morse kids, Gerry's brother."

"What are you doing here?" Janie scowls at me.

"I'm going to be on the ski team," I say.

"You can't," Janie says. "You're too young. You have to at least be in the seventh grade."

"Who says?"

"That's just the way it is," she says.

"Well, I'm going to be on the ski team," I say.

I've decided since she says I can't and isn't being very nice about it, I darned well *will* be on the ski team.

Tommy Moore, Bill Marolt, Cherie Gerbaz, Sharon Pejack, my brother Gerry, and a few other kids straggle into the room and listen to me argue with Janie. Finally, Sally, who I find out later is the president of the ski team, says, "Okay, let's call the meeting to order. It seems like we may have some new business to discuss along with the travel and housing arrangements for the race in Steamboat this weekend."

"What new business?" someone says.

"I think we should discuss whether or not we should let some of these younger kids join the ski team. First though, we should make the plans for the weekend."

They talk for a while about the travel plans for Steamboat Winter Carnival: who is going to be staying at whose house, which parents are going to lend their cars, and who is going to drive. Finally, when they finish with the Steamboat business, they began talking about whether us "little kids" should be allowed on the ski team.

"Heck, he's only old enough for Class V," one of the guys says. "How old are you anyway, Morse?"

I look at him and say, "I'm nine. I really want to be on the ski team."

He laughs and says, "Nine, huh? I guess nine must be old enough if you want to be on the ski team that much."

"I do," I say.

The others laugh. I'm embarrassed. They talk about it for a few minutes and decide I can join the ski team under certain conditions, because it might be good if us "little kids" get an early start on learning how to ski race. Then, Sally says, "Okay, it's settled. Terry, you can join the ski team. "Buuuttt," she says, "here are the rules. First, you have to come to practice after school at least three days a week and one full day on the weekends. Second, you have to ski four events. Third, you can only go to races that are close to Aspen and if we have enough room in the cars to take you. Fourth, you have to have your parents' permission. And fifth, you have to do well in school. If Miss Helmcamp tells me that you are getting lazy because you are tired from ski practice, you're out. If you think you can do all of these things, then you can join."

I look at her and nod my head, trying to figure out how she knew I was in Miss Helmcamp's class.

"Yes," I say. "I can do those things. But what is skiing four events? I thought the ski team did slalom and downhill on the Big Mountain."

Everyone in the room laughs, and I'm embarrassed again. How should I know what skiing four events is? I've never been on a ski team. Sally looks at me and says, "Skiing four events means you have to ski slalom and downhill, which you know, and cross-country skiing and ski jumping. You'll have to get some cross-country skis if you don't have any. We have some extra jumping skis that MJ or Tommy has grown out of that you can use."

Again I think for a minute and look at my brother Gerry and say, "Gerry doesn't have to ski cross-country. He doesn't have any cross-country skis." Then I look up at Sally and say to her, "He doesn't ski cross-country, he only skis on the Big Mountain. He says he only skis gates and bumps."

Everyone laughs. I look back at Gerry who is laughing too. I don't know what is so darned funny.

Sally says, "This is a new thing for you. Spider thinks all the guys should ski four events because it will make them stronger. Most of the races have four events. Gerry has to ski four events too, he just borrows some cross-country skis from MJ to do it."

"Who's Spider?" I say.

"Gale Spence, our coach, stupid, you know that." Gerry says.

"Oh, yeah," I mumble.

"Well, what about Gerry skiing cross-country?" I push my point since it's my brother we're talking about.

"I ski cross-country. I'm not really good at it. It's pretty hard. I only do it so I can ski downhill and slalom," he kind of whines.

"Okay," I say. "I'll ski four events. Now, when can I start?"

"Just show up at the slalom hill on Wednesday after school with your downhill skis, and we'll tell Spider you're coming. Now, if there is no other business, I'll call for a motion to adjourn," Sally says.

I look at the clock on the wall. Its 4:20. I've missed the bus. I say to Gerry, "Can I walk over to the Jerome with you to meet Dad?"

"Sure, but we're going to have to hustle because all this talk about your joining the ski team has made us late."

Gerry says good-bye to his friends, grabs me by the arm, and we hustle out of the schoolhouse up the street toward the Hotel Jerome.

When we get to the Jerome, we go to the ski school desk. Ginny Chamberlain runs the ski school desk. She takes reservations for classes and private lessons. Her desk is next to the "Bamboo Room," a lounge where the ski school meetings are held each afternoon after the skiing day is over. We talk to Ginny for a few minutes while we take the ink stamps she uses for the ski lesson tickets, and stamp dates on every loose piece of paper we can find on the desk. Ginny is about to get grumpy. Before she can get worked up, my dad walks out of the ski school meeting with the rest of the ski instructors.

"Okay, kids," he says, "let's go home." Gerry and I follow him out to the Jeep, climb in, and prepare for the cold ride home. As usual, we freeze our asses off.

~ ~ ~

When we get home, I say to Dad, "Guess what?"

"What's that, Terr-Ass?"

"I'm going to be on the ski team," I say.

"Mmmmm, that's great. When do you start?"

"I have to go to practice three days a week after school and one day on the weekends." I'm getting more excited about it as I speak.

"And guess what?"

"What's that?" Dad says.

He's in the house now and has taken off his big, dirty sheepskin coat. I'm following him into the kitchen with my coat and galoshes still on.

"I have to ski cross-country and jump too."

"Hmmmm," he says as he goes to the kitchen cupboard and pulls out a glass. I'm still for a moment while he makes a drink. I know he doesn't like to be disturbed when he makes his drink. He sets the glass on the counter by the refrigerator. It's a highball glass. That's what he calls it. A "highball glass." I never could figure that one out because I can't see what a glass has to do with high balls. It doesn't have anything to do with baseball, and it for sure doesn't have anything to do with bulls because their balls hang down low. I think it's a stupid name for a glass.

He walks to the cupboard over the broom closet and gets out the Bellows Partners Choice, his favorite bourbon. He takes it over to the glass and pours in two fingers. He says, "two fingers is just the right amount." He holds up his hand with two fingers squeezed side by side so I can see how much that is. Then he opens up the freezer and grabs a handful of ice and drops it into the glass on top of the bourbon. It clinks and rattles as he takes his index finger and stirs the ice and the bourbon together. Then he opens the cabinet over the refrigerator and takes out a box of Triscuits. He stores the crackers over the refrigerator because he knows Teddy and I can't get into them without a chair. He grabs a handful of Triscuits and looks down at me. I'm still standing there looking at him with my coat and boots on.

"Take off your coat and stay awhile," he says to me.

"But I want to tell you about the ski team," I say, "I have to ski cross-country and jump too. I don't have any cross-country skis, so we have to find some somewhere. I can borrow an old small pair of jumpers from Tom Moore or MJ Elisha. And I have to get some boots to fit the cross-country skis, so we have to get those too. And..."

"Wait a minute," my dad interrupts. "Where are we going to find you cross-country skis? Neither Aspen Sports nor Magnifico Sports sell cross-country skis, and I don't think you can find any around here."

"I don't know, but we have to find some somewhere or I can't be on the ski team." I say. I figure he'll help me somehow.

"Let me think about it. It means you won't get home until late, so you'll have to figure out your homework schedule. You can use the skis you have for your downhill and slalom, and you have the jumpers handled. You can use your alpine boots for the jumping skis, so you are all set there. That leaves the cross-country gear. Let me talk to Gale Spence, and we'll figure something out."

"Gee, thanks, Dad," I say with a big grin.

I go out to the porch and take off my coat and boots. Third grade is looking up.

~~~

Several days later, Gerry and I meet my dad at the Jerome after ski team. We have to lug our skis most of the way down Mill Street because it hasn't snowed in a while, and there are a bunch of little rocks on the street from all the cars. Sometimes after it snows, we can ski all the way from the slalom hill down to the Jerome if we get a good start up on the mountain. We have to be careful though, because sometimes cars come across from one of the side streets. If they do, we have to turn into the snow banks real fast so we won't get run over. Having to move out of the way of a car stinks because we lose our speed, then we have to pole the rest of the way to the Jerome.

The sun has gone down and it is getting colder. The ski school meeting is over, and my dad will be in the Jerome Bar having a drink with one of the people in his ski school class. We lug our skis and poles down Mill Street and stop at Elli's shop. Elli is Fred Islen's wife. She has a sports shop across the street from the Jerome. Fred is sort of the co-director of the ski school with Freidl Pfeifer. He's not really a director, but I like to think he is because I like him better than Freidl. Freidl is really the director, but Fred is a better skier. It seems unfair that Freidl is the real director when Fred is a better skier.

We take our skis off, cross the street, leave our skis in the snow bank in front of the Jerome, and go in to find my dad. Just as we are walking in, he is walking out and says, "There you are! I've been looking all over hell and gone for you two. Why are you so late? Come on, we have some work to do before we go home."

He walks toward the Jeep. Gerry and I grab our skis and poles, and run after him. When we get to the Jeep, we set our skis in the back with the tail ends under the front seats so they won't fall out. I climb in the back and Gerry gets in the shotgun seat. When I'm settled in my seat, I notice there is another pair of white skis next to my dad's Head skis, the ones he uses to teach with. The white skis look very long.

My dad drives down to the end of the block and turns right next to Matthews Drug Store. I think he is going to stop there for something, but he drives right by. I wonder where he is going and by the time I am finished wondering, we are parked out in front of the school. My dad gets out of the Jeep and says, "Come on, boys, we have to get this done before it's too dark. Gerry, bring that pair of white skis and follow me."

Gerry wrestles the cumbersome skis out of the Jeep, and we fall in step with my dad along the sidewalk and around to the back of the school.

"What are these skis?" Gerry asks.

My dad looks at us and says, "They are old Tenth Mountain Division white elephant skis. The ski troops used them during the Second World War in Europe. They're now surplus, and I picked these up over at the Thrift Shop for fifty cents. I figure we can make them into cross-country skis."

Gerry stops. He puts the tails of the skis on the sidewalk and stands them up. They are about a foot taller than my dad, who is six foot two. I look up at the tips of the skis. The skis are twice as long as I am high and higher than I can reach with my arm by a good amount. Gerry says, "Who is going to ski on these? They're too long for anybody. They're too long to be jumping skis. And look how wide they are."

My dad looks at him as if to say, "Don't say that so loud, somebody may hear you," and just keeps walking. Gerry grabs the skis and follows. It's dusk as we go into the school's heating plant, a small decrepit wood building where they store the coal that is shoveled into the furnace to heat the school during the winter. It is also a tiny shop with a table saw. Dad is already playing with the machine. He speaks to us as he is working almost like he is talking to himself.

"Okay, kids. First we have to set the fence. Let's see, these skis are about four inches wide so we should be able to take about an inch off each side. Then we would have a nifty set of skis about two inches wide. Just right." He sets the fence about an inch away from the blade and turns on the saw.

"Gerry, give me one of those skis."

Gerry hands him a ski. My dad runs it through the table saw and takes about an inch off the side. He then reverses the ski and takes about an inch off the other side and does the same with the other one Gerry is holding out for him. He turns off the saw, picks up the four scraps, and stands them in the corner.

He takes the skis from Gerry and gives them to me.

"There you go, Terr-Ass," he says. "Here's your cross-country skis. You'll have to clean the Fast Ski off the bottoms with sand paper and burn in some pine tar, then they'll be as fast as any of 'em."

"You may as well get used to the weight, because once you get set up with bindings and boots, you'll have to be skiing on them as fast as you can."

I take the skis and heft them.

Well, at least I can carry them, I think.

"Gosh, thanks!" I say, not knowing if I should say "thanks" or "no thanks." But beggars can't be choosers. If it means I have to ski on cross-country skis twice as long as I am tall, so be it. At least I will be able to be on the ski team.

I struggle out the door, catching the ski tips on the doorjamb, and fumble my way back to the Jeep in the darkness, my dad and brother walking in front of me. In that moment, I decide that I'm very happy and that something good will come of it all. As I get in the Jeep, I say to my dad again, "Thanks a lot. These are really great. It was a good idea to cut them in half. They would have been too heavy for me to ski on otherwise."

As he gets in the Jeep, he says, "You're welcome, son. You'll have to have Spider help you with the bindings and boots."

I can see the red tip of my dad's cigarette between his fingers when his hand is on the steering wheel, and I know that all is right with the world.

~~~

The next day after school, I walk to practice with my cross-country skis. All day kids have been laughing at me. One kid said, "Terry, your skis are longer than a jousting pole." I don't respond too much to them because I know the skis will be good enough if I can find some bindings and boots. Also I know that a jousting pole is really called a lance. If anybody knew anything about the Knights of the Round Table, they would know that. And besides, I know they are right. The skis are longer than a jousting lance.

I get up to the ski hill where we are supposed to be skiing slalom that day. I haven't had to carry my slalom skis, but only these white elephant skis that have been run through a table saw and have no bindings. My slalom skis and poles are in the snow bank where my dad left them for me on his way to work this morning. I had to carry the cross-country skis from school. Usually I am supposed to take my skis to school and then carry them to the slalom hill. That's what all the big kids do. Since I'm just joining the ski team and have to get all my stuff together, my dad is helping me out a bit.

Spider Spence, our coach, sees me lugging the massive boards up to the base of the slalom hill, and he says to me, "Hey, Morsely, whatcha got there?"

"These are my cross-country skis!" I blurt out proudly.

"Wow," he laughs. "Those are great. You can grow into them for the rest of your life," he laughs. "Come on over here and let me look at them."

I take the skis and show them to him. He looks at them and then me.

"Who cut them down for you?"

"My dad did it last night at the school coal shed."

"Good idea."

"I need some bindings and boots," I say.

Spider looks at me and says, "I may have an extra pair of bindings down at the shop. Tonight after practice, bring the skis down to the shop and we'll look for some. Tomorrow you can to go the Thrift Shop to see if you can find some old boots or shoes with a big edge on the side so the bindings can hold your boots on the skis. Like this but wider."

He shows me the edge on his ski boot where the stitching goes along the side of the boot toward the toe.

"Okay," I say.

"Now, go get your boots and skis on, and start climbing the hill so you can practice with everyone else. And be quick about it."

He hits me on the butt with his ski pole as I turn and walk off to get my boots and skis on.

I begin climbing the hill listening to the banter of the big kids. I quickly understand that none of them have names that I have known. Tommy Moore is "Golf Bags," MJ Elisha is "Ebwah," my brother Gerry is "Horsely," and Mike Baar is "Mick." Others are called only by their last names, like Bill Marolt is called Marolt. Most of the girls are called by their names Cherie for Cherie Gerbaz, Sharon for Sharon Pejack, and Roine for Roine Rowland, except that Roine is called Batsy sometimes, and Sharon is Loglegs.

Spider calls everyone anything he wants to when he is talking to them. He looks at you and says, "Hey, fig lips! How do you take this gate, high or low?" Or "Hey, lug nuts! Stay on your line. You came out of that gate too low!"

All the big kids are giving Spider back as good as they get. While packing up the hill looking at the slalom course Spider has set, they are saying in loud voices things like, "Who set this slalom anyway? These gates are tighter than a snake's ass!"

"Hey, Spider, we want you to come up and forerun this bamboo jungle!"

To me they are saying things like, "Hey, little Morse, by the time it's your turn to run, the ruts'll be so deep you'll feel like you're running a luge and we won't find you until morning, cause we won't be able to see you until you are spit out on the bottom."

I listen to the banter; I feel the snow under my skis and the frosty afternoon air on my reddening cheeks, and know I can add this to the several other homes I have.

~ ~ ~

I go to find some cross-country boots the next day, and walk to Aspen Sports, the sports shop owned by Gale "Spider" Spence and John Oakes. I amble into the store and look for Spider. Then I remember he's at practice where I am supposed to be, except Spider told me yesterday to find some boots for my cross-country skis.

John Oakes sees me out of the corner of his eye while he is speaking with a customer. I see him say something to the customer and come over to me.

"Hey, Morse," he says, "Gale told me you need some cross-country bindings."

He goes over to the cash register, reaches under the counter, and pulls out an old pair of Rottefella three-pin bindings.

"These should work. Take 'em with you when you go to the Thrift Shop to look for some boots," he says.

"Gee, thanks!" I say.

I take the bindings, careful not to lose any of the pieces out of the box, then head off to the Thrift Shop in the basement of the Independence Building. I walk in the door and see Louiva Stapleton there. She is Don Stapleton's mother. Don is Gerry's age. She doesn't know me really well but clearly knows who I am. "Aren't you one of the Morse kids?"

"Yep," I say.

"What can I do for you today?"

I show her the Rottafella bindings and say, "I'm looking for some boots my size I can fit into these bindings."

Louiva looks at me, "I'm not sure we have anything here that would be your size that would fit into those contraptions. What are they for, anyway?"

I explain about the ski team and skiing four events and
that I have to have cross-country skis so I can ski on the team
and the whole line of crap that leads up to my being there. Of
course, she knows about most of it because she knows most
of the kids on the ski team even though her kid, Don Neal
(she calls him that), plays basketball and doesn't ski.

Finally, she takes me to a stack of shoes piled up in the
back of the store and says, "Look through the shoes and
boots on the shelves first, and then paw through these if you
don't find anything on the shelves."

"Okay," I answer.

I really have no idea of what I'm looking for, and decide
if I see it I'll know it when I see it. So I start looking for shoes
or boots that would fit me within a size or two. It is an
exhausting search. I find nothing on the shelves and start in
on the large pile at the back of the store behind the shelves. I
locate a pair of ski boots that will fit me, but the soles are too
stiff. I continue my search. Finally I come up with an old pair
of work boots that look like they have enough space on the
edge of the sole for the edges of the binding to catch and
hold the toes of the boots on the skis. I'll have to drill three
holes in the sole for the binding pins but I think I can get
Spider to help me with that. They are only about two sizes
too big, but I figure that'll give me a year or two to use them
before my feet grow out of them. I'm very satisfied with my
find and take the boots up front.

"How much are these?" I ask Louiva.

She takes them from me and has a good look at them.

"Hmmm," she says, "they don't look like they have
much life left in them. How about twenty-five cents?"

In all my hurry to get to school this morning, I forget to
think about paying for the boots if I found any. I search my
pockets and come up with a dime, a nickel, and a penny. I put
them on the counter and look up at Louiva.

"How about sixteen cents?" I say.

"That sounds about right," she laughs.

I take my new boots and head back to Aspen Sports to see if I can get Spider or John to show me how to mount the bindings on the skis.

When I get back to the shop, Spider is still up on the slalom hill with the ski team but John's in the shop. I show him the boots and how they fit into the bindings well enough for me to use them as cross-country ski boots. John takes them and tells me he and Spider will mount them up for me, and I can pick them up after practice tomorrow.

By Friday I'll have cross-country skis, and I'll really be a member of the Aspen Ski Team. I'll have the skis I need to practice, I think. *Now all I have to do is sand the Fast-Ski off the bottoms of my skis and burn some pine tar into them.*

I say goodbye to John and head down to the Jerome where I know I will arrive early enough to hassle Ginny Chamberlain at the Ski School ticket desk before the Ski School meeting is out. It has been a good day's work.

~ ~ ~

Pine tar smells like the pine woods in the high country. It's got to be one of my favorite smells. I've sanded all the Fast-Ski off the bottoms of the white elephants and sanded the edges down where the saw cut them. It took me a good while to do it because I had to use every little corner of the sand paper I had, which was only one sheet for each ski. Luckily the Fast Ski wasn't coated too thick. Now I am putting pine tar on the white elephants. I'm at Aspen Sports where Spider has lent me a blowtorch to use when I apply pine tar to the bottoms of the skis.

Spider said to me, "Pine tar works into the pores of the wood and seals the bottoms of the skis so they will slide on the snow. It also helps hold the wax on the ski." Then he showed me how to dribble the pine tar on the bottoms of the skis from the can. I'm heating the pine tar with the torch making sure not to hold the torch over the pine tar too long so it doesn't catch fire.

The pine tar goes on smoothly. The heat thins it out and helps it fill the pores of the wood. I then wipe off the excess with an old rag. The whole shop smells like we're up in the high country in spring when the pines wake up and the sap begins to run in the trees. When I am done, I set the skis outside the shop to cool off in the freezing air. When they've cooled off, they'll be ready to wax and use. As I finish the project, I'm quite proud that I haven't caught anything on fire or burned down the store.

Tomorrow we have cross-country practice, so I'll get to try them out. I hope I'll be able to make them slide across the snow like Tom and MJ do. They're both good cross-country skiers. They're skinny and can go fast. I'm not as tall and skinny as they are, so I'll probably be lots slower but I don't care. Ski Team is loads of fun and I'm happy to be able to ski with "the big kids" and hear them calling each other names and griping about the slalom course and stuff.

As I come in the back door from setting my skis out, Spider asks me, "You done there, Fish Lips?"

"Yep, I am. And I think I did it the way you showed me."

"Good," he says, "because tomorrow you get to try them out. Make sure you're on time to practice."

"Okay," I say. Then, "I have to go now because my dad has to leave early right after the ski school meeting."

"Hey, Morse," Spider says as I am walking out the door.

I turn around, look at him an instant and say, "What?"

"See ya," he says.

Chapter 27

Spring 1955

Rebuilding the house is finished now. Mom has done most of the work decorating the new rooms added to the house. With the exception of a few things I don't like—the stupid ceramic parrots on the hall table, the yellow tile in the bathroom, and the yucky green refrigerator in the kitchen— the house looks beautiful. Mom made the draperies for the windows in the different rooms.

In our room the walls are rough-sawn pine that came out of the Lenado sawmill. My dad put the planks on the wall in a style he called batten board. Mom stained the room a peaceful light grey color. She painted a large bureau that Gerry uses for his clothes. She also painted the headboards for our beds. The headboards and the bureau are done in the "Peter Hunt" style. I'm not sure exactly what Peter Hunt style is, except I think Mom said it is some old New England style that she likes because it reminds her of the East.

The headboards stick up above the beds about three feet and are curvy. Mom painted them a dark bluish-greenish with a dull red border. Then she mixed up some linseed oil, turpentine, and varnish, put some brown powder in the mixture, and brushed it over the colored paint. She called it a "brown antique glaze." It made the headboards look old. The mixture smelled a bit like the pine tar I used on my skis. Dad attached the headboards to the bases of our beds he'd made from rough fir. The bases hold the box springs and mattresses.

~ ~ ~

Everything was going along fine until Christmas when I got this bow and arrow set. Santa Claus (ha ha) knew how much I like Indian lore and left this present for me under the tree. I was really happy and excited about the gift except I couldn't use it until summer. I put it away and forgot about it . . . until this morning.

Today is Sunday. With no ski team practice, I'm at home trying to figure out what to do with myself. I'm bored because it's yucky spring weather out, snowing and sleeting. I'm tired of winter weather and don't want to go out in it. I'm sitting at my desk in our new room, cleaning up.

For some reason, all of a sudden I remember Santa's bow and arrow Christmas gift. I get them out of the closet, where I have put them, behind a few shirts and hanging pants, to look them over. The bow is formed from beautiful yellow hickory, the grip is genuine leather, and the bowstring is real honest-to-goodness gut. The Indians used buffalo gut to make their bowstrings. I wonder what animal gave up his guts for this string. Maybe a pig or something. Probably not a cat. They say it's catgut, but I don't believe they'd kill a bunch of cats to make bowstrings. We don't eat cats, so it would be a big waste.

I take the gut string, put it on one end of the bow, and try to bend the bow so I can get the string to hook on the other end. The wood is too stiff for me to bend far enough to get the string in the end notch. I sit down and try to figure a way to bend it so I can get the string on the end where it belongs and get the bow strung. When I can't figure it out, I take the bow downstairs to Gerry who is eating a snack at the kitchen table. I ask him, "Hey, can you help me string this bow?"

"Is that the one you got for Christmas?"

"Yeah," I say. "Pretty cool, huh?"

"Sure," he says, "Let me help you. I know how to do that."

He stands up, takes the bow from me, and puts the string on the end he has resting on the floor. He steadies the bow and the string with the end on the floor and puts his knee on the middle of the bow and pulls the other end towards him. He slips the string over it. Slick as can be.

"Wow," I say. "Can you teach me how to do that?"

"Sure, but you may not be tall enough and strong enough to do it."

So I try it a few times and finally, when I really struggle with all my might, I get the bow strung myself.

"Thanks," I say and head back up the stairs.

Back in my room, I fit one of the arrows in the bowstring and pull it back a bit. I would love to really pull it back and let the arrow fly to see how fast it hits the target. Then I realize there is no target. I head back downstairs and find a cardboard box out in the garage by the trash cans, take it upstairs to the bedroom, and set it on my bed in front of the headboard. Standing at the end of my bed a little ways back, I load up the bow with an arrow. I don't pull back very far because I'm not sure what will happen. I let the arrow go and, faster than I can blink, it is lodged in the box.

Wow, I think, *this is cool!*

So I load up and shoot a few more times. Then I wonder if I can hit the box if I am further back across the room. I back up until I'm by Gerry's bed, clear on the other side of the room. I load up an arrow and let it go. I don't pull the bowstring back far enough, so the arrow drops on the bed making a scrape on the bedspread. Again I load up, pull back farther, and let it rip. The arrow zips across the room and lands right in the box. I'm having fun now. I shoot a few more arrows, then one misses the box and hits the headboard.

Uh oh! I go over to inspect the damage where the arrow hit and see a small dent in the headboard. Actually, it's a medium-sized dent. There'll be some sort of hell to pay for this, but I don't think about it too much because Dad doesn't whip us anymore. We're too big for a whipping now. Besides, I'm having fun imagining myself as an Indian and the box a buffalo that I'm taking down. The only thing that's missing is a painted pony. I shoot a bunch more arrows into the box without hitting the headboard again and end the session proud that there's only one dent in the it.

Maybe I can cover that up with my pillow, I'll just have to see, I think. Walking over to take a look at the situation, I realize it's too high on the headboard to be hidden with my pillow. Perhaps I can camouflage it by putting something on top of my pillow to cover the offensive hole. I move the box to get it out of the way so I can solve the problem. The problem suddenly gets huge. Once I have moved the box, I see about twenty other holes in the headboard where the arrows have passed all the way through the box, and come out the other side into the headboard.

Ooooohhhhh shit, I think. *Now I'm sure gonna catch hell.*

I don't know what to do. After a moments thought, I take my logical strategy and do nothing. I'll let this problem set a bit until I can come up with a good reason for the holes now marring the beautifully painted headboard.

The day passes. After dinner, Gerry, Teddy, and I are upstairs getting ready for bed. We said goodnight to Mom and Dad. Sometimes Dad comes upstairs to say goodnight, but tonight he won't because we've already said goodnight downstairs. I get into my pj's. I don't like pj's and am thinking pretty soon I won't wear them anymore. The pj bottoms get twisted on my legs and bunched up on my butt. The pj top twists around my neck, and the arms may as well be cut off anyway because they are so short on me. I would rather sleep in my underwear.

Teddy loves pj's and has his on. His bed is next to mine with a table and a lamp between our beds. Mom has painted this table in Peter Hunt style like the rest of the furniture in the room. As Teddy gets into bed, he looks over at my headboard.

"What happened to your headboard?" he asks.

"Gerry, come here and look at this," he says. "Man, Terry, you're gonna catch hell! Mom painted these headboards specially."

Gerry walks over. "Oh brother. Man, are you screwed. You're gonna catch so much hell for this. Way worse than all the stuff I catch hell for."

"It really wasn't my fault," I say. "It just sorta happened. How was I supposed to know the arrows would go all the way through the box?"

Gerry looks at the flier on the left side of the headboard and says, "What about this one? You must have seen it. Why didn't you stop when you saw what the arrows would do?"

"I dunno," I say. "I guess I thought is was only that one. I figured I could cover it up with something. Then, when I moved the box, there were all these other holes."

Teddy is already in his bed, laughing to himself. Gerry walks over to his bed laughing and says, "Good luck with that one, buddy. I'm glad I'm not you."

There is nothing I can do about the damage, so I leave things as they are. Part of our chores are to clean our room, make our own beds, vacuum the upstairs, and clean the bathroom. I figure Mom won't be upstairs for a few days because it's usually a few days before she comes up to inspect our room, and she was just up here yesterday. I hope I can think of something in the meanwhile.

~~~

When I get home from school today, I know right away that the cat is out of the bag and I've had it. Mom doesn't even talk to me. She just looks at me and begins to cry.

Uh! Oh!, this'll really get bad.

Dad goes on the warpath when I do something so bad that mom cries.

I go upstairs to work on my homework, a story I am writing about an Indian brave called Red Wolf. I'm upset at the moment and don't feel like working on the story, so find myself staring off into space.

At dinner, Dad doesn't say anything. Mom is so upset, she is having dinner in bed. Dad is busy trying to calm her down and forgets to tear into me. He leaves the dinner table and goes into their bedroom to talk to Mom. We get up and clear the table, then do the dishes like we're supposed to. By the time we're almost finished, Dad comes in with Mom's dishes. I can hear him talking to himself as he walks upstairs to survey the damage. I hear the f-word and a few others that he doesn't say too often. I know it might be best for me to stay on high alert in case I have to hightail it. I hear him shout down the staircase, "Terry, you get your ass up here right now!"

Too late. I don't know if you have ever heard my dad when he is angry for real, and I don't want to wish it upon you if you haven't. I have no interest in watching your blood freeze in your veins. That's how I can describe what your body feels like when you hear him shout you up the stairs when he's really pissed off.

I am so afraid, I can't move. Then I realize I really can't move.

Gerry says, "Well, don't just stand there, you better get going. It'll just get worse."

How can it get any worse? I think.

Teddy says, "You're really gonna catch hell now."

I spit back, "Don't you think I know that? Besides, you said that last night."

I head upstairs to take what I've got coming. He may smack me around a bit, he's so mad. I can hear it in his voice.

Oh well, how bad can it get? He always feels sorry after he gives us a whipping, and besides, he quit that with me when I was six.

~~~

203

Time slows down, and I remember the last time I was disciplined. When I was six, Dad was mad at me for doing some stupid ass thing I can't remember. He took me into his bedroom to give me a whipping. The first thing he did was take his belt off to give me what for. Before he actually put the belt to me, he always would double it back on itself and grab both ends. He would put his hands together so the two sides of the belt would open up, then pull his hands apart really quickly so the sides of belt came together with a loud snap, which scared me more than the whipping did. He snapped the belt a loud pop or two, and I started crying.

"Quit your crying," he said, "and take it like a man!"

All of a sudden, something became very clear to me. I would take it like a man. Then we would both see who won the battle of wills. I knew he could tan my hide good, but he couldn't tan my mind, let alone tame it. I stopped crying and went silent. He gave me a few hard whacks with the belt. Usually after one or two good whacks, I'd start crying; then he'd give me one or two more token whacks, and it would be over. This time, I didn't cry, and he gave me a good licking. Lots more whacks than usual and much harder. Finally he said, "Why aren't you crying?" I knew he wanted me to start crying so he could stop.

"You told me to take it like a man," I said. "And that's what I'm doing."

My dad put the belt down and gently shoved me toward the door and never touched me again.

But tonight I'm pretty sure he'll raise holy hell. I know he and Mom worked hard putting together a beautiful home. It seems all I can do is tear it up. Knowing that makes me feel worse than any whipping.

I shuffle upstairs into the room and there's Dad sitting on my bed.

"Come here," he says. He looks into my eyes. I immediately shift my gaze to the floor. He puts his finger under my chin and lifts my head up and says, "Look at me when I am talking to you. Now what were you thinking? Didn't you think ahead enough to see that the arrows would easily go through cardboard? What did you think would stop them?"

"I dunno," I mumbled.

"I really don't know what to do with you. You go downstairs and apologize to your mother. You'll have to live with these arrow holes in the headboard; they're not easily fixed. It will be a good reminder for you to start using your head. Now go on. Get downstairs and talk to your mother."

This was the worst punishment he could ever give me. First, he doesn't give me a whipping, then he doesn't shout at me, and finally he tells me I have to go downstairs and face Mom. Not that I dread that really, it is just that I feel so bad about doing such a stupid-ass thing.

I go downstairs and talk to Mom. I don't need to go into all the details, but I say I'm sorry, and Mom sobs and tells me what a devil I am and that I have to live with the holes in my headboard. I'll see them every night before I go to bed and maybe that will make me think a little about how hard other people work to make my life nice. Lots of stuff like that, which I listen to but makes me feel worse than Dad does. Finally she says, "Now you get up to bed and in the future start using you head."

I walk up the stairs, feeling really, really bad. Gerry and Teddy are sitting on Gerry's bed waiting for me.

"What happened?" they say.

I don't say anything, so they ask me again. "What happened?"

"Nothing," I say.

I take off my clothes and hop into bed in my underwear. No more pj's for me.

Teddy says, "I don't know how you got away with that one."

Gerry says, "Man, if that had been me, I'd be hanging by my thumbs from the cottonwood tree."

They had no idea how it would be for me to sleep in my bed under those arrow holes for the rest of the nights I would spend in that house. I roll over away from my brothers and take a long time to go to sleep.

Chapter 28

Summer 1955

This past school year, Miss Helmcamp taught me to like reading a whole lot more than I already did, and she got me interested in math and science. Also she told me I'm too rambunctious and need to have lots to do to keep me out of trouble. This spring when I was rambunctious in class, she made me stay after school and help Mr. Garrish and Mr. Quam help them with the janitorial work. Sometimes this made me miss the bus, which I caught trouble for at home. The first time I had to help was when I did a dumb thing and called Paul Coble a "stupid shit" on the playground when Mr. Gann was walking by. Mr. Gann took me in to Miss Helmcamp and told her she needed to help me clean up my mouth.

"Miss Helmcamp," Mr. Gann said, "See if you can do something with Morse here. His vocabulary of swear words is monumental, but he doesn't seem to know the right time to use them. We've gotta get him to clean up his mouth."

Miss Helmcamp looked at me and said, "Honestly, Terry. We've talked about this before, and here we go again."

I looked down and shuffled my feet some like I do when I've done something wrong.

"Yes, ma'am," I said.

"I'm leaving him in your hands," Mr. Gann said to Miss Helmcamp. "See if you can do something with him."

She nodded to Mr. Gann, still looking at me, and said, "I've got just the thing for you. I'm going to have you stay after school and help Mr. Garrish and Mr. Quam clean the schoolhouse every time I catch you swearing. Maybe that'll cure you."

After school she took me to meet the school janitors and told them they had a new helper and explained that I could help them any time she caught me swearing. She thought this would be a severe punishment and would cure me from swearing all the time. It didn't work. Actually I liked helping Mr. Garrish and Mr. Quam. They're nice and let me do everything they do. I emptied the trash baskets and mopped the floors. Mr. Garrish gave me a big floor mop and a bucket of sawdust mixed with some kind of oil that helps pick up all the dirt and dust.

"Here," he said, "spread this sawdust on the floor like this." Then he showed me how.

"Then with the mop, you push down the aisles between the desks. You have to move the desks to make new aisles so you can mop under each row."

"Okay," I said.

I spread some sawdust on the floor and went over it a couple of passes then began moving desks. Once I had them moved, I threw more sawdust, mopped and did another row. It wasn't so bad.

Mr. Garrish and Mr. Quam took a liking to me and let me do just about everything to help them out. One day Mr. Garrish offered me chewing tobacco.

"Here, Morse," he said. "Have a chaw of this. It'll make hair grow on the bottoms of your feet." He pulled a little corner off his plug and handed it to me.

"Uh, I don't think I better," I said.

"Ah, go ahead, it won't hurt you."

So I took the small bit and said, "How do you chew this stuff? Like gum?"

"Sure, that'll work," he said.

I stuffed the tobacco in my mouth and chewed it. It was like trying to chew tea leaves. It was all loose in my mouth.

The more I tried to chew, the more broken up it became. Then I had so much saliva in my mouth that I had to swallow. The tobacco juice didn't taste very good going down, so I spit the tobacco out in one of the wastebaskets.

"Not bad for a first try," Mr. Garrish said. He and Mr. Quam were laughing. "Lucky you spit it out, otherwise you'd probably be puking by now." Mr. Quam said. "That stuff is pretty powerful."

"It made me dizzy," I said, "but I don't think I have to throw up."

It usually took me an hour to help Mr. Garrish and Mr. Quam, so I was done by 4:30. I finally got the hang of looking to see if any adults were around before I let loose with a string of swear words, so I only had to clean the school four or five times.

~~~

We found out that Mom is pregnant again. She is having another baby in December. We're all surprised because that means there will be five of us kids now. Jennifer will be five years old when the new baby is born. I'll be nine this September. You can see my mom has a bigger stomach. She keeps saying, "Gads, I'm going to have to get bigger clothes. This baby is growing so fast."

~~~

I've started having these strange dreams. I've had two since last winter. Sometimes they are so real I think I'm actually awake. Other times I know I'm dreaming, but I am thinking about the dream while I'm dreaming. It's like I'm awake and participating in the dream.

It is night. Blackness all around. Yet he can see the space immediately around him. It must also be day. He is a sturdy, average-sized young blond boy with unruly hair and is running down a slight incline on a dirt street in a town of dirt streets. His slender legs churn across the greyish-yellowish dust, avoiding the deep potholes. He kicks up rocks, dust, and pebbles with his worn tennis shoes. Running, running, running.

He is terrified, a feeling so foreign to him it makes his stomach roil. He wants to stop and vomit up his fear, to leave it all on the street in one nauseous puddle, but he dare not. He dare not stop because he knows his pursuer will be on him in a flash. He pumps his young arms in rhythm with his legs and his lungs.

"Faster !" his body shouts out. "Faster!"

Muscles ache, lungs burn, and his pounding heart seems to explode in his head.

He looks back. It is a mistake. It costs him precious time. But now he has a clear vision of the monster that is chasing him. His fear increases, if that is possible. His pursuer is a dark, shadowy figure. A wraith. It floats in the shadows of darkness cloaked by the very dark that it travels through. It is gaining on him. Always gaining, gaining.

Before him, a dust devil kicks up in the street and whirls around him, pulling him to the side of the street and back to center. Slowing him more and more and more. The shadow figure is almost upon him. The boy looks to the left to see an abandoned, ghostly house that has its own stories to tell. He looks to the right and sees the same haunted house. Running, running, running. He cannot get past the house. His feet are moving, but his body remains trapped in front of the house. He chances another look back and sees the cloak of the wraith floating out at its sides and knows he is about to die. He cannot outrun the shadow figure. It is upon him, throwing its cloak around him, and driving him to the ground in the darkness, the inky black darkness, darker than dark. He disappears, swallowed up by the shadows.

I wake in bed, drenched in sweat, knowing I have just had a nightmare, one I cannot shake from my head. I lie in bed staring into the dark and wonder what the world will be like if the monster kills me and eats my flesh. What will the world be like if I am dead? What will happen to me? Not my body. I understand my body will rot away back into the earth that it is made from, like the ranch animals I have seen die. But *me,* where will I go?

Will anyone know I am gone? What if I am a dream in someone else's dream? What if I wake up and realize that I am just a dream being dreamed by another me? All these questions and more go through my mind. I cannot figure any of them out, and I'm frightened. I'm frightened by the wraith, the thought of dying, and the thought that I do not really exist, that I'm just a character in someone's dream.

These thoughts of death have been with me all winter, and I can't shake them. I haven't told anyone about them. They will think I'm crazy. I know about birth and death because of the ranch animals, Grandpa dying, and Mom having babies. But I can't figure out my place in it all and how it relates to me. I hope these dying dreams will go away or that I will figure something out so as not to have to think about them anymore.

The same sturdy, young, blond boy is standing on a rocky outcropping of shale overlooking Maroon Creek. He looks down. There is an almost vertical drop to the riverbed. How far is it? One hundred feet? Two hundred? To his young eyes, it is simply a long way. He looks down and has a feeling of fullness in his body. He is not afraid. He takes one step forward and jumps out and begins to fall into the chasm of the river valley. He pulls his arms in beside his body and picks up speed as he plummets toward the earth and water below.

He arches his back, extends his arms out from his sides, and begins to glide horizontally up the river valley letting the thermal currents on the side of the riverbank push him upward. He is out of the river valley and soars into more thermals over fields of hay and alfalfa. The air is warm and crisp, perhaps dry. The sky, a cerulean blue seen only once every few years when the temperature is exact, when the humidity is exact, and when the eye can see deeply into the clarity of an atmosphere devoid of dust, exhaust, and the molecular detritus of man. He is a golden eagle, a great blue heron, a raven. Soaring, diving, gliding. The incredible freedom of flight.

His body feels every light buffeting air current, the updrafts freeing him of all gravity, the downdrafts sucking him back to earth. He gains speed, going down, down, down. Then he arches heavenward once again and, using the speed, he floats upward in great spirals, then downward once more rolling, diving, playing with the elements, the currents, with gravity. He is doing a dance in the heavens, knowing viscerally the unimaginable lightness of flight and of being. His body feels as if it were an image of who he is, suspended in the sky like a hologram, then given the power of life, the power of movement, the power of flight.

Joy fills him. He is more than whom he knows himself as. He knows this but cannot yet understand it. After some time playing in this other world contained in his dream world, he alights on the earth and comes awake.

I am awake and lying in my bed. I keep my eyes closed and do not move. I do not want the feeling of flight to leave my body. I savor the moments as they tick by. Just being, just being, just being and that wonderful space of the pure, the honest; of sharing life with the birds in flight and with all the creatures on the earth who are also in flight, their own flight but flight nevertheless.

My mind begins to question why I have these dreams. How can they be so real that I feel them in my body as if they were truly happening when I am fully awake? I cannot answer this, nor can I understand what the flying dreams are saying to me, only that they are joyous and make me feel complete and very happy.

Chapter 29

Summer 1955

We're in the Denver airport. I'm dressed in a sport coat, a shirt, and a necktie that Mom has gotten from somewhere. Our whole family is dressed up because we're flying to Boston to spend the summer in the East. Dad has a job working as a carpenter. We're living in a house we're renting on a street down from Granny's house. I'm very excited to go on an airplane for the first time in my life. So are Gerry and Teddy. Soon the pilot will call us onto the plane, and we will take off into the wild blue yonder.

We're waiting inside a building called a terminal, standing in a line in front of a door called a gate. We're flying on a plane called a DC-6. It has four motors. I guess it has that many motors in case a couple of them don't work, you have extras. My dad says it will take about eight hours to get to Boston. We'll have lunch on the plane. When we're in Boston, I think someone will pick us up at the airport and drive us down to Granny's house on the Cape.

Gerry, Teddy, and I are screwing around. Dad says, "Quit screwing around and stand still."

We stand still for a minute or two, then start screwing around some more, doing things like Gerry messing up my necktie and Teddy bending over, pretending to tie his shoe but untying mine instead. Stupid stuff like that. Pretty soon a man at the gate takes our tickets. The line moves forward as we go out a door, walk across some pavement, up a set of stairs, and into the plane. Dad shows us where to sit and tells us, "Now settle down. No horseplay or the stewardess will let me know and there will be hell to pay."

I guess he doesn't trust us. We sit down in a row next to each other. Of course I have to sit in the middle because Gerry wants to sit on the aisle, and Teddy wants to sit next to the window. Gerry wants to sit in the aisle so he can look at girls. He'll be fourteen in a few weeks and looks at girls now. Actually he's been looking at girls for a while. He isn't much fun to fool around with any more because he thinks he is too big to play with Teddy and me.

So here I am, stuck in the middle. I've brought a book along to amuse myself during the long flight. The book is about Frank and Joe Hardy. They are these two kids who are amateur detectives and solve mysteries and crimes. Its written by a guy named Frank W. Dixon. He's written a bunch of Hardy Boy books. I've read six so far. Now I am beginning the seventh. It's called *The Secret of the Caves*. I don't know what it is about yet because I haven't started it.

The motors start, and the plane moves across the pavement to the runway. The plane vibrates, and the motors make a loud, low hum you don't notice after a while. The stewardess comes and tells us to make sure our seat belts are fastened. Then the plane moves faster, and pretty soon it is going faster than our car. It begins to vibrate more, then suddenly, it feels like there is nothing under us. The vibrating stops except for the motors, the plane tilts upward, and we are off the ground! My stomach feels like it does in my flying dreams as the plane lifts quickly. Then it settles into a steady climb for a long time before leveling off.

Teddy is glued to the window. I can only see a bit of the view around his big head. Gerry isn't looking out the window because he can't see past Teddy and me.

Pretty soon my neck gets stiff, and I sit back in my seat and read my book. Before I know it, the stewardess is next to our row and Gerry is shaking me asking me if I want any lunch. I've fallen asleep.

"Wake up," he says. "You want some lunch?"

I rub my eyes, yawn, and say, "Sure."

Teddy is still looking out the window. I suppose he has looked somewhere else because he would have a sore neck if he were staring out the window all this time. The stewardess serves us a real good hot lunch. It's as much as a regular dinner. There is even a piece of chocolate for after dessert. After lunch I read some more and sleep a bit. Finally the plane lands in Boston where Uncle Neddie meets us. We all pile in his car and drive down to Cape Cod and Granny's house.

~~~

We've have been at the Cape for about a month and have settled into our rental house a mile's walk from Granny's. We've met some new friends our age named Paul and Steve Chesley. Their house is a five-minute-walk from ours and is on Bass River. The Chesleys have a boat, water skis, and fishing tackle, so Teddy and I play with them whenever we can. Gerry is always off with some older kids.

Granny's house is the same as I remember it from last time I was here. I love spending time with Granny, even though the first thing she did when I was here for two days is ask me to go out and weed the vegetable garden.

"Turnip," she said. She is always making up new names for me. "Come with me. I need some help this morning."

So we went out to the garden house and Granny found a trowel and a rake, then took me over to the garden. After she explained what she needed, she turned me loose, told me to finish it up and do a real nice job, so I could go fishing in the afternoon.

After that first gardening experience, I scoot in and out of the house so she can't catch me so often to do work. I think she has my strategy figured out because lots of the time at dinner she will say to me, "Terry, could you come over in the morning and help me out for just a minute before you go play with the Chesleys?"

"Okay," I say, but I'm not really happy about it because it means work in the garden or around the house pretty much all morning.

~ ~ ~

I've finally learned to swim right. My dad told me, "It's time for you to learn to swim properly." He and I had gone down to Bass River and climbed on Uncle Bud's sailboat.

"Okay," my dad said, "you jump in the water and grab hold of the side of the boat. When you get set, work your way around to the bow, grab on to the anchor line, and follow it out in the river. Then let go and swim back to the boat."

I wasn't too sure of his logic but didn't say anything. I did what he said and jumped in the water. I worked my way around the side of the boat to the anchor line and followed it out for a ways in the river. The only problem was that the anchor line went down as well as out. I followed it down hand over hand to the bottom of the river. When I reached the bottom, I wasn't sure what he wanted me to do next. I was running out of air, so thought it might be smart for me to go back up.

I pushed off the bottom with my feet and hit my head on my dad's stomach as he was coming down to rescue me. When he didn't see me coming up, he jumped in after me, clothes and all, to pull me up from the bottom. When we hit the surface, he was sputtering and looked a little scared. After he saw I was okay - maybe a little water logged - he said, "Maybe that wasn't such a good idea."

"Maybe not," I said.

He helped me over to the boat. We climbed in, then out onto the pier, and walked back to Granny's house. After the story got out, everyone pitched in and helped me learn to swim right.

~~~

Today the Cutters are at our house having lunch. Since it's a windy, rainy day, Edward and Timmy went to the glass museum with Aunt Mary Leigh. We stayed here to visit with Uncle Neddie and Aunt Helen, which we're not doing because they sent us upstairs while they sit in the living room with mom and dad having some fish sandwiches and a "toddie." Gerry, Teddy, and I ate lunch earlier with Wendy Cutter and are upstairs fooling around, playing Crazy Eights and seeing who can cheat the most.

Soon we begin to get bored playing cards, because we all know how the others like to cheat. Gerry says, "I wonder where Wendy is?"

Gerry wanders out of the room to find our cousin, and in a short moment they come back together.

"She was in Jennifer's room," Gerry says.

We greet her with a "Hi, Wendy," and she sits on the edge of one of the beds. Wendy's wearing a yellow pull-over dress with a flower print and some tennis shoes with her hair in a ponytail. She is pretty good looking but not beautiful like some other girls I've seen. We talk a bit and finally we are all bored. Finally Gerry says, "I have an idea. Let's play strip poker."

"What's that?" I say.

Gerry explains that we have to play a game called blackjack and whoever loses the hand has to take off a piece of their clothes.

"We've never played blackjack," Teddy says.

"I'll teach you as we go," Gerry explains.

"I don't know if I want to play," Wendy says. "I'm the only girl here."

Gerry replies to her, "Don't worry, you're older, so you will probably win anyway."

We start the game. I lose the first hand with two low cards, so I have to take off a shoe. Teddy loses a shoe and a sock by losing two hands. Next, Wendy loses a hand and has to take off her shoe. The game goes on, and I can tell something is not quite right because Gerry and Wendy keep losing. Gerry says, "Two tens beat an ace and a jack, because two tens is a pair."

I see he's lying because he's grinning. Wendy acts like she believes him and now has to take off her dress. She's lost her shoes and socks, her hair barrette, and the belt she had tied around the dress. She has nothing left to take off.

"I'm not going to take off my dress," Wendy says.

"You have to," Gerry replies. "Besides, I had to take my shirt off."

Teddy and I are still pretty much dressed because Gerry and Wendy are no longer paying attention to the cards we draw. We see where this is going and keep our mouths shut.

Wendy takes her dress off and is left in her underwear. Gerry loses the next hand and has to take off his pants. Then Wendy loses the next hand and has to remove her bra. Teddy and I stare at her with our mouths open. Her boobs are small, pointy things with big red nipples. You can tell that they aren't full grown yet, but we can see they are big enough to be real boobs.

She loses the next hand and has to take off her underpants. Down there she has a patch of light brown hair. I can feel a tingling in my body, and I watch Wendy with my full attention as she stands up and says, "Ta Da!" She turns around like a dancer showing us her butt, side, and her front.

I look at Gerry and can see he is looking at her too; only he is like, *really* looking at her. I can see that something's happening in his underpants because they are sticking out.

We keep staring at Wendy, enraptured as she dances about for a moment or two, her little boobs wobbling up and down like Jell-O squares on a plate. Suddenly we hear footsteps, and Uncle Neddie shouts as he's coming up the stairs, "Wendy, come on, it's time to go."

Wendy looks horrified. She quickly grabs her underpants and puts them on followed by her dress. About the time she gets her dress on, she realizes she has forgotten her bra. She doesn't have time to deal with it, so she just hands it to me. I look at her like, "Are you crazy?"

"Do something with it!" she says. "Quick!"

I hide it under the pillow on my bed. Wendy is putting the ponytail back in her hair just as Uncle Neddie comes down the hall. Gerry has his clothes back on, and Teddy and I are still in our bare feet without our shirts on.

Uncle Neddie comes through the door and says, "What have you kids been up to?"

"Just playing cards," Gerry says.

Uncle Neddie doesn't see that Wendy is a little bit of a mess and says, "Say goodbye, Wendy. We have to get back to Boston."

Wendy smiles, we say our goodbyes, and she and Uncle Neddie head downstairs. We follow them to say goodbye to Aunt Helen, because we know that Mom and Dad will be upset if we don't use the manners they are trying to teach us.

"That was a good look!" Gerry whispers as we head down the staircase.

I think of Barbie Lewis and the school bus and wonder how big her boobs are now. Since I have Wendy's bra under my pillow, it's easy for me to remember how big her boobs are. Maybe I'll give it back to her, and maybe I won't.

After seeing Wendy without her clothes, I start noticing more things I didn't when I was little. I notice Teddy hanging around the girl who lives across the street. Her name is Mary Griffith, and she has boobs popping up in the T-shirts she wears. I try to get Teddy to do stuff with me, but mostly he hangs around with Mary. I think he wants to try to get her to play cards, too. I spend more of my time at the Chesleys' house hacking around. We go fishing, go out in the rowboat on the river, and generally do a bunch of small adventures around Bass River.

~~~

About a week after the "Great Card Game," as we now call it, Teddy and I are at Granny's house. She has buttonholed us to do some work in the garden. I've already done a bunch of garden work, painted a shed, and done lots of errands for Granny, so you can see why I'm getting a little tired of it. But I do it anyway because I really like Granny and see she's getting too old to get down on her knees to pick weeds out of beds of lettuce or rows of peas.

Teddy, as usual, is off dreaming about something, so I end up doing more than my half of the work.

When I finish with the weeding, I go inside to tell Granny she can come out and inspect my work if she wants. She likes to inspect my work so she can tell me what a good job I've done, even though sometimes I skip a few weeds here and there. She looks at the garden and tells me that the garden is better than ever this year, and wouldn't be half as nice, nor half as productive, without my great care. We're walking back to the house, and she says, "I have a surprise for you and Teddy tomorrow."

"Really," I say. I'm expecting her to say something like "We're going to go up to Nauset Beach for a picnic" or "We're going up to Harwichport to have lunch on the pier." She knows I love doing both, and we've done both a few times this summer. Instead she says, "You both are going deep-sea fishing for tuna tomorrow."

"Wow," I say. "Really? You're not just joking? I don't believe you. I have always wanted to do that."

"Yes," she says "You've done such a good job helping me out this summer, I want to do something for you. I've reserved two spots on a tuna trawler that will pick you up at the pier at 4 o'clock tomorrow morning. You can sleep here tonight. There will be a few other folks on the boat, but you should have a chance to catch a tuna. They're running off the coast."

"Oh, man," I say happily. "That's great! I can't wait!"

~ ~ ~

Granny is shaking me by the shoulder to wake me up.

"Time to get dressed," she says.

I wipe the sleep from my eyes, yawn a big yawn, and hop out of bed in my underwear. I don't wear pj's anymore like I already told you, so I jump right into the clothes I set aside last night. Jeans, a short-sleeve shirt, a sweatshirt, and my socks and sneakers. I'm on my way downstairs to eat breakfast even before Teddy's feet hit the floor. A few minutes later, he follows me downstairs, we have a quick breakfast, and soon enough we're standing on the dock watching the trawler come up the river. As it pulls alongside the pier, the captain jumps off the bow and says, "Which one of you swabbies is coming this morning?"

"We both are," Teddy says.

The captain says, "Come aboard, and we'll head out to the sound and see if we can land a few school tuna. What's your names?"

We tell him our names and he tells us his name, which I immediately forget. We hop aboard the boat, the captain turns the motors up, and the boat leaves the pier. I wave to Granny and blow her a kiss. It is still dark out, and the rumbling of the engine, and the gentle rocking of the boat, puts me to sleep in the seat I have settled into at the rear of the trawler.

When I wake up it's light, and we're surrounded by ocean. A gentle easterly breeze ruffles my hair as I look over the side of the boat to watch the waves on the blue water. The trawler is moving up and down, climbing to the top of one gentle wave and sliding down its backside time after time. Although not too big, the waves are high enough to make the boat rise and fall noticeably. I turn around to see Teddy sitting on the other side of the vessel gazing out at the ocean.

There are four other people aboard besides the captain: three men and one woman. They all are wearing shorts, short sleeve shirts, and baseball caps. Teddy and I don't have hats because we have lots of hair on our heads. The lady is wearing a sweater and has a visor tangled in her hair. They say good morning to me and ask me my name, where I come from, and lots of questions like that. We talk for a while and pretty soon the captain comes out and says, "It's time to put the lines out."

His helper, who he calls "mate," helps him bait some huge feathered hooks and set the lines. The rods are in cuplike holders that sit in front of two chairs in the back of the boat. The captain and the mate feed the lines out for a long way in back of the trawler, then set the drag knobs on the reels so the lines will stay where they are unless a fish hits the lure and runs with it. When this happens, the line will whine off the reel, the rod will bend, and we'll know we have a fish.

The captain heads to the steering wheel, puts the boat in forward, and we move slowly through the water looking for fish. Nothing happens for some time. I get bored of watching the rods to see if they are going to bend. I begin noticing the ocean. The water is green next to the boat. As I look seaward, it turns dark blue and then to black on the horizon where the ocean meets the blue sky. There are some clouds in the sky, and the wind has shifted gently, now coming out of the south.

I look at Teddy to see him talking to one of the men. Just as I stand to go over and join their conversation, both of the lines start screaming off the reels. I look at the rods and see them bending. The captain cuts the engine and yells to his mate, "Set the hooks, mate, set the hooks!"

The mate runs to the back of the boat and one after the other grabs the rods, gives them a hefty tug backwards, and sets the hooks. He motions to Teddy and the other guy to sit in the chairs. He pulls the rod out of its cup and hands it to the big guy, quickly showing him how to pull back on it and reel in the line. Then he gets the other rod for Teddy. He sets the end of the rod into the seat cup between Teddy's legs and shows him how to pull back on the line with his arms and back, using his feet to push against the back of the boat. This way Teddy can use all his strength to reel in the big fish.

Teddy is excited and pulls back on the rod, rocking back on the chair, then moves his body forward. As he moves forward, he quickly reels in the line that he gained by pulling back on the rod. He does this a few times, then, begins to get into a rhythm. He pulls back slowly, using his legs to help him, then leans forward to reel the line in. Pull, reel. Pull, reel.

He does this for what seems like an hour but is only a few minutes. I watch the man next to him. He's doing the same and is much stronger, so it looks easier for him than it does Teddy. As he is pulling back the next time I see the rod go slack and know that the fish has broken off the line. I hear him say, "Shoot! I lost him."

The mate comes over and pats his shoulder and says, "We'll get another if all goes well."

He reels in the line on the man's pole and sets it back into the rod holder on the back of the boat. The man goes back to the others and tells them what a gigantic fish he had on the line and, "If he just hadn't...and I know he was a fighter...and it didn't feel like a tuna, more like a huge swordfish." And so on. I wonder to myself if this is how many stories get started - by the "near misses" and the "if only I's."

Teddy is still working his fish in toward the boat. I see he is really tired. It's been more than twenty minutes since he hooked the fish. Finally I see it swimming back and forth, ten or fifteen yards from the boat. It looks humongous.

"Reel it in closer," the mate says.

Teddy reels the magnificent fish in until it is right up at the rear of the boat. The mate leans over the side with a gaff and hooks the fish under the gill. The captain is beside the mate with another gaff. The mate picks the tuna's head out of the water so the captain can get his gaff under the other gill. Meanwhile the fish is slapping back and forth, trying to get free. The captain gets a hold on the tuna's gill, and together they bring it up and slide it smoothly into the bottom of the boat. It's a large school tuna flopping all over the bottom of the boat. The mate grabs a stick that looks like a baseball bat and hits the fish real hard on the head. The fish goes quiet with death.

"Good job, kid," says the captain.

"Yeah," I say. "Good job. Are you tired? What was it like? How big do you think your fish is?" I can't stop asking questions.

Teddy grins proudly. "Man, that was hard. My arms are killing me."

We talk some more about how it was to catch the fish, and are wondering if there are any more in the ocean for us to catch right now and who will be up next. The captain is setting out the hooks once more, and, before we know it, we are trawling again. The mate weighs Teddy's tuna, then sets about beheading and gutting it so we can take it to shore without it spoiling. When he's finished, he slides it into the hold. The fish looks much smaller without its head, but it's still big.

"One hundred and twenty-five pounds," he says looking at Teddy. "Not a bad catch for a young lad."

Teddy grins from ear to ear and tells the others about landing the fish and how it felt to have it on the line, and lots of stuff that I didn't listen to because I was just watching the lines, hoping for another tuna.

It is shortly after that both lines go off again. I am next to one of the rods, looking out to sea when it happens. The line spins off the reel with a high-pitched whine. The mate jumps beside me and says, "Don't touch the line. You'll be burned."

He clicks the drag lever on the reel, quickly grabs the rod, and yanks back on it to set the hook. I've already climbed up in the chair as the mate has indicated. He hands me the rod after setting it into the seat cup. Luckily I've been watching Teddy, so know what to do as the mate has his hands full dealing with the other rod.

I pull back on the rod, and reel in the line as I let my body lean forward getting ready for the next backward pull. I'm too short for my feet to hit the back of the boat, so have no leverage to push back with my feet. It's a struggle for me to use only my arms and back to pull, but I'm so excited about the fish I don't think about it. Slowly my body moves into the rhythm of pulling back and reeling in, pulling back, releasing my muscles forward, and reeling in. All the time I'm looking out to the ocean, watching the angle of the line on the water, watching the waves move up and down in reference to my chair. I do my one chore, pull back and reel in smoothly, while watching the angle of the line change as I bring the fish closer.

Suddenly my line is singing and spinning off the reel. The fish is on a run. I'm afraid all the line will play from the reel before the fish stops running. The mate comes over and adjusts the drag on the reel. The line plays out slower until finally the fish stops running.

"Adjusted the drag. Now keep pulling, and I'll get something for your feet," the mate says as he backs away. I begin the methodical pull-reel rhythm again, my arms and back burning from the effort. Soon the mate comes back with a milk crate and sets it between the back of the boat and my legs.

"Here," he says. "Put your feet on this and use it for leverage when you pull."

It becomes easier to pull now that I have my legs to help me. I chance a look over at the guy next to me, and he is pulling as well. I can tell his fish is almost up to the boat because there is commotion around him and the mate is next to the boat with his gaff.

"It's a blue shark," I hear the mate shout up to the captain. "Whaddya want to do with him?"

"Big?" says the captain.

"Looks bigger than the tuna, maybe 150 or 200."

"Better cut him loose. Not enough free space to make it safe."

The mate leans over the boat with the gaff and pulls the shark a little closer. With his other hand, he takes a pair of wire cutters from his belt and cuts the line as close to the mouth of the shark as he dares get. The shark floats for an instant as the mate unhooks the gaff, then, with a splash of his tail, is gone. I watch this drama at the same time I'm concentrating on my fish. I hear the man next to me say, "Aw, darn. I would have loved to land a shark."

Time goes by and twice the mate asks me if I want a hand or if I want someone else to take over. I refuse him. He gives me a drink of water and spreads some sun tan cream on my face so I don't totally fry in the sun. I thank him and keep pulling and reeling. My back is aches, my arms are tired to the point that I can't make my fingers work right. My legs ache. I have blisters on the bottoms of my feet where my feet are wedged on the top corner of the milk crate.

I'm just about done in. I want to quit but refuse to. This is my fish, and I'm going to get it all the way to the boat no matter what. Time passes slowly; each backward pull becomes a century, each forward reeling too short a time for rest. Finally, somewhere through the fog of my tiredness, I hear the mate say, "There he is!" He is pointing to sea only about fifty yards out. I can see the angle of the line has changed and know the mate is right.

"Now reel him in next to the boat real easy so I can gaff him." By now the captain is back with us. I reel the fish closer with the last bit of energy I can muster. The mate gaffs him, turns him, and the captain gaffs him. Together they sling the fish up into the boat, and it flops lazily on the deck. It looks as tired as I am. It's a large school tuna that looks to be a bit smaller than Teddy's. I'm too tired and excited to care about size or weight. It's enough that I have landed my first deep-sea fish.

I'm getting pats on the back from the older guys, the lady, and Teddy. The mate says, "You were at it for forty five minutes, lad. We didn't think you'd be able to get it in after it ran out the line. Good job." I grin and sit down next to Teddy while the mate sets out the lines again and guts my tuna.

It's lunchtime, and Teddy and I are hungry. The mate passes out sandwiches and a Coke to everyone. We eat while the captain trawls for another school of tuna. The afternoon drags on, and the others hook into some fish, a shark, an albacore, and a few small fish that I can't remember the name of. No more tuna. The captain says, "Sorry, folks, we've gotta head in now if we're to be back by dark, so we'll trawl on the way. If we find any more tuna, we'll have at 'em but only if we cross over 'em."

We trawl back across the sea, the boat rising and falling gently on the waves, the breeze still blowing from the south. The sun is lower on the western horizon, and the few clouds that dot the sky show the faintest shades of red and pink when we enter the mouth of the Bass River. As we move on the quiet waters of the river in the sunset hour, I think about the life of the tuna I've caught and how it can feed folks. I don't know what they plan to do with our fish, but I have my own plan. I don't want to see the day's catch go to waste. I walk over to the mate and ask him, "What will happen to our fish?"

"Dunno," he says. "Depends on whether you have a freezer and want to keep it. Don't think you'll have room for two though, unless you have a couple of big chest freezers that are empty."

"What do you usually do with them?"

"Usually," he says to me, "we take them up to the fish market and sell them to the owner. Sometimes we sell them to the processing plant in Harwich, and sometimes we give them to anyone on the boat that wants them."

"I think it would be good if you give mine to the fish market. Maybe they could give it to someone with a freezer or someone who needs some extra fish. I don't want them to sell it though. They should give it away. We've already paid for it once."

The mate laughs and says, "That sounds like a good idea. I'll tell the captain."

We tie up at the dock, and everyone is there to greet us. Granny, Mary Leigh, Mom and Dad, and even Gerry. All are curious. We unload off the trawler, the mate bringing the two fish carcasses. Mary Leigh takes a picture of Teddy and me holding the two tunas by their tails with the headless necks resting on the pavement.

It is loads of fun: there are tons of questions and explanations. Finally the captain tells the mate it's time to weigh anchor. I look at the fish and then at the mate. He turns to the captain and says, "Don't think they want the fish, but the lad here wants us to give 'em to the Bass River fish market so they can slice 'em up and give 'em away to folks." The captain is about to answer him, but the mate sends him a look that makes him stop. The Bass River Fish market is less than two full blocks in an almost straight line from the dock.

The mate picks up one of the fish and puts it on his shoulder and starts walking. The captain picks up the other and follows. It occurs to me that the mate is now the captain and the captain, the mate.

Chapter 30

Fall 1955

Mrs. Anderson is my fourth grade teacher. She's a nice old lady whose husband has died. I like her because she takes care of business in the class. Right now Mrs. Anderson has finished reading a chapter of *Huckleberry Finn* by Mark Twain. I like the story because I can imagine myself as Huckleberry Finn - always getting in trouble. It seems I have lots of practice at that.

The Jameses have moved to town, and Spook is now in my class. His real name is Nathan. He's friends with me and Tony Vagneur and Richard Sabbatini. Spook lives across the street from Richard, on Third Street and Hallam. He lives in the big white house that Freddie and Ricky Henry used to live in before Freidl and Bunny bought the ranch to the west of ours. Theirs borders up against our old ranch. Well, I guess I should say Pfister's. I'm getting used to the fact that we no longer own the ranch; still I roam around all the time just like I used to, because I'll be damned if I won't. I do my best to stay out of trouble, so, for now I am pretty free.

In school we're learning multiplication tables. We have to learn them up to 15. I know them now all pretty well up to 12, and have to learn the last three. I have this great idea about multiplication tables, which I am working on at home to surprise Mrs. Anderson. It might be a way for kids to learn their multiplication tables quicker and have some fun doing it.

The idea came to me a few days ago when I was up at Fred's house. (He and Ricky like to be called Fred and Rick now, but Bunny still calls them Freddie and Ricky). I walked over to his house through the lower fields of Pfister's ranch. Fred and I were looking at a quiz game he had. The game is on a board that has a bunch of questions in one column and a bunch of answers in another. You have to match up the right answers with the questions. As I looked at it, I got this idea that you could do the same thing with arithmetic.

~ ~ ~

So I'm at home now working on this idea. I have some office paper I got from John Oakes that is "legal size." I've made two columns with a ruler and made boxes on the paper all the way down. In the boxes on the left, I've written the multiplication tables like 8 x 6 or 9 x 5 and so forth. On the right column, I have written the answers to all the multiplication problems but have mixed them up so the correct answers aren't next to the problems. With a punch, I've made a hole just to the left of each of the problems and just to the right of each of the answers. Then I punched two holes at the top of each page so the pages fit on two paper clasps that I have poked through the bottom of a Monopoly box. I've glued them so they won't move. Now I have pages with the problems and answers on them with little holes next to each; the papers clamped on the flat surface on the top of the bottom of the Monopoly box.

Underneath, on the backside of the box, where you can't see them, I've put a bunch of wires in a random order going from the problem side of the box to the answer side of the box. I've punched small holes in the box for the wires to feed through, matching the holes on the box with the holes on the papers above. So, on the top of the box, there are the pages of multiplication table questions and multiplication answers, all of which have holes next to them where little wires are sticking out of the box below.

The wiring underneath the box is set up so that each wire runs from a problem to its correct answer. Like the wire from 9 x 5 goes to the answer 45. I'll wrap the ends of the small wires with aluminum foil, so they will be larger and very easy to see.

I'm going to use electricity to make it more fun. I know that you have to complete a circuit to make a light go on or a bell ring. I learned that when I was bothering Kenny Broughton as he was helping us rebuild our house. He also taught me that you can touch a "live wire" with your thumb and finger to see if you have "juice." I got a pretty good jolt when I did that. Like when I cut the lamp cord with the scissors. I sure found out that line had juice.

I have an old electric bell that I got from Freddie Fischer at Fischer's Fix-It yesterday after school. He gave me the bell for a nickel because he didn't know if it worked. I brought it home and borrowed a nine-volt battery from the shop in our garage. I've made two wands with pieces of bailing wire that I've twisted together and hooked them to the smaller wire that I've used to wire the back of the box with. Then I've hooked up the two wands to the battery. When I touch the two wands to the wires on the bell, I complete the circuit and sure enough the bell rings. So I'm ready to go.

I take the wands and touch one to the foil end of the wire that goes into the box from the question side. Then I touch the other wand to the wire by the correct answer. RRRRiiiiiinnnnnngggg. There you go. Instant correct answer to the problem. Of course, if you don't get the answer right, the bell doesn't ring.

After the finishing touches, I hold my breath, and test the whole first page. Sure enough, it works! I test it for all the sheets from one to fifteen and have all the right answers wired to the right problems, so it all works really slick. All I have to do now is make sure there is always juice in the battery.

~ ~ ~

Today I've lugged my "arithmo-solver" to school to show Mrs. Anderson and the class. When it is time for arithmetic, I raise my hand and say, "Mrs. Anderson, I have this real nifty way for people to learn their multiplication tables faster. I have it with me. Do you want to see it?"

She looks at me like she thinks something's up, but I say, "Really, it's something I made over this weekend and it really works!" She looks at me and says, "Okay, let's see what you have."

I go out in the hall, get the arithmo-solver from my bag, and set about doing a demonstration. I show the other kids how to use it and how it works and all. Mrs. Anderson says, "Who helped you put this together?"

"No one, I did it myself," I say. I'm a little insulted, but I don't let it show. Then the kids start in on me and pretty soon I just say, "Fine don't believe me, I don't care."

Then Mrs. Anderson sees that I am serious about having put the little project together and becomes more impressed than anything.

"This is really amazing," she says. "Where did you learn about the electric circuits?"

I told her about what I learned from Kenny Broughton, how I bought the bell from Freddie Fisher, and that I borrowed the battery from home. Then I explain to everyone, because now the whole class was listening, how I got the idea and built the contraption.

In the end, everyone believes me and thinks it's a cool way to learn multiplication tables. I'm happy everyone likes it and decide to leave it at school so everyone can use it to learn with. Mrs. Anderson says, "I'll get a battery from Mr. Lewis so you can take your battery home."

"Thanks."

A few weeks later, on our school's annual Math Day, our class wins the school-wide contest to see who can do their multiplication tables fastest. What an exciting day!

Chapter 31

November 1955

Earlier this fall I read a book about Squanto, an Indian who was captured by the English and kidnapped to England. He learned how to speak English and, after some time in England, came back to America with an expedition led by a man named Captain Demer. I am more and more interested in the lives and lore of the American Indians, especially how the American Indians used every part of the deer or the buffalo they hunted.

I learned from some of my library books that the Plains Indians killed buffalo for meat, but they used all of the buffalo for their clothing, tools, and housewares. I read that the most prized clothing was made from the tanned hide of deerskin. The Indians began tanning their hides by rubbing salt on the hairy side. They then rolled it up in a bundle, buried it in the ground, and let it stay there all fall and through the winter. The next spring they dug the hide up to finish the tanning process. The hair would fall off the hide so easily from its winter burial that it was easy to turn it into a soft, comfortable material for clothes. I finished reading about this almost magical process and decided to try it.

~ ~ ~

About a week ago, I put my plan in action: to make some deerskin clothes out of a deer hide the same way the American Indians did. Since we eat venison all the time, getting a deerskin is not a problem. My dad had just shot a big buck, and he gave me the hide for my experiment. I followed the instructions in the book, and went to bury it. My dad said, "Terr-Ass, if you're gonna plant that hide, you better take it out by the compost heap where the soil is softer."

The ground was frozen and digging was hard. I finally used a pick to break through the layer of frost to softer dirt and dug down another two feet to set the hide in the soft, black loam under the compost heap. I covered the hide with dirt, ceremoniously, thinking of the Indian way. Next spring I'll dig the hide back up and see what's happened to it.

I'm teaching myself more Indian crafts. For my birthday, I got this cool little loom used to make beaded Indian ornaments, like bracelets, edging for vests, moccasins, and hatbands. At the moment I'm making a bead bracelet using the original Indian patterns I studied in some of the library books. I like the Navajo and Sioux patterns best because they seem the sharpest and most symmetrical to me. The bracelet I'm making is my first, and is a traditional Navajo weaving style with bright red, yellow, blue, green, black, and white beads. I should finish it tonight and will wear it to school tomorrow to show my friends.

~ ~ ~

I'm wearing the finished bracelet on my wrist at school today. Everyone is asking me where I got it. I tell them, "I made it last night on my bead loom."

"No way!" they say.

The girls especially like the bracelet, which gives me an idea.

Spook James is convinced I didn't make the bracelet, so I say to him, "Okay, I tell you what, tonight I'll make another one like this one with different colors and a different pattern. I'll bring it to school tomorrow and, if you like it, I will sell it to you for a dollar."

"Fine," Spook says. He's smiling because he doesn't think I'll show up tomorrow with the beadwork.

"Just make sure you bring a dollar," I say. "If you don't, I'll sell it to the first person who wants to give me a dollar for it." I'm pretty sure he'll bring a dollar because there are several girls who definitely will want it.

~ ~ ~

I was hoping to get home earlier today so I could work on the bracelet. Unfortunately Dad had to have a drink in the Jerome Bar with a client. They got to listening to Walt Smith and Freddie Fischer playing jazz and "stayed for another round." While I was waiting, I started on my homework because Ginny Chamberlain had closed the ski school ticket desk. I'm staying up late to complete the bracelet after finishing my homework, a project on Yellowstone National Park. Tomorrow Spook James will eat his words!

"Wow," Spook says the next day, "You really did it."

"Yep," I say, "I did. Now where's my dollar?"

He reluctantly searches his jeans pockets and finds a lone dollar. I hand over the bracelet and Spook hands over the dollar. He has a big grin on his face. I can see he is happy with his purchase. Suddenly it occurs to me, "If I can sell one to Spook, I'm sure I can sell a bunch of them to others." Immediately I start soliciting orders.

For the next two weeks, I have plenty to do in the evenings after I finish my homework. I stay at my loom and, by the time I've run too low on beads to make any more bracelets, the fad has started to wear off. I close up shop and am happy with the fifteen-dollar profit I made on the little venture.

Chapter 32

Winter 1956

Ski Team is the most fun I can think of.

"Hey, Peach Breath, peg me down one of those bamboo poles."

"What for? This course is already crookeder than a snake's ass!" I look down the hill at Spider. He shakes his head.

"Don't give me any of your lip, Flap Jaw! Just toss me a pole."

I toss him a bamboo slalom pole.

Each day the team and I are on the snow. Ski jumping one day, cross country skiing another day, slalom more days, and downhill skiing on the weekends. We "pop" off the thirty-meter hill. We kick and glide up hills, around corners and downhills, until we are breathing hard and our hearts are pounding like jackhammers. We thread through slalom gates, changing rhythms to fit the gate combination, lost in the moment. We do our downhill "non-stops" on Ruthie's Run, tearing up the mountain, weaving through the moguls, over the summer roads, taking air, and zooming down through Spring Pitch to the bottom. Then we're back on the lift to do it all over again until our legs are jelly and our bellies growl with hunger. Through all of it, all the thinking and the not-thinking, the knowing when to pour it on and when to lay back, the only thing we can do wrong is to give up.

"If something is difficult, it means you work harder and use your head to be good at it. You don't give up, you don't quit." Spider says.

I hate to lose. I don't know what it is inside me that makes me feel this way, but I never want to be last. Even second or third in some races upsets me. I know the competition. Jere Elliot from Steamboat Springs is a good skier. He beats me in the slalom and downhill races most of the time. So does Richard Sabbatini. Jere Elliot sometimes beats me in cross-country. When he does, it makes me mad and makes me want to learn how to go faster.

"Jere Elliot is a good little athlete" Spider says. "He's a tough little son of a gun, but you can beat him if you work at it. All you have to do is ski faster and don't give up."

For some reason I like cross-country skiing best. I've realized, even when I win a race, I'm looking for ways to win the next one by more. I find myself wanting to win not because winning gives me a little gold medal or a stupid trophy with a plastic base, but wanting to win because I'm curious as to how much I can take. How long can I go my fastest without giving up? When will my lungs burst? When will my legs buckle under me? Last winter I wanted to learn to ski cross-country. This winter I want to learn how to ski faster.

~ ~ ~

We're on the slalom hill today practicing slalom. I'm just finishing my run down through the gates. Spider is timing us, "Not bad, Morsely. You've gotta stay on your downhill ski more coming out of the gates so you can pick up some speed."

"Okay."

Spider looks up from his watch at me and says, "By the way, we have cross-country on Friday. Why don't you stop by the store after practice today before you go home."

"Okay,"

After practice I ski down Mill Street all the way to Aspen Sports and find Spider in the repair shop putting his skis away.

"You want to see me?" I say.

"Yeah, come here. I've got something to show you."

Spider walks to the back of the shop, rummages around in a pile of skis, and pulls out a pair of blue Swedish Sandstorm Traveler cross-country skis.

He hands them to me and says, "I ordered these in for you because I thought you could use some skis that fit you better than those old Army white elephants. So, here's what we're gonna do. I'm going to mount these up with the new boots and bindings that I also ordered in for you.

"Wow," I say. "Thanks, but I can't pay for them. I don't have enough money, and I don't think my dad will be able to buy them either."

"I've thought a bit about that," Spider says. "I've got an idea that you would do a pretty good job around the shop here polishing the rental ski boots and cleaning things up after closing. It means you will have to work in the afternoons and on the weekends after practice. If you want, John and I will hire you, and you can work to pay for the skis and boots."

I'm floating. My body feels light and my mind is working fast. Not only am I able to get some new skis that will help me ski faster, but I also have my first real job. Well, it's not really my first real job, but sort of. I mowed Mrs. Ferguson's lawn four or five times last summer and she paid me fifty cents a time, so I guess that might have been my first job. But this will be for the rest of the winter every day after practice. "Thanks," I say to Spider. "This will be really great!"

~ ~ ~

It's Friday, and I'm heading out to the cross-country course with my new cross-country ski set up. I'm really excited to see what difference it will make in my being able to keep up with the big guys.

Probably none, I think. *But we'll see.*

Ever since I started skiing cross-country in third grade, I've never been able to keep up with the older guys. I feel slow and clumsy on my white elephant skis. Everyone leaves me in the dust. It frustrates me and makes me sad. I've ended up crying a few times, I have been so mad. Each time I tried harder to keep up and always at the end of the cross-country course I can't see anyone who has finished except maybe Richard Sabbatini and Dave Durrance who are even slower than I am. That is if they come to practice. Often it's almost dark when I finish. It makes me stinking mad.

The cross-country course starts and finishes over by the old Ute Cemetery on the east side of town beyond the Glory Hole where Piss Pot Allen used to live. His cabin got torn down a year or two ago. The old run-down cemetery has a bunch of Civil War soldiers buried there along with a bunch of old-time miners. In the winter you can only see the tallest of the grave markers, and in the summer it is overgrown with dandelions and thistles. The wooden grave markers are grey with years and the carving on them faint. Many look like the silhouettes of old barns leaning, ready to fall. The course skirts the edge of the cemetery and heads east out toward Stillwater Ranch where the Roaring Fork River meanders across the flat valley floor heading west of town, where it picks up speed as it falls down valley to meet the Colorado River down by Glenwood Springs.

I put on my skis with the rest of the team. They're laughing and joking, "Hey, Morsely where are your skis? How're ya gonna ski on those puny things? Don't you know that x-c skis are supposed to be twice as tall as you are? Better get back on those white elephants." Or, "Hey, speed, whatcha waxin' with today? Swix blue and Elmer's glue? You don't think those sticks are going to make you go any faster do you?"

"Yeah," I say, "you'll be thinking twice when you eat my dust."

We start out together, the big guys pushing each other and sticking their ski poles in between each other's legs, each of them fighting for a position in the line of skiers. I hang back at the end of the line. It is foolish for me to try to get up front. I'll just get pounded.

Off we go, past the graveyard and around the hillside, weaving through the sage on rolling hills toward the Roaring Fork River and Roger Dixon's Stillwater Ranch. The snow is cold and dry. It hasn't snowed all week, so the tracks are hard and fast. Our wax, Swix green, is perfect for the snow temperature. It gives us good grip when we kick, and lots of speed when we glide.

The sun has dropped behind Aspen Mountain to the west, and it is the quiet time between sundown and dusk when the light begins to fade from daylight to lighter shades of grey. Shadows grow from dark to darkness as night slowly falls. The air has the snap of a clear winter day's end, when the sun sets and the air drops ten degrees in ten minutes. In an instant you feel the temperature change on your cheeks and exposed wrists. The in-between times of dawn and dusk are my favorite parts of the day.

As I ski, I am getting the feel for my new skis. I'm skiing much faster. Around the corners and over the bumps, I ski without having to fight the immense length and weight of the white elephants. I work hard and heat up. My breath comes to me deep and smooth. I'm relaxed, gliding across the snow effortlessly, as if the skis are a part of me rather than foreign objects I must do battle with. I see I'm losing distance on the older guys, but more slowly than before. I'm resolved to forget about keeping up with them. I'm paying attention to the feeling of lightness in my body.

We ski across the back of the Stillwater ranch and turn toward town, heading into a hilly section with quick uphills, corners, and downhills. I realize going uphill is much easier. The skis are lighter, and it is as if I can ski up the hills the same way I can ski on the flats, smooth and relaxed. The rest of the big guys are ahead of me but not totally out of sight or sound. I can hear the swishing of their skis and sometimes the breathing of those who are working so hard that they're out of breath. I stay with the feelings in my body, with the sound of my skis, the sound of my breath. Soon I'm back at the cemetery only a short time behind the older guys.

The group is taking off their skis and yakking about the snow, the course, and the temperature when I slide to a stop next to them. They're as surprised to see me as I am to see them. I can see on their faces they know something important has changed. I'm not quite sure what it is but nevertheless I am happy with myself when MJ Elisha says to me, "Hey, Morsely, you skied fast today. Good job!"

It is the first day since I have begun skiing cross-country that I finally feel like I'm at home on my skis. I'm determined to keep the feeling within. I can't wait to thank Spider and John for the opportunity to be able to ski on some real cross-country skis rather than white elephants.

It isn't even dark out yet. I love the feeling of walking back to town in the early dusk.

Chapter 33

Spring 1956

I wish fourth grade weren't winding down so fast. Mrs. Anderson, my favorite teacher, has encouraged me explore ideas that fascinate me. She shows interest in what I'm doing outside of school, like exploring Indian lore and fishing. Still, I irritate her when I cut up in class. I've had to stay after school twice this spring to write one hundred times on the black board, "I will not cut up in class." I suppose she thinks if I write it down enough it'll sink in and I'll turn into an angel. On the other hand, maybe she likes that I'm not an angel.

Now that we've learned about nouns, pronouns, adjectives, adverbs, and prepositional phrases and have memorized more vocabulary, Mrs. Anderson has us writing stories. Of course I have written stories about Indians and fishing. They and skiing are my top favorite things.

~ ~ ~

It's spring and the end of the ski season. Just after the ski school meeting, Dad, Gerry, and I are headed home from the Jerome. Dad pulls out from his parking place in front of Matthews Drug and suddenly turns left on Monarch Street. He drives up Monarch and turns left on Hyman Street, across Mill Street, and pulls the Jeep up in front of Louie's Spirit House, which Dad calls "Louie's Liquors." Louie's Liquors is owned by Louie Pastore and is the only place in town where my dad can get his favorite Bellows Partner's Choice Bourbon. Louie is a short, good-humored man with curly black hair. He's always nice to me when Dad sends me in to fetch a bottle of Partner's Choice.

Usually, either Gerry, Teddy, or I stop by Louie's Liquor when Dad runs out of bourbon.

"Here for your dad's bourbon?" Louie always says.

He puts a fifth of the bourbon in a liquor bag.

"I'm not supposed to do this, you know. Tell your dad next time he'll have to stop by himself," Louie says, as he puts the bagged bottle into a grocery bag to fool Dirty Herwick, the sheriff, if he sees me.

"Yes, sir," I say.

I walk down to the Jerome, carrying the bottle in the grocery bag.

But today we are sitting in the Jeep, and Dad says, "Forgot to have you pick up my hooch. I'll just be a minute. Sit tight."

Louie's Spirit House is a small white building next door to the White Kitchen, a café housed in another small white building. The locals show up in the mornings to drink coffee and tell lies about what they've done yesterday or are going to do today.

Next to the White Kitchen is a third white-faced building which houses E.H. Tideman's. Tideman's is a hodgepodge of a store. He stocks candy, newspapers, comics, canned foods, some cheese, bread, fishhooks, and fireworks.

Tideman is an old man who grows grumpier each year. He is suspicious that us young kids will steal from him. I learned my lesson about stealing back when Richard and I got caught at Matthews Drug. In the back room Tideman has a never-ending card game. Old timers come and go, some hanging around, some playing cards.

To the left of Louie's Spirit House is a big brick building called the Aspen Block building. There used to be an old drive-through garage on the corner of Hyman Street and Original Street. The old red sandstone building is one of the original buildings built in Aspen in the mining days. It has one or two businesses on the ground floor and lodging rooms on the second floor.

Dad says goodbye to Louie Pastore, puts up the collar on his sheepskin coat, and puts his gloves on. He grabs the bottle which Louie has put in a bag and twists the bag at the top around the neck of the bottle. Holding the bottle in one hand, he pushes the door open and comes out to the Jeep.

"All right, kids," he says. "Let's go home."

When we get home, Mom is in the kitchen cooking dinner. I'm fooling around in the kitchen putting off my homework while Dad makes his drink.

"How'd your day go, Mouse?" Dad asks Mom.

"Fine," she says. "What about yours?" She always likes to hear about his day first, then she knows how much bad stuff to tell him if there was any on that day.

"Great, had a good day on the slopes." He stirs his drink with his forefinger, sticks it in his mouth, sucks off the lingering bourbon, and heads across the kitchen to the cupboard. Today it's Ritz crackers. He grabs a few, and then turns back to Mom.

She turns around to him, gives him a kiss, and says, "I got a call from Hazel Dixon today."

"Really?"

"Yes, she told me Roger passed away two days ago. Heart attack."

"That's a darned shame," Dad says.

I hear Roger's name and say, "What happened?"

Mom hasn't seen me in the kitchen. She gives Dad that, "What do I say now?" look.

Dad picks up on it and says, "Well, son, Roger Dixon has passed away."

"He's dead?"

"Yes. According to your mom, he died two days ago."

I'm dumbfounded. I've grown to like Roger. He's taught me to fish and been very nice to me. My head starts to buzz, and I feel strange. I'm really sad.

"Hazel is thinking of selling Stillwater," my mom says. "I told her not to do anything rash, but she has her mind set on it. She has too many good memories there to visit alone in the summers."

"That's just a darned shame," my dad says again.

I hear Mom behind the buzzing in my head. Her words don't register. I can't quite believe Roger is dead. I'll miss fishing on the still water the ranch is named for if Hazel sells. And I know my dreams about dying are bound to return.

It's just a darned shame, I think.

Chapter 34

Early Summer 1956

It's a weekend in late May, and the ground is plenty soft enough now. I remember the deer hide I buried out by the compost heap last fall and dig it up to see what is happening to it. It smells bad and has lots of maggots and bugs on it. Maggots are eating at the remains of the rancid meat on the hide where my dad's skinning knife left bits of it. Large clumps of the hair have fallen out and the hide is softer, but it doesn't look like I imagined it would. I must not have left it in the ground long enough or the instructions were wrong, because the method does not appear to be working.

I've brought the whole project into our garage and am trying to scrape the hair off the dirty, smelly hide. It doesn't just fall out the way I read it would. I realize the deerskin isn't cured right, and it's never going to be suitable for making leggings and moccasins. I set it on the garage floor next to one of the trash cans headed for the dump, and I think maybe I'll try again when we get another deer. I sit on a toolbox and think about my interest in Indian lore. I've tried tanning the hide. That didn't work out so well. My other explorations have. I did beadwork last winter and have collected a bunch of arrowheads and other ancient stone items around the ranch.

For years I've been poking around the ranch for arrowheads and other artifacts because I know the Ute Indians summered in the Roaring Fork Valley. I found a nearly perfect obsidian arrowhead by the south side of the pond, two other stones that are some kind of tools, and a tomahawk head.

Last summer after Pfister bought the ranch, he had a Cat skinner dig another lake on the northwest side of the property. It's a bigger lake than our pond. We call it the "lower lake." He didn't give Adair Rippy the job, which was too bad because we all like Adair Rippy. This new guy would get madder than hell if we came over there to watch.

"You kids'll get run over by this D-8," he would say. Then he would spit a big lougie of tobacco juice and say, "Now, get!"

So we'd run up on the hillside a bit out of the way to watch him with the Cat. Gerry and Teddy only went down and watched once or twice because they got bored with the whole thing and didn't like the new guy.

After the Cat skinner left for the day, I'd head over to where the new lake was taking shape and look for arrowheads and other Indian artifacts. The area had been an old Ute camping spot. I found another tomahawk head, some more arrowheads, a few stone scrapers, and several other tools. My two prizes were two perfectly formed arrowheads, one of pure obsidian, the other of pure flint. I cherish these because I know the Utes had to trade for the flint and obsidian not found in the Roaring Fork Valley.

It's harder for me to find Indian artifacts since we've sold the ranch and I'm not supposed to wander as much. I've looked every place on the ranch I can imagine, so maybe I have to look other places in the valley if I'm to find anything new. I think about it and realize that unless I stumble onto something, finding more Indian relics may be a problem because most of them would be on private property. In the end, I decide I'm more interested in the ski team and fishing than I am in finding more Indian arrowheads.

~ ~ ~

I've been fishing as much as possible since fishing season opened. The freezer is full of rainbow and brook trout. Depending upon where I've been fishing, I either bring home a lot of fish or just a few. I still go to Stillwater Ranch but have to sneak in now because Roger Dixon died last winter and Hazel sold the ranch to some guy who doesn't like to have kids around, especially me.

"I've heard about you Morse kids," he said to me the first day he caught me fishing on the river. "You stay off this property."

I couldn't argue the matter because it wasn't my property. Every now and then I still sneak over to the ranch and take a few casts for "the Big One."

~ ~ ~

School gets out this week. I'm fooling around the playground waiting for the bus, hoping that Mr. Lewis will drive today and take Barbie along so we can get her to take her clothes off. I see some of the kids playing marbles. It's still marble season. I'm not playing today because I've been winning more than losing and I'm getting bored with it. I have two huge cans of marbles and think that's enough to last me a long time. I'm not sure what I can use marbles for besides playing marbles. But I save them anyway because you never know.

Then, out of the blue, I get this thought that it might be a good idea for me to get a job for this summer because I need some money. Sometimes Dad or Mom gives me a little bit of money to buy a fishing fly or two, but usually my dad says, "Money is tight, son. Maybe next week."

I figure if I have my own money I can buy what I need without having to ask Mom and Dad. That way I won't be disappointed because they don't have any extra to give me. The more I think about it, the more I think it's a real good idea.

When I get home, I wander around to the backside of the house and find my dad fixing one of the shutters that has come loose during the winter.

"Where do you think I could get a job?" I ask him. I'm still half thinking about whether this is a good idea or not.

My dad looks at me and says, "You want a job? I'll give you a job around here if you're looking for something to do today."

I see maybe I shouldn't have asked him, because he'll put me to work around the house. I do enough work around the house to be permanently tired of it. I say to him, "No, not work around here. I mean a real job where I can earn some money for myself."

He looks at me and says, "You sound serious. Why don't you go down and talk to Guido? He's always looking for someone to wash dishes. He hired Teddy last summer, so he'll probably hire you if he needs you."

Guido is Guido Meyer. He owns Guido's Swiss Inn, a restaurant in town. My dad helped Guido build a big second floor on top of the building to make it an inn as well as a restaurant. My dad says Guido is a "character." Guido always carries a bunch of money in his pocket. One time Guido was checking on the addition that dad was building and accidentally dropped his wallet on the floor. Dad and another workman counted around $4,000 before Guido came back looking for his wallet. Dad said that they hadn't even stopped counting. I knew if Guido had that much money in his wallet, he would have enough to pay me some of it.

"Okay," I say, "I think I'll go ask him." I start to walk off.

"Wait a minute," my dad says. "Here, gimme a hand with this shutter." I look at him and see that he doesn't need a hand but is just buying time while he thinks up another project for me to help him with around the house. Something like raking the yard or cleaning the garage.

"I gotta bike into town," I say and scoot around the corner.

~ ~ ~

The next thing I know, I'm in the kitchen at Guido's restaurant asking a Hungarian man named Jimmy where I can find Guido. Jimmy speaks with a very heavy accent, so I have a hard time understanding him. I can barely figure out his name is Jimmy. Finally Jimmy gets tired of trying to explain to me that Guido is out in the bar. He leaves and before long brings Guido.

"What do you want?" Guido says.

"I want a job," I say.

"Who are you?"

"Terry Morse."

"You're Wendy's boy, huh?"

"Yep."

His wife Trudi comes into the kitchen on an errand of her own. She takes one look at me and says, "You're Teddy's brother, aren't you?"

"Yes," I say.

"Come to think of it, you look like Teddy," Guido says. "Where is he? Is he going to work for us this summer?"

"I don't know. I just need a job. I didn't ask him about what he is doing."

Guido looks down at me and says, "Trudi, he wants a job." Then to me, "How old are you anyway?"

"Almost ten," I say.

Trudi looks at me and says to Guido, "Well, why not, he looks like he can do something, and Teddy did good work for us last summer. He and that Rowland boy. Where is he?"

Guido says, "I haven't spoken with either Teddy or the Rowland boy."

"You ever wash dishes?"

"All the time at home."

"Come here, and I'll show you," Guido says and walks over to a long silver counter with a large hump in the middle.

"This is the dishwasher." He explains to me how it works and shows me how to load and unload the trays and how to dry the silverware after it comes out of the dishwasher so is doesn't have spots on it.

"When you want to come to work?" Guido says. "My other dishwasher didn't show up yesterday. Damned bum. So Jimmy has to do all the dishes, pots and pans, and is working until midnight just to keep up. When can you start?"

"School gets out on Friday," I say. "I guess I can start on Saturday."

"What about coming in after school to help out for a few hours this week so Jimmy doesn't drop dead? Maybe you can come until six or seven."

Since it is already almost June, the sun isn't going down until about 8:15, so it will be plenty light out after 7 o'clock for me to ride my bike home.

"I guess I can do that but I'll have to ask my mom and dad."

"You come Monday after school. Don't worry about your mom and dad, I'll talk to them," Guido says. In his mind, it's final. He turns to go back into the bar.

"Well, just one more thing," I say shyly. Guido turns around. Trudi is looking at me as well. I'm a bit embarrassed, but I get up my courage and ask, "How much will you pay me?"

Guido says, "We'll pay you a dollar an hour," and looks at Trudi for her agreement.

"Guido," Trudi says, "I think he will be a hard worker. We give him one dollar and twenty-five cents an hour."

I like Trudi already.

"Okay," I say, closing the deal, "but one more thing. The dishwasher is too high for me to load the dishes into it. What shall I do about that?"

Guido hadn't noticed that, but it's a monkey wrench in the works. He looks at me and says, "Come here," and takes me over to the dishwasher.

"You're too short," he says.

I think, *That's what I just I told you.* But I don't say anything.

"Here," Guido says. He walks over to the outside door and on the stoop is a stacked pile of wooden milk crates. He brings one back and says, "Stand on this. Let's see if it is high enough."

I stand on the crate, open the machine, and move a dish tray into it. Then I get down off the milk crate and move it to the other side of the machine so I can open the door and pull the dish tray out. Guido is already out the door and walking back with two more milk crates. He lines them up on the floor so I can walk on them from one side of the machine to the other.

"Good," he says. "You can use these. They should work fine, eh?"

"Yes," I say, not knowing if they will work or not. I let it ride because he thinks they will and has given me my first real summer job. Guido pushes the crates underneath the stainless steel counter on the dish machine where they are out of the way and says, "We'll leave these here, so you have them when you need them."

"Thanks, Mr. Meyer," I say.

"My name is Guido," he says. "And her name is Trudi," he says, looking at Trudi. "You call us that."

"Okay," I say.

"So, we see you Monday after school. What time does school get out?"

"3:30," I answer.

"Good, you be here by quarter to four. That gives you plenty of time to come from school. And we'll figure out later which days you will have off during the week, eh?"

"Okay, Guido," I say. "Thanks a lot."

I fairly fly home on my bike. A dollar and twenty-five cents an hour! All the way home, I am figuring in my head. A buck twenty-five times eight is ten dollars a day. Ten dollars a day times how many days? I couldn't do the math till I knew how many days.

When I get home, I find my dad.

"Guess what? I got a job," I blurt out.

"Really? That's great! Tell me a little more."

"Don't think you'll get too tired?" he says when I have finished my monologue.

"Nope."

My dad grins and says, "Good for you."

~ ~ ~

We're at dinner, and I've told everyone at the dinner table that I have a job. Gerry is not impressed because he's had a job for a couple of years. Teddy is wondering why I went and got a job. He worked for Guido last summer and knows all about Jimmy. He's a bit miffed that I have gotten a job with Guido and says to me, "I'm going to work at Guido's this summer, too."

"Have you asked Guido?" I say.

"Well, not yet, but I'm gonna."

"Well, you better hurry up, because I start after school on Monday," I say.

After dinner, Teddy asks me and I tell him again about everything I did. He thinks about it.

What finally happens is Teddy decides he'll go down to Guido's and ask him if he can work there again this summer. As it turns out, Jack Rowland doesn't want to work this summer, so there's no problem. Guido and Trudi schedule us so I work with Jimmy part of the week, Teddy works with Jimmy part of the week, and Teddy and I work together part of the week. That way, Guido can have Jimmy doing other stuff that is too hard for us to do, like stocking the bar and washing all the real big heavy pots and pans. Everyone gets a day or two days off so we won't get worn out. Teddy and I like the arrangement. I can't wait to get started and watch those hours, days, and money adding up.

Chapter 35

Summer 1956

Working for Guido is harder than I first thought it would be, although he is fun to work for. He doesn't get too mad if I screw up, and he pays me every two weeks. I now have a Social Security card so Guido can deduct taxes from my pay. It seems like the government takes a lot of your hard-earned money for taxes. I've been getting about $125 per pay check before they take out taxes. After taxes, I make about $110 or $55 per week. I think Trudi is paying me more than $1.25 an hour because the numbers don't add up when I figure them. By the end of the summer, I hope to have saved about $600. That really is a fortune for me. I'm saving my money to buy a new pair of shoes I've seen at Magnifico Sports. They are made in Europe and look real rugged, with good leather instead of tennis-shoe canvas. Since my feet are growing and I'm now a size eight, I'll need a new pair soon.

~ ~ ~

So far this summer I haven't had time to look for any more Indian relics. In all honesty, I'm not too interested in looking for them right now. If I'm not too tired and have time, I prefer to fish - on weekends, in the evenings, after work. From time to time, I sneak over to Stillwater and try to catch the "Big One" out of the hole by the pines. So far with no success. It's been three years since I first saw him. I know he's still there because I've seen him, although I don't know how long fish live, so maybe he'll be gone before I catch him.

When I'm not fishing, I try to practice playing my guitar when my chores don't get in the way.

Heather will be a year old in a few months. Mom has shown us how she wants us to take care of Heather when we babysit. We boys feed, change diapers, and play with her. Heather is an easy baby so isn't a problem when I take care of her. She likes being tickled and bounced around.

Gerry, Teddy, and I fool around a lot doing stupid things, but when it's time to be serious, we make sure we know what we are doing so we don't get hurt or hurt someone else. As you can imagine, that isn't the way it always goes. I have all sorts of bumps and bruises all the time from falling off my bike when I am jumping things or riding where I shouldn't, like trying to ride across the Roaring Fork River where it passes through Aspen over on the east end of town.

Gerry is worse than I am. He's always getting banged up. This last winter he broke his leg skiing. He was in a cast most of the back end of the winter and out for the rest of the ski season.

To make matters worse, one day we were riding to school in the Jeep. It was a clear day, but it had snowed a couple of days before. Dad had plowed the road and it needed a little cleaning up. He figured he'd set the plow down on the spots where the snow needed a little moving and knock the drifts back as we headed down the road. Everything went well until Dad picked up some speed. Up ahead we saw a drift that needed clearing. Dad put the plow down and hit the drift going about a thousand miles an hour. The snow didn't move as quickly as it should have, in fact, it barely moved at all. The tip of the plow blade stopped dead in the drift, causing the Jeep to spin completely around. It happened fast and was fierce. Teddy and I were both thrown out of the Jeep into the snow bank on the far side of the road. Gerry was thrown out of the passenger seat. His cast caught under the Jeep's instrument panel, and he ended up half in and half out of the Jeep with his head resting on the road. His cast was broken. Luckily he did not re-break his leg.

Dad collected Gerry, Teddy, and me back into the Jeep, got it unstuck from the snowdrift, and said, "Son of a gun! Wonder what we hit there. You kids all right? Teddy, I'll drop you and Terry at school, and take Gerry up to the hospital for a new cast, after I check in at the ski school." We drove down the road, turned on to the Maroon Creek Bridge, and Dad lit up his cigarette like he always does.

~ ~ ~

I don't have much time to goof off anymore. I have pretty much given up on traipsing around the ranch. Pfister has a new foreman for the ranch, so Ed no longer works there. The new man is Art Kuen. Maybe Pfister hired him because they both have a first name of Art. The Kuens are from Europe. There are two brothers who are younger than us, and who will probably take the bus to school. Art Kuen works for Pfister, but he's also going to work for Friedl making a chair lift on Friedl's ranch if it works out. They live in the bunkhouse Pfister built west of where our old chicken coop used to be. All the Kuens are fatter than we are. We are all pretty skinny.

I've gotten to town to play with Richard Sabbatini once in awhile. Last time I was there, we got in a fight. Richard's mother blamed it on me and sent me home. It wasn't really all my fault, but Richard started crying because I pounded him pretty good. He doesn't like to wrestle or get rough. Of course, I'm used to it because I am always fighting with Gerry and Teddy who beat me up all the time. Mom and Dad won't listen to me when I tell them. They just say, "You work it out." When Teddy complains, it's a different story: Gerry and I catch hell. When I get bigger, I'll throttle him. (Get that, a new word from Mrs. Anderson; throttle. It means I will get the better of him and make him be quiet. Subdue is another word Mrs. Anderson uses. Throttle also means suffocate. But I won't do that. I don't want to see him suffocate. I guess I'd have to be really mad to suffocate him. Maybe I could suffocate him just a little bit so he runs out of breath for a few minutes, gets scared, and leaves me alone from then on). So one day I may throttle him just part way. For now, I get beat up on pretty good.

Anyway, I beat up on Richard and his mom came out shouting at us, mad as a hatter. (That's another one I learned this year. Mad as a hatter. Mrs. Anderson says it is a saying about insane people who worked in a hat factory). Richard was crying, and Thelma got mad as a hatter and sent me home. I wasn't allowed to play with Richard until school started.

I played with Spook some but not too much. When I did, we always got in trouble for something or another. Spook's dad is an artist and doesn't pay too much attention to him. It seems like his mom always has to deal with the problems that Spook creates. She likes me and likes me to play with Spook because, even though we get in trouble, it's usually nothing too bad.

But mostly I'm at Guido's washing dishes. I'm glad I have a job, but some days I'd rather be goofing off. On my days off, sometimes I go to the Hotel Jerome swimming pool. Mom bought us a membership this summer. She has some free time to sit at the pool and socialize with her friends. She wants us to keep up our swimming since we all know how to swim now except Jennifer who is just learning, and Heather, who is of course too small. It's kind of fun for a couple of hours. The only trouble is that Mom uses it as a lure to get us hooked into working after we get home from the pool. She tells us that since we got to go swimming, we need to help her do this, that, or the other thing. It's usually gardening, cleaning, or lawn work, not my most favorite things to do when I have time off.

We found out we can sneak out of our room upstairs and not have to go through the house to do it. When Dad built the addition on the house, for some reason one of the big beams that came out of the Tippler mine was left to stick out beyond the roof about a foot. The roof around our room is flat gravel and tar and is over part of the living room. We have a door in our room that opens out on the roof in case we have another fire.

If you go out the door from our bedroom, and go straight ahead by the fireplace chimney that comes up from the living room, you run smack into where the beam sticks out past the roof line. Just to make it better, the beam has a huge, old, rusted, bent spike coming out of the end. One day Gerry, Teddy, and I were goofing around on the roof, and we got looking at this set up. Gerry says, "I bet I can swing on that spike and drop to the ground."

"Bet you can't," Teddy says.

So Gerry gets down on his knees and slides his legs over the side of the roof. He grabs the spike and hangs down from it. I go over to look, and see he is only about two feet off the ground. He lets go and, presto, he lands right on his feet and walks back to where we can see him. Teddy and I try it, and both of us figured it out right away. I have a longer jump to the ground, but it isn't so far that I can't do it.

"Cool," Gerry says. "Now we have a way to sneak out if we want to."

Chapter 36

Summer 1956

Tonight at dinner, Dad says, "Mouse, it's about time for those kids to learn how to handle firearms."

"Oh, Wendy," Mom says. "What do they need to do that for? It'll just give them another way to get hurt."

"It's something they need to know." Then he says, "Okay, boys, tomorrow we're gonna teach you to shoot." The subject was closed, as simple as that.

~ ~ ~

Saturday afternoon Dad rounds us up, collects the .22 rifle, the shotgun and his 30.06, and takes us out behind the house where we will learn to shoot. We set some old beer cans on a couple of rocks near the pond, and Dad explains how the firearms work, how to load them, how to fire them, and how to use them safely.

We start by shooting the .22. It is a pump-action rifle with a barrel magazine holding 15 bullets. Once loaded, we will take up a prone position and plunk away at the cans. Of course Gerry goes first because he is the oldest, then Teddy, and finally me. We use up a little more than a box of ammo before we really start getting the hang of it and can hit the cans consistently.

As soon as Dad sees we are hitting cans and are comfortable using the rifle safely, he picks up the .20 gauge double-barreled shotgun. It is a breech-loading Parker that Popeye gave him. He loads the shotgun, and we're ready for action. Dad explains carefully the differences in using a shotgun and a rifle. He shows us the safety and the two triggers, one for each barrel.

Teddy goes first because he's most anxious to shoot the shotgun. He thinks the .22 is too tame, nothing more than a kid's squirrel gun. Dad lines him up and shows him how to shoot kneeling with your elbow on your knee so you can steady the weapon, and tells him, "Fire at will, son!"

Teddy takes his time aiming the shotgun toward the cans, and when he is ready, he pulls the trigger. KABOOM! The shotgun blast knocks Teddy back on his ass. I'm glad I have my fingers in my ears because it makes one hell of a racket. Dad quickly grabs the shotgun from Teddy and breaks it at the breech. Smoke is coming from both barrels. Teddy has pulled the back trigger instead of the forward trigger and set both barrels off at the same time. Gerry and I roll on the ground laughing. Teddy's in a daze. He picks himself up off the ground and says, "Quit laughing! You try it if you think you're so smart!"

Gerry stops laughing long enough to fire off both barrels one at a time. He sends a couple of the cans flying.

My ears are ringing. I ask my dad, "Do you have any more cotton to put in my ears?"

"Oh, yeah," he says. "Your mom gave me some for your ears. I forgot." He pulls out a few cotton balls and gives them to each of us. We pull them apart and stuff them into each ear.

I get set and fire the shotgun. I shoot one barrel, barely hold my balance, and get a good kick in the shoulder from the blast.

"Hold it tighter into your shoulder," my dad says. "It won't kick so much."

I do and fire the next barrel. I'm happy to see that the cans are mincemeat.

Gerry takes another turn with the shotgun, then we each spend some time firing off a bunch of rounds from the .22, and the shotgun. The Maroon Creek Valley echoes like a war zone. Finally Dad says, "It's about time to go in. The light is getting bad. Do you want to try the 30.06 before we shut 'er down?" He's told us that the 30.06 is a WWI Springfield model 1903. Dad has added about four inches to the back of the stock so it fits him. He's a big man and has a long reach.

Teddy is still recovering from his shotgun blast and shakes his head. Gerry and I both want to try it. Dad loads one bullet into the chamber and helps Gerry get set in the prone position. He gives him a few pointers on sighting then says, "Fire at will!"

Gerry hesitates a minute, then pulls the trigger. The big rifle roars. I'm looking at the cans, and I'll be darned if he doesn't hit one, knocking it up in the air.

"Good shot, Gerry!" my dad says.

"Yeah, good shot," I repeat.

Gerry grins and passes the 30.06 back to my dad. I'm next and I take the rifle from him and try to fit it into the crotch of my shoulder. I get it all snugged in and find I can't reach the trigger. The stock is too long by about six inches. Dad looks at me and laughs, "Terr-Ass, looks like you'll have to take your turn in a couple of years when you've grown into a string bean." He takes the rifle from me and says, "Okay, kids, that's enough for today. I'm sure Mom's got dinner, and it's probably cold by now. We walk back up to the house, and Mom says, "Finally. You're late for dinner. It's on the table and probably cold."

Chapter 37

Early Fall 1956

I've decided that ten years old is old enough to stop celebrating my birthday with a party. This year I tell Mom I want to celebrate by having scrambled eggs and coffee cake for breakfast. She's worried I'm not inviting my friends over and thinks I've done something to alienate them. I assure her that I still have friends, it's just that I don't want to have a stupid birthday party with everyone bringing gifts because they think they should or having a good time because it is a birthday party and that's what you do at birthday parties. I figure if someone wants to give me a gift, it doesn't have to be my birthday for them to do it. Any old day will work for that.

I'm now in fifth grade. Mrs. Houston is my very pretty teacher. I like her a lot because she is the nicest teacher I've had so far. Sometimes I think about kissing her, which is stupid because I'm just a kid and she's married. Besides, I can see she's pregnant because her belly is beginning to show. She'll have a baby sometime in the winter, and we'll have to have another teacher.

Mrs. Houston is smart. She knows if she challenges me with a problem, I'll set my mind to work on it to figure out the answer, not just to please her, but also to satisfy my curiosity. About a week ago, Mrs. Houston said to me, "Terry, here's a little problem I want you to solve."

"Okay," I say, "what is it?"

She says, "Who said *je pense donc je suis?*"

"Hmmmm, I don't know," I said. "But I know it is French because I have heard Fred Henry talk French. He is learning French from Madame Kecheid after school, and he tells me some of the words and pronounces them like they do in France. I know that *je* means I, but that's all I know."

Mrs. Houston said, "Well, that is your challenge. When you know who said those words and what they mean, you come back and tell me." She hands me a slip of paper with the saying written on it.

"Okay," I said.

So, I'm asking lots of people, even teachers, but no one seems to know what the phrase means. I'm going to the library to see if I can find it there. The library is located in the Wheeler Opera House building next to Beck and Bishop's Grocery store. Mrs. Braun is the librarian who is nice but strict. If you goof around in the library, she disciplines you. She tells you to be quiet, and if you are really goofing off, she kicks you out. I go up to her desk and say, "Mrs. Braun? Do you know who said, *"Je pense donc je suis?"* She is from Germany, and I can see that she doesn't understand what I am asking her because I don't pronounce the phrase correctly. I show her the paper that Mrs. Houston has given me.

She looks and asks me, "Is this for school?"

"Yes," I say. "Mrs. Houston told me I should try and find out who said this, but I am not sure where I can find out."

"If it's for school, you'll have to find out yourself. I am sure Mrs. Houston wouldn't like me giving you the answers to her assignments."

"It's not exactly an assignment," I say. "It's more like a problem that she's given me to solve."

"You'll have to work on it yourself," Mrs. Braun replies. She picks up some books and heads back into the stacks.

I'm miffed because I can tell she knows the answer and just won't tell me. I look in the card catalogue under *French* and *je pense* and everything else I can think of. After spending an hour, I give up, seeing there is no way to find the solution in the stacks without having more information. I decide to go about it in a different way.

I know Fred takes French lessons from Madame Kecheid, so I figure if I ask Fred to ask Madame Kecheid what the phrase means, then I can solve the puzzle. Better yet, if I can get Fred to take me to one of his French lessons maybe as a guest or something, I can ask her myself. That way I would know that Fred hasn't forgotten part of it or has changed something just to fool me. I remind myself to ask him next time I see him, and set the problem aside for the time being.

~ ~ ~

Guido has needed me to work more than he thought. I go into town to help him on Saturdays so Jimmy can have a day off. I've already made more than $600 over the course of the summer. I've saved it all and have decided it may be time for me to buy that pair of new shoes that I have seen at Magnifico Sports. I need new shoes because of this situation with my bike.

It's really not cool to have fenders on your bike. The high school kids customize their bikes. They take the fenders off and turn the handlebars down really low. Then they turn the brake levers around so you have to work them with your thumbs instead of your fingers. They do other stuff like put cards on the spokes and take the chain guards off.

I've taken the fenders off my bike. I turned my brakes backwards, but it didn't work for me because in that position I couldn't stop fast enough. While I was putting my brakes back to their proper position, I got this great idea: instead of using my brakes, I could stick my foot between the steel back tube of the bike frame and the back tire with my sneaker sole against the tire. The further in the gap I pushed my foot, the more the back wheel would slow down. I could use my foot for a brake!

I practiced my new technique until I could stop on a dime. If I stopped the back wheel really fast, it acted like the emergency brake on a car, throwing the bike into a spin, spraying gravel, and skidding to a stop. It wasn't long before my right sneaker was worn down through the sole and into my socks. So I taped the shoe up with adhesive tape. It was worth it. I imagined myself as a daredevil spewing gravel and stopping my bike in a skid just before plummeting off a cliff.

Of course Mom isn't amused and says she isn't going to buy me another pair of sneakers because the ones I have should have lasted a year.

~ ~ ~

So, today's the day. I head over to Magnifico's Sports to buy some new shoes. The salesman, Gene Mason, helps me find the size I need in the cool-looking leather shoe I really like. They're not cool for school but fit and feel great. They will be harder to run in but will be much warmer in the winter.

Gene Mason says, "These are good shoes so you should take care of them. You'll need to put some Sno Sealer on them to keep the water from wrecking the leather this winter. If you don't have any at home, bring them in and I'll do it for you"

"Thanks," I say. "I know we have some Sno Sealer at home because we use it for our ski boots."

"Good," he says. He rings up my purchase on the cash register, and I pay. I wonder how I'll get the shoes home. I'm on my bike and don't want to have to carry the shoes in a bag if I don't have to. Gene gives me my change and, as I leave the store, I see a rucksack on the wall next to a rope and an ice ax on display. Suddenly I get a great idea. "Mr. Mason, do you sell those packs?"

"Yes, we have several in the back. Not much use for them around here, but Mike (Mr. Magnifico) thought we might be able to sell a few of them to the tourists who come to town and want to climb around in the mountains."

"People climb the mountains?" I ask. "Why don't they just ride the lifts?'

"They aren't climbing Aspen Mountain, they're climbing the fourteen-thousand-foot peaks, like Maroon Bells and Pyramid Peak."

"They climb those peaks?" I say.

"Sure. If you are careful, you can walk all the way to the top. But when you do, you need to carry some water and lunch and maybe some rope or first aid kit or other things. The rucksacks are a great way to carry things and still have your hands free."

I think about this for a moment, then realize I have seen pictures of the soldiers in the Tenth Mountain Division skiing with rucksacks. Of course that's the best way to carry your gear.

"Wow, how much are they?" I say.

"They're pretty expensive. You probably don't have enough money to pay for one."

"I've been working for Guido all summer and have saved some money," I say. "I could use one to carry my shoes home, and it would be real handy to carry stuff whenever I'm on my bike or if I want to go hiking."

"Let me talk to Mike," Gene says.

He disappears to the back of the shop, and I hear him climbing the stairs to the little office where Mike Magnifico does the paperwork. A few minutes later Gene comes down and says, "Mike says we can sell you a pack for our cost plus ten percent if you don't let on that we are giving you a big discount like that. He thinks it might be good business if you were wearing the pack around town and people pick up on it."

"Hmmmm," I say, "that actually may be a way for you to sell more stuff."

"That's the idea," says Gene.

Gene tells me the price plus tax. I think about it for a moment, then, decide to buy the La Fuma rucksack. Gene helps me get the it properly fitted, and I leave the store with the rucksack on my back, shoes packed neatly inside, and about $150 poorer. It's a huge amount of money for me to spend, more than I have ever spent by far. I'm happy with my purchases, a new pair of shoes, a new ruck sack, and a new way of carrying things on my bike.

When I get home, I say to Mom, who is fixing dinner, "Mom, come look at what I bought with my work money."

"Just a minute, let me get some potatoes in the oven to bake."

I stand with my pack at my feet and watch as she picks out six potatoes from the sack in the cupboard under the kitchen counter. She washes them, pokes holes in all six of them with a fork so they won't blow up, and puts them in the oven. When she is finished, she says, "Now what do you want?"

"I want to show you my new shoes. You have to turn around while I get them out and put them on."

She humors me. I get the shoes out of the pack, sit down on the floor, and put them on. I stand up and hold my pants legs up so she can see.

"Okay, turn around," I say.

She turns around and looks at my feet.

"Oh! Those are horrible! They make your feet look like a...I don't know what. You'll have to take them back. I can't believe you would buy shoes that clunky."

"But," I say, "they are really comfortable. They're leather, and they are really good quality. They'll last me a long time. I got them a half size too big so I have some room to grow in them."

"No," she says. "I can't stand them. You'll just have to take them back. How much did you pay for them anyway?'

I don't tell her how much I paid because I'm crushed by her response. *Here I went clear into town, bought and paid for my own shoes, and this is what she says*, I think. *And now she wants me to take them back.*

"I'm going to ask Dad," I say.

"It won't do any good, because I'll tell him I want you to take them back. Sneakers are just fine for you, and they must be less expensive than those clunky things."

I nod as if I'm saying okay. I'll wait to talk to Dad.

When Dad gets home, he's not in such a good mood because they had some trouble setting roof rafters at the job site. One of the workers dropped a rafter and nearly clonked Dick Wright on the head. I speak up, and the moment the words come out of my mouth, I know I'm not picking the right time to talk to Dad.

"Dad," I begin to explain, "I went to Magnifico's and bought a pair of shoes with my own money today. Money from Guido's."

"What a day," he is already saying to my mom, not listening to me.

My mom says, "Don't start with your dad, Terry. He's tired and had a hard day."

Suddenly my dad is paying attention and says, "What's this about?"

My mom says, "He went to Magnifico's and bought these hideous shoes that make his feet look like I don't know what...like duck's feet. I told him he had to take them back. They are probably far too expensive."

"They do not," I blurt out. "Here, look." I hold up my pants legs. "Besides I paid for them myself."

My dad looks at my shoes. "They look fine to me, but you have to do what your mother says."

That's the end of it. He's too tired to deal with me and is not going to take argue with Mom about such a trivial matter. He turns away and opens the liquor cabinet for his Partner's Choice. I know the conversation is over and feel humiliated by the whole event.

After all, I think to myself, *it's my money. I earned it myself. Just because she doesn't like the shoes, doesn't mean I don't.*

~ ~ ~

The next day, I ride to school with my rucksack and shoes. Although I get some strange looks walking into school with a rucksack, no one teases me. I wouldn't care if they did, because it's a great way to carry stuff on my bike.

After school, I go over to Magnifico Sports and tell Gene Mason that I have to bring the shoes back.

"What for?" Gene asks.

"Because my mom doesn't like the looks of them."

"That's too bad," says Gene. "I think they're fine. And they are good, rugged shoes for a young kid like you."

"Sorry," I say as I put the shoes on the counter. "I'm keeping the rucksack though, no matter what."

"Good," says Gene. "Give me a minute to figure out how much money you've got coming."

While Gene is figuring, I look around the store. The more I look, and the more I think about having to return the shoes, the more upset I get. I work myself into a small frenzy. I think, *I'm really mad at my mom for telling me what I can or can't do with my hard-earned money that I had to sweat for over that steamy dishwasher at Guido's. I washed a lot of dishes, pots, and pans for that money.*

That's when I get another idea.

"Hey, Gene," I say. "What about me getting some other shoes?"

"Well, you could try that," he says.

I start looking at the boots on the wall, and my eyes land on a shoe that is an obvious mountain shoe. It comes up around the ankle, looks lighter than most of the other boots, and isn't as wide at the toe as the shoes I bought. They have a treaded sole, rough leather, and lace up with eyelets and hooks. Maybe Mom won't notice them if I don't mention I bought them, and I'll just let her figure it out after I have worn them for awhile.

"What about these?" I say to Gene. "Do you have any of these in my size? What are they anyway?"

"Those are called *kletter shue*," Gene says. "That's German for a light rock-climbing shoe. It's not as heavy as the mountaineering boots." He points to a pair of mountain boots. "Let me see if I have a pair your size."

He goes to the back of the store, and I can hear him rummaging around a bit until he finally comes back with a box.

"You're in luck," he says. "Here, try these on."

I take the box, sit down on the bench, and try them on. They're a nice comfortable fit. Not quite like the other shoes, but I like them just the same.

"What happened to your sneakers?" Gene asks me. He is pointing to the trench in my right shoe.

"Oh, that," I say. "That's from braking on my bike." I explain to him how I use my foot as a brake on the back tire.

"Wow," he says. "Don't do that with these kletter shue because you may wreck your bicycle tire as well as your boots. The soles on these boots are much harder than the sneakers. It may prove to be a real problem if you try to brake your bike that way."

"Okay," I say. I am a bit torn about buying the kletter shue in place of the other shoes because I know my mom would rather have me buy sneakers. Then I think, *To heck with it! It's my money. I earned it, and she's not going to tell me how to spend it. She should be happy I'm buying shoes and not some stupid toy or another.*

I look at Gene and say, "Do you think there is room enough for me to grow some in these?"

He feels where my big toe is and says, "I think so. You have quite a bit of extra space there. We can try a half size larger if you want."

We do and find I'm swimming in them, so go back to the original pair.

"I'm going to take these," I say. "I think they will work really well."

"What about your mom?" he says.

"I have decided it's my money because I earned it at Guido's, and I'm going to spend it the way I want to."

Gene looks at me hard, smiles, and says, "Okay, let me figure out the difference in price." Then he goes over to the cash register and does some figuring. "The boots are a bit more expensive than the shoes, so you may owe me a bit. I'll tell you what, there's only about five bucks difference. I'm sure Mike wouldn't mind if I gave you a small discount on the boots. Let's just call it even."

"Gosh," I say. "Thanks."

This time I'm more clever about my approach to keeping my shoes. "Can you throw these sneakers and the shoe box away for me?" I say. "I think I'll wear my new boots."

This way Mom can't make me take them back because I won't have any other shoes for school. I ride home, and the first thing my mom says to me when I get there is, "Did you take those hideous shoes back?"

I say "Yes" as I walk past her in the hall and go upstairs to do my homework.

When she finally does notice my new footwear, our conversations about shoes are a distant memory.

Chapter 38

October 1956

Yesterday after school, Mrs. Houston called me up to her desk and said, "Did you find out who said *Je pense donc je suis?*"

"No, but I found out that it means *I think therefore I am.*"

"Good. That's a good try. The man's name is Rene Decartes. He is a French philosopher, and he makes philosophical arguments for the proof of one's existence lying in the ability to think from moment to moment. It gets complicated, and if you are interested, I suggest you look it up in the encyclopedia and read about him. I have one more small problem for you to solve." She handed me a small piece of paper and said, "Now run quickly before you miss the bus."

I sprinted down the hall, out the door, and caught the bus just as it was leaving. Once on the bus, I looked down at the paper. "Who developed the formula $E=MC^2$?" it read.

Ugh. How am I ever going to solve this one? I don't even see any numbers in it. It must not be math.

~ ~ ~

For a while this morning, I was trying to figure out Mrs. Houston's problem with no luck. So now I'm working on a new project I've been thinking about for a while. I'm in the barnyard with a huge piece of cardboard Dad brought home from his job. It must be four feet wide and eight feet long. I'm using it for a human kite! I've cut two hand holes far enough apart so I have to stretch my arms to get my fingers through and hold on. I'll put it on my back, and it will be a wing in the wind.

There is a massive thunderstorm coming. I've been waiting for a few weeks for just such an opportunity.

I look up. The thunderheads have tumbled over the ridgeline. It's raining up on the saddle. Lightning shoots through the rain soaked clouds, sometimes hitting ground, other times disappearing in a flash of white and yellow that lights up the whole sky. The wind is blowing in violent gusts picking up small sticks, forgotten leaves, hay, and dust, driving them through the air. They pelt the side of the garage where I'm waiting for the right moment to begin my experiment. I peek around the side of the garage and see the barnyard detritus skidding across the ground, swirling in violent dust devils that die as fast as they are born. Soon there's a lull in the wind.

Now is the time, I think.

I scoot out to the barnyard, hold on to the cardboard wing with both hands, face the direction of the wind and hoist the cardboard over my head. The wind picks up, and I run into it. All at once there is a brilliant flash of light, my hair stands on end, thunder roars in my ears, and the wind catches the cardboard. My arms are ripped upward as the raging gust picks me off the ground, catches the underside of the cardboard, and tumbles me over. I fly through the air, holding on to the cardboard for dear life. I'm five feet off the ground, rolling and flipping in a state of pure horror and joy. Suddenly my body is slammed viciously into the ground.

My not-so-trusty wing drags me across the barnyard— through dirt, over rocks and across puddles of water—before it rips apart and flies into the heavens in two large pieces. I lie on the ground taking stock, the rain pelting my back, and finally realize I am more or less in one piece. Both hands are bleeding on the palms and fingers, my blue jeans are ripped, and my T-shirt is not salvageable.

Not bad, for the first try. I think. Then, *What am I thinking? First try?* I limp toward the house and know there will be no second try. If I were supposed to fly, I'd have wings.

~ ~ ~

A week after my "Great Flying Experiment," Dad and I are headed out hunting. Dad comes upstairs, shakes me awake, and whispers, "Come on, Terr-Ass, time to go."

I get up quietly, careful not to disturb Gerry and Teddy, who said last night that they didn't want to come, put on my jeans and shirt over my underwear, and head downstairs. Dad has fixed a piece of buttered toast and a glass of orange juice.

"We'll be home about breakfast time," he says.

I know we won't, because the sun won't be up until about 7:15. It won't be light enough to shoot until at least 6:30.

I sit down at the kitchen table, bleary eyed. I eat while Dad gets the 30.06 and the bullets. We bundle up in coats, hats, and gloves. Dad takes a last sip of his coffee, we put our dishes in the sink, and go out to the Jeep.

The Jeep starts right away this morning without having to push it. We head across the barnyard, through Pfister's corrals and up toward the saddle. Dad and Pfister made some agreement when Dad sold the ranch so he can still go hunting on the property. Pfister is pretty good about it because he knows Mom and Dad don't make much money and need the venison.

The sound of the Jeep in the aspens breaks the morning stillness as we drive higher and higher. We break out of the aspens and move into the pines. They seem to hush the engine noise. When we reach the saddle, the light is changing from full darkness to pre-dawn grey. I love the way shadows become objects at this time of day.

Dad stops the Jeep and whispers, "We'll walk down the hill to the meadow and wait for the light."

We make our way quietly through the pine trees, hearing only the muted crunch of dry needles under our boots, down to the tree line on the edge of the meadow. There we wait in the dew-wet grass. Dad shakes out a cigarette, puts it in his mouth, but doesn't light it. The red glow and smell of smoke will spook any deer in the area. We squat at the tree line watching the darkness lift. The scene below comes to life in the soft light.

Scattered nimbus clouds float in the sky, purple, red, and orange. A crisp breeze fans its way up through the meadow below us, and the smell of pine is strong. The last of the yellow field flowers give notice of coming snows. Meadow grasses and stands of aspen spill down the slope. The small birds begin their morning chirping, and I hear the rodents moving on the forest floor. Serenity in the high country.

The sun is almost up; Dad elbows me quietly and nods his head toward a shape in the meadow. A big buck has come into the open to graze. Slowly my dad takes the unlit cigarette from his mouth and puts it behind his ear. He never stops watching the buck. He's been holding the rifle in his left hand with the butt on the ground, his hand around the upper stock. He slowly shifts to a sitting position. The buck senses the movement, stops grazing, and picks up his head. Dad stays motionless. The buck goes back to grazing. Dad continues to move into position. He brings the stock into his shoulder, sights down the barrel of the powerful rifle, and squeezes off the shot. It all takes less than a minute.

The buck lifts its head, pauses, and falls on its side. It is a clean shot to the animal's heart. I say a prayer for it in my mind the way the Indians did when they killed a buffalo. Again I am saddened by the death of the creature, and again I know we will have some meat for the next months of the coming winter.

We gut the animal. Dad walks back to the Jeep and drives it down through the meadow where we heave the animal up onto the hood. We tie it to the fenders with a rope, get in the Jeep, and drive down the mountain in silence. When we arrive at home, we unstring the buck and hang it in the garage using the whippletree and a pulley that Dad has rigged to a cross beam for this very purpose.

The smell of breakfast hits us before we take off our boots. Everyone is at the breakfast table, and Teddy says, "How'd ya do?"

"Dad shot a big buck. Clean shot. Hit the ground right away. We gutted him and came home. Simple," I said.

That night, I discovered it isn't all that simple. After being dormant for some months, my dying dreams are back again.

Chapter 39

Early Winter 1956

It's December. Aspen has changed this past summer. I've only recently noticed it because I was busy working at Guido's all summer. Aspen Sports has moved to a new location on Cooper Avenue next to the Red Onion. Their old store on Mill Street next to the Little Percent Taxi is now the office for the Aspen Ski Club. Natalie Gignoux started the Little Percent Taxi in a small building across the alley from the Golden Horn on Mill Street.

Natalie is an interesting lady, to say the least. She will give you a taxi ride at any time of the day or night. A couple of times, like on Fourth of July weekend, I worked late at Guido's. It was too dark to ride my bike home, so I went over to her office and banged on the door loudly. It must have been at least eleven o'clock at night.

"What'd ya want?" I heard from inside the small building.

"Uh, I need a ride home, Miss Gignoux."

Natalie said, "Hang on a minute." She let me into the cramped front room as she lit up a cigarette and made some coffee. While the coffee was brewing, she ran her hands through her hair and said, "Watch the coffee while I get out of my bathrobe." She ambled to the back of the building and I heard her say loudly over her shoulder, "When the coffee's done, pour me a cup."

"Okay," I said. When the last of the coffee dribbled into the carafe, I poured a cup. Natalie came out, grabbed the coffee and her car keys off the counter, and said, "Okay, lets go."

I followed her out of the office, and together we loaded my bicycle into the trunk of her taxi. We started out of town toward our house.

"How're your dad and mom?" she said.

"Fine." We began talking about my family, work, when the snow will come, and all sorts of stuff. Pretty soon we're at the house. We unloaded the bike, I gave her fifty cents for the ride, and she is back off to town. I was happy not to have had to ride my bike all the way home in the dark and cold.

~ ~ ~

Just before Thanksgiving, Bob Gibson gives us a concert at the school auditorium. He sings songs he calls "ballads" and "folk songs." Everyone loves his music. I think it's a new trend. The high school kids talk about getting guitars and learning to sing folk songs. Some of them probably will. We have some excellent musicians at the school. King Fisher, Freddie Fisher's son, plays the trumpet. Of course Freddie Fisher is famous for playing the clarinet. He used to have a popular band called Freddie Fisher's Schnicklefritz Band. Then he lost all of his money when he refused to pay income taxes, and moved to Aspen to live a simpler life. Another good musician is Greg Livingston who plays the clarinet. Bob Gorsuch and some other big kids have guitars and play some of the Kingston Trio songs like "Tom Dooley" and "MTA."

Everything with the big kids is "cool" or "neato" or "hep." They're new words that everyone is beginning to use as much as they used to use swear words. Which reminds me, I don't use swear words in public much anymore because some of the adults have started calling me a "foul-mouthed kid." I've learned that if you are going to swear, you have to do it when adults aren't around to hear you. Unless you are on a working job, that is. Then, if something happens, sometimes it's okay to swear. I hear Guido swear. He says stuff like, "Those goddamned beatniks are nothing but bums. They ought to get rid of the lot of them." Guido doesn't like beatniks. Beatniks is a new name for older kids who sit around, play guitars or bongo drums, drink lots of coffee, and talk about weird stuff they think is important. There aren't many beatniks in Aspen as far as I can see.

In Aspen the older kids talk about cars and girls. They are all about old enough to drive legally. Of course Dirty Herwick, our sheriff, knows most of the kids drive whether they have a license or not, especially all the kids who live on ranches out of town, most of whom have been driving since they could reach the clutch and brake pedals on the floor. When Dirty Herwick catches them, he says, "You better come down to the office and get a license next time you want to drive in town."

"Okay," they say. It usually takes them two or three more times of being stopped before they do.

~ ~ ~

Sandy Sabbatini, Richard's dad, and Bert Bidwell have started a new ski shop called the Mountain Shop. Now there are three sports shops in town if you don't count Briggs Blue Ski Rental. Mr. Briggs doesn't really count because he only rents skis during the winter. He has painted all his skis blue so nobody will steal them. You can't miss them on the mountain. Painting the skis blue is smart because they are easy to see in the snow if you fall and your ski comes off.

Sometimes Gale and John send me over to the other two shops to see if there are a lot of people in them. Gale says, "Hey, Little Horsley, why don't ya head over to the other shops and see how busy they are. I want you to check out the competition."

I take up the secret mission and walk casually around to the two other places and check them out. Gene Mason is always nice to me and treats me really well, even though he knows I won't buy anything. He remembers me and asks me about my kletter shue and the LaFuma pack that is pretty much glued to my back.

Bert Bidwell is another story. He's usually pretty grumpy. I can't tell if that's the way he is, or if he just seems that way because his eyebrows are thick and hang over his eyes. He knows I won't buy anything at his shop because he knows I'm on the ski team. Spook James and Richard buy their ski equipment at the Mountain Shop so Bert and Sandy get some business.

Neither shop is as busy as Aspen Sports, which is good. That way I will always have boots to polish. This year I'm going to help MJ, Bill Marolt, and my brother sweep up the shop.

~ ~ ~

Ruth Whyte quit being a gym teacher and is now running the Aspen Ski Club. Her job is to keep track of all the business stuff about the club. She was a good gym teacher, but I don't think she liked working with some of us kids who were pretty rambunctious. She is nice to me, so I don't sass her. Besides, I think she volunteers her time to take care of the Ski Club.

~ ~ ~

Our family is getting larger. I have two brothers and two sisters. Gerry is 14, Teddy is 12, I'm 10, Jennifer is 6, and Heather is almost 1. Yep. You guessed it. Mom is pregnant again. She is going to have another baby in July. When the new baby is born, I'm not too sure how the sleeping arrangements are going to work out. Right now the three of us older boys sleep upstairs in the boys' room, Jennifer sleeps upstairs in the old room that Gerry used to be in, above the room that she was in when she set the house on fire. Of course, that was re-built. Heather sleeps in the room Jennifer used to sleep in downstairs, the one that was burned and rebuilt. When the new baby is born, I not sure where it will sleep. I guess Mom and Dad will figure it out.

Chapter 40

December 1956

It's Christmas vacation from December 23rd until January 2nd. Teddy and I are working with Jimmy at Guido's. I barely have time to get my coat and hat off when Helen, one of the Swiss girls who works as a waitress, says, "Little boy, run downstairs and get the whipped cream out of the walk-in. I need to refill this small can for desserts." She always calls me "little boy" because she can't remember my name. Helen is stiff, like she has a stick up her butt.

"Okay," I say. I hang my coat on the hooks by the back door, then head for the stairs to the basement.

The bar, kitchen, and restaurant are on the first floor at street level. On the second story are the rooms my dad built for guests to stay in. In the basement there is a walk-in refrigerator, a walk-in freezer, two huge storage closets, and an area where Guido and Trudi make all their breads, salad dressings, whipped cream, and baked goods. The whipped cream is stored in the walk-in refrigerator.

I walk down stairs, open the door to the walk-in, carefully leaving the door open halfway because there is no handle on the inside. As I search for the big bowl of whipped cream, I hear Guido's footsteps running down the stairs and through the basement to one of the storage areas. Out of the corner of my eye, I see him as he passes by saying, "Gotdamn it. I tell those girls a hundred times to keep these refrigerator doors closed."

SLAM! Guido slams the door. I am now locked in the refrigerator. I run to the door and pound on it, yell for Guido to come open the door. It is to no purpose. He has passed by without hearing me. I hear him clomp up the stairs, fortunately forgetting to turn off the light. At least I can see. I know it is only a matter of time before someone comes to the refrigerator to get something, and I hope it's soon.

Time passes, no one has come, and I'm getting cold. I wait, and I wait, and I wait. Still no one comes. I'm now shivering in earnest. I wonder if I can die of exposure or hypothermal or whatever they call it. I look around the refrigerator to see what there is to eat, thinking maybe I can warm up if I eat something. Cherries are the only things that look easy and appealing. I take a handful out of their crate and dip them in the whipped cream. Mmmmm. Pretty good. Having nowhere else to put the pits, I spit them on the grated floor.

More than an hour has gone by, and I am now really, truthfully, fully cold. Not your "I've been out in the snow too long playing around" cold but more the "riding up the lift first thing in the morning when the temperature is 10 below and I can't get into the Sundeck to get warm fast enough" cold. I'm tired of cherries and whipped cream, I'm tired of the walk-in refrigerator, and I'm tired of wondering if anyone is going to come downstairs and open this darned refrigerator door.

Another half-hour passes. This is no longer funny to me. At first I thought it might be a good laugh. You know, a "Guido locked me in the refrigerator so I didn't have to work for half an hour" sort of thing. But this long? I'm cold, and I'm not laughing.

Finally, as near as I can tell, almost two hours have passed, when the door opens and Guido sticks his head in the refrigerator and says, "Where have you been? I need you upstairs."

My teeth are chattering, and I say to him, "Guido, you locked me in here when you ran by and slammed the door!

How the hell am I supposed to get out when there is no latch on the inside to open the door?"

"Mein Got," he says. "Did I do that? That was a couple hours ago." Then he looks at me closer and says, "Boy, you are all purple. Come upstairs, come on, quickly." I can hear him saying under his breath, "Scheissel, Wendy will kill me if I freeze one of his kids to death."

I laugh to myself knowing that I'll survive, but knowing I now have some great leverage to use in any future negotiations with Trudi and Guido.

"Trudi," Guido says, "Get Terry some cocoa. He got locked in the walk-in!"

I notice Guido doesn't say who locked me in. Not wanting to lose my leverage, I say, "Yeah, Guido ran by and slammed the door shut more than two hours ago. I'm freezing."

"Schatzi," Trudi says, "What are you thinking? You know that door has no handle on the inside. You always have to look to see if someone is in there before you close the door." Then she rattles off a bunch of stuff in Swiss-German or Switzer-Dutch or whatever the Swiss speak. I don't understand it, but I get the gist of it and know it translates to something like, "What in hell are you going to say to Wendy, you stupid oaf. He'll be madder than the devil if we send this kid home frozen."

So Trudi sits me down and coddles me with some cocoa and wraps a coat around me.

"You sit here for a few minutes," she says.

I sit next to the dishwasher watching the dishes pile up from lunch, which is now in full swing. Soon I figure it's a better idea to get going on the dishes than sit wrapped in a coat watching them pile up. I take the coat off, get my milk crates situated, and start working. Soon I'm warm again, and I'm making progress on the huge pile of tourists' Christmas vacation dishes.

~~~

I'm getting ready to leave work and go over to the Jerome to catch a ride home with Dad, when Trudi comes up to me and hands me an envelope. She says, "Here's a little something to warm you up. I'm sorry Guido locked you in the walk-in."

I take the envelope and say, "It's okay. I know he didn't do it on purpose. I just got a little cold."

As I get ready to say goodbye to Trudi, Guido walks upstairs from the basement carrying an armful of French bread and says, "Who left all those cherry pits on the floor in the walk-in? Don't you know someone could slip on them?" He is addressing everyone and no one in the kitchen. I pipe up and say, "I did. I got hungry in there after you slammed the door on me." Everyone in the kitchen laughs, and Guido slinks off out to the bar.

"Good night, Trudi," I say.

'Gut night," she says.

Walking over to the Jerome, I peek inside the envelope and see a twenty-dollar bill. I am excited and take it out of the envelope to finger it. I have never made twenty dollars so quickly.

"Not bad pay for two hours in the cooler." I say to myself as I stroll into the Jerome Bar.

~~~

Dad's having a drink with Shorty Pabst and Freidl Pfeifer, to talk about Buttermilk, the new ski area that Freidl wants to build on his land next our old ranch. I hear Shorty say to my dad something about possibly getting the financing for the project arranged through a banker in Wisconsin named Bill Brumdner.

I listen to their conversation and wish my dad had known Shorty when he tried to start Tiehack because we would still have the ranch.

Chapter 41

Winter 1957

With five kids in the house now, Mom finds she sometimes needs help getting things done, so she uses some of the money she earns at Elli's to pay Albina Gerbaz to help her clean the house once a week. When it's a weekend day, Albina usually brings her son, Jimmy Gerbaz, who is two years older than me. We fool around for a couple of hours while Albina does some cleaning.

Today Jimmy is at the house, and we've made a really cool snow fort in the space between our garage and the road out to the barnyard. There is a big red rock, and some pine trees Dad planted when we first had the ranch, which we use as cover. In the fort, we've made a shelf where we can line up snowballs to pelt Teddy and Gerry when they get home later, if Jimmy is still here. If Jimmy leaves, I'll just pelt Gerry and Teddy myself. We're almost finished with the project when Dad comes home early from skiing. He's had a private lesson all morning and wants to get a few things done around the house before another lesson tomorrow.

It's probably about two o'clock when Dad drives up and parks the Jeep in front of the garage. I can see he's in a hurry because he's parked the Jeep facing in toward the garage instead of turning it around so he can push it down hill in the morning if he has to. I say, "Why are you parking that way?"

"Terr-Ass, I have to try to get a few things done before the ski school meeting. The Jeep will still be warm and should start up fine."

"Oh," I say as I make another snowball.

Jimmy and I pat down the sides of the fort to make sure it won't collapse, if it gets hit by a big snowball. We stand back to admire our work.

"This is great," Jimmy says.

"Yeah. It's ready to go. Stocked with snowballs, high enough to kneel down behind the walls, and even shelves for the ammo."

We go on admiring our handiwork; then Jimmy says, "Too bad there's not a heater in here. I'm getting kind of cold."

"Yeah, maybe we could rig something up," I say.

I think about it for a few moments, then say, "I've got an idea. We could get some gasoline, put it in a pan or something, light it on fire, and let it burn like the torches you see in those movies about Roman times. It would just sit there and burn. That would sure heat the place up."

Jimmy looks at me like I'm a genius. "Yeah, that's a great idea. Let's try it!"

"Okay, come with me."

We leave the fort and walk over to the back of the Jeep. I get in and lift out the five-gallon jerry can of gasoline which is about half full. I set the can on the ground next to the Jeep, and head into the garage to find the old steel pot that we used for a dog dish when Wendy and Pan were alive.

After setting the pot down by the gas can, I have Jimmy help me pour some of the gas into the dog dish. Just as we finish, Jimmy's hand slips on the Jerry can, and we dump a whole bunch of gas on the snow. I don't think much of it because it's in the snow, so it probably won't make a difference. I head back into the garage, rummage around for a box of matches, go back outside, and say to Jimmy, "Here, hold these while I put the top back on the gas can."

I hand him the big box of strike-anywhere matches and turn to put the top on the gas can. The next thing I know Jimmy has lit a match and is dropping it into the snow.

WHOOMP! Up goes the gas on the snow. It quickly spreads to the dog dish. Instantly there is a huge ball of flame shooting upward. The surrounding snow and the dog dish are engulfed in flame!

"Damn! Jimmy," I shout. "What are you doing?"

I realize the heat of the fire can blow up the gas can, and the gas can blowing up will probably blow up the Jeep, and the Jeep blowing up will probably burn down the whole garage. Something tells me I can't panic, I mustn't panic. I have to deal with this catastrophe.

"Jimmy!" I shout, "Start throwing snow on the flames. Hurry. I have to move the gas can!"

I charge in behind the flaming dog dish and grab the gas can, pulling it well out of the way. Somehow it doesn't explode in my hands. When I have it far enough away, I scoot back to help Jimmy throw snow on the dog dish before it catches the Jeep on fire. Finally we are able to suffocate the fire. I pick up the dog dish and hear the heat hissing against the wet of the snow on my gloves. When the dog dish is cool enough, I ditch it back in the garage. Jimmy and I throw more snow on the exposed gravel so my dad won't see the burned spot when he goes back to town. I check the Jeep to make sure it didn't get scorched. Not that it would make any difference. The paint is all scratched and chipped off the tailgate, and there're lots of places where there is a nice layer of rust growing. You probably couldn't tell if it were burned or not.

"Whew!" I say to Jimmy, "that was a close call."

Only then do I tell Jimmy my visions of the Jeep blowing up and the garage burning. Jimmy looks at me and doesn't say anything. I see his mind ticking as he processes what I have said. Finally he says, "Yeah, that would have been a hell of a mess. I'll bet your dad would have been mad if we had burned down the garage."

~ ~ ~

A few weeks later Fred Henry and I are skiing on Aspen Mountain. Just the two of us. We've been tearing up the trails at the top of the mountain all morning, skiing all the runs from One and Two Leaf all the way over to and Buckhorn and North American. We've been skiing on Lift #3, which they put in just above Spar Gulch in 1953. It is a double chair and faster than Lift #1 and Lift #2. It's the end of the day, and we have just finished skiing down Spar Gulch and around the catwalk above Niagara.

"Shall we go all the way down Little Nell?" Fred asks.

"No, let's go down Schuss Gully, and we can jump off the roads then cut back to Little Nell to the bottom."

We ski down to the top of Schuss Gully, the trail that takes you from Little Nell over to the slalom hill, where we run gates after school. The plan is to ski about halfway down Schuss Gully, jumping a couple of the summer road switchbacks. Then we'll cut back to Little Nell to the bottom. We're stopped on the top of Schuss Gully.

"You go first on the upper road and I'll go first on the lower one," I say to Fred.

"Okay." He pushes off and skis down to the summer road. He jumps, takes air, and lands about thirty feet down the hill where he stops and waits for me. I take off, get some good air, and land with a loud "thwack" as my skis hit the snow.

We ski down to just above the next road and stop.

"Okay, your turn to go first," Fred says.

I nod and push off, picking up speed as I head straight for the road. When I hit it, I instantly know I'm in trouble. I didn't see the ridge on the downhill side and am thrown high in the air. As I look down, I realize I hit the road way too fast and I'm going to land in the flats. No man's land. I hang in the air a few seconds before gravity makes its inevitable pull. I come down, hitting hard on the flats with a loud crack. I'm dazed, not knowing if I'm dead or alive, but knowing my right leg is broken. I hear Fred shouting, "Wow, did you get air on that one!"

Fred skis down to me, tries to stop, but loses control and plows into my legs. Pain shoots through my right leg, and now I know if it wasn't broken before, it sure is now.

I look at him and howl, "You idiot! Don't you know how to stop?"

"Sorry," he says.

"Sorry, my butt. You broke my leg."

"Sure," Fred says. "Fat chance of that. I didn't hit you that hard."

"It really is broken," I say. I'm in real pain now. "You have to go down and get the ski patrol. I can't ski down."

"If I do that," Fred says, "who's gonna watch to make sure no one else hits you?"

A good thought. I'm not thinking too clearly.

"I guess I'll just have to chance it.'" I say. "Go now, because the lifts will be closing in a few minutes."

Fred skis off. I'm alone on the slope with the sun behind Shadow Mountain and my breath turning to fog. My leg throbs something fierce. Each heartbeat brings along with it an electrical surge of pain. Minutes turn to hours. I wonder if Fred is too late to catch the patrol. Will I have to spend half the night here while he searches for someone to drag me off the slope? What if another skier comes off the road and piles into me? Sunlight turns to dusk. I'm cold and frightened by the thought of having to stay on the freezing snow much longer.

When the ski patrol finally comes I am freezing half to death. They load me in a meat sled and take me to the bottom where I'm loaded into our ambulance, an old converted Chevy station wagon. Up to the hospital I go.

I haven't been to see the doctor for anything serious since I drank that ink four years ago. Well, there was that other time....actually lots of times. Sure, I've had to see the doctor to get stitched up a few times and some knocks on the head and stuff, but nothing serious or interesting enough to have a hospital visit.

Doc Lewis is no longer in town, and Dr. Houston is our doctor. He fixes me up with a cast and some crutches, and I'm out the door an hour later with my mom who has come down to pick me up. I can now count myself in the group of eight other people in our school who have broken their legs this year, including my brother Gerry, my friend Tony Vagneur, Don Neal Stapleton, Fleeta Rowland and others. On the way home, my mom, who is starting to grow the next baby only says, "Gads, what am I going to do with you Terry?"

Chapter 42

Spring 1957

It's spring, the snow has melted, and my broken leg has healed. When it warms up more, I'll be able to ride my bike to school without freezing my butt off. I do try to ride on the warm days. The handlebars and brakes are back in their correct position, so I'm not tempted to use my kletter shoes for braking.

At the moment I'm walking up our road after getting off the bus. I'm thinking about lots of random things as I walk. I am wondering why fads come and go so quickly. For example, the beatnik fad has already been replaced by the hot rod fad. Now the high school kids talk about cars, hoodlums, and movies they think are cool, like "The Asphalt Jungle." Regular old haircuts have been replaced by the latest fad haircuts I think are pretty stupid. One is called a flat top. It makes you look like your head is shaped like a coffee can or a jar. Then there is another one called a "duck tail." This requires long hair and a lot of grease. They slick the hair to the back of the head so it looks like the ass end of a duck. Or for a while it was a big fad to go to the Rexall Drugstore and buy a small bottle of cinnamon oil which you would put toothpicks in. Then, after the toothpicks have been in the cinnamon for a couple of days, you take one out and suck on it like you have a toothpick in your mouth, except it is full of cinnamon.

As I walk, I realize I'm not interested in cars or any of the new fad stuff that Gerry's and some of Teddy's friends are always talking about. I'm more interested in ski team, fly fishing, tying flies, bicycling, and those sorts of things. It seems like I'm interested in different things than my friends, so I spend more time goofing off by myself than I do with the other kids. Of course, living out of town has something to do with that.

School is generally boring, although I did have fun doing a project on Yellowstone National Park for Miss Goodrich, who replaced Mrs. Houston when she left to have her baby. To add to the boredom, Miss Goodrich has made us all turn our desks so our backs are to the windows. She thinks too many of us get distracted and don't listen well because we are always looking out the windows. Even though this could be true, I would prefer to look out the window. I miss Mrs. Houston. She made school much more interesting with all the little problems she challenged me with. I still haven't figured out the last one.

Soon it will be summer, and I'll be back working at Guido's.

Chapter 43

Summer 1957

Mom had another baby on July 3rd! They named him Christopher, and they call him Toby. I can never figure out why Mom and Dad give us two names. Teddy is really Edward. My real name is Dexter, and they call me Terry. The girls all have only one name, but the boys mostly are named one thing and called another. Toby is a cute little thing and doesn't cry too much. I'm sure it'll only be a little while before we will be feeding him Gerber's baby foods when we are babysitting him. Now we just have to feed him his bottle of formula. All he does is eat, sleep, pee, and poop. We babysit quite a bit because Mom and Dad have become more social without the ranch to worry about. They like to get away from "this mad house."

Toby sleeps downstairs in the bedroom next to Mom and Dad's, and Heather has moved upstairs where she sleeps in Jennifer's room. Now there are five of us upstairs, two in "Jennifer's room" and three in "the boys' room."

~ ~ ~

Today I arrive at work to see Guido talking to an old man with a long, white beard. The man wants to buy a loaf of Guido's bread. I've seen him around town but don't think he's from around here. I'm afraid Guido will call him a bum and kick him out of the restaurant. I move closer so I can hear what they are saying.

"…and I came over the pass from Leadville the other day when it snowed. It was colder 'en hell," the old man was saying. "Must've been six inches of snow on the pass. Don't know how my car made it over with the tires bald as they are, but I know some tricks yet."

"How long are you in town?" Guido asks.

"Only passing through today. Have to go out to Ely for the funeral…Sell me one of those loaves of that French bread that you make. I love that stuff."

"What about your brother? What was his name? Darrell?" Guido ignores the request for the bread.

"Oh, he's long dead. Died over there near Idaho Springs fooling around with the claim he had over there. Cave in and a timber stove his head in. That was some time ago. Surprised you never heard about it."

"Sorry to hear that," Guido says as he gets a couple of loaves of bread from the counter where the waitresses cut them up for the dining room. He hands the loaves to the old man who now has taken his hand out of his pocket.

"How much?" he says.

"Nothing. Here you take this." Guido hands him the loaves. I look at the old man and notice he has a large roll of money in his hand. I don't know how much it is, but it is really a lot of money. He stuffs it back in his jacket pocket and puts the loaves under his arm. He shakes Guido's hand and says, "Thanks. I'll see you next time I'm through."

Guido nods, and the old man walks out the door.

"Who was that?" I ask Guido.

"Just an old friend," he replies.

~ ~ ~

A few days later Guido says, "Come with me. I need to show you how to make Roquefort dressing. None of the girls make it right."

In the basement, Guido shows me how to turn on the big mixing machine and the attachment that grinds the big blocks of cheese. He unwraps a block and drops it into a flat pan attachment above the grinder.

"You take a mangle and push down on the cheese to get it through. Sometimes the cream backs up into the tray and ends up here on top," Guido says.

"If the cream backs up, you have to be careful when you push the cheese through so you don't splash the whole mess everywhere." He continues, "Start with this, and make two batches. We'll be busy tonight and need it all."

I think for a moment Guido is giving me a raise of sorts by elevating me, giving me the responsibility of making salad dressings. First salad dressings, then sous chef. I'm on my way up.

I'm on my second batch and half way through adding blue cheese to the concoction, when Guido comes down to see how I am faring.

"How's it going down here?" Guido asks.

"Great," I say as I push down on the mangle.

I look over at Guido and see that he is all dressed up. He has on a wine red velour shirt and khaki pants.

"Are you going somewhere?" I ask, knowing he is, because he doesn't have on his usual blue shirt covered by a full-length apron.

"Going to a Chamber meeting. I'll be back in about an hour or so. When you finish this, you go up and do the pots and pans. Jimmy can't come in until four o'clock. He has to see the doctor."

"Okay," I say.

I don't notice that the cream has backed up in the grinder, and there is a messy puddle of cream, cheese, and seasonings now swirling around in the grinder pan. Further, I don't notice Guido leaning over to see how much I have left to do before I give a mighty push on the mangle. The smelly concoction squirts up and lands in puddles on Guido's face, shirt, and chinos. He sputters as the dressing dribbles off his chin. I know I'm fired. I bite my tongue and turn my head away so he can't see I'm busting up with laughter.

Guido swears, "Damn it! I told you to be careful with that!"

He must have shouted louder than we both thought because the upstairs went immediately quiet. No clanging of dishes, no background conversation.

"What's happened down there?" Trudi shouts down the stairs as she comes running. Guido turns around about the same time Trudi hits the bottom stair landing. She looks at him, the blue cheese dressing dribbling down his face, shirt, and pants, and bursts into laughter. I am relieved because I can start laughing, too, which I immediately do.

"You should see yourself!" Trudi says through her hysterics.

Guido grumbles something in Swiss and walks by her and up the stairs.

Trudi watches him go and says, "I really shouldn't laugh, but he looks so funny!"

I nod, still laughing, as she continues, "You finish here, then get the pots and pans done. He'll be fine after his meeting."

Just before it is quitting time, Guido walks by me and says, "The dressing tastes pretty good."

~ ~ ~

There is a big vacant lot close to Guido's Restaurant where a carnival has set up. I've never been to a carnival, so after work one day, I go over to see what it is all about. It is confusing. The amusement rides are clanging, banging, and squeaking. Men and women are shouting, "Step right up! Step right up!" hoping to get you to throw darts at balloons or hoops over bunny rabbits or to play some other game of chance. I wander around and watch people pay a quarter only to lose, and pay another quarter, to lose again.

Finally I stop my wandering, settle down, and watch some big men whom I have never seen before throwing baseballs at small wooden milk bottles that are stacked in pyramids of three, on several wooden stools. The men throw three baseballs trying to knock all the bottles down. Some of them hit, and some miss. However, the ones that hit only seem to be able to knock the top bottle, and maybe one or two of the bottles below, off the stool.

As this happens time and time again, it occurs to me maybe the bottles are glued or nailed together and to the stool so they won't fall over no matter how many times they're hit.

I walk over to the man running the show, who has a name tag on his vest that says Brad or Brent or something like that. He's taking money from this one guy, who is pretty tall and somewhat fat. I say, "Mister, I've been watching this game, and the bottles on the left side of the stool must be glued together and to the stool somehow, because they aren't falling off when they should be."

"Get lost, kid," the man says.

"No, I've been watching it."

The men are gathering around listening to me mouthing off to Brad or Brent. Some of them are laughing, and some are watching to see what will happen.

"Go on, get! You little punk."

I start to give in and walk away, but before I do, I give him my last shot, "This is a cheat. The game is rigged. That guy couldn't knock the bottles off no matter what because they're glued or nailed together."

"Get out of here," Brad-Brent growls.

But the game is over. Now all the men are milling around trying to figure out if the game is rigged or not. Finally one of them says, "If they're not glued down, let's see you knock them all off."

Brad-Brent glares at him and says, "Yeah, you think I'm gonna do that for you? And have to set them all up again so this lunk head can just throw a few balls and miss them again? No way."

"That proves it," the guy says. "This game is rigged."

So Brad-Brent goes over to a stool at the edge of the booth that no one hardly throws a ball at and knocks the bottles off. They all fall off the stool.

"There, are you satisfied?" Brad-Brent spits back.

The men stand around thinking about it and decide maybe the game isn't rigged. But I've been watching it, so I say to Brad-Brent, "Yeah, well, I still think it's rigged."

I'm about to walk off, when the big guy who has been playing says, "Well, at least let me throw my baseballs."

Brad-Brent steps back, and the guy winds up and hurls the first ball with all his might. It hits smack in the middle row on the left side of the stack. All the loose bottles fall off the stool, but two on the bottom row don't. The one stacked on top is broken in half, and half of it is hanging from one of the bottles beneath it.

"See," I say, "I told you it was rigged. They are glued together or nailed down.'

"This booth is closed" Brad-Brent says. He pulls down a canvas over the front of the booth and tells us, "Go away. The booth is closed."

He walks off behind the booth quickly. The guy shouts after him, "I want my money back!"

Brad-Brent keeps walking. The men begin to wander off talking about what a cheat the place is and how they aren't coming back any more. I admit to myself that the carnival is a big disappointment, and I certainly won't go back.

Two days later the carnival leaves town, and the event is forgotten. I wonder why people would try to cheat others that way.

~ ~ ~

I'm at the library looking for something to read. I've finished all the Hardy Boys books, at least until Frank W. Dixon comes out with another. Mrs. Braun is checking in some books as I walk up to her desk.

"Do you have any new adventure or mystery books?" I ask.

She looks up at me over her glasses and says, "No, nothing that would interest you, I think."

My eyes wander down at the books on her desk. On the top of the pile is a book showing the formula on the cover jacket, $E=MC^2$. There it is right in front of me! The formula that Mrs. Houston gave me last winter before she left, the puzzle I forgot about and didn't solve.

"I'll take this book if I can," I say to Mrs. Braun.

"Well, that is a pretty difficult book," she responds. "You may want to try something different."

"Who wrote it?" I ask.

"It was written by a man named Albert Einstein. He is a famous physicist."

"I'd like to check it out if I may."

Mrs. Braun carefully stamped the due date in the inside cover and handed me the book.

"Good luck."

Her words followed me as I joyfully walked out the door. I only wish I knew how I could tell Mrs. Houston that I had finally solved her last riddle.

Chapter 44

Fall 1957

Mrs. Frost, my new sixth grade teacher, is walking back, forth, and up and down the aisles while she tells us how things are going to be in her classroom this school year. She is notoriously the hardest teacher in school and doesn't put up with horseplay in her classroom. While she is talking, I begin to fool around with someone who is sitting next to me, not paying attention to what Mrs. Frost is saying. Her voice drones on until…in the next instant, I feel like all the hair on my head is being pulled out by the roots. Some Indian warrior is trying to remove my topknot. Pain screams through me. My head jerks back, and I'm looking up into the face of Mrs. Frost who has crept up from behind and ambushed me.

She looks down and says, "Okay, Mr. Morse. Your reputation precedes you. I know you are a troublemaker, and I have some very bad news for you. You will NOT act up in my classroom. You will NOT talk out of turn and you WILL get straight A's every grading period or you WILL have me to deal with in a way that will be your WORST nightmare. Do we understand each other?"

I look up at her, horrified. No teacher has dared lay a hand on me that way. Sure I have been whipped a lick or two in second grade by Mr. Gann, but that was different. That was just for show. This is serious business. I'm actually frightened.

"Yes," I say.

"Yes, what?" she says, glaring at me.

"Yes, ma'am," I say.

"My name is Mrs. Frost."

"Yes, Mrs. Frost"

There is absolute silence in the classroom. Every pupil in the class is looking at us, surveying the carnage. In less than two minutes into the new school year I have been laid to waste.

"Now you sit up straight and pay attention. Tomorrow I want to see you come in here with clean fingernails. Your hands are a mess."

"Well, that's because…" I begin, hoping to tell her that I was always working on my bike and other stuff, and it was almost impossible to keep my nails clean except in the summer when I am washing dishes all day.

"I don't want to hear it!" she breaks in. "Just have clean nails when you come into my classroom tomorrow."

"Yes, Mrs. Frost."

I can see right away that things have shifted once again in my world.

Oh well, I think, *it could be worse.*

Although, in the moment I can't think of how.

~ ~ ~

Robert Rubey is a new student in our classroom. He's very smart. In fact he is so smart, he probably knows as much or more than most of the teachers in the school. Robert and I have become good friends and are interested in a bunch of stuff. Robert knows how to do many things but sometimes isn't too practical about putting different things together. This is where I come in. I'm curious. If I come up with some knucklehead idea for us to do, Robert usually knows how to put together most of the parts separately from each other, but not how to put them all together to make something monumental happen.

Today we are at his house, which, by the way, is the same house that the Groves lived in when we had the fire in our house at the ranch back in 1953. Robert's dad, Bill Rubey, and his mom, Marion Rubey, bought the house from the Groves when they left Aspen. We're in Robert's room on the second floor of the house. It's a small room on the south side of the house with a window over his bed on the west wall. The window overlooks a small patch of weeds between his house and the neighbors. The room is crammed with electronics, magazines, books, tools, and various other mad scientist kinds of things. There is a shortwave radio, a record player with gigantic speakers, an oscilloscope, an amplifier, and a chemistry set.

Robert and I are fooling around with the oscilloscope. Robert explains to me it is used for troubleshooting problems with electronic equipment. Then he goes into an explanation that I don't fully understand because some of the electronic terminology is new to me. I've never seen an oscilloscope before today. Robert explains the theory behind the machine as we hook it up to his radio and turn it on. The screen gives off a green, glowing wave. Robert makes some adjustments to stabilize the wave, then turns on the radio. It takes me a moment to understand that the oscilloscope is really useful if you are fixing lots of electronic equipment. It's interesting but not too useful to me.

We move from that to another subject that comes up as I spot one of his books about chemistry experiments for kids.

"Let's do some experiments," I say to Robert, picking up the book and thumbing through it.

He looks at me like there is something on his mind.

He says, "The stuff in that book is really boring, like making a vacuum in a milk bottle by lighting a piece of newspaper on fire and sucking a boiled egg into the bottle. Dumb stuff like that. But there is one thing I have been wanting to try but just haven't done yet."

"What's that?" I ask.

"I want to make gunpowder."

"Wow!" I'm excited now. "How're we gonna do that?"

"If you mix charcoal, sulfur, and saltpeter together in just the right proportions, it's gunpowder."

"Hey, that sounds great!" I say. "Lets try it! We could make some great bombs!"

"I've never done it, so I'm not sure it really works. I've only read about it."

"Okay, we've gotta try this!" I say.

In the next few moments, we are on our way to Tompkins Hardware to buy sulfur and charcoal. We then stop at the Rexall Drugstore to buy saltpeter. We collect the items and head back to Robert's room, our new chemistry lab. Robert opens the charcoal, and I open the bags of sulfur and saltpeter. Already we are smelling up the house.

"I wonder how much of each we should use in the mixture?" I say to Robert.

"I have no idea, I just read about the chemicals."

"Well, let's start with equal parts. We've gotta get something to mix it in and something to grind up the charcoal with," I say, looking around Robert's room for some good things to mix the chemicals in.

Robert says, "Just a minute."

He disappears, and in a few minutes comes back with a cocktail mixer thing-a-ma-jig, a pan, and a smaller pan that looks like an angel food cake pan. Robert shows me the bigger pan and the cocktail mixer thing-a-ma-jig and says, "We can use this cocktail muddler and pan to mix it all together in."

"Where did you get this pan?" I ask him, pointing to the smaller pan. "It looks like an angel food cake baking pan like my mom uses."

"It came from my sister's doll cooking set. It should work fine."

Robert puts some charcoal in the larger pan and starts crushing it up. He crushes it real fine and soon has quite a pile of it. We dump it into the smaller pan. I carefully measure out equal parts of sulfur and saltpeter, then put them into the small baking pan with the charcoal. We have about a quarter of a teaspoon each of my ingredients in the small pan, and Robert dumps in a bunch more charcoal.

"How much did you put in?" I ask.

"I don't know, probably about three tablespoons. You need more charcoal than sulfur or saltpeter," Robert says.

"Why?"

"I don't know," he says. "Mostly because I ground it all up, and it's already in the pan."

This sounds logical to me, so I say, "We need to keep track of what we are doing, otherwise we will never know how to make it next time. Do you have a pencil and paper so we can write down what we do?"

"No problem for such a great science experiment," Robert says. He rummages around his room and finds a pad and pencil.

"Now what?"

"We should test a little of it and see if it sparks, I guess," says Robert.

Robert has a small pocketknife he has been using to strip wire with next to his radio. I pick it up and carefully put some of the gunpowder on the blade. Meanwhile, Robert finds some matches and lights one. I pass the blade through the flame, and the powder ignites, but weakly.

"We've gotta make this more powerful," I say. "Should we try more charcoal or saltpeter or both?"

"Let's try sulfur first. If that doesn't work, we'll add more saltpeter. We have a ton of charcoal here. Maybe it's too much. I don't think we should put any more of that in."

We fool around with the mixture for about half an hour until we think we have it just about exactly right. Now the powder is flashing quickly, and the flame has white on top and a blue base.

"Okay," I say. "One last run. Let's add just a bit more sulfur and a hint of charcoal, and I'll bet we have it!"

Like two mad scientists, we add the final touches to the concoction. When we are all set for the last run, I put some powder on the knife blade. I am so excited that I forget I'm still holding the cake pan full of powder rather than setting it on the shelf away from the test. Just as I remember to set the pan aside, Robert runs the flame underneath the knife blade and WOOSH!

The small mound of powder flashes upward, sending a burning spark down into the cake pan I'm holding in my hand. Suddenly there is a huge flash of white light as the whole pan erupts in flame. It is burning in my hand, and I say urgently to Robert, "What shall I do with it?"

"Geez I don't know. Throw it on the bed. It's going to burn your fingers off."

It's already burning me, so it doesn't take much persuading for me to drop the flaming pan on the bed.

"Whoa!" I say, almost screaming. "Now what? We're gonna burn the house down!"

Robert looks at me confused because I am looking at him just as confused. Then both of us grab the bedspread and blankets from the bed and wrap the whole mess up to suffocate the fire. By now the gunpowder has spent its energy, and the flames and heat are transferred to the blankets and bedspread, making it easier for us to extinguish.

Robert quickly opens the window to let the smoke out so it doesn't go throughout the whole house. We then throw the whole mess out the window, run downstairs, out behind the house, and stamp the remaining flames and heat out of the now-worthless blanket and bedspread.

"I guess the gunpowder works," says Robert.

We both burst out laughing, both from the comment and the relief that we haven't burned his house down. After a few minutes we stretch out the bedding to survey the damage, which is formidable.

"Looks like you won't be using these again anytime soon," I say.

"Hmmm, no, I don't think so."

"What're we going to do with this mess?" I wonder.

"Well, we could take it back upstairs and put it on the bed and see if anyone notices it," Robert says.

"Good idea. I'm sure you want to sleep with these huge holes and the smell of smoke for the rest of your life!"

"Well, it was just a thought," he says.

We take the bedding back upstairs trying to figure out how to get rid of the evidence.

I look around the room, and my eyes land on the speaker boxes in the corner. Robert and I have come to the same conclusion in an instant without saying a word. I go over to one of the speakers and tilt it forward to see how the back is fastened on.

"We'll need a Phillips screwdriver," I say.

Robert hands me one from his tool kit. Fifteen minutes later we have the offending bedding stowed in the two speaker cabinets, and the backs securely in place. The smell of smoke is still in the air but is tolerable.

"I wonder if the speakers will still work?" I say to Robert.

"Let's see," he says.

He turns on the radio and turns up the volume enough so we can hear that they are working at least well enough to have pretty good sound coming through.

"I guess they can stay there for the time being," Robert says.

Chapter 45

December 1957

School gets out for the Christmas holidays tomorrow. We have a new source of amusement which someone, I don't know who, has come up with. We call it "skitching." I don't have ski team today, and decide to ignore my parents' instructions to take the bus home after school, when Spook says, "Hey, let's go skitching".

"What's that?"

"Come on," he says, "I'll show you."

We walk toward Main Street to get a couple of blocks away from school. There are very few stop signs on the streets of Aspen. Those that exist control traffic turning onto or crossing Main Street. The rest of the streets don't have any signs at the intersections. People bust on through them without stopping unless another car is coming from the side street. Then the one who is the closest to the intersection has the right of way. We had a good early snow over Thanksgiving and have had one or two storms since, so the streets are snowpacked and slick.

When we reach Main Street, Spook says, "Okay, when the next car slows down for the stop sign, we'll run up behind, grab the back bumper, crouch down with our heels on our butts, and slide along behind the car. It's a great way to get around town."

We wait on Garmish Street or maybe it's Aspen Street. Presently a car pulls up to the stop sign. Spook and I run over to the back bumper all hunched down so the driver won't see us in his mirror, and grab onto the back bumper. The car takes off across Main Street up toward Aspen Mountain, and we slide on our feet with our butts on our heels going what feels like fifty miles an hour. We are laughing and shouting as the car turns onto another street and heads towards Independence. After six or seven blocks, the car slows down like it is going to park, so Spook and I drop off, slide a little further, then stand up, and walk off. We're laughing and joking about the fun and how fast we were going.

We walk around town looking at people and into windows until we end up in front of Tomkins Hardware. Spook says, "Hey, you gotta see this! They just got this in the window yesterday, and it's the latest thing. I've never seen it before but I heard some of the kids in the high school saying that they just HAD to see the box in Tomkins Hardware window."

We step over to the window and look in. There sitting on a stand is a box with glass on the front and what looks like snow flakes covering the faces of people who are talking and moving on the glass.

"Holy moly," I say. "What is that?"

Spook says, "It's called TV. That's short for television."

"Whoa," I say, "that's cool."

We stare in the window for a long time watching the people and the snow. I feel like I should know what the box is for, but I don't. I ask Spook, "What's it for?"

"I don't know. I guess you can watch it, and they tell you the news. Then there are like short movies that are supposed to make you laugh."

"Yeah," I continue on with the idea. "It looks like a miniature movie. I'll have to ask Robert if he knows about TV. I'll bet he does and just hasn't told me about it. He knows a bunch about electronics, and this looks like an electronic."

We watch some more, and finally Spook says, "I've gotta get home. I was supposed to go home right after school and help my mom with something, but it looks like I might have just missed that."

Suddenly I realize that I might miss my dad at the ski school meeting because Spook and I have been farting around so long. I watch Spook run after a car, grab on and skitch back toward the direction we came. I run down the street, turn the corner by the Rexall Drugstore, run past Louis', past Tideman's, turn right by Beck and Bishops, and run down Mill Street to the Jerome. I catch my dad just as he is heading toward the Jeep.

~ ~ ~

It's New Year's Eve, and Teddy and I are washing dishes at Guido's. The restaurant has been busy since breakfast. Guido needs us tonight because the night dishwasher didn't show up when our shift was done. Guido asks us, "Can you work tonight? I'll pay you extra. That bum didn't show up for work." Guido calls anyone who is irresponsible a "bum."

"All right," we say, "but we've gotta call our mom to make sure it's okay." Teddy goes off to the bar and calls home. Mom and Dad are going to a New Year's Party, and Mom says, "How will you get home? We'll be late and won't be able to pick you up. How late are you working?"

"Just a minute."

Teddy puts down the phone and comes back to the kitchen and says to Guido, "How long are we going to work? How can we get home?"

"Maybe you can work until nine," Guido says, "then, if you can't get a taxi from Natalie, I'll take you home."

Teddy goes back to the phone and gets parental clearance, and we go back to work. Guido is right when he says he needs us. The dishes are piling up faster than we can send them through the machine. Teddy's loading, and I am unloading. I put the dishes on the shelves separating the stoves and the sous chef counter in between drying and storing the silverware. As soon as we catch up, he then sends more through the machine. We have no breaks and are sweating from the work and the heat in the kitchen.

Trudi walks by and looks at us. "You're sweating. I'll get you something to drink." She hustles out to the bar and returns with two Cokes.

"Thanks," we say in unison.

As the night wears on, Trudi comes once more with Cokes, and shortly thereafter Guido walks by and says, "You like glog?"

He's looking at Teddy, so I don't reply. Teddy says, "Sure."

I can tell he has no idea what "glog" is. Guido leaves for the bar and returns with two cups of glog.

"Careful, it's pretty hot."

He walks off to the bar and continues doing whatever it is that he is doing. We take a sip of the glog and realize it is hot spiced wine suitable for the Christmas season. I don't much like it. Teddy is relishing his cup. We return to the dishes. What seems likes half a minute but is really half an hour or more goes by, and we are hard at the dishes, silverware and glasses. If we get a short break, we help Jimmy with the pots and pans.

Teddy says, "Did you finish your glog?"

"No, I don't much like it."

"Can I have it?" he says as he takes a big gulp from my cup. "I like it."

Not long after, Guido returns to the kitchen and makes the rounds. He checks the chef's cooking, the sous chef area where Helen is cutting up some French bread, and comes over to us. He notices that our cups are empty and says, "You want some more?"

Teddy says, "Yes, that stuff is really good."

"It's Trudi's special recipe," Guido says as he walks back to the bar with the empty cups. He returns quickly with two more and sets them on the counter where we're working. "This should get you through the evening."

Teddy blows on his cup and sips it gingerly.

"Wow, this stuff is good," he says.

I take a small sip from my cup to reconfirm that I don't like it enough to drink it no matter how good it will make me feel.

It's late when we manage to finish the last of the dishes. Teddy's looking and acting real happy. The glog has put him in the Christmas spirit.

Guido comes into the kitchen and says, "You guys can go home now, it's late. I have to take you because Natalie is off somewhere with the taxi and doesn't answer the phone."

Teddy's weaving back and forth trying to stay standing straight. He's drunk as a waltzing piss ant. He looks at Guido with a big grin on his face and says, "Thatss probaly good."

We head outside, Guido taking Teddy's arm to steady him now that he realizes Teddy is three sheets to the wind. I walk on his other side just in case his list throws him too far away from Guido's grasp. We pile him in Guido's Jeep and head out to the ranch. Guido isn't saying much because the wind rushing through the front of the Jeep is noisy, and he is thinking. I can tell he is wondering what Dad will say when he brings Teddy home drunk. Dad doesn't get mad easily, but when he does, you don't want to be within twenty miles of him. Dad won't be mad at Guido because he has a drink or two every evening, and besides, Teddy is thirteen and it's probably about time for him to get drunk.

When we arrive home, Guido seems relieved because Mom and Dad aren't there. Guido stops the Jeep and goes around the side to help Teddy out. He says, "You can get him inside?"

"I think so," I say, not knowing how I'll lift him out of the snow bank if he falls down. Guido hops back in the Jeep, turns it around, and takes off. I can tell he wants to get down the road and onto the highway before he passes my parents if they are on their way home.

Teddy and I are standing in the driveway. He's singing and weaving back and forth and slurring his song so it's hard to recognize. I point him toward the walkway and say, "Come on, this way. We've gotta get inside before we freeze our butts off."

Somehow I'm able to get him into the house and upstairs. He falls on his bed, still singing and mumbling. I take his boots off but don't bother trying to help him with his clothes. He is already gone to the world.

The next morning Teddy appears sometime after breakfast. Dad has already wormed the whole story out of me, so when he sees Teddy, he says, "Rough night at work last night?"

Teddy only mumbles something to the affirmative and stumbles into the kitchen to see if there is anything that will help cure the Guido flu.

Several days later I'm with Dad when he sees Guido on the street. He stops the Jeep next to Guido and says, "You could have at least taken him inside and put him to bed." Guido has a sheepish look on his face and replies, "I do that next time."

They both laugh; Dad shoves the gearshift forward, and we take off for home.

Chapter 46

Winter 1958

I don't have ski team today. It's Sunday. I've been fooling around outside and head into the garage to see if I can amuse myself there. I see the vacuum cleaner in the garage, where it shouldn't be. It should be in the house where it belongs. Gerry must have dragged it out here to clean up his mess.

I look at the vacuum cleaner and get this great idea. Since I'm now interested in electronics, I should explore how vacuum cleaners work. I gather up some tools and begin taking the vacuum apart. No, it wasn't plugged in. I'm not that stupid. Remember I learned all about that when I cut the cord on the lamp.

It takes me a good while to get the thing apart. There are hundreds of screws and bolts in the machine. It takes more than an hour to get it completely torn down to the essentials: a motor, a fan, a container, and a bunch of accessory parts that go here and there to make the thing complete. It's noon by the time I finish. I've been careful to put all the pieces in specific piles so I can remember where they go and in what order they must be replaced.

I head into the house to grab a sandwich. Yep. Still peanut butter and jam (I like strawberry jam best now), but not on Wonder Bread. Mom's read somewhere that wheat bread is much more healthy, so now its wheat bread. It took awhile to get used to it. I finish wolfing down my sandwich and gulping my milk and head back out to the garage.

When I arrive at the site of my great electronic investigation, Dirty Peter Morse is lying half in and half out of the parts. I wake him and shoo him away. In the process, he mixes parts, screws, nuts and bolts around like a Mix Master. I shout at him, and he runs out of the garage. Looking at the mess, I wonder if I can get the parts back in their respective piles, and think *this is going to be a pain in the butt*, I get down on my hands and knees and go to work. It takes me a long time to straighten things out as nearly as I can remember them.

Once the parts are sorted, I take time to figure out how the machine works. Let's see. The motor drives the fan that sucks the air and dirt into the cylinder where the bag is, the dirt goes into the bag, and the air is filtered out the exit port. Pretty simple.

I begin to put the contraption back together and find it takes me longer to get it re-assembled because I have to find homes for many of the screws and bolts by trial and error. Finally, when I am finished, I plug it in, turn it on, and test it out. It seems to work all right. I suck up a few small piles of sawdust and some screws and bolts.

Oops, I think, *I wonder if those go to the vacuum.* Just about that time, I see a part on the floor that looks like a flywheel. It's round, shiny, and is the right size to fit into the vacuum cylinder. I shut the machine off and take a good look at the part to make sure it's a vacuum part and not something Dad or Gerry are working with. Nope. Definitely vacuum. I set it down and turn the vacuum on again. It seems to work just fine. I decide the part must be some extra gimmick built in the machine so they can charge more money for it. If the vacuum works without the part, then it must not be necessary. I suck up one or two more screws, turn the machine off, and chuck the round part in the trash.

That was fun. Time will tell if the part is critical. I'll just have to keep an eye on things to see if the vacuum keeps working, I think.

~ ~ ~

I've watched the machine carefully from the day I took it apart early in the winter, and it still seems to be working. It has developed a little squeak when it shuts down but still sucks up the dust just fine.

My latest electronic experiment is building a radio. Just after I got the vacuum cleaner back together I purchased a subscription to *Popular Mechanics*. There I saw an ad for a company called Heathkit. Heathkit sells radio kits, parts, and many things an electronics buff needs. I sent for a catalogue thinking it would be interesting to buy one of their radio kits and build my own radio.

Not long after I received the catalog, I ordered a clock radio. It was expensive but didn't break my bank account that was growing from all the summer work and extra time at Guido's. I was excited and looking forward to the day the radio kit showed up at the post office. Every day at noon I'd leave school and run up Galena Street to the post office located in the Elks Building. I had to hustle to get to the post office, check the mail, run back, and eat my lunch before school started for the afternoon.

Today Mr. Ware, our postmaster, says to me, "What are you looking for, Morse? You expecting a bag of money?"

"No, I'm expecting to get my radio kit. I'm gonna build a radio from all the parts," I say.

"That sounds like a big project," Mr. Ware says. "I hope it gets here soon, but sorry, not today."

I go back to school disappointed but looking forward to my trip to the post office tomorrow, when I'm sure the radio will arrive.

~ ~ ~

For the past two weeks I've been sitting at my desk soldering capacitors and transistors, working with circuit boards, and fitting cathode ray tubes. Tonight I hope to complete the radio. I'm finishing the last touches and will soon fire it up.

It has been a fun, interesting project. I've had to learn to read the electrical blueprints, figure out all the parts' names and their purpose, and where they go in the radio. Now it's late at night. Gerry and Teddy are asleep, so I'm quiet, trying not to bang around too much so as not to wake them. I feel like the mad professor with my desk light on, huddled over my creation, parts and tools lying around, and an extension cord just waiting to send one 110 volts of electricity racing through my newest invention.

I make the last adjustments to the chassis and plug the radio in to tune it. The first thing I hear is static! I am walking on air, I'm so excited. The radio is actually making noise! This is a good sign. I fiddle with the tuning by inserting a small plastic rod into the housing that covers the frequency tuning parts. I twist it to the right some and twist the channel indicator knob on the front of the machine. Nothing happens. Silence. I'm disappointed and think I have broken something. I twist the little rod to the left. I repeat the process with the channel indicator knob. Static. Another little twist to the left. Then, MUSIC! Wow, am I excited. I turn the channel indicator knob to KOMA, 102.7 in Oklahoma City. It's the strongest channel that we can pick up in the Aspen area that plays rock and roll. I hear Fats Domino singing "Blueberry Hill." I turn up the volume as loud as it will go so I can hear the music. *I found my thrill on Blueberry Hill. On Blueberry Hill where I found you. The moon stood still...*

Gerry and Teddy both roll over. Teddy continues sleeping, but Gerry wakes up. I turn the volume down right away. Gerry gets out of bed and comes over to my desk. I think he is going to give me a slug on the arm, but instead he says, "You finally got that thing going, eh?"

"Yeah. We're listening to KOMA."

"Cool. We need a radio up here." He checks out the guts of the radio that still don't have the case around them.

"Yeah," I continue, "and it has a built-in clock with an alarm and everything."

I point to the radio's feature hoping he will become too engrossed to realize I've woken him up. We listen to a few more songs like "Jailhouse Rock" and "That'll Be the Day". Then Gerry says, "What time is it anyway?" He looks at his watch. "Holy moly, it's one fifteen. We better call it a night."

I turn off the radio, turn off my desk light, and crawl into bed just before Gerry turns off his bedside light. I can hardly sleep, I'm so excited that the radio is together and actually works.

Chapter 47

Spring 1958

We listen to KOMA on the radio every night before we go to sleep. The radio is on the lower shelf of the table between Teddy's and my bed where, if I wake up at night, I see the radium glow of the hands. They tell me it's time to roust myself out of bed or, if I'm lucky, to return to my dreams for another few hours.

Lately I have been dreaming more. My dreams are not often about death. I've thought about death and have figured out that it really doesn't matter what happens after I die because the world will go on without me like it does every day. Hundreds of thousands of people die every day. I don't even know their names. When Grandpa died, I remembered him once in a while. Now I only think of him when I am remembering the past and my trip to Cape Cod when he was still alive or when I go fishing and admire the hexagonal bamboo rod he gave me that was his father's before him. That's all I have left of Grandpa: just a few memories and a fishing rod. Why should it matter what happens after I die? The fact of the matter is only a very few people will remember me. After a generation or two or three, the only thing that will remain of me is perhaps a faded photo and one or two stories. I am at peace with the thought. It seems right.

My dreams are now strange and ones that I keep closely guarded. The night before last I had this dream...

The boys are walking down Hallam Street. I am with them. I am above them, watching them. I am watching myself. It is Spook James, Richard Sabbatini, and me. We are goofing around on the street, punching each other in the arm, teasing each other about saying something stupid in school, daring each other to do things that we know we would never do. That kind of stuff. It's spring and warmth has replaced the winter cold so we are wearing our jean jackets. We kick rocks on the dirt street as we head toward school on Hallam Street. I see us stop in front of Mrs. Griffith's house.

"That house is haunted," Spook says.

"No, it's not. It's Mrs. Griffith's house. I've seen her go inside," Richard says.

"It is, and she's a witch."

I watch the two as they have their conversation.

"Well, you're wrong. She is just an old ugly lady who doesn't have any family and lives there by herself."

"How do you know?" Spook continues. "You may think you have seen her, but it might have been someone who was lost and went to the wrong house. I've watched the house from my bedroom window, and no one has ever gone in or out."

"I bet she lives there. My dad and mom said she was just an old lady with no family."

"Yeah, if you are so sure, then why don't you go up and knock on the door and see if she answers?"

"No, I don't need to," Richard says. "I know she lives there."

Spook looks at me.

"Why don't you do it?"

"Why don't you," I say.

"You're just chicken!" Spook is now taunting me.

"Fine," I say, "I'll go knock on her door. It's probably like Richard said. The house isn't haunted." There aren't any broken windows or anything.

I walk across the street and open the broken, weathered gate on the low picket fence in front of the house. The house looks abandoned, in need of paint, fixing, and attention to the weeds growing in the yard. There are a few bushes alongside the house beginning to leaf out. I climb the steps to the front door and look back at Spook and Richard. They signal me to knock. I'm feeling frightened but knock anyway. Tap. Tap.

Tap. I know no one inside can hear the soft knocks. I find courage and knock loudly. TAP. TAP. TAP. Nothing. I knock again, knowing I can give up after the third time because it is plenty of time to be on the stoop to show Richard and Spook that I'm not a chicken.

Suddenly the door opens and before me is a very small old lady. She's wearing a light blue apron with faded dark blue flowers. She's very short and has a mess of long grey hair flowing down onto her shoulders. She doesn't look scary at all. She looks like a friendly old lady.

"May I help you?" she says.

"Uh, no," I stammer. "I must have the wrong house. I was looking for Jimmy."

"Well, he doesn't live here. It's just little old me. Would you like to come in?"

"No thank you, ma'am. I've gotta go."

I turn and jog down the steps toward the street as I hear the door latch and at the same time Richard and Spook beginning to laugh and to talk about who is right and who is wrong. We amble further down Hallam Street, and my dreaming turns to other things.

~ ~ ~

I didn't think much of the dream until yesterday, when I rode my bike into town to meet Spook at his house where he and Richard were fooling around waiting for me, so we could go fool around the Smuggler Mine dumps. I bumped into them coming from the backyard.

"Come on," Spook says. "Let's go to the mine dumps."

As we walk from his yard out onto Hallam Street, a weird feeling comes over me. I feel light headed, my ears are buzzing, and I have trouble focusing my eyes. I feel like I've put my tongue on a nine-volt battery. We walk past Mrs. Griffith's house. Spook says, "That house is haunted."

Richard says, "No, it's not. It's Mrs. Griffith's house. I've seen her go inside."

"It is, and she's a witch." Spook says.

I watch the two as they have the conversation. I realize events are unfolding exactly as they were in my dream the night before last.

"Well, you're wrong. She is just an old ugly lady who doesn't have any family and lives there by herself."

"How do you know?" Spook continues. "You may think you have seen her, but it might have been someone who was lost and went to the wrong house. I've watched the house from my bedroom window, and no one has ever gone in or out."

I am now electrified and can't stand it. I break into their conversation and say. "I know what you are going to say and what's going to happen."

Richard and Spook both stop talking and look me. I continue, not caring. The words tumble out of me.

First, Richard, you are going to say, "I bet she lives there. My dad and mom said she was just an old lady with no family."

Then, Spook, you are going to say, "Yeah, if you are so sure then why don't you go up and knock on the door and see if she answers."

And then Richard will say, "No, I don't need to, I know she lives there."

Spook looks at me. Richard looks at me. I can tell they are surprised and mystified all at the same time.

Then, Spook, you're going to say to me, "Why don't you do it?"

And I will say, "Why don't you?"

And then you will say, "You're just chicken!"

And then I'll say, "Fine, I'll go knock on her door. It's probably like Richard said. The house isn't haunted because there aren't any broken windows or anything."

Now they are both staring at me in silence.

"So," I continue, "why don't we save ourselves the time, and I'll just go knock on her door. She'll come out and ask me if she can help me, and I'll make up some excuse like I am looking for a kid named Jimmy or something, and then I'll just leave. Then the issue will be settled."

Without waiting for them to comment, I turn, walk through the gate, knock on the door, and everything happens just exactly as I dreamt it the night before last. As I walk down the stoop and onto the sidewalk, I hear Richard and Spook arguing about who is right and who is wrong and who said what and that sort of thing. I walk over to them and say, "Let's head into town."

~ ~ ~

I've been dreaming about events before they happen. This is more frightening to me than the death dreams. It is possible for me to understand death whether or not I accept it. These dreams I don't understand. I've resolved not to tell anybody about them before I can understand them, especially after the circumstances with Richard and Spook at Mrs. Griffith's house.

Oftentimes it happens during the day and not in a dream. I have a feeling in my body that tells me if something is dangerous to me, or something bad will happen if I take a certain action. If I ignore the feeling, I always regret it, because I make a stupid decision and something bad happens. It is all very strange and at the same time exciting, because it keeps me busy trying to understand why it is happening to me and what it means. I get exhausted thinking about it.

~ ~ ~

My concern with understanding what is happening with my dreams and my feeling of knowing things has taken most of my energy this spring.

To bring you up to speed: Mrs. Frost is still "riding herd" on me. I'm doing well in school. Robert, Spook, Richard, and Tony are still my friends. I've ordered another Heathkit radio, a short wave radio. I've lost interest in collecting Indian relics but do love my marvelous collection of arrowheads. I've been babysitting Toby. Teddy and Gerry get out of it whenever they can. Teddy's in junior high and Gerry's in high school, so I'm now just the dumb kid getting in their way.

That'll change, like everything else does.

Chapter 48

Summer 1958

Teddy wants to be called Ted now. He thinks Teddy is dorky and sounds like a kid's name. Ted and I are working at Guido's again this summer. Today we both have the day off and are outside playing with some model plastic cars. He and Gerry make plastic models, gluing them together with glue that makes you dizzy if you smell it too long. They paint them and put decals on them to make them look authentic. We've been having races with Ted's cars but are now bored.

"Ted," I say. "I've got an idea! Here's what we should do. We should pretend a plane crashes into one of your cars and creates a huge car wreck."

"What do you mean?"

"Well," I continue, making it up as I go, "we could get one of Gerry's planes and sail it out over one of your cars and have it crash into the car and the whole catastrophe can blow up in a huge fireball."

"Wow," Ted says, not thinking of the demise of his car, just that of the plane.

"How would we make it blow up?"

"Well," I go on, making it up as I go, "I have these cherry bombs and M-80s that I squirreled away from Fourth of July. We could put one in the plane and one in your car, light them, then sail the plane into the car. With luck, both the firecrackers will blow at the same time."

"Wow, that'd be a sight. It would be like a real catastrophe. What about Gerry's plane though? He'll be really mad if we blow up one of his models," Ted says.

"Ah, he's got so many, he'll never miss one. We'll use an old one that's behind some of the other ones."

"Well, what about my car? I don't want to have one of my cars wrecked."

"Look at it this way," I say, "if your car gets blown up, then you can tell Gerry that we were trying to blow up your car and it accidentally blew up the plane, too. Then he won't be so mad."

"But I don't want to blow up one of my cars."

"Come on, it'll be fun," I say as convincingly as I can.

We argue the points back and forth until Ted finally agrees it would be a very cool thing to watch. We go upstairs and trade the cars we were playing with for a Chevy Impala which is nowhere as cool as the others. I select an old Hellcat Fighter that Gerry has stuffed behind a B-52 Bomber and a Lockheed F-94 Starfire. We decide the scene of the accident should be up on the hillside north of the house.

Since it is late July, the grasses are all brown and dry so the wreck will be easy for us to see at a distance; and far enough away so we don't get sprayed with the shrapnel from the explosions. We spend some time discussing all of this and finally settle on a location. Ted puts a cherry bomb in his car. I tape an M-80 to Gerry's plane. Our plan is to light the fuses, have Ted move back out of the way, and after counting to three, I'll toss the plane in the direction of the car hoping it will stay airborne long enough to blow up just as it gets to the car. We have figured that a three count on my part should make up for the difference in the lengths of the two fuses.

We do a dry run and it looks like everything is a go.

"Okay," I say, "all men to your battle stations."

"Aye, aye, sir!"

We move into position.

Ted says, "Ready to ignite."

He lights a match. I have to set the plane down to light a match but get it done and pick up the plane.

"All ready here," I say.

"All ready here," Ted says. Then, "Fire!"

We both light our fuses. Sparks fly from the fuse, and I count one thousand, two thousand, three thousand. Ted moves back laterally on the hillside, far enough away so he can see but not be strafed. I toss the plane on the three count. It doesn't quite glide but at the same time doesn't act like a missile. It does a lazy float toward the car. As it lands a few inches away from the car, almost simultaneously the cherry bomb and the M-80 explode. There is a huge roar and plastic is flying everywhere. Thankfully I have put my hands up to my face to protect my eyes, and I feel the plastic shards cutting into them. I look through my fingers to see Ted running further across the side of the hill.

It takes us half a minute to regroup. When we do, we jump up and down yelling, "How cool was that!" and "What an explosion!" There is nothing left of the two models that resemble a car or a plane. We're congratulating ourselves as we walk over to the smoldering grass where the car once sat. We assess the damage. Impressive. Nothing left of anything. Just the way a real crash would be. After a moment, I notice to my left that the grass is burning in a small area up the hill from the bombsite.

"Ted! Look, the grass is on fire!" I say.

In just an instant the spot has turned from a small circle into a major blaze as the gentle wind nudges the flames across the hillside. I run up to the fire and start stamping it out. Almost as quickly as I stomp, the fire spreads and spreads and spreads.

"Darn it!" I shout at Ted. "Come and help me!" I look up, and Ted is headed down the hill.

"What the hell! Where are you going?" I shout.

"I'm going to get the hose to put out the fire'" he shouts back.

"No, the hose won't reach, you dummy! And besides, there isn't time. Even if it would reach, by the time you got it up here the fire will be burning Pfister's house! Now come back and help me!"

He sees the logic of this, comes running, and helps me stomp out the rapidly growing fire. For what seems like days, we are stomping on flames, on embers, and on charred earth. Everywhere we look, the flames are expanding in an ever-widening circle. We stomp out the flames on one arc, and they get worse on another.

"Don't quit!" I say. "If we don't get this out, it'll hit the oak brush on the other side of the hill, and next thing you know we really will have burned down Pfister's house."

Ted nods his understanding, and we stomp on the flames like madmen. The soles of our shoes are so hot we almost cannot stand it. Our hair is singed and our clothes are covered in black soot. Finally the wind shifts, and the fire begins to burn itself out with no fuel to consume. We quickly take advantage of this and stomp some more. We battle the small blaze for about a half an hour before we finally have it contained and under control.

"If you want to get some water on it, I'll stay here and watch it so it won't get going again," I say to Ted.

"Okay." He strolls down the hill. Presently I see him pulling the hose across the driveway and up the hill. He gets to a point that is about a hundred feet away from where we are and says, "I guess you were right. The hose won't reach."

"Fill up one of the Jerry cans, and lug it up here with a smaller pan so we can throw water on some of this."

"Right."

He takes the hose back down into the driveway, finds and fills a Jerry can, and lugs it back up the hill. I walk down to help him and soon we are sprinkling water on the ashes. The fire is out. We stomp it some more and water it down until we think it isn't hot enough to start up again.

We're down in the driveway looking at the carnage. We have burned a huge portion of the hillside.

"Wow, that was a close one," Ted observes.

"Yeah," I say, "but it sure was fun except the fire part of it. That was pretty scary. We're really lucky it didn't get into the scrub oak. Then there'd a been hell to pay."

"I wonder if anyone will notice it," Ted says, half to himself.

"Probably not," I laugh. "We've only charred about half of the county. Shoot!, Whip Jones can see this from clear over on Highlands! But I'm sure Mom and Dad won't notice it."

Ted is regarding me hopefully as I look down and try to figure out what I am going to do with my scorched and blackened tennis shoes.

Chapter 49

Fall 1958

We caught holy hell for burning up the hillside. There was trouble from all sides. First Mom gave us hell and then gave us the "wait until your dad gets home" speech. When Dad got home, the first words out of his mouth were, "What happened up on the hill?"

When I told him what we had done, he wasn't too mad but said, "You're darn lucky the fire didn't get into the oak brush or Pfister would have lost his house."

"I know," I replied. "It was a pretty stupid thing to do. But you should have seen it. It was almost as good as the Fourth of July."

Dad glared at me, then went into the house shaking his head. I thought things would be fine until Harold Hall drove by on the way to his caretaker house. Harold Hall is the new caretaker for the ranch, is mean as hell, and doesn't like us Morse kids at all. He calls us "a bunch of juvenile delinquent brats." It's real clear that he has no idea what constitutes juvenile delinquency and what is just good old fun.

He and his wife Jean have three real honest-to-goodness brats, Dickie, Larry, and Stanley all of whom are younger than us kids. Harold treats them poorly. Jean just stands by and whimpers. None of us give one damn about Harold, but we feel sorry for the kids.

If anything goes wrong on the ranch, Harold tells Pfister, "It's those damned Morse kids again."

He doesn't know what a fool he makes of himself by doing that, because Pfister already knows how far we will take things, and what sort of mischief we get up to around the ranch. Pfister has finally become resigned to having us roam about as long as we don't tear things up. We've come to a truce. That is until Harold Hall took over from Art Kuen.

~ ~ ~

Gerry got into it with him the day after Ted and I burned the hillside. Gerry didn't officially have his driver's license but still drives around on the ranch. The day after Ted and I burned the hillside, Gerry was driving Mom's car, a 1956 Ford station Wagon, up the road hell bent for leather, leaving a rooster tail of dust the whole way from Highway 82 to the house. Harold must have just turned off the highway and followed him up through all that dust. When he got to the house, he found Gerry and me out in the garage.

"You're driving too goddamned fast up the road," Harold said. "I'll have your ass if I ever catch you doing that again."

We couldn't believe he had the guts and the stupidity to say anything like that to us. He had no idea what we were capable of if we got rousted.

Gerry looked at him and said, "You're on private property here, get the hell off," and went back to what we were doing.

Harold didn't say anything, just turned and left. As he was leaving, Gerry said to me loud enough so Harold could hear, "Now, there goes a first class asshole."

I agreed.

Harold walked back out to his car, and that's when he saw the scorched hillside. He came back and said, "You little shits burn the hillside? Art is going to love to hear you damned near burned his house down."

"It wasn't even close," I said. "The fire didn't even get over to the oak brush." Besides, we had it under control. We had water up there." Which was true, just that we had it up a little late in the game.

"Well, Art is going to hear about it." He stomped off.

And of course Pfister did head about it. Once he did, he had a word with Dad. Dad had another word with us. By the time this had all transpired, too much time had passed for any of us to have any interest in it. Dad said to Ted and me, "You two stay out of trouble, stay off the ranch, and away from Harold Hall."

We gave him our most sincere "Yes, sir" and soon forgot the whole thing. I remembered the incident the next weekend when I found myself on the top of Tiehack, roaming the ranch. At least I've paid attention to two of the three. Haven't gotten into trouble and haven't seen Harold Hall for a whole week.

Chapter 50

Fall 1958

It's very late. I've just finished soldering the last transistor onto the circuit board of my Heathkit shortwave radio. This afternoon I climbed up in the cottonwood and attached a copper antenna wire high in the tree that I then stretched and attached to the peak of the roof over our room. Using a book with some formulas for determining antenna lengths, I figured out the length of antenna wire needed to pick up the frequencies of the shortwave radio. I made a pretty close guess at the length needed and stretched it for sixty feet. About in the middle of the main antenna wire, I spliced in another wire running from the main antenna wire into our room through the window next to my desk. Fortunately I had purchased a hundred-foot roll because I have only about two feet left.

I was just as excited to buy this shortwave radio as I was the clock radio. I started going to the post office about ten days after I ordered it to see if it had come in. Each day Mr. Ware would say something to me like, "Nope, not today" or "You're gonna walk your legs off coming over here from school every day just to get the same answer" or "How'd that first radio turn out?"

I'd tell him that I don't mind walking because I'm excited to get the radio. I would have to carry it home on the bus and leave my bike at school. But that didn't matter, once it was in my hands, I wasn't about to let go of it. Finally it arrived. Building this radio has gone much faster than the clock radio, as I have a better idea of the components and what they do.

The shortwave radio almost functions the same as the clock radio except there are more working parts that allow you to pick up a broader band of frequencies from much farther away. This is the way it works: You have an antenna that brings the signal to the radio. The signal then passes through its series of filters made of wire coils and capacitors to isolate the radio frequency. From there, the radio waves are routed through a crystal or diode detector that translates the sound waves into the amplitudes that can be recognized as voice or music the same as when they are broadcasted. The amplifier amplifies the sound so you can hear it through a speaker or earphones, if you have any, which I do not.

Now I sit at my desk with the radio almost completed. After I have the last pieces soldered to the circuit boards, I hook up the antenna and plug it in. I see I have juice from the red, glowing power light. Good. I begin to tune the set so it picks up the radio waves on the frequencies reserved for shortwave transmissions. I have another little plastic wand that I am using to fine-tune the frequency bands. I work on the tuning, and become very discouraged after half an hour. I don't seem to be able to hear any incoming signal. I recalculate the antenna length, check my soldering joints, and look for any cracked transistors or capacitors. Nothing. I'm getting tired and upset. Not good. When I get tired and upset, I sometimes loose my temper and after that, who knows what will happen? Sometimes I just walk away and sometimes I get destructive, destroy what I am working on, and start all over. However, I know that destroying the radio is not an option for a couple of reasons. First, it cost me too much of my hard-earned money. Second, it has taken me too long to build, and third, it will take me too long to get a replacement. It's not like wadding up a piece of paper, so I hold my temper and give it one more try. I fiddle this way and that. Finally I hear it!

Static! Now I really *am* excited! I turn up the volume and turn the tuning rod to the right. I hear, "This is the Voice of America broadcasting from Quito, Ecuador. Next up, the news."

"*Imagine that! Quito, Ecuador!*" I think. It makes me shiver. Listening to someone speaking into a microphone thousands of miles away, and at the same time they are speaking, I am hear them thousands of miles away. I realize I really don't know how a radio works even though I know how to build one. I simply cannot imagine how someone's voice can be captured as a sound wave, then transported thousands of miles through space by some force that is incomprehensible, and translated back into that person's exact voice on the receiving end. I mean, I know about atoms and molecules, electrical forces and waves, and most of the insides of the radio, but it's still a mystery. What a marvel it is to think I can hear someone's voice from clear across the ocean.

I realize I don't know where Quito is. I leave the radio on after listening to it for a few moments, and sneak downstairs to get the World Geographic Atlas Herbert Bayer gave my dad and mom last Christmas. Herbert Bayer is a famous artist who designed the book. He and Joella are friends of my parents who come over to the house quite a bit.

Back at my desk, I open the atlas to a map of the world. I know that Ecuador is in South America, so I find it on the map, then after a short search I find Quito. Quito, Ecuador is a very long distance from Aspen, Colorado. It amazes me to think my radio can pick up a signal broadcast from that far away.

I listen to the Quito station a little longer, then, try to tune the radio to another station. I find Radio Free Europe broadcasting from Munich, Germany! I'm extremely excited that my shortwave radio actually works and can pick up stations from all over the world. I listen to these radio stations broadcasting in foreign languages and wonder what the commentators are saying. What are the countries like? What are the people like? What are they doing at this moment? How do they live? What do they look like? Do they have radios? Thousands of thoughts race through my mind. It feels like I am going through some small mouse hole into a whole other world. What wondrous mystery. I wish I had a transmitter as well as a receiver, then I could actually talk to people across the oceans. Wouldn't that be an adventure! I listen and change the channels until I am too tired to continue. When I finally hit the sack, it's early in the morning and I sleep like the dead.

Chapter 51

Winter 1958–59

The sun is less than fifteen minutes from disappearing behind the ridgeline of Howelsen Hill in Steamboat Springs, Colorado. The winter air still holds some of its noonday heat. It dissipates with each passing minute. I'm in the starting gate of the Steamboat Winter Carnival cross-country ski race.

Three...Two...One...GO! I leave the starting gate, skiing as fast as I can. In a very short distance I'm breathing hard. I shuttle across the flats and ski around a right-hand corner, out of sight of the starting gate. I'm relieved to be out of sight of the people at the start, the person behind me, and all human contact. The person in front of me I'll see on the next straight stretch where the course goes across a hay field. My breath is now coming in short gasps, and my muscles are tight. I see myself as I was last summer, sprinting across the barnyard trying to run faster than Gerry and Ted.

I realize, when that picture comes into my mind, that I have to slow down and be more relaxed, because this race is much, much longer than a mere sprint across the barnyard. It is five kilometers. Rather than slow down, I try to relax my body so it is easier to glide across the snow.

After a fashion, my body begins to cooperate with my mind. I begin to see things I have not seen before while cross-country skiing - little bumps in the terrain, little aberrations in the tracks, the steepness and definition of the uphills. I see the gradual transition of the land rising to form the hill, the middle steep section and the top of the hill as it rolls over and forms itself into a downhill. My body feels the gentle demands of the transition, the increasing demands of the mid-section and upper section, over the top, and then time for a moment's rest going down the other side. It's a small realization that there are hills within hills, and it's a realization that helps me ski each hill faster.

The sun is fully down. The drop in temperature is instantaneous. I chase my breath down the track as it blasts out in front of me in small puffs of grey steam. Although I am very warm from exertion, I feel the temperature change on my cheeks. I ski across a long field, through the sage which I can smell even in the cold air. I feel at home and alive.

Presently I see the skier who started thirty seconds before me. I'm excited and agitated, something stirring inside me. I can't put my mind on it in a way that forms itself into thoughts. It is a hidden, profound, innate feeling coming from a dark place in me that I cannot see into. It is as if this skier has taken something precious from me that I have to get back. Almost instantly my body is working harder. Rapid breath. Muscles driving me forward. Skiing faster. My mind tells my body to slow down or it will explode. I back off but have almost caught up with him. Settling into a smoother rhythm, I pass him.

"Hut, hut!" I say as I come up behind him. He steps out of the track and I whiz past, looking ahead for the next skier, my mind and body now on a search-and-destroy mission that I feel coming from those dark depths. I don't know the words for it, but I know I have unleashed the competitive wild beast inside, letting it out to run in the world, free for the first time. It is frightening. And, I love it.

~ ~ ~

I'm working at Aspen Sports after ski team practice. Gale is in the back working on skis, fixing broken edges, waxing the bottoms, and getting them ready for people the next day. He's holding a spring-loaded wood clamp that he uses to hold repairs in place when he is fixing broken edges on the wooden skis. Oftentimes people hit rocks when they are skiing and knock out an edge. Generally some wood comes off the ski at the same time. Gale is good at fixing wood. He splices a piece back into the side of the ski and puts on a new edge. The ski is as good as new. Now he's watching from the repair shop out across the retail shop at a young woman who is looking at skis in the ski rack.

"Hey, dog-breath," he says, "come over here."

"You talking to me?" I say. "For you, it's Mr. Dog-breath. Show some respect."

Spider laughs and says, "Just get over here, wiseass."

I go over to him behind the counter. Spider drops his voice and says conspiratorially, "Here, take this clamp and go clamp it on that lady's butt."

"No, I'm not going to do that!" I say, half laughing because I can picture the surprise on her face if I did it.

"Go ahead. It's all right. I know her!. She'll think it's funny," Spider eggs me on.

He hands me the clamp and pushes me out from behind the shop counter.

"Go on," he says, "it's a practical joke. She's an old friend from Armenia."

"Yeah," I say, "Like that uncle of yours who's the Armenian truck driver."

I know just about all his stories about "my uncle from Pakistan and my old Aunt Liz from East Jesus Junction." I'm not about to go slam a clamp on the butt of some lady I don't even know.

I look at Spider like he's crazy. But then he is always doing crazy stuff. Just a few days ago he sent me next door to the Red Onion.

"Hey, Morsely," he said, "go over to the Onion and pick up the steaks that I had Kuster make up for John and me. They should be on the cook shelf where the waitresses pick up the meals."

So I went over to the Onion, walked in the back door, and up to the heat counter where the food is waiting to be picked up. I saw a couple of plates with steaks on them. I made sure all the trimmings are on the plates, picked them up, and walked out. No one said a word to me, so I guessed they must be the right plates. I took them back to Spider and John, and they sat down and ate them.

Just about the time they finished their dinners, Kuster came in from the Onion with a box of tomatoes. He stood in the back door where he had a straight line of fire and began throwing them at Spider and John, shouting, "That's for the steak! That's for the potatoes! That's for the bread!" with each tomato he hurled at them.

I was hiding down behind the shop counter so as not to get hit. There were tomatoes all over the store. Everyone was laughing so hard they couldn't move as Kuster walked out the back door.

Now I find myself with the clamp squeezed open in my right hand down by my side, shuffling over to the woman, pretending that I am looking at skis as well. She looks at me then turns half sideways to look at the skis again. It is too perfect. I have a direct shot. She's wearing the latest ski fashion: stretch pants, leaving no doubt as to where her butt is.

In an instant I feel my hand moving up and slapping the clamp on her butt. Mortified, I turn and walk quickly away. I can't believe my hand did that. In less than an instant, there is pandemonium. The lady is shouting at me. She is swearing at me. She is jumping up and down with has one hand in the air above her head and the other hand trying to reach around and grab the clamp off her butt. She looks like a bull rider going for the eight-second bell. I've stopped in my tracks to watch her. Gale and John are laughing uproariously, hiding in the safety of the repair shop.

About the time it occurs to me that the lady will soon stop jumping up and down, and come after me when she gets the clamp off her butt.

In the next instant, the clamp comes whistling through the air as the woman snarls at me, "You little shit!" and rushes by me and out the door.

Gale and John are still in the repair shop laughing so hard they can't speak.

"What was she so mad about?" I say, "I thought you said she'd think it was funny."

"Well, wouldn't you be mad if some young punk sidled up to you and clamped Big Bertha on your butt?" Gale says.

The thought had not occurred to me.

"I thought she'd laugh. You said you knew her and that she'd think it was funny. She should know you are always pulling stunts like that," I say.

"Know her?" John laughs. "I've never seen her in my life!"

"I don't know her," Gale chimes in. "She's just a customer in the shop looking to buy some skis who you've chased away by slamming a clamp on her butt! I ought to dock your pay for a pair of skis!" Gale says. Both he and John are now laughing harder than ever.

"Probably cost us a couple of hundred dollars. Guess you'll have to work some overtime to make that up." John says.

They're still laughing. I'm standing in the middle of the shop feeling bad because I probably have given the lady a black and blue spot on her butt that will last for a month.

"Well," I say, turning back to my work, "she did have a real cute butt."

Chapter 52

April 10, 1959

I'm in my seventh grade fifth period class right after lunch. Mr. Ralston, the superintendent, enters our classroom to speak with Miss Krogmeier. A chill runs up and down my spine. I know something bad has happened. I know it's not something I did but something that will seriously effect me. Without a word I stand up, and at the same time Miss Krogmeier makes eye contact with me. The room is silent, and the rest of the class is looking on. By the time Miss Krogmeier starts to beckon me to her desk, I am already halfway there. Mr. Ralston, unaware that I know something has gone badly wrong, takes me out into the hall.

"What has happened?" I say.

"You have to take the bus home after school. Your mom called and said plans have changed because your dad has had a ski accident and is in the hospital."

"How bad is it?"

"I don't know. I'm just passing along the message."

I can see he's lying to me, trying to protect me from the seriousness of the accident. I know I'll get no meaningful information, so I don't try.

~ ~ ~

I've come home, and I'm in the kitchen having a peanut butter sandwich and a glass of milk. I fix my gaze on the grain of the knotty pine on the kitchen cabinets. It's swirling around a knot like a whirlpool. I follow it around and around. I know I am about to be sucked into a whirlpool I may never be able to swim out of. At the moment, there is nothing I can do. I know my dad's had a serious accident but don't know what it is nor the true magnitude of it. If it involves the ski hill, it could be anything. Gerry and Ted weren't on the school bus. I don't know where they are. Of course Gerry could be anywhere. He has his own wheels now.

I continue staring at the wood. It's silky and yellow from years of kitchen smoke. Kitchen smoke and aging. The growth rings speak of the years I've had with my father. I sense I'll never do anything with him again as a son, not that I've ever done that much with him. A few hunting forays. A laugh here and there. A family picnic up Castle Creek or Old Snowmass. He was busy. He worked hard. Very hard. Tears run down my face. I miss him and know that my life has changed in some fundamental way. Forever. My relationship with him has smoked over, like the walls of the kitchen. I'll never be able to see clearly into his heartwood again. And I am aging like the wood I stare at.

~ ~ ~

It is later. I don't know the time, but it is fully dark. My mom drives up in the Ford. I still sit on the chair in the kitchen, staring at the cabinet doors. I stand and face her. She is a wreck of too many tears, too much information, and too many impossible decisions facing her.

I think I should hug her, but do not. She and I have never been hugging close. I ask her, "What's happened to Dad?"

We are alone in the kitchen. She's taken off her winter coat on the porch and has no reasonable excuse to avoid my question, even though I can see that she doesn't want to talk.

"Your father has had a horrible ski accident," she begins. "One of the people in his ski school class has run into him. He's broken both legs very badly, broken his ribs, torn the ligaments in his elbow, and a thousand other things that I can't even remember. Dr. Oden doesn't know what to do. They're saying he may lose his legs. They're broken so badly, it may be impossible to set the bones well enough for them to knit and heal. You boys are going to have to take care of things around here while we figure this mess out."

My mind flashes, *All the king's horses and all the king's men...*

Mom is crying fully. Tears stream down her face. I want to go to her, comfort her, comfort myself, but I know it is the wrong thing to do, so I stand still waiting for her to finish.

"And besides that," she says, "I'm pregnant. How am I going to deal with all of this?"

She turns, walks into her bedroom, and closes the door.

...could not put Humpty Dumpty back together again.

I'm in shock. It's clear that Dad will be in the hospital a long, long time. It's clear that Mom, however strong, is not equipped to deal with this situation on her own. Yet, she will have to. We all will have to. It is new territory. Alien territory.

Seven, by the clock on the stove. Dad's accident and Mom's pregnancy: what a mess. I rummage through the refrigerator unsuccessfully for something to serve as dinner. I give up on the idea before it's had a chance to fully develop. Mechanically I pull out a loaf of bread and the half-gallon container of milk. I make a peanut butter sandwich, throw it on a plate, pour a glass of milk, and sit down at the kitchen table to eat. I hardly taste the sandwich and don't care that I have forgotten the strawberry jam. Gerry and Ted are still not home.

~ ~ ~

I'm upstairs on my bed, confused, lonely, and frightened. Confused, because I know my life is at a crossroads, and the signs pointing the directions are as obscured as road signs in a blizzard. Lonely, because I know I have no one to guide me or help me make the inevitable choices I know are ahead. Frightened, because I don't know where to turn to get answers. Mom is beside herself, and will be long past the time I've made choices that may impact my life forever. My dad is simply unavailable.

I know up until now my life has been simple, choices easy. It is an easy thing to make good choices when life is comfortable and basic needs are provided for. What happens in times of monumental stress? I know I'm about to find out. Then I think of my dad and mom. If I'm thinking these thoughts, what are they thinking? I have only me. They have themselves, their situation, and six children to consider. It is too much for me to comprehend. I decide not to think about it. It is all I can do to contemplate how I can rearrange my little world to make it work.

9:05 on my clock radio. The front door bangs as Ted and Gerry stomp their boots off. Moments later they are upstairs. Their faces are serious.

"What're we going to do?" I say.

"I don't know," Gerry says. "We'll just have to figure it out."

Ted doesn't say anything.

I take off my clothes and get into bed in my undershirt. I'll take a shower tomorrow morning. It's a long time before I go to sleep.

Chapter 53

Late May 1959

I am sitting at the awards assembly with the rest of the junior high and high school. The principal, coaches, and the teachers are giving awards for the sports teams, academic accomplishments, and special recognition. I'm given an award for my grades which have been straight As. I had decided to study this year, and actually had a good time learning new things in science, math and English. That's all well and good, but the most important thing I learned is, knowing I have done the best I can is most satisfying. No one can teach you that. You have to feel it inside.

Mr. Ralston says, "This year we have a new and very special award for the students in junior high. This award is for excellence in leadership. This year we are proud to announce that the recipient is Terry Morse."

I am frozen in place until Tony Vagneur pokes me in the side and says, "You've gotta go up there and get the award."

I walk to the front of the gym, shake hands with Mr. Ralston, thank him for the certificate he hands me, and return to my seat. During the rest of the ceremony I try to figure out why I would get an award for leadership. I haven't done anything to deserve it. If the truth be known, I've been more of a disruptive force in the classroom than a leader. I conclude I've received the award because the teachers and administration want me to feel like a leader so I won't be such a troublemaker.

It's a good idea, but probably won't change who I am. I get into trouble either because I am bored or curious and can't resist the urge to explore. Having figured this out, I realize that the award is nice but doesn't really mean much to me. I'll keep being who I am until I grow tired of it, then I'll be who I am in another way. It's important to me to be who I am, not what other people think I should be or what they think I am.

Chapter 54

Summer 1959

The boy-man has been walking, walking, walking. Body in pain. Mind in pain. Yellow dirt from the roads he has travelled has stained his feet and ankles so they are no longer white. The soles of his feet are black with the dirt from the oily highways he has trod upon. Walking and growing and dreaming. His skin no longer fits him. His bones are pushing against each other, ripping at the ligaments and cartilage and muscles, pushing their way heavenward with no accounting for the expense, the confusion, the pain. No auditor is crunching the numbers here. His mind cannot keep up. Or his mind is too far ahead. Or his mind is not in his body. He is not in his body. He is beside it, watching it grow, watching it do things that his mind sometimes, coming out of the mists, wills it to do or not to do. He does it anyway. There is a fog about him like the early morning mists rising above a mountain lake in late fall. In the freezing before the sun comes up, there is clarity. When the sun comes up, the fog rises and it doesn't leave during the day. Clarity only returns in the freeze of the night. In the small interstices of sweet silent sleep, tucked in between the nightmares and daymares of his confused existence. His body has become an antenna transmitting the world around him into knowings. Many of the things he knows because he feels them in his painful, growing body. There are certain sensations for thoughts sent to him by others. There are special sensations sent to him from the earth and from the ethers. He does not talk about this. It is his secret, silent in the mists. In his dreams he sometimes sees the others telling him what to do, what to say, how to act. Sometimes he heeds, sometimes he doesn't. He only knows that his days are passed in hours of fatigue and fogs so real that he cannot separate dreams from waking reality. He walks onward through the mists of his mind, each day performing the physical movements he is expected to do for his job, for his school, for his family, for the others in his life, not knowing or remembering why he is doing them, only that he must.

~ ~ ~

Dad is still in the hospital. He's been there since his accident four months ago. Dr. Oden operated on his right leg to try setting the bones. The left leg was easier and didn't have to be cut open. The ribs and other injuries have to heal by themselves. Dad has contracted osteomyelitis in his right leg, and Dr. Oden doesn't know what to do about it. His leg is a horrendous mess. No one has said but somehow I know Dad contracted the osteomyelitis due to unsterile conditions at the hospital. The damage has been done. Dr. Oden is not experienced enough to have operated on Dad. The hospital is too small for the magnitude of my dad's problems. He should have been sent to Denver immediately, where there are better hospital facilities and more experienced doctors.

~ ~ ~

Mom is at her desk paying bills. She has already told us, "You boys will have to chip in with your jobs. There is no money for anything but food and clothes for the little ones." Fortunately we all have jobs, Gerry works for Henry Pedersen the landscaper, Ted works a construction job, and I run the Aspen Meadows Tennis Club catering to the vacuous elite. Mom worries about money all the time. After weeks of arguing and paperwork, Dad is getting Workman's Compensation of four hundred twenty dollars a month. Popeye is sending us two hundred dollars a month. Six hundred twenty dollars a month for Mom, six of us kids, and a seventh on the way.

It seems like a summer of living in a dream and wakefulness at the same time. There are times this summer when I don't know who I am. In my free time I've been goofing off with Spook. We are walking the edge but not getting in trouble...yet. I'm running wild, and I know it.

Chapter 55

Late Summer 1959

Gerry is seventeen. A year ago, before Dad had his ski accident, he and Gerry went to Grand Junction where Gerry used some of his work money to buy a 1953 Studebaker Coupe. The car looked like a rolling wreck, but Gerry's proud of it.

Gerry said, "Just wait until I finish with it. It'll be boss."

He dropped the engine and the dashboard, put in a 383 hp Corvette engine, a new transmission, a tachometer, and other necessary gauges. He rewired the electrical system, changed the manifold exhaust system, and beefed up the rear end.

Now a year later in the late afternoon alpenglow, I watch Gerry install the dashboard and hook up the remaining electricals. "I've almost got her done," Gerry says. "Just have to hook up these last few wires, and then we can turn her over and see if she works.

I look at the makeshift winch he's rigged on the ceiling beam in the garage, the chain and pulleys now hoisted back to the ceiling tied off and out of the way. His toolbox is pushed up against the wall tightly so he can pass between it and the car that has been in the garage more than out of it since last fall. I watch him twist the ignition wires together. My brother is a pro.

"Now," he says, "let's see if we can get this baby to turn over."

All evening I have listened to him mumble about tachometers, magnetos, and alternators. I've understood none of it, so I'm happy to hear he's finally ready to turn her over. I look inside at the metal floors, devoid of carpeting, covered with grease and dirt. The dashboard, made of stained plywood, hosts an array of dials and switches giving it the look of an airplane cockpit.

"Get in!" Gerry says.

I get in and sit in the bucket seat.

"Here goes!"

He turns the ignition key, flips a few switches, pumps the gas, and hits the starter button. The engine roars to life. I don't mean it starts. It ROARS. Gerry is grinning from ear to ear. He pumps the gas pedal a few times and the engine revs up.

"Slicker 'en hammered whale shit!" he says.

"Wow!" I say. "It works!"

"Of course it works! That's because the Master of Motors has worked his magic. Let's see if we can get her to go. Guess I should hook up the mufflers to the manifold pipes before I go too far, but let's take her down the road."

Gerry backs the car out of the garage, revving the engine to keep it running. He wants to break in the engine slowly so he doesn't send the rpm's too high. He turns around, puts the car in first gear, and we head down the road. Gerry is ecstatic. It's the first time he's torn an engine out of an automobile and replaced it.

We motor down the road slowly until we get to the bottom. "Guess I better stay off the highway until I get the pipes on," Gerry says. "Dirty Herwick will hear me all the way out here if I don't."

He's right. We start back up the road, and I look at Gerry. I can see in his eyes what comes next. He is about to put the pedal to the medal just to test the power. Not a second later, we are fishtailing up the road, dirt and rocks flying off the back tires, and the car accelerating with G forces that neither one of us has ever anticipated.

"Whoa!" he says and takes his foot off the accelerator. "Guess she has enough power!"

"Guess so," I say. My stomach's in my throat.

We park out in front of the garage and head into the house as darkness falls. I ask him, "When will it be completely done?"

"She's not an it, she's a she," Gerry corrects me. "Geez Terry, I don't know. I'm out of money. I have the exhaust system so I can get her street legal, but I need a new rear end gearing, and the inside needs to be finished. Probably never."

I nod as though I understand, which I almost do. We go in to make something for dinner.

Chapter 56

Fall 1959

Dad is home from the hospital, either in bed or in a wheel chair. He and Mom are in the living room. I'm in the kitchen and hear him say, "Damn it! I'm not going to let them amputate my leg, and I'm damn well not going to spend my life in a wheel chair!"

"Gads, Wendy, just what do you think you're going to do?"

"I don't know, but we have to figure it out. Maybe the best thing is to go into Denver and see what the doctors at Denver General have to say."

I make some noise and walk upstairs. I don't want to hear any more.

~~~

I'm upstairs sitting at my desk. I look at the scattered projects in and on top. The old bead loom sitting in one of the nooks unused. Beaded out. Buried in my mind like the deer hide in the compost heap. I reach up, turn on the shortwave radio, and tune it to KOMA to listen to some of the latest songs.

They asked me how I knew
My true love was true
Oh, I of course replied
Something here inside cannot be denied...

I keep looking around, as though there might be a clue somewhere, a clue that will help things get back to normal: the remains of the fly-tying vice; a few feathers floating into the cracks in the wood and behind the radio; papers, letters and books piled on each other haphazardly; an E string for my guitar, sometime I should put it on the guitar and begin playing again; an errant marble, escaped from the number ten coffee can. It's all nothing but flotsam and jetsam from a previous life. Pre-accident. Pre-pain. Pre-confusion. Still, I have my skiing. When I'm skiing cross-country, my head seems to clear, the mist lifts, and my vision returns. I can see. I can see.

They said someday you'll find
All who love are blind
Oh, when your heart's on fire
You must realize
Smoke gets in your eyes...

I suddenly open my eyes. Blind love, but I can see. I have a crush on Sarah James, Spook's sister. She's a year younger and beautiful. She has long black hair, big round brown eyes, and an entrancing smile. Today she wore a plaid Scottish skirt with a dark green, blue-and-black pattern, and a white, long-sleeved shirt that fit tightly over her almost woman-breasts. I had trouble keeping my eyes off her.

Sarah is a mystery. Some days she talks to me and is very nice. Other days she ignores me completely. She walks away swinging her hips. For some reason it makes me crazy. I know she likes me, but it's difficult because Spook and I are good friends. She's seen me when Spook and I do all the stupid stuff guys do to get in trouble.

I sit at my desk totally confused. I pick up my math book and begin my homework. The music plays on.

Chapter 57

Later Fall 1959

It's Saturday, and we are at the height of a Rocky Mountain Indian summer unlike anything I've experienced. The leaves are stunning reds, oranges, and yellows offset against the backdrop of the green pines. It has been a warm, cloudless autumn.

Albina Gerbaz is helping Mom clean the house. They're yakking in the kitchen like women do. Jimmy is here with Albina. We are fooling around outside while Mom and Albina get their work done.

"Hey, Jimmie!" I say, "you ever smoked cigarettes?"

"No."

"Either have I. Do you wanna try? I think we should try it out."

Jimmy says, "I'm not supposed to because of my asthma,"

"Aw, one puff or two shouldn't hurt anything. I know where I can get some of my dad's cigarettes. I saw a pack in the hall closet yesterday where he must have left them before his accident. I'll go and get them."

I walk inside, and Jimmy follows. Sure enough, the cigarettes are on the shelf tucked beside an old Ajax can. I take the pack and put it in my pocket.

"He thinks he's lost them, so he'll never miss a couple."

"I don't think we should," Jimmy says.

"Fine. You stay here by yourself, and I'll go try a ciggy by myself."

I walk toward the kitchen.

"Where ya goin'?" Jimmy says.

"I'm goin' to get some matches, then I'm gonna have a smoke."

I go into the kitchen and open the drawer next to the refrigerator. I rummage among the rubber bands, pencils and pens, scraps of paper, a deck of cards that we never use, an old can opener which always ends up in the wrong drawer, scissors, and all sorts of other junk. I find the box of Diamond Strike Anywhere matches. I open the box, grab a handful, and head back outside. Jimmy follows me.

"Okay, I've got the cigarettes and matches. Are you coming?" I say.

"I guess," he says.

I have no idea where the best place to smoke one or two cigarettes would be. We wander off the reservation and end up alone in the corral at the back of Pfister's barn. Harold Hall is not to be seen.

"Let's go up in the hay loft," I say.

"Okay," he says.

We walk through the back of the barn, past the stalls, to the loft ladder. The loft is full to the brim with hay. We climb the ladder and find a seat on one of the bales.

"Okay," I say to Jimmy, "we've gotta be careful because of all this hay."

I take two cigarettes out and hand one to Jimmy. I strike a match on the zipper of my jeans like I've seen Dad do when he forgets his Zippo. Wooosh, the match bursts into flame. I hold it for Jimmy while he takes a big puff and coughs up a storm.

"SSSSHHHH!" I say. "If Harold is around, surer than hell he'll find us."

"Can't (cough cough) help (cough) it (cough cough)."

I let it go and light up my cigarette, the match now burning down close to my fingers. I shake my hand, the match goes out, I let it cool, then drop it on the loft floor.

In the meanwhile I've taken a healthy drag on the Lucky Strike and have my own coughing fit.

"You're not so darn quiet either," Jimmy says.

"Sorry (cough cough). It (cough cough) just went down the wrong way (cough cough)."

I take a few more puffs and say, "Not bad, once you get the hang of it."

I look down at my feet in the hay and see the burnt match lying on the loft floor cozily nestled in random stalks of hay that cover the floor here and there. We smoke happily until our cigarettes are headed toward our knuckles, our heads spinning, and our stomachs churning. I look at Jimmy who's turning a shade of light green. I'm trying to get my bearings, stop my head from spinning, my stomach from rolling, to bring my general constitution back to normal, when we hear a truck driving up the road into the barnyard.

"Oh No!," I whisper, "that's Harold Hall. We've gotta get out of here."

I get up and weave my way for the ladder. Just as I put my foot on the first stair, I see Jimmy about to put his cigarette out on the hay bale.

"No," I whisper loudly, "bring it with you and hurry up!"

Jimmy does a double take, hops off the bale, and follows me down the ladder. I hear the Jeep pulling up outside the shop on the other end of the barn. I know we're in trouble but somehow hold myself together enough to make my way over to the door by the rear stalls. I open it quietly, and we go outside, Jimmy still holding his burning cigarette. It's then I realize I've left the pack of Lucky Strikes on the hay bale in the loft.

Nothing I can do about it now, I think to myself.

I point to the back fence and whisper to Jimmy, "Quick, we'll run across the corral and hop over the back fence, then head up the hill into the aspen trees."

Jimmy doesn't say anything. I can see he is spooked. The danger has cleared our heads. I stub my cigarette out in the dirt and horse shit of the corral. Jimmy stomps his ciggy and off we go at a lope to the corral fence, over it, and up into the aspens. Once we hit the tree line, we duck down in the grasses behind the aspen trees and look back down on the barn. We don't see Harold. Relieved, we fall back on the grass.

I am lying flat on my back looking, up at the light filtering down through the tree branches. I feel strangely alive. In an instant I become lost in the light above me. It breaks into shards and daggers that shoot themselves into the leaves so violently the leaves become a translucent green with great halos of light surrounding them. They quake and shimmer with the gentle breeze flowing up, down and around the small branches. Sunglow yellows, orange yellows, red yellows blend with orange reds and shocking reds, born only of the crisp nights, and warm autumn days of a high country Rocky Mountain Indian summer.

If I were thinking, I would be thinking *how utterly, breath taking, stunningly beautiful.* But I am not thinking. I am simply feeling. The vision above me becomes an imprint in my mind as clear as the names my parents have given me. Dexter, Terry, Terr-Ass, Son, and not to forget, You Little Shit.

My gaze rests on the white bark of the aspen trees where the branches have been stripped clean by lack of light, wind, and the process of their natural growth. Eyes stare back at me from everywhere. Eyes in the sunlight. Eyes in the shadows. Eyes in the trees where branches have fallen, leaving eyes staring at me, through me, and into me so intensely I disappear into them.

I am lost. What am I doing? What am I thinking? *Je pense donc je suis.* If I can think am I? What is I? But I'm not thinking. I'm only feeling. If I am feeling, am I? Being with the light, the colors, the trees, and the wind. Is it good to think about these moments, feel these moments, this nature, these questions I have been grappling with ever since Mrs. Houston gave me that insane problem. I know the answer lies somewhere; is it in these trees that I lie beneath? In the shards of light? In the autumn reds, yellows, and oranges? No. I don't want to think about it, rather only feel it. I am lost in all the beauty.

Presently Jimmy says, "What should we do now?"

I'm startled back to the day and the problem at hand: how we get from where we are, back to the house without being seen by Harold. I figure out the route and jump up.

"Let's go," I say.

We trot along the hillside, head north until the barn disappears from view, then cut to the east across the lower fields, and hit the driveway about halfway up to the house. We travel quickly because we both know it's late.

"We're on the road now, so he can't do anything to us for walking up the road," I say.

"No, I guess he can't."

'Dang," I say, "I'm glad you didn't try to put that cigarette out on the hay bale. We would have burned the barn down. I've had enough problems to last me a lifetime without burning Pfister's barn. Burning his hillside was enough."

"I might have if you didn't stop me. I was afraid he would smell the smoke," says Jimmy.

I shake my head and say, "What do you think he'd a smelled if you lit the barn on fire?"

Jimmy thinks about this a while and says nothing.

~ ~ ~

It is about five days after Jimmy and I had a smoke in the hayloft. I've ridden my bike home after school and have tons of homework. I walk in the door and Mom says, "Your dad wants to see you."

Uh Oh. I think. *Here it comes.*

I walk into the bedroom and find my dad lying in bed with his legs up. He has a bandage resting lightly on the open wound caused by the osteomyelitis in his right leg. He looks at me and says, "Terr-Ass, next time you want to smoke, come and see me. I don't recommend your smoking because it weakens your bones, and you could very easily end up like this. And you should have had the sense to take the cigarettes with you so Harold wouldn't find them in the hay loft."

I am ashamed that I've brought this down on Dad when he is in the condition he's in. I can't look him in the eye.

"Now go do your homework," he says.

I look up at him and take in his full situation. Broken up in pieces, not being able to walk, a family to feed but unable to work, a pregnant wife and six kids that are all hell on wheels. In that moment I make the decision that I'll never be a smoker.

Chapter 58

Spring 1960

The man-boy is walking, walking, walking. Back into the mists. He is more man than he is boy in his body. Full height. The shadows surround him as he looks out from them trying to make sense of the world beyond. He cannot. There are two new insane people in his family of insane people. One is a baby. One is a grown woman. Where did they come from? He doesn't care. He cares only about walking. He knows if he walks far enough, he will pass through the forest of mists. Mists that crowd his mind, his senses, and his body. For he is man walking. He is man-boy walking. Still a child with his fits of anger. Still a child with his inner tears. Still a child with his inner fears. He has his determination. It is all that keeps walking. He sees young people, middle-aged people, old people. People teaching, people learning. People sitting, standing, running, stopping, doing something, and doing nothing. He does not care. What are friends in the mist if not those who walk alongside him for moments and let him know that it is all right to keep walking? He may not know them, he may not see them except for that once. Walking in the mists. He is reading, he is thinking, he is feeling, he is living…all in the mist.

The mist enshrouds him, cloaked in a disguise as more mist. He passes through it. Seasons change, red glowing autumn into windswept white frozen winter. He passes through it. Time moves but relative to what? Or does time move? Or does he move creating time in his wake? He doesn't care, he just walks. He walks to school. He walks home. He walks through the cold and into the snow. He walks through December and Christmas. He walks through his studies, his skiing, his work, his family, his friends. He walks through his teachers. All of them are but misty apparitions of a life he cannot find.

One night the man-boy has a dream. He dreams of being in the forest. He is now running. He is being chased by a black bear. He knows he must get to the other side of the forest and out into the green meadows beyond. He finds himself lost and running. The bear is running behind him. His foot catches a root and he falls. The bear is upon him but does not molest him. The bear sniffs tentatively. The man-boy lies still. The bear says to the man-boy, "Turn over and look at me. Remember your past, and you will know who I am. I am you. I am life. Come, embrace me."

The bear lowers his head down to the man-boy. The man-boy, frightened to be so close, backs away on his elbows. The bear laughs and changes into a raven and flies high above the forest, taking the man-boy's eyes with him. The man-boy can see the forest from above through the raven's man-boy eyes. He sees the paths that lead to the edge of the forest. Then he sees only darkness.

The next morning in his dream the man-boy arises and begins walking, walking, walking. Next to him is the bear and above him is the raven. The bear says to him, "I am Bear. I am you, and you are me. Where do you walk?"

The man-boy answers Bear, "I don't know where I am. I only know I must walk until I am no longer in this mist".

The raven flies down from her heights and says, "I am Raven. I am you, and you are also me. I have your eyes. You have my eyes. Your man-boy-Raven eyes have seen the way, why do you not take it? You must walk."

The man-boy answers Raven, "My eyes do not see in this darkness."

"Look deeper," Raven says as she flies up again, up, up, and up until he can no longer see her.

Still he walks, plunging deeper into the darkness until he feels under his feet, in the black of the blackness, the smoothness of a path. He begins walking on this smoothness, blind now in the inky darkness, careful with each step. Bear is no longer beside him. It is a path he must walk upon. Walking and walking. Time is without time. The mist lightens slowly until one moment he realizes he can see down the path and the fields beyond the forest and the green of the grasses and the blue of the skies. He is on the edge of the forest. He sees Raven flying in the distance. He turns and sees Bear retreating back into the forest.

The man-boy wakes from his dream.

~ ~ ~

I am upstairs at my desk. It is spring, and the school year is almost over. I am doing my homework and have taken a break. Suddenly I see the paper in front of me. I read the math word problems. I sit back in my chair and look around my small world. I am seeing things that I have not seen for a long time, and things that I do not remember having. The shortwave radio is dialed to the frequency of Radio Free Europe but is not turned on, so I hear nothing from its speakers. There is a Mad Magazine lying on top of it. I pick up the magazine and leaf through it, pausing to look at Spy vs. Spy, my favorite. I find myself chuckling. Mid-laugh, I am shocked at how good it feels. I haven't laughed for a long time.

I turn around and look at our room, the "boys' room." Ted is sitting at his desk, working on a drawing. Gerry is not here. I notice there is a Johnny Mathis record playing. I remember Gerry bought a record player. He and Ted have been buying some albums and 45s that they like. Ted likes Johnny Mathis, who is singing,

Look at me, I'm as helpless as a kitten up a tree
And I feel like I'm clinging to a cloud
I can't understand, I get misty, just holding your hand
Walk...

The feeling is back, and something else. I know I will be okay, Dad and Mom will be okay, Gerry and Ted will be okay and the young kids will be okay. The song courses through me. I realize I have walked through the mist, but I am no longer helpless as a kitten. The impact of the realization punches a hole in my chest, and I become giddy and elated. I continue looking around the room, seeing everything for the first time through my Raven eyes. I am very happy.

~~~

I didn't sleep much last night. After I began seeing and feeling again, I stayed up for a long time, looking at things on my desk and around the room. Now it's the beginning of fourth period, right before lunch. I walk into the math room and see Mrs. Smith sitting at her desk. I look at her and say, "Hi, Mrs. Smith."

She looks at me and says, "Hello, Terry. How are you doing today?"

I can see she is confused by my presence.

"Fine," I say, and I walk to one of the desks in the second row. Mrs. Smith looks at me strangely as I walk by and says, "Terry, where are you going?"

"What to you mean?" I say. "I'm going to have a seat for class."

Some of the other kids are coming into the room.

"Come here," Mrs. Smith says.

I walk over to her desk and face her.

"Yes?"

She is looking at me carefully. I am not sure I understand her look. It is as if she is trying to discover something about me. Who I am or if she has seen me somewhere else before.

"Don't you remember you have math out in the hall with the self-taught module?" she says.

Then I remember I've been kicked out of math class for the year for mouthing off and cutting up in class. Then I realize I've started to sit down in the classroom. Something has shifted within me causing me to forget I am no longer welcome here. Things are different today. Life has more clarity. It is as if a dense fog has lifted, and I can see things that I haven't been able to see for weeks and weeks.

"Oh," I say, looking at Mrs. Smith, obviously confused. "I'm sorry, I forgot."

I turn and walk out of the classroom to find my space in the hall, the table holding my math lessons. I begin my work.

An hour later the bell rings for lunch, and kids fill the hallway. I mark where I am on the Self Teacher and stand up to go to lunch. Mrs. Smith is behind me when I turn around.

"Terry, could you come into the classroom for a minute?" she says.

"Yes, ma'am," I say and follow her inside.

"Take a seat."

Mrs. Smith has long black hair that she wears up, beautiful brown eyes, and a pretty face. I look at her eyes and decide they are placed just where they should be on her face, not too far apart and not too close together. I decide she is pretty not just because she has a stunning smile or beautiful eyes, rather she is pretty because all her features are in proportion to each other and are placed on the oval of her face precisely where they should be to produce a pleasing symmetry.

I sit down and wait.

"Are you all right?" she says.

"Yes."

"It's just that you look different today. Are your independent studies going well? You know you have a test coming up at the end of the year that you will be expected to pass."

"Yes, ma'am. I know. I'm on the second month of the algebra section. I think I know all the word problem lessons pretty well. I was able to get through that section with little difficulty."

"Are you sure you've completed all the eighth-grade-level chapters? You know algebra is a ninth-grade level."

"Yes, ma'am."

"What's this 'yes ma'am' stuff? Usually it's 'yeah' and you're off in a huff."

"I don't know," I say.

"Look, Terry, you know you have been a huge problem in this classroom and that's why you are out in the hall. You would be taking all your classes out in the hall if all your subjects lent themselves to it."

"I have, really?" I am surprised by this.

Somewhere in the far reaches of my mind I remember this: the interruptions, the inconsiderate talking out of turn when the teacher is talking, the general bad attitude about school arising partly from boredom and partly from I don't know where. I haven't been happy at school. I've spent the year in a fog, so much so that I hardly remember the school year going by.

"Yes, ma'am. Sorry."

Suddenly tears are running down my face. I fight to control myself, my emotions, my demeanor in front of her. I blurt out, "I'm sorry I have been such a pain in the ass this year." Then I wipe my face and gather my composure. I make a move to leave.

Mrs. Smith says, "Terry?"

I turn and look at her full on.

"Welcome back."

I leave the room to find my lunch.

~~~

It's later in the day and I'm on my bicycle heading home. Usually the wind is in my face in the afternoon as it moves up the valley. Today, thankfully, there is no wind. In the calm I think about Mom and Dad. They're in Denver. Dad has gone to Denver General Hospital for more operations on his right leg. The doctors will try to reset it. The osteoporosis has caused problems with the healing. His left leg is mending, his ribs are better, and the pain in his right lung has abated with the reduction of bruising. His elbow is also healing pretty well, although he has nerve damage that the doctor says will get better over time.

Mom has had to hire some help for the little kids and the housework while the rest of us are at school. She spends most of her time taking care of Dad and trying to help him make decisions about the best way for him to progress. Somehow she is managing the whole mess and is doing it all on six hundred and twenty dollars a month. I can't understand how she's able to do it, but she does. It helps that Gerry, Ted, and I have jobs in the summer and after skiing in the winter. We use the money to buy our clothing and sports equipment.

I haven't spoken with Gerry and Ted about the fact we are living on a shoestring, but they must know. I know because I've seen both the Workman's Compensation check and the check from Popeye on the small living room desk where Mom keeps track of the money she spends. I snuck a peek at the ledger and know what she's been doing to make it all balance out. I suppose I shouldn't have done this, but I did, so it's done and now I know the whole truth about it.

My mind turns to my conversation with Mrs. Smith before lunch. It dawns on me I have been more than a "little shit" at school. Instead of Terry, I'm being called Trouble. I know some of the kids and teachers say it in jest, but underneath there is a reason for it and they mean it. I think of the stupid things I've done over the year out of boredom and to be noticed. The truth is that Mom and Dad just aren't there for us older kids anymore. I understand they have serious stuff to deal with, but it has left Gerry, Ted, and me to fend for our selves. Mom puts her attention on the rest of the kids who are not old enough yet to be as impacted by the situation.

With Mom and Dad having such a hard time, I realize, as I ride the last stretch of road up to the house, that they don't need me causing problems to give them more to worry about. I decide a change is in order.

Chapter 59

Summer 1960

Gerry turns eighteen in a couple of days. He's working for Henry Pedersen again this summer, Ted is working construction, and I'm running the Aspen Meadows tennis courts.

It's been a wet June, so I've had to sweep the courts more than usual. It's good luck that today is clear, sunny, and warm. All four of the tennis courts are reserved from opening at seven thirty, until closing at seven thirty this evening. I open up, get the first folks out on the courts, and begin stringing a Dunlop racket with premium gut string.

As I finish the racket an hour later, the courts are turning over. Two hard-core singles players are running a little late finishing their hard-fought third set. They're regulars and excellent players. There's a foursome of women waiting for them to finish. One of the women approaches me and says, "There are players on court two that we have reserved for 8:30. You need to go kick them off so we can start our doubles. I have to be at the hair dresser's at 9:45, so we can't be wasting time while they finish playing a point."

"Couldn't you start play on court one, then switch to court two as soon as they finish? They're playing a wicked match of singles, and I'm sure they will be finished by the time you get warmed up," I say.

"No. We reserved court two, and that's where we want to play."

"Okay," I say. "Just give me a second to finish tying off this string so I don't lose the tension."

I hate doing this sort of thing. I know the players on court two have played a couple of minutes over their time, but they've had a terrific game and are battling it out to see who takes the set. Disturbing their flow could wreck the whole day for them. I slowly tie off the string on the racket, take it out of the racket vice, set it on the counter, and walk out toward court two. Just as I'm walking out on the courts to deliver the bad news, the singles players walk toward each other to shake hands. The match is obviously over. I turn and start walking back.

The woman looks at me and says, "Go on, Terry, tell them to get off the court. Right now."

She doesn't realize it, but she's raised her voice enough for the folks now playing on court one to notice. I continue walking back into the shop. As I pass the woman, she says, "Wait until Lefty hears about this. You are uncooperative and insubordinate!"

"Sorry, ma'am, but if you look, you'll see their match is over. The court's all yours."

She gives me a huff and joins the other three to spend their hour patting the ball back and forth into the net and past out-of-bounds lines. I'm beginning to dislike this job and the clientele who frequent the place. I'll be looking for another job next year.

Then Bill Marolt comes through the door.

"What's up, Morsely?" he says.

Bill takes care of the grounds at the Aspen Meadows, mowing the lawns, making sure everything is properly trimmed and watered, and that there isn't any trash lying around.

"Not much," I say. Then I think to ask him. "Are you going to be taking care of the Meadows next summer?"

"I don't know yet. I'm going to CU in the fall and don't know what I'll be doing next summer. Why?"

"Well, I thought if you aren't going to be doing your job next summer, maybe I could have it."

"What about the tennis club here? This looks like a pretty easy job," Bill says.

"It is," I continue, "but I may want a change by then. I'll be going into high school."

"I gotta get back to work," Bill says, "but I'll keep it in mind. By the way, I heard Gerry ran Henry Pedersen's backhoe into the pond up on Red Mountain. That guy drives everything too fast. Was Henry mad?"

"Ya think?" I say, "but he's not going to fire Gerry. They lost an afternoon because they had to get one of Gerbaz's Cats up there to pull it out."

Bill laughs as he is walking out the door. "That brother of yours is something else."

~ ~ ~

Gerry and I get home from work at the same time. He comes tearing up the road in his Studebaker as I get off my bike and lean it against the fence. Dad is still in the Denver hospital, and Mom is in Aspen getting things together before she leaves for Denver again tomorrow or the next day. We're not sure who'll be staying at the house with the little kids while we're at work during the day. Gerry and I are in the kitchen rummaging through the cupboards and refrigerator when Ted gets home. We talk a little bit about work, and then Gerry says, "Hey, lets go out and shoot the .45."

This is Dad's Colt 1911 .45 caliber service revolver that came home with him after the war.

"Great idea," Ted and I both say.

Gerry goes to the gun rack on the porch and gets the pistol. I grab a box of ammunition off the top shelf of the porch closet, and the three of us head out to the backyard to take some potshots. Ted has brought some cotton from Mom's bathroom to stuff into our ears so we won't be half-deaf when we finish.

Gerry loads the clip with eight rounds and chambers a round in the barrel. He aims at a clump of dirt where the moles have molested the lawn and fires at it. A puff of dirt shoots up. We each take turns blasting away at something, laughing at each other for missing, praising each other for a hit. After several rounds of fire, I say to Gerry and Ted, "This is kind of boring. We really don't know if we are hitting something or not, we just think we are. Let's get something we can see break, a bottle or something."

"Good idea," Ted and Gerry both agree.

We head up to the house to collect some empty bottles and grab a few more bullets. When we return, we hear Jennifer calling to us, "What are you guys doing?"

"We're having some target practice," Gerry shouts.

I look to see where Jennifer is standing to make sure she is out of the way, so we don't accidentally shoot her. She is nowhere to be seen.

"Jennifer," I shout, "where are you?"

"Up here," she says.

I look up and see her on the roof over our bedroom.

"Damn," I say to Gerry and Ted, "she's up on the roof!"

"Hey, get down off there," Gerry shouts.

"I'm fine!" Jennifer shouts back. "I want to watch you shoot."

"You be careful up there," Gerry says.

Ted and I fling a few bottles down the bank where we can see them, but far enough away so we won't step on broken glass while we are on the lawn, just in case we hit them.

Gerry chambers another bullet and fires the pistol at one of the bottles. He misses, so he takes another pot shot out of turn.

"Hey," Ted complains, "it's my turn."

"I had to have an extra practice shot to warm things up," Gerry says.

Ted blasts one of the bottles to smithereens.

"Ha! The first direct hit!"

"You mean the first lucky hit," I say.

We shoot more rounds until the bottles are mere debris. Ted reaches down on the grass behind him and picks up the two ceramic parrots that have been sitting on the breakfront table that stands at the bottom of the staircase.

"I brought these ugly parrots along just in case we need them," Ted smiles.

"Good thinking!" Gerry says. "I hate those stupid things. They're a pain. They fall over if you even breathe on the table as you walk by."

"It's my turn to shoot," I say.

I know there'll be problems if I don't demand my place in line immediately. There are three of us, and only two parrots.

"No problem," Gerry says. He doesn't think I'll hit one.

Ted tosses them down the bank. I take the pistol from Gerry, aim down the barrel, and squeeze the trigger. The bird explodes into a thousand gaudy pieces.

"Wow, nice shot," Ted says. "I'm next."

"Not even close!" Gerry exclaims. "I'm next and you know it." He takes the gun from me and blasts three shots at the second bird before Teddy can say anything. All three shots miss.

"Ha!" says Ted. "Now it really *is* my turn, and you miss two turns because you took three shots."

Gerry surrenders the pistol.

Ted takes a shot and misses. I am about to tell him it's my turn, but he does the same as Gerry and takes another shot. This one is dead center. The bird is demolished.

"Waaaaahhh!" I hear. I look at Gerry and Ted to see who has made *that* frightening noise. Both of them are looking at me. Then as one we all three turn and look for Jennifer. She has disappeared from the roof. We hear her crying and take a closer look. She's now on the lower roof lying flat out on her back.

"Damn!" Gerry says. "She fell off the roof!"

"Jennifer, don't move! We're coming to get you!" I scream.

If she moves to the side another foot or two, she will fall another ten or twelve feet to the ground. Gerry, Ted, and I sprint up to the house. I've taken the pistol from Ted and put the safety on as we are running.

"Shit, shit, shit!" Gerry says. "She's supposed to be watching Heather and Toby. Terry go find out what the the kids are up to while Ted and I get Jennifer off the roof."

We all run into the house. I holler out for Heather and Toby, while Gerry and Ted race up the stairs to get Jennifer. Heather and Toby are playing dress-up in Heather's room and are just fine. I tell them to keep having fun and that I'll be back in a minute. I head upstairs and meet Gerry and Ted as they bring Jennifer into the bedroom. She's walking on her own but is holding one arm with the other and is still crying.

"I think she's broken her arm," Gerry says. "I'll have to take her to the hospital. You guys stay here and feed the kids while I'm gone. I better get going before Mom gets home. It won't be as bad if I'm already at the hospital when she gets here. And for Chrissakes, Terry, get that pistol cleared and put away."

I look down at my right hand and see I am still carrying the pistol.

"Okay," I say.

"Want me to come with you?" Ted says.

"No, you stay here and help take care of the others. You and Terry make up some story about why Jennifer was on the roof. Mom'll kill us if she finds out we were shooting, especially at those stupid damn parrots. And, Jennifer, if you say anything about this, I'll kill you, and if you're not dead, Ted and Terry will kill you. And if you aren't dead after that, we'll feed you to the fish in the pond."

Jennifer starts crying again. "I won't, I promise. Just don't shoot me!"

Gerry piles Jennifer into the Studebaker and heads to the hospital. Ted and I round up Heather and Toby, get them to clean up their mess, and fix them some dinner. We're about finished feeding them when we hear a car drive up. I run over to the outside door and look out.

"It's Mom!" I shout.

Mom walks into the house carrying some packages.

"Will one of you go out to the car and get the rest of the groceries?" she says.

"Yeah, I will," I say.

I head out to the car and bring in two bags of groceries and set them down on the kitchen counter. Mom comes back into the kitchen after dumping her packages in her room and stopping off at her bathroom to pee.

"Where's Jennifer?" she says.

I look at Ted, hoping he will say something. He pretends to be interested in making sure Toby finishes the last of his broccoli and potatoes. I know he isn't going to answer, so I say, "She had a little spill and broke her arm. Gerry took her to the hospital. He should be back any time."

Well, anytime in the next eight hours, I think.

I look at Mom. She doesn't look surprised. She shakes her head and says, "What am I going to do with you kids?" And before taking another breath she says, "Heather, quit playing with your food and eat it!"

I know that will be the end of the conversation about Jennifer's broken arm. Mom is already thinking about some bigger concern. I wonder how long it'll be before she notices the ugly green and yellow parrots have disappeared from their roost on the breakfront table.

~~~

I tell Lefty I have to go to Denver for a couple of days to help my mom with dad. Lefty has a few things to say like, "I thought you wanted to work," and "I'm going to take the time out of your pay" and "You should have thought of that before you decided to work here."

I have a few choice words for him to the effect that if he thinks he can find someone to do the job better than me, good luck at it because I'm the most reliable guy he'll ever find. He knows this is true. The door is always open at seven thirty in the morning, the clubhouse is always clean and neat, and the books always balance at the end of the day. Finally he realizes that he is being an ass after I remind him that my dad has been in and out of the hospital for over a year and that life isn't easy for my mom at the Morse homestead. She needs someone to keep her company once in a while going to Denver.

Lefty, stepping out of character, acquiesces.

Mom and I have an uneventful trip to Denver. We check into a motel close to the hospital, then, head over to Denver General to see my dad. He's lying in bed with his right leg in light traction to ease the pressure on the bones and ligaments while he's recovering from his latest surgery, a bone graft just below the knee. They've taken some bone from his hip, and grafted it to the thin strip of bone below his right knee, in hopes of getting ahead of the osteomyelitis. He is in good spirits, hoping that this operation, and a huge dose of antibiotics, will take care of the problem. I'm standing at the door behind Mom when he says, "If this doesn't take care of it, the doc says there is nothing more he can do. The leg may have to go. He's doing some research on some special techniques they are toying with at Massachusetts General Hospital. If all else fails, maybe we can do one last try with their experimental surgery."

Mom looks at him. She begins to cry. "Honestly, Wendy, this all just stinks. You've been in and out of the hospital for a year and a half, and the Ski Company is barely speaking to you. You've had I don't know how many operations, and they're bitching because their insurance rates are going up. When something like this happens, you can really tell who your friends are."

"I know, I know," Dad says. "We just have to get through this with both of my legs if we can. It's bad enough that I'll never be able to do the things I used to, let alone walk right."

"What are we going to do?"

"We'll figure it out. For now, we just need to keep doing what we are doing until I can get on my feet again."

Dad finally sees me.

"How're ya doin', Terr-Ass? Glad you could come down and keep your mom company."

"Fine," I say. I look at him lying there in the bed, all grey from his operation and from all the weeks of medications, hospital beds, and no fresh air.

"How's the rest of the crew? You taking good care of things?"

"Sort of," I say.

Jennifer has let the cat out of the bag to Mom about being up on the roof when she broke her arm. Luckily she hasn't said anything about our Wild West show. I figure I may as well tell Dad the story, or at least part of it.

"The little kids are fine," I say. Then in the same breath, "Jennifer fell off the roof and broke her arm. But other than that, everything is going well. I guess Mom probably told you about Gerry running Henry Pedersen's backhoe into the pond on Red Mountain. But that's all cleaned up now. They got it out with Gerbaz's Cat, and they've finished the job. Lefty is a pain in the butt. He thinks he's pretty hot stuff. In fact, most of the people who are playing down at the

Meadows think quite highly of themselves. I'm tired of it. I don't care for the phoniness."

Dad says, "You can always work somewhere else next summer if you don't want to work at the Meadows. So Jenni-fuzz broke her arm, eh? Is it serious?"

I see Mom rolling her eyes. I can hear her saying to herself, *Gads, they are so cute when they are babies, but after that...*

"Not really. The doctor said it was a clean break, and she should heal just fine."

"What was she doing on the roof?"

"I'm not too sure. Gerry, Ted, and I were fooling around in the backyard, and I guess she wanted to see what we were doing. She must have thought it would be fun to watch from the top of the roof. Luckily she didn't fall all the way to the ground. She just hit the deck on our floor and stayed there. She could have bounced off that and gone all the way to the ground."

"You mean she was clear up on the top of the roof above your room?"

"Yep."

"How in the name of..., how did she get clear up there?"

"Climbed. It's not hard. We do it lots of times."

"Well, you kids stay off the roof. And tell Jennifer I'm sorry to hear about her arm. Hope she heals quickly. What else is happening?"

"Not much besides that. Gerry is still working on the Studebaker. Ted is trying to figure out how he can look good for the girls, and I'm just trying to stay out of too much trouble. It's harder nowadays because we can't roam around the ranch so much anymore because Harold Hall is such an asshole and..."

"Terry," Mom interjects. I know she is talking about my language.

"Well, he is. And anyway, people in town are getting a bit more concerned about us kids exploring the abandoned houses around town, the silver mines, and that stuff. Spook and I have been run off a couple of times. It's like everyone is getting more afraid we're going to bust something up or get hurt. Even two years ago it wasn't that way."

"Son, the town is changing. Skiing in the winter and the Music Festival in the summer is turning Aspen into a resort town. It's becoming well known, so business owners are making more money from the tourists who are spending time there. They don't want a bunch of wild kids fouling things up for them."

"Yeah, well, they don't even have a sense of humor any more. A couple of weeks ago, Spook and I bought some firecrackers at Tidemann's store. He was really grumpy and told me that we couldn't look at the comic books. He told us to take what we bought and hit the bricks. I could see through the door at the back of the store he had a card game going. We walked out, but I stopped in the door and watched Tidemann go back to his card game. It made me mad to be treated like that, so I tossed a firecracker into the store. It was just a small one but loud enough to make them all jump. Spook and I were laughing and running hard by the time Tidemann limped out the door swearing and shaking his fists at us. He shouldn't have been so nasty in the first place."

"Terr-Ass. You can't be doing that sort of thing anymore in town. First of all, you could cause damage or a fire, and the next thing you know, we'll have to get you out of jail."

"Yeah, I know. But that's about the only thing I've pulled since I got kicked out of class and put out in the hall last year. I spent most of the school year out in the hall. Half of the time it's not even my fault."

"You better wake up and fly right because all this nonsense is too hard on your mom."

I'm duly chastised, and sit down in a chair at the end of his bed. He and Mom spend some time talking about things at home, and how Mom wants to have a woman named Carol Carlson move into the guest room by the kitchen that they added onto the house before Dad got hit. Carol would help Mom with the new baby, the housework, and kids. I listen for a while, then wonder how in the name of the Almighty they are going to pay a live-in person to help. On the other hand, I know it is all too much for Mom, even if us three older ones do all we can and are on our best behavior. School hours, athletics, and activities just don't make it all possible. Luckily Ted will get his license in September, so he can help drive when Gerry can't.

It's all difficult and confusing. I keep feeling guilty. I wonder if my brothers feel the same way. The older three of us want in some way to be responsible, but we want our freedom. Having to do all the chores around the house, take care of the little ones, and deal with school, work, and sports is just a bit more than we can handle. Ted is better off than Gerry and I because the only sport he does is football in the fall, and I'm not all that sure he likes it. Gerry and I play football in the fall, ski in the winter, and Gerry does track in the spring. Gerry and I work at Aspen Sports in the evenings after ski practice, and he drives me home in the freezing Studebaker which is every bit as cold as the open Jeep. Since Dad isn't driving, Gerry uses the Jeep when the Studebaker is torn apart in the garage. Then we all have summer jobs. All of that and … girls.

~ ~ ~

I excuse myself and take a stroll around the hospital. I walk in all the areas I'm allowed, and then head outside and walk the streets near the hospital. A couple of hours later, I go back and Mom is getting ready to return to the hotel.

"I've got a couple of things I want to do in the morning," I say to Dad, "so I'll probably see you after lunch."

Mom looks at me questioningly. "What do you have to do?" I can hear in her voice that she expects an answer because she doesn't want to worry about me goofing around in Denver and have to pick me up in jail.

"I'm going to a music shop. I've decided to get a new classical guitar. My other guitar is a steel-string, twenty-five-dollar thing I got on the Cape four years ago. I think I want to learn to play better instead of knowing a few sloppy chords."

Mom looks at Dad, and he shrugs his shoulders tiredly.

Chapter 60

Summer 1960

I haven't told Mom and Dad their friend Edgar Stanton, who is involved with the Aspen Music Festival and is a very good guitar player, as well as an excellent piano player, has spoken with me a couple of weeks ago. I was riding my bike behind the Meadows and through the sagebrush field, past the festival music tent, on my way into town after work when, for some reason, I decided to stop and take a peek inside the tent. There I saw Edgar Stanton down by the stage, testing his recording equipment. I walked down to see what he was doing and to see the reel-to-reel tape machine.

"Hi," I said.

"Hi," Edgar Stanton said. "Aren't you one of Wendy's boys? You Morses all look alike."

"Yes, sir. How does that machine work?"

"You like music? What's your name anyway?"

"Terry."

"I'm Edgar Stanton. Nice to meet you, Terry."

"Nice to meet you, too."

I tell him that I'm interested in electronic stuff, have built a radio, that I have a cheap guitar that I can't play very well, and I'm really interested in how the tape machine works. He wants to know how Dad is doing and how Mom is doing, so I go into all that business. Finally he looks at me and says, "So, you are interested in playing the guitar better, eh?"

"Yes, sir."

"What kind of music do you like to play?"

"I only know a bunch of chords and some folk songs that I don't play very well. I'm thinking I'd like to learn to play classical guitar and Spanish guitar," I say.

"It just so happens I play the guitar a little, too. And it just so happens I play classical guitar. Maybe we should get together, and we can both learn to play better. What would you think about that? We could meet once a week when you have time."

"I have a job, but I get two days off a week and I finish at 4:30 every day," I say.

"Do you know where I live?"

"Sort of. You have that house on Red Mountain that looks like a lunch box, right?"

He laughs. "I guess it does look a bit like a lunch box. If you want to ride your bike up to my house, maybe I can help you learn a few things. I have two guitars, so you wouldn't have to carry your guitar with you, only the sheet music. You know how to read music?"

"I've been playing the trumpet in band for a few years. I'm not very good, but I can read music a little."

"Well, if you know the basics, I can teach you the rest."

"That would be swell."

"What kind of guitar do you have?" Edgar asks.

"It's just a cheap steel-string learner guitar. I want to get a new one, a good classical guitar. I have to get it in Denver next time I'm there."

"You let me know what you decide. If you do get a new guitar and want to learn to play better, call me, and we'll see if we can make it work out."

I thank him, say good-bye, decide not to go into town, and head toward home.

~ ~ ~

The next morning in Denver, Mom and I part after breakfast.

"You be careful today," she says.

'Yeah, I will."

I don't tell her that I'm headed for Larimer Street, the seedy part of town where all the pawnshops are.

~ ~ ~

One day, earlier in the summer, I was at the Jerome pool sneaking a quick swim. The lifeguard, an older kid named Swede Larsen, noticed I was in the pool but didn't have a summer pass. He was playing a beautiful Spanish melody on an equally beautiful classic guitar. When he finished playing he set the guitar aside, and asked me to get out of the pool. I tried to distract him by asking him questions about the guitar, the music, and where he learned to play, trying to get him to forget about the fact that I was swimming illegally. We began talking, and after half an hour or so, I got all the information I could ever want about Spanish guitar music, classical guitars, and where to get one. He told me about a pawnshop on Larimer Street in Denver that carried great guitars at very cheap prices. He didn't let me get back in the pool.

~ ~ ~

This morning I'm on a twenty-block mission to find a pawnshop. I walk north on Bannock Street, take a left on 14th Street, then a right on Larimer Street. I'm nervous because there are quite a few bums and drunks on Larimer. Some of them are hassling me for loose change, and others are mumbling at me. It's the first time I've seen bums on the street. I've seen poor people, of course, right in Aspen. We're pretty much all poor. But we have homes. These are people without homes. All of them are men. They look like they haven't had a bath in months. I pass one or two stores with guitars in the windows, but they aren't the right shops. Finally I am so nervous I duck into the next shop I come to with guitars in the window.

I have no idea what I am looking for, and no idea how much I should pay, except the information that I was able to get from Swede Larsen, which was not much.

"What're you doin' in here, kid? What can I get you for?" says a small, bald man wearing glasses. "You're pretty brave walking down here by yourself. But then you're pretty tall. Any of the bums hassle you?"

"Not too bad, but they do make me nervous," I say.

"Well, don't worry about them. They're harmless for the most part. They may shout at you, but most of them aren't violent."

I'm not reassured.

"What do you need? Want to sell something?"

"No thanks. I'm actually looking to buy a classical guitar. I don't know much about them, but I would like to get something with a good sound."

"You have come to the right place, young man," Mr. Baldhead says. "Just so happens I have some fantastic guitars here for sale at very good prices."

He continues to give me his sales pitch and show me a bunch of guitars, none of which I like. Either they have the wrong shape, or they don't sound good or they are beat up.

"I guess I don't see what I need," I say.

"Well then," he says, "let me show you a couple of new guitars that I happened to get the other day from a guy who just had to sell them. They're not on pawn, so they're a bit more expensive." He goes into the back room and returns with two Goya guitars. I look inside and see they are made in Sweden. I always expected the best guitars to be made in Spain.

I say to him, "I thought the best guitars are made in Spain."

"A lot of them are," he says. "But the wood in Scandinavia is excellent for the pine soundboards. These guitars have a wonderful tonal quality." He plucks the strings.

The guitar vibrates with full-bodied notes that resonate and linger in the air. He sits down on his stool behind the counter and plucks at the strings, tuning the guitar. After it's tuned, he plays. And he plays. And he plays. A half-hour concert is happening right in front of me. I wish I could play the guitar as he does.

Suddenly he catches himself and stops mid-piece.

"Yes, see, it's a good sounding instrument. This one is a Goya Grand Concert, and this one, he points to the one which is just a bit smaller and has a less robust shape at the bottom of its curved body, is a G-15 Concert. You play the guitar?"

"Not really, but I have a learner guitar, and I want to learn how to play classical guitar. There's a guy at home who plays and is willing to teach me."

"Good, good. I think the G-15 would be better for you in the beginning. It is not so difficult to handle and not so expensive."

"How much is it?" I ask.

"It's new and is worth at least $140 to $150. I can sell it to you for $125."

"That seems like a lot of money to me." My guess is, he probably got it for less that half that from someone who took it off a delivery truck or something. I've heard that's how most of these shops stay in business. But I don't really know, so I test the waters.

"What about a case?" I say.

"I have a few good hard cases. They range in price from $25 to $50, depending on the size and how good the case is."

"I need a hard case. It doesn't have to be fancy, just sturdy."

He says, "How much do you want to pay?"

"I'll buy the guitar for $75 and the case for $15 if you throw in some polish for the guitar."

"No, no, no." He is laughing at me. "It is worth much more. I can give you a case for $30. For both, because I like you, $125. And you are robbing me at that."

"Shoot," I say in a sad voice, " I guess I can't afford it. I don't have that much money."

"How much you have? Maybe we can figure something out."

Now I suspect that he's gotten the guitars for free and any profit is a huge profit. But in all honesty I have only $110 with me, and I'm not sure he will go for that.

"$100. I'll give you $100 for the guitar, case, and polish. I have $110, but I need $10 to get home." I start for the door.

"Because I like you and you want to learn," he says, "I'll sell the G-15 to you with the case and polish for $100 even."

We finish the purchase. As I am walking out the door, he says, "Turn right when you leave the store and go to 16th Street at the end of the block, then take 16th to the east for a few blocks before you turn south. It'll be safer for you. Especially with the guitar."

"Thanks. And thanks for the guitar. I think I'm going to love it."

"You're welcome, and good luck with it."

I head back to the hotel where I am to meet Mom for lunch. I'm happy with my new guitar and getting a reasonably good deal on it. As I walk, I wonder, *How did he know I was going to have to walk east and south of here to get to our hotel?* It was as if he knew exactly where I was coming from.

~ ~ ~

When I arrive at the hotel, I stop at Mom's room to let her know I'm back. I knock on her door. She answers my knock. "What do you have there?"

"A new guitar. It's a good one, and I got it for a steal."

"Where did you buy it?" she says.

"I got it at a pawn shop over on Larimer Street."

"On Larimer Street? Don't you know that part of town is dangerous? Whatever possessed you to go there?"

"It's a good place to get a good guitar for a good price." I explain.

"Honestly, Terry." She shakes her head.

Chapter 61

Summer 1960

Mom and I are home from Denver. Dad will be in the hospital for another few weeks while the doctors monitor the success of his latest operation. Ted and I are in the kitchen talking about the upcoming weekend. Gerry drives up, rushes into the house, and heads for the stairs.

"Where ya going in such a hurry?" Ted asks.

"I've got a date with Presh, and I'm late," he says.

"It's a little early for a date," I say.

"I know. We're going up the pass for a woodsie. I am supposed to pick Presh up at 6 o'clock."

"Hmmmm," I say to Ted, "guess he is a little late."

In a few minutes, Gerry is showered, dressed, and downstairs in the kitchen.

"When will you be home? It's your turn to do the dishes tonight," Ted says.

"That'll just have to wait," he says. He dashes out the door. We hear the Studebaker throw gravel as it accelerates down the driveway.

Ted and I look at each other, wondering who'll do the dishes. Carol comes into the kitchen with Heather and Toby following. She's carrying ten-month-old Valerie, whom she hands off to me, and says, "Watch her while I make these two some dinner."

What about Ted and me? I think.

Carol reads my mind and says, "Maybe if you and Ted are nice and do the dishes, I'll make some for you."

I look at Ted, and for once we agree. Doing the dishes is a small price to pay for having someone cook dinner.

After dinner I go upstairs, lie down on my bed, and read. Ted comes up later and goes to sleep. I read until it is late, turn out the light, but don't fall asleep right away. Some time has passed when I hear Gerry come quietly in the front door. I know something is up the moment I hear him creeping up the stairs. Usually when Gerry comes home late he stomps up the stairs normally, waking up half the household.

"Sssshhhh!" I hear him saying. "I think they're asleep."

I'm not about to contradict him because I am curious about the second voice. In the starlight, I see Gerry crossing the room with a girl coming behind him. "Presh, come over here," he says and leads her across the room to his bed. They kiss and make little noises, then start taking off their clothes. Soon they are lying on the bed naked, making big noises. Amidst all the groaning and heavy breathing, I hear Ted rustle in his sheets and know he's awake.

"What was that?" Presh whispers.

"Nothing, just one of my brothers turning over in his sleep. They always do that. Now, sssshhhh,"

When they are back at their noises, I whisper over to Ted.

"You awake?"

"Yeah. What are they doing over there? Sounds like more than kissing."

The noises from Gerry's side of the room get louder even though both he and Presh are doing their best to contain themselves.

"That's because they are not just kissing, they're screwing," I whisper.

"No, you think so?"

Just about that time, the passion across the room crescendos. We wait for a few minutes for the commotion to subside.

"Oops," Ted says aloud, "I guess you're right. You'd think they'd be quieter about it so they didn't wake us up."

"I think it's be nice if Gerry shared the wealth as long as we're awake," I half whisper.

I hear Gerry stifle a laugh and Presh giggle quietly. It's obvious they've heard me.

Soon I see Presh sit up in bed, her bare breasts reflecting in the ambient light. She hops out of bed, giggling, and puts on her panties and bra.

"And you told me they were sound sleepers," Presh says. Gerry is getting dressed.

As they walk from the room, Presh teases, "Maybe some other time, boys."

I hear Ted sigh.

Chapter 62

Fall 1960

Dad's back from the hospital in Denver. He's getting around on crutches. The surgery was only partially successful. The bone graft took, but his right leg is still too weak for him to stand on unsupported.

We're sitting in the kitchen having breakfast, and Dad says, "I wonder where I put my watch. I took it off the other day when I went to shower, and haven't seen it since. It's driving me crazy."

"I haven't seen it," Mom says.

Suddenly a vision pops into my mind. I see Dad's watch in his dresser drawer nestled between his T-shirts.

I blurt out, "It's in your bureau under your T-shirts on the left side of the second drawer down."

"You been in my bureau?"

"No, I just have a sense that's where it is."

"Well, I'm glad someone knows where it is," he says.

We finished breakfast and the conversation was forgotten. The next day, I overheard my dad speaking to Mom, "...and I'll be darned if I didn't find it under my T-shirts. Can't imagine how it got there unless I set it down while I was putting on a clean T-shirt. Well, anyway, I've found it, that's all that counts."

"Mmmmm," my mom says.

So I was right. How did I know that? This is happening to me more frequently, and each event goes much farther than mere coincidence. I don't understand it, and I want to know more about it, to investigate it further, but I don't know where to turn. Where to find books, whom to ask that won't think I'm crazy. I'll keep it to myself until I can find out more about what is happening in my mind.

Chapter 63

Fall 1960

Finally I'm in high school. Ninth Grade. The Sadie Hawkins Dance is over, and I'm walking Coral home. We leave the school and go up Francis Street toward her house. No moon, no streetlights, few house lights. The Milky Way is a light brush stroke on the night's dark palette.

"Let's see how many constellations we can identify," I say.

"Mmmm," Coral says.

She starts naming the ones she knows: Ursa Major, Ursa Minor, Draco, Orion and so forth.

"They're beautiful, aren't they?" Coral says.

"Mmmmm," I say.

We stand in the cold night air and look toward the heavens until we become chilled. Then we kiss, linger, and kiss some more, before we walk the rest of the way to her house.

The dance ended at 11:00. It is well after midnight by the time we get to Coral's house. Neither one of us is ready to end the evening, so we sneak into her house downstairs to the family room. We sit on the couch and kiss some more. With a mind of their own, my hands begin to wander. Coral doesn't seem worried. Soon my hands wander under her shirt, slowly around her side, and up her back. Then her bra is undone and hands have wandered back to the front and are touching her breasts.

This is new to Coral, and her insincere protests turn into tender sounds of pleasure. My hands wander some more and we get pretty mussed before Coral decides that she doesn't want to take it any further.

"It's getting late," she says.

"Yeah, it must be about one, I probably should get going because I have to walk home."

We kiss and fool around some more, then break it off, and Coral stands up and says, "Okay, time for bed."

Wow, I think, I'm gonna get lucky! Then it occurs to me that this is my cue to hit the road. We sneak up the stairs to the front door where we kiss goodnight, and I head home. On the way, I replay the events in my head. The dance, the stars, and the heavy petting. A perfect night. Maybe Coral and I are now officially dating.

~ ~ ~

Several days after the Sadie Hawkins Dance, it's clear that Coral and I are dating. I've decided to try to keep my mouth shut in school so I stay out of trouble, at least at much as possible. I'm doing this by giving myself more to do. Since we are studying astronomy, I've developed another one of my great ideas. I stay for a minute after science class and buttonhole Mr. Simons.

"Does the school own a telescope? I'd like to see the stars more clearly," I say.

"No, we don't," Mr. Simon says. "It would be fun to have one though, wouldn't it? If we did, we could see the craters on the moon or look at some of the larger stars in the constellations like Rigel in Orion and Sirius in Canis Major. It would be easier to distinguish all seven stars of the Pleiades, the seven daughters of Atlantis."

"Wouldn't it be great if we could get a telescope?" I say.

"Yeah, it sure would. But I don't have the funds in the science department, and I'm not sure the school can afford it. Telescopes are expensive."

I persevere, "What do you think you could see with a four-and-a-half-inch reflective telescope, for instance?"

"Hmmmm" Mr. Marsh says, "Surely a lot more than you can see with the naked eye or a set of good binoculars. I don't know if you could see the canals on Mars, but I'm sure you'd be able to see many more stars and constellations than you can see otherwise."

"How much do you think one would cost?"

"Gosh, Terry. I have no idea."

"Well," I say, "Let me show you what I found."

I take one of my Popular Mechanics magazines from my still-surviving La Fuma backpack and open it to the page I've marked with a piece of scrap paper.

"Here," I point to the page. "We can get a real good reflector telescope kit with a 4.5 inch mirror and a 1.25 eye piece with the tube and the tripod with an equatorial mount for a mere $50 including shipping. This is probably a $400 telescope. Of course, I would have to grind the glass and send it back to the company for the mirror coating, but in the end we could have a great telescope for not much money compared to what they cost assembled."

"How do you go about grinding the mirror?" Mr. Marsh asks me.

"They send you two round flat pieces of glass that are about seven-eighths-of-an- inch thick, along with some sort of resin wax and a bunch of different grades of corundum powder. You heat up the wax and pour it over one of the pieces of glass, using the mold that's included in the kit. The resin wax sticks to the glass. Before it cools down completely, you cut crosshatches in the resin so when you grind the mirror, the water and corundum will flow off the resin as it is used. When the resin has cooled and you're ready to begin grinding the lens, you wet down the resinated piece and sprinkle coarse grit corundum on it. You take the blank glass and grind it by moving it back and forth across the resin-covered glass. You hold the blank, which is going to become the mirror, halfway on the resin glass. Then you move it back and forth four or five times, then turn it thirty degrees, repeat the grinding motion, and turn it again. You continue like that until you grind the whole blank. As you grind it, you will see that it is pitted. This means the corundum powder is cutting the glass. You grind it until it becomes concave, then you use finer grits of corundum on the resinated glass. When the mirror is the exact concavity you want, you finish it and polish it with extra-fine corundum powder. Then you return it to the company so they can mirror it. They send it back, you mount it in the tube, fix the ocular to the tube, and, presto, you have a telescope for $50 plus shipping." I realize I'm out of breath.

Mr. Simons grins.

"Where did you learn all this?" he says.

"I want to see if I can see more of the stars, so I decided to call these guys up at the number listed here in the ad. I talked to someone about it, and that's what he told me. I took notes."

"You've sure done your research," Mr. Simon says.

"So, do you think you could ask the school board or Mr. Kelly or whoever you need to ask if they can find the $50 to buy it? Then I would grind the lens, build the telescope, and the school could own it after I finished as long as you will let me use it when I want to." I've planned that closing line.

"Sounds reasonable and very enterprising," says Mr. Simons. "Let me see what I can do."

"Thanks," I say, and head off to my next class knowing I'm late and not caring!

~ ~ ~

After our last class, Richard says to me, "What are you doing after school? Tony, Stephen, and I are going over to the Koch Lumber Company to check it out. Stephen says he knows a way in that he found with Spook last summer. You should come with us."

"I'd like to," I say, "but I have to go up to Edgar Stanton's house to play guitar."

"You're playing guitar?"

"Yeah. I thought you knew that. Edgar Stanton's been helping me out since earlier in the summer."

"Oh," Richard says, "well, you're gonna miss out on some fun."

Chapter 64

Fall 1960

A few weeks later after school, I do go over to the Koch Lumber Company with Tony, Richard, and the rest of them to see what they are up to. The Koch Lumber Company is a collection of old boarded-up and seemingly abandoned buildings located on the south part of town. We fool around in the buildings we can get into, looking at the old furniture, wood, and some old office equipment. It is really nothing special to me, but my buddies like to hang out there, so I don't mind coming along. I hear some glass breaking and know that someone has tossed a rock or a wrench through one of the last remaining windows. Most of the windows are boarded over, as are the doors. We stay there for an hour or so, then move on to other things. I head home on my bike, mildly disappointed that it is not as exciting as Richard had made it seem a few weeks ago.

~ ~ ~

Spook is home from Steamboat, where he now goes to school at Whitman Gaylord, a small private school, for the weekend and has called me to see if I want to come into town and goof around. I tell him, sure, and head into town on my bike. It's Saturday morning. I meet Spook at his house and leave my bike there. Spook doesn't really have a bike. Actually, he has one, but he is always doing something to it, and every time he does, it doesn't work for a long time. Then somehow he'll fix it or get some help fixing it, and he'll ride it for a while until he has some harebrained idea about how to make it stop or go faster or how to make it louder than you can by clipping cards to the spokes.

We walk toward town. We haven't gone too far, making our usual foolish conversation, when Spook stops in the street and says, "Let's do something new. The same old stuff we do is boring."

"Good idea," I say. "What do you want to do?"

"I don't know, just something."

I've had an idea for about a year but haven't had the opportunity to act on it. I needed someone who is game to come along in case there's trouble.

"I've got an idea," I say.

"What, let's hear it!"

"Well, about a year ago I was fooling around below Shadow Mountain, and I stumbled across a mine shaft that is overgrown with bushes. It has an old ladder that goes straight down into the ground for a long way. We could go and explore that."

"Sounds better than what we're doing," Spook says. "Lets do it."

"We'll need a flash light and some rope," I say. "If the wood on the ladder is rotten and one of the rungs breaks, we should be tied in at the top. And it's darker than a snake's butt down there."

"Who cares, let's just go do it. I've got some matches, we don't need any flashlight."

"Are you crazy? What if there's mine gas down there. You light a match, and you'll be blown to smithereens," I say.

"Hmmm, hadn't thought of that," Spook says. "Guess we should go collect our equipment."

We head back to Spook's house to round up a flashlight and an old climbing rope. In a few minutes, we're headed for Shadow Mountain. When we arrive at the end of Fifth Street where it dead ends into the mountain, I take off through the serviceberry bushes and stomp around for about ten minutes before I locate the hole in the ground.

"I think this must have been an air vent for some of the mine tunnels that go beneath Aspen. Maybe it's that one."

I point over to a place on the side of Shadow Mountain where there's a mineshaft that's now caved in. We look back at the tunnel and see the ladder going down into the darkness below. I search for something to tie the rope to. There's a small pine about ten feet away that looks like it will work, so I wrap the rope around it several times and tie a good knot in it.

"Who goes first?" I ask.

"I'll go first," says Spook.

I don't argue with him since it's his equipment.

"Tie the rope around your waist real good so if a rung breaks, you don't fall into the hole. We don't know how deep it is to the bottom."

Spook ties himself in and without saying another word, turns on the flashlight and steps on the first rung of the ladder, testing its strength. It seems to be all right, so he eases down to the second and third. As he disappears from view, I lie on the ground with my head over the shaft to see what's happening. In a few moments, I can only see the light from the flashlight bouncing off the walls, and a sliver of Spook. A pants leg here, an arm there, a foot on the rung. Suddenly I hear him shout, "Shit!"

"What's wrong?"

"Everything's cool. One of the rungs broke and I thought I was going to fall. I hit the one below and it held. I'm going down further."

"Take it easy. That wood is probably rotten down there where it's moist year-around," I shout.

"How'd you know it was moist down here?"

"Never mind. Can you see the bottom?"

"Not yet."

I wait for what seems like an hour, then hear Spook shout, "I'm out of rope. I think I'll untie the rope and go down a little bit further."

"Spook! Don't you dare untie that rope. It's too dangerous."

"Ah, it'll be okay."

I know he is up to his usual, dancing along the knife-edge. I stand up, grab hold of the rope, and pull it up as hard as I can so he will be unable to get the knot untied without more slack.

"Damn it, Morse! What are you doing?"

"You come on up now. No more rope, no more descent," I shout.

Slowly it sinks in, and he starts up the ladder. I pull the rope up as he comes.

When he gets to the top he says, "I was just kidding."

I know the crazy goof ball isn't kidding but let it pass. It would be just my luck to have to tell his mom that I left him at the bottom of some air vent tunnel, and she might like to go fetch him.

"Now it's my turn," I say.

I know I won't be able to see anything besides rock walls because I'm now sure the actual mining tunnel is well below us.

I check in with myself and find everything ready to go, so I tie off and head down the shaft. It is a wholly uneventful adventure for me. Down to the end of the rope, shining the flashlight to see if I can see the bottom, which I cannot, and back up.

We grumble about not having been able to hit the bottom and discuss how much rope we need to bring next time.

"I'm hungry," Spook says. "Let's head into town and find something to eat."

After a revolving door trip through Matthews Drug and the White Kitchen, neither of which have any counter space, we end up at Pinocchio's.

Pinocchio's is a beer and pizza joint on Cooper Street where you can always get a good pizza or hamburger. We walk in and take a seat.

"What can I get you kids?" the man behind the bar says.

We glance at the menu and decide to split a pepperoni-and-sausage pizza.

"We'll take a pepperoni-and-sausage pizza," I say.

"What to drink?"

Spook says, "I'll have a draft beer." He hasn't missed a beat.

"Me, too."

The bartender walks off and sends the order back to the kitchen. The next thing we know, there are two cold beers on the bar in front of us.

"Cool," I say.

We take a long sip and put our elbows on the bar like we know what we're doing. We're both fourteen and have another four years before we can drink beer legally, but if this guy is willing to serve them up, we're willing to drink them.

By the time our pizza arrives, we've quaffed down the first beer and the forlorn empty glasses beckon the bartender to quiz us, "Another?"

"Sure," we say in unison.

This could turn out to be a really interesting afternoon.

We chat about the great adventure just passed and what a total bust it was. As we sit discussing the adventure, it becomes more dangerous and exciting with every sip of the story-telling elixir in front of us. The pizza runs out before we run out of topics to catch up on.

Spook tells me how Whitman Gaylord School is the shits, being away from Aspen is the shits, and everything is generally the shits except the great pussy he is getting in

Steamboat. He goes on and on about it all, and I realize he has just as many sails in the wind as I do.

I tell him how school here is the shits and boring, and how Aspen is the shits because you can't do a lot of stuff we used to be able to do without getting into trouble, and how I've got a new girlfriend who puts out enough.

The bartender comes by and sees the last piece of pizza lingering on the platter.

"You guys done?"

"No, we're gonna finish this pizza here," Spook says.

"Want another beer?"

"Sure."

"Where's the bathroom?"

Of course, I know where it is because I've been in Pinocchio's a hundred times, but for some reason it's slipped my mind. The bartender says, "Back there where it's always been, Morse."

I am sobered by the fact that he knows my name. This is a dangerous situation. If he knows my name, he knows my parents, too. They would not be happy knowing that I was getting served beer on a Saturday afternoon in the middle of town. But, because I'm two beers to the wind, I have become virtually bulletproof, and I let this roll off me. I head back to the bathroom noticing my compass is off and my boat is listing dangerously side to side. I take a nice long pee and head back to the bar. Spook's head is hanging a little low from the neck. It looks like he is contemplating his beer rather seriously.

"What do you see in there?" I ask.

"Not a whole hell of a lot."

We have a couple more sips of beer and talk some more about old times and about what we are going to do over the summer. Stuff like that. We are both pretty drunk.

"You kids done?" the bartender says.

"Yeah, probably," I say.

He sets the tab on the bar and says, "I'll get it when you are ready," and walks off.

Suddenly I have this sinking feeling that something's wrong.

"Spook, you got any money?"

"No, I thought you'd buy since I'm the guest from out of town."

"Darn! I don't think I have any money with me."

We get in a discussion about the tab, if it is correct, who is going to pay, and whether or not we deserve a free beer since we've been the only customers in the bar for the last hour or so. While we're talking, I feel someone approaching the stool next to me. I turn to see Harry Baloney now sitting at the bar eying my beer.

Harry is a county employee who cleans streets with the water truck whenever someone tells him they need cleaning. He is a character and somewhat of a lush. I look over at him and give him his opening, "How're ya doin' Harry?"

"Same old Baloney," he says, "heh heh heh."

Then he takes his finger and pokes me in the ribs hard enough I think I've been shot. I turn on my stool and start to say something when he holds up his finger in front of my face and says, "This is an index digit. There are many things one can do with an index digit. It can be used to point, like this." He points his finger at the bar mirror.

"Or it can be used as an aid in exclamation. Like this." He holds his finger in the air and says, "Aha!"

"Or it can be a nose picker. Like this." He sticks his finger in his nose.

I try to stop his rambling. "Harry, what're you doing today? No street washing?"

"Now let me tell you about the street washing," he says. "Here's what I figured out."

He reaches down the bar and grabs a cocktail napkin and rummages around in his pockets for a minute before coming up with a stubby pencil.

"Okay, now watch this. I figure that I can spray water on the street at a velocity of about, let me see… well, let's say it's an average day, not after a parade or nothing." Then Harry begins talking mostly to himself, but sometimes looking up at me while he goes through the math and the physics of spraying water on the street. He's explaining to me all the formulas for velocity, nozzle drag, water viscosity, and a bunch of other stuff that I don't understand. A half hour later, he has filled four bar napkins with mathematical and physics formulae.

"And that," he says, stabbing his index digit into the latest napkin, "is how you spray the streets down to get them clear of rubbish. And, I might add, that any god-fearing, truck driving, high-end street sweeper needs to know to get his job done properly. And that's why they hired Harry. Because Harry knows how to get it done! Now, how about buying me a beer?"

I turn to look at Spook. He's gone. Nowhere to be found. I know he's left for a reason. He really doesn't have any money, and now it becomes my problem.

Damnit! I think. What am I going to do now? Harry sure doesn't have any money.

I stand up and have to hold the edge of the bar to keep from falling over. Once I've gotten off the swaying boat and am standing firmly on terra firma, I begin rummaging in my pockets. I remember leaving my wallet at home because I didn't want to ride to town with it in my back pocket. Usually I keep it in my backpack because it hurts my butt after sitting on it for a few miles. I realize my thoughts are wandering.

Through the haze, I remember I might have some money after all. Or maybe not. I rifle through my pockets once again, and my hands come across some paper-like substance. I pull it out: twenty bucks. I have no idea how it got there, but here it is. Good enough for me. I look at the tab and at the bartender. I say, "Give the street mathematician a beer. On me," and drop the twenty on the bar over the check.

As I weave out the door, I hear Harry saying, "How ya doin', Harry? Same old Baloney! Damn I love that!"

Chapter 65

December 1960

Dad's gone to Massachusetts General Hospital. His last operation in Denver didn't work out as they had hoped, so the doctors in Denver referred him to two doctors at Mass General who have had some luck using new techniques. The surgery Dad is now recovering from involved taking a large portion of his gastrocnemius muscle from the back of his lower leg, wrapping it around to the front of his leg, and attaching it to the bone on the interior side of his leg so the muscle tissue can serve as support for the weakened bone. The hope is that this, coupled with another bone graft, and a skin graft to cover the open wound, will allow the leg to heal completely and he'll be able to walk without crutches or a cane.

We'll see. I don't have much hope. It seems to me that they have been messing around with it for too long, and nobody really knows what they are doing. On the other hand, over the past twenty months Dad has shown his strength. He's been stronger than an ox. All the surgeries, drugs, and therapy would have killed a normal person, but he has come through it better than I can imagine. Part of me is still angry the accident happened, part of me feels sorry for Mom and Dad, and part of me wants it all to be over so I can get on with a normal life. Then I think, perhaps this *is* a normal life.

~ ~ ~

Coral and I are dating. Before the snow fell and I could still ride my bike home, Coral and I went to her house to "do our homework." We always said hello to her mom, shared a few words, then headed downstairs to the garden-level family room and got down to business. We turned on the TV to Dobie Gillis, Hawaii Five-O, or some other program, loud enough to cover the noise we made but not so loud that we couldn't hear if her mom or sister came downstairs. We'd sit on the couch and make out until it got too steamy and Coral put the skids on everything. I resigned myself to petting, hoping the Senior Prom might be the magical night.

Whether I get any on Prom Night or not, my life is full. I'm still playing guitar with Edgar Stanton at his house on Red Mountain: preludes, etudes, and short classical pieces. I spend as much time as I can spare each day practicing. The telescope lens is taking shape. I've ground it enough so I can see the concavity in the mirror. I should be finished in a few more weeks and will send the glass off to be mirrored. I'd like to build a two-way radio, so I'm studying to get a ham radio operator's license. I need to know Morse code, which I'm teaching myself. I picked up a little telegraph key from Fisher's Fix-It shop and am practicing with it. I know all the letters up through T.

And I'm still working at Aspen Sports. Spider and John are good to me, helping me with ski equipment, keeping my spirits up when I get depressed about the situation at home, and generally helping me to stay on an even keel. Spider won't be coaching this year. The sports shop is a great success, so he has to pay attention to the business. The new coach is Tom Carter. He's a nice enough guy, but nowhere near as much fun as Spider. He inspires me about as much as watching grass grow.

Gerry, Ted, and I are "holding down the fort" while Mom and Dad are back east. Gerry has had to plow the road using the battered old Jeep. Carol Carlson takes care of the little kids while we are in school or at work. When we get home, we fix dinner, clean up the kitchen, do our homework, and fool around some before falling into bed, tired as an all-day plow mule.

Gerry's Studebaker is torn apart again. He's put a 471 GMC blower on the fuel system with three two-barreled carburetors mounted on top. He's had to cut a hole in the hood to accommodate it. He changed the gearing in the rear end so it will take the extra power. The car is a beast. There is not one in a two-hundred-mile radius that can touch it.

~ ~ ~

One day Fred Henry and I were goofing around at his house, when I saw an article about go-karts in a magazine. I said to him, "Hey, Fred, I think we should build a go-kart. It wouldn't be too hard if we can get all the right parts."

"Yeah, that would be fun," he said.

"We can get the parts lined up this winter and build it next summer."

"You know what?" Fred said, "my half-brother Peter has an old go-kart that he was given for his birthday this summer. He never got it to work, and ended up taking the engine off to use on the lawnmower. Maybe we could buy the frame from him. That would give us something to start with."

"Let's talk to him about it," I said.

We went in search of Peter. We found him, made small talk, and then I said, "Peter. I saw that old piece-of-crap go-kart you have out in the garage. You ever going to fix it up and use it?"

"No. It never would run, so we used the engine to replace the one on the lawn mower after it broke."

"Looks like the tires are rotting too," I continued. "And there are a couple of cables on the thing that are bent. Too bad. It might have been fun to have something that worked."

"Yeah," said Peter, "but I don't have time for it anymore. It's almost winter, and that means it's time to ski."

"True enough," I said. "So, what are you going to do with all the junk metal? Scrap it?"

"Yeah, I guess I'll take the tires off and maybe use them for something, then just take the rest to the dump next time Freidl goes."

"Tell you what," I said, "if you take the tires off and keep the frame here in your garage for the winter, I'll pay you five bucks for it. I don't have the money with me, but I'll bring it over tomorrow."

"What do you want to do with it?"

"Nothing much, I just hate to see all that metal go in the dump when there may be something I can make out of it," I say.

Peter was thinking about things to be made out of metal, other than a go-kart and was having difficulty considering just what those may be. Then he clearly realized having five bucks now for something he was going to scrap anyway is much better than having nothing now and wasting the time trying to figure out what I'm up to. "All right," he said, "but you have to bring the five bucks tomorrow for sure. If you don't, the deal's off."

"Deal." I reached out and we shook on it.

Fred and I went back to his house. He and Rick live in a small structure on the property separated from the main residence. They have their own space with a little kitchen, a bath, and two bedrooms. We were in Fred's room talking about the go-kart idea.

"I'll do some research on engines," Fred says. "Maybe we should get another Briggs and Stratton since there is already a mount that fits it on the kart frame."

"Naw, McColloch is the best," I say. "Heck, they invented the two-cycle engine so they could sell their oil. You think they'd make a bad engine for chain saws and small machines? Nope. They need to have the best small engines in the world so they can sell lots of them to people who will buy their oil. I read that in Popular Mechanics."

"Fine, you do it then," Fred says. "You think you are so damn smart about it, Mr. High IQ. You probably don't know what IQ means anyway."

"Duh. Intelligence Quotient,"

"Do you know I had an IQ test when I applied to Deerfield? Bet you can't guess what mine was."

"Probably not," I say

"It's 161. That's pretty high. Einstein had a real high IQ."

"So what? No one knows how high Einstein's IQ was because he never took a test. They didn't even have an IQ test back then. Besides, people can have real high IQs in some things and be stupid in others. Let's get back on the subject, which is go-karts," I say. "We need to do more research on the engines, so let's both do some work on it while you are gone at school, and when you get home for your Christmas vacation we can talk about it some more." We both agree and resolve to do our homework.

~ ~ ~

Ted and I are in the bathroom, getting ready to go out with our dates. Ted has his driver's license now, so I'm hitching a ride into town with him. I'm wearing jeans, shirt, sweater, and my usual climbing footwear. I stand in front of the mirror and comb my hair. Ted butts in front of me. I'm just about to push him out of my way, but I stop mid-push. "Christ, what happened to you?"

"Whaddya mean?" he says.

"Well, what are you wearing?"

He has on chinos, a white shirt, a tweed sports coat that I've never seen before, and an ascot. I look down at his feet. Penny loafers.

"You're not going to town looking like that, are you? You look like...like, I don't know what. A Tweed Bag. A-a-a tourist!"

"If you want to get the girls, you gotta look good," he says.

"Maybe if you were in Detroit or somewhere. What's that around your neck?"

"An ascot, you idiot."

He admires himself in the mirror and says to his reflection, "One thing about us Morses, we've got the looks."

He turns and walks out of the bathroom, saying, "Come on if you're coming. I'm leaving now."

I don't know whether to stay and puke in the sink or to follow and get a ride into town.

Tweed Bag. That's a good name for him. Think I'll use it from now on.

Chapter 66

Winter 1961

We're in Steamboat for the Winter Sports Carnival. Today we skied the giant slalom and the cross-country events. Richard is here. He placed in the giant slalom, and I won the cross-country race. At dinner tonight, we were told is that there is a meeting in Bill Marolt's room. Guys only. Richard and I have come to the meeting like all the others.

Everyone gathers in Marolt's room, some of the guys sitting on chairs, some on the bed. I'm leaning up against the wall next to the window. Richard is on the other side of the room, sitting on the edge of a table.

Someone says, "Okay, the first order of business is to initiate the freshmen into the ski team. When we turn the lights off, we're gonna have a circle jerk. The first one to come will be this year's team captain."

I'm a little confused, so I ask, "What are we supposed to do? I've never heard of a circle jerk."

They all laugh, and someone says, "You stupid little shit, you're supposed to pull your pud. The first one to come becomes the team captain."

"Oh," I say. Something-besides jerking off with other guys-doesn't feel right.

Someone turns the lights out, and I hear the other guys rustling their clothing and zippers. I stay standing, leaning up against the wall. I decide to trust my feelings of distrust. Soon the others in the room are making noises like they are masturbating and saying, "Uh, and Oh, and Ah (groan, groan)."

I smile to myself, because now I am sure they're trying to mess with Richard and me.

Suddenly the lights come on in the room. Everyone has their pants on. They look at me and then at Richard. I'm leaning up against the wall with a cynical grin and my pants zipped. Richard is leaning against the table jerking off with his pants down.

The guys laugh hilariously. They call Richard "Captain." He doesn't think it's funny. He pulls his pants up and heads for the door, embarrassed and ashamed. One of the upperclassmen stops him and says, "Don't worry about it. It's all in good fun. They got me when I was a freshman too. It's just something we do to welcome freshmen to the team. So, stick around; we have some business to handle."

Richard looks at him and decides to stay. He looks at me like, "How the hell did you know, traitor?"

I shrug my shoulders and wait to see what is next.

Chapter 67

Winter 1960

Gerry and I have just finished work at Aspen Sports, and we're late for dinner. With Dad home, Mom is back to cooking dinners for us older ones. I think it makes her feel more like a mom.

Gerry says, "We're late, so we better get movin'."

We lock the shop door and head out to the car. The Studebaker has been running pretty well these days now that Gerry has it back together, and has figured out the rear-end gear ratios and the fuel mixture for the carburetors and blower. We hop in, and Gerry fires up the engine. It rumbles like a growling Savanna cat. He feathers the gas, and the car roars to life.

Gerry releases the clutch, the tires shriek on the pavement, and we are off. We head out of town, Gerry accelerating as we go. By the time we hit Seventh Street, we're going sixty miles an hour. Gerry double-clutches and downshifts. Rounding the corner on Eighth, he hits the gas, and the car leaps forward. We flash through the two blocks, another double-clutch, downshift, and an almost immediate acceleration around the corner and it's a straight shot to the Castle Creek Bridge. As we power through the last turn, out of the corner of my eye, I see a car lurking in the shadows on Hallam Street.

"Gerry," I begin, "I think Baker…"

Before the words leave my mouth, Roy Baker, Aspen's finest, blue light flashing, siren wailing, and horn blowing, speeds after us. Gerry punches it. He downshifts to second gear and floors the accelerator, demanding the engine to perform. It does. Tires squeal, and the car pounces forward. We cross the Castle Creek Bridge. I look back and see Baker is just leaving the intersection of 8th and Hallam. We're already three solid blocks ahead. Gerry does a power shift into third and lays another patch of rubber as we accelerate to fourth gear.

We pass the Maroon Creek turn-off six hundred yards past the Castle Creek Bridge. I see blue pulses of light reflecting off the snow. Baker is not in sight. We hit the mile straightaway to the Maroon Creek Bridge. Gerry shifts to fourth. We're still accelerating. We are going at least a hundred miles per hour. Cottonwood trees zip by on the left, the golf course a blur on the right. When we hit the Maroon Creek Bridge, I look back and see Baker coming out of the slight bend by the Maroon Creek turn-off, his police cruiser at top speed.

Gerry is focused on driving. He's never driven the Studebaker this fast. The narrow Maroon Creek Bridge is frightening at the speed we are going. We're on it only for seconds before we hit the end of the bridge, streak past our road turn-off, and Gerry kills the lights. We're driving toward the airport at one hundred and thirty miles an hour with no lights.

"What the hell?" I say to Gerry. "Can you see anything?"

"Not much, but I know about where the road goes."

"You might want to slow down just a bit. I'm sure he can't see you at this point."

"Good idea," says Gerry. He lets off the gas, and the lightning machine torques down. We're a mile ahead of Roy Baker. We pass the entrance to the Buttermilk Ski area and Rick and Fred's house. Gerry downshifts to third, then to second, avoiding the brakes so the brake lights don't glow red, and makes a ninety-degree turn onto a dirt road that heads to Zoline's ranch and Caudill's house beyond. We ease down the dirt road, trying not to kick up dust. Two hundred yards down this side road, Gerry turns the Studebaker around.

We sit, engine idling, and wait. Will Baker figure out what we've done? It seems like minutes, but it is only a few seconds before we see Baker scream by the intersection, lights on, blue light flashing, and siren wailing. We wait for a short minute, then pull out and slowly return to the highway.

Gerry drives fast, lights out, to our road turn-off on the west side of the Maroon Creek Bridge. We make the turn and drive the rest of the way home in the dark and park the car in the garage. We're both pumped with adrenaline.

"What a gas!" I say.

"Yeah, that was bitchin'!" Gerry says.

We walk into the house and see everyone at the table eating.

"You're late," Dad says.

"Sorry, got delayed at work,"

We wash up and serve ourselves dinner. We talk about the day and what is going on around the house. The usual dinner chatter. The others are on dessert, and Gerry and I are just about finished with our dinner, when there's a knock on the door. My gut lurches.

"Who can that be?" my dad says. "Terry, you go see."

I already know who it is. I walk slowly to the door, open it, and see Roy Baker standing, one hand on his gun and the other on his hip. "Where is he? I know he's here, because I saw the car in the garage. And I felt the engine. It's hot. I know he's here."

I look at Baker dumbly and say, "Who?"

"Your brother! Where is he?" Baker's so mad he stutters.

"Well, if you mean Gerry, he's eating dinner."

"Who is it?" Dad shouts.

I shout back, "It's the cops!"

"It's dinner time. What the hell do they want?"

I can hear him getting up from the kitchen table. I step back because I know this is going to get interesting.

My dad limps over to the door. Even with his accident, my dad is a large man. He is well over six feet, raw-boned, and has laser blue eyes that can burn through about anything. I know from many years of experience that you can make him mad, but you never want to truly piss him off.

"Good evening," my dad says gruffly. "What can I do for you?"

"Your son has been speeding. I chased him half way to Glenwood Springs. I was going over a hundred and couldn't even stay close to him. I know he's here because I seen the car in the garage and felt the engine. It's still hot."

I could see my dad starting to simmer. He doesn't appreciate the fact that Baker went into our garage. It's private property, and he has no business there. Dad says, "Which son are you talking about? My kids are home here eating dinner."

"The hell, you say," says Baker. "I chased that kid driving that Studebaker all the way from town. I'm here to arrest him for speeding."

Now my dad heats up from simmering to boiling. No one interrupts his dinner with a "to hell, you say" and a threat of arrest. I can see him trying to decide whether to hold the lid on it or let Baker have it. I see he is going to land somewhere in between.

"Look, mister, I don't give a damn what you think you saw. My sons are here in the privacy of my home eating dinner. I don't like to have my dinner interrupted. It's family time. I also don't like you trespassing on private property. My garage and my house are private property, and you are at the moment trespassing in the worst way I can think of. Now, if you don't get the hell out of here and down the road in less than thirty seconds, I'm going to be on the phone to Guido, (Guido is the magistrate now), every one in the city council, and that is after I call Loren Herwick (the Sheriff) up here and have you arrested for trespassing. Now get your sorry ass down the road before I get mad!"

Baker stands in the entrance dumbfounded. He understands he's on very thin ice and has the common sense to back off. By now Ted and Gerry are both standing with me, watching the exchange. It is something out of the Hatfields and McCoys, only Baker has come without his kinfolk. He should have brought them.

He looks at Gerry. "I'm gonna get you one of these days soon."

My dad gives him his worst evil eye and says, "Are you threatening my son?"

Baker realizes that he has opened his mouth once too often and begins backing out the door.

"No, Sir, I'll be leaving now."

Dad looks at him as he walks out.

"Don't let the door hit you in the ass, you little pipsqueak."

Then he turns to Gerry as we go back to the table. "What in the name of hell did you do now? Christ, you're getting to be a royal pain in the ass. That damn car is gonna either get you killed or in jail."

"Well, do you want to hear the whole story?" I cut in.

"Yeah," Ted pipes up.

"Well, we got off work, and we were a little late because I had to mop the floor tonight and..."

I went through the whole story with all the little details. When I finished, Ted was laughing, and my dad was chuckling.

"He fell for the oldest trick in the book," my dad says.

I realize, after finishing dinner and heading upstairs to do my homework, that Gerry is walking on the edge. And he likes it.

Chapter 68

Spring 1961

Winter is over. Dad has tried to work for the ski school, but it's not working out. He's been talking to Fritz Benedict, who's suggested that Dad should get into the real estate business. He's letting Dad use a little office in his building on the corner of Cooper and Hopkins Streets. It will be good for my dad to have some work after all this time. He's been in and out of the hospital for the last 36 months and has had 39 different operations. It's amazing that he's still functioning. The doctors say that he can walk, but is not to do anything strenuous with his leg, being as weak as it is. It won't get much better, but at least he has both legs.

I finished grinding the telescope lens, and we sent it off to be mirrored. When we got it back, I mounted it in the telescope tube, put the ocular on, mounted it on the tripod, and tried it out. What do you know! It worked! Now we can see the craters of the moon and tons more stars.

I'm doing time-lapse photography of the heavens. The first set of photographs I took showed the stars moving across the sky with bands of light streaming behind. I saw a picture in an astronomy book that gave me the idea to take a photo with the camera lens focused right on the North Star. I was intrigued to see all the stars circled in a big arc around the North Star. I love learning new stuff.

~ ~ ~

There's been a big scandal in the school that I am a part of. Apparently the guys have been fooling around the Koch Lumber Company. They broke some more windows, and some things have gone missing. The Koch Lumber Company is private property, so sneaking into the buildings is trespassing. I've only gone with them three times, but I'm still involved in the scandal.

A few days after the last lumber company visit, which I was in on, Richard comes up to me at school and says, "Did you hear the latest? The FBI is here investigating a break-in and vandalism at the Koch Lumber Company!"

"What?" I say. "Why? We haven't really done anything bad. Sure we sneak in there, but I sure haven't vandalized anything. Unless there's stuff I don't know about. I've only been over there three times."

"I don't know, but I heard they are questioning everyone. They'll probably ask us about it, too. I guess they may arrest somebody if they find out who did it."

"Dang," I say. "This is not good."

"No kidding," says Richard.

We see Tony down the hall and stroll over to ask him what he knows. He says, "Apparently someone did some serious damage a few days after we were there last time. They found the Playboy magazines and the cigarettes. We're all pretty scared."

Several days pass before I'm called to the principle's office. I go down the hall, shaking in my boots, and enter the room. Mr. Kelly is there and introduces me to a man who says he is an FBI agent. I am almost pissing my pants and immediately forget his name.

"As you know, I'm here investigating the break-in and the vandalism to the Koch Lumber Company," he says.

I immediately think to myself, *How would I know what he's doing before he tells me? I mean, of course, I know, but that's only because I have heard the rumors. He doesn't really know I know, he's only surmising that I know."*

"Some person or persons have broken into the property and caused some damage, which has not gone unnoticed."

He continues, "I am here to ascertain the guilty party or parties. So," he pauses. "What can you tell me about this?"

My mind races back to the first grade and the caper at Matthews Drug Store. There is no sense in lying. Lies are always found out or suspected at some point. So I say, "I don't know much. I have only been there three times. Twice last fall and once this spring. I know that a bunch of guys meet there, but I'm not at all sure what happens."

"Tell me what happened when you were there." He's trying to be serious and stern with me. I sense he already knows I'm not the culprit, but he has a job to do and needs to do it right.

"Well, the first time I was there, a few kids and I went in through the broken door in the back of the building in the middle, and looked around at the furniture and stuff that was left there. We didn't take anything, only looked at stuff and imagined what it was like back when the place was open. One of the kids tossed a rock or something through one of the windows that hadn't already been broken, but that's about it. We were there for about an hour. It wasn't that interesting."

"What else?"

"The last time was this spring about ten days ago or so. We went over there again and went to a different building that I had never been in before. We hung out there, looked at Playboy magazines and some of the kids smoked. I don't smoke, so all I did is look at the magazines."

"Anything else?"

"Nope."

He asks me a few more questions, and then tells me that I can go. As I leave, I wonder if we are really in trouble, or if they are just trying to scare us so we don't go into the Lumber Company any more. Either way, it's working.

Later in the afternoon, Tony, Richard, and I compare notes. None of us really knows what is happening because the FBI agent isn't saying anything about the vandalism or what happened. We decide we will just have to wait to see what becomes of it.

After about two weeks, we don't hear any more. No one is arrested, there is no mention of it in the newspaper, and no one is talking about it at school. We decide they just got someone in there to scare us. I take it to heart and stay away from the Koch Lumber Company.

~ ~ ~

While the great Lumber Yard Investigation fizzled out, I've found a new potential for Terr-Ass: the clothespin gun. We dismantle a clothespin and re-assemble it reversing the spring on the pins. Then we tape the thin ends of the clothespin together, creating a trigger devise. If a Strike Anywhere Kitchen Match is stuck in between the two arms of the clothespin (where it rests quite nicely) and the spring trigger is pulled, it snaps down and back, hitting the head of the match and lighting it, at the same time it sends the match flying about twenty or thirty feet. It is a terrific portable flamethrower. The contraption is actually quite ingenious.

I don't know who figured it out, but we have been fooling around with these gizmos for a few weeks now, shooting them at each other and off into space. Everyone is pretty careful with them, and no one has gotten hurt, no clothes have been burned, at least too badly, and in general it's just been fun.

Today, things changed. Stephen Kellogg and I are fooling around, walking down Galena Street after school. He has his match gun with him and is firing matches out into the street once in a while. We're having a loud-and-obnoxious good time. As we walk by the Arrow Shop, Stephen shoots another match. He must have loaded the match crookedly, because out of the corner of my eye, I think I see the match hit the window outside the entrance to the shop. The window is at an angle abutting the doorframe, allowing the door to be set back from the sidewalk. I think I see the match bounce off the window, where it is deflected right into the store landing in the center of a table that has a bunch of earrings attached to little cardboard price tags.

"Stephen," I say, "I'm pretty sure that match went into the Arrow Shop."

"No, it didn't, I saw it go down the sidewalk somewhere."

"No," I say, "I really think it went into the Arrow Shop. We need to go back and see. If it went in and we don't get it, it's bound to start a fire."

"You can go back if you want, but I'm sure it didn't go into the store."

Shoot, I think, *this is going to be trouble.* I know I should run back to the store and check it out, but for some reason I keep walking.

We go about our business of nothing much at all, just wasting time, and goofing around town. After a fashion, I ride my bike home to start my homework. I'm not home more than half an hour when Dad gets home.

"Terry!" he shouts upstairs.

"Yes?" I shout down the stairs.

"Get your ass down here."

My heart is in my shoes. I know trouble is on the way, but I can't imagine what I've done this time. I go down to the kitchen.

"Follow me," he says. He walks into his bedroom and closes the door after me. I now know this is serious.

"What in hell were you doing this afternoon with that Kellogg boy?"

"Nothing, we were just fooling around town."

"Do you call starting a fire in the Arrow Shop fooling around?"

News travels fast in Aspen. How did he find out about that?

"No. But I didn't start any fire."

"Tell me what happened."

I explain. "Stephen and I were walking down the sidewalk on Galena Street. He had a match gun."

"What's a match gun?" my dad interrupts.

I explain to him what a match gun is, how it works, and keep talking, "So, we were walking down the street and Stephen is shooting off his match gun from time to time, and he shot one that I think I saw bounce off the window. It might have gone into the Arrow Shop. I couldn't be sure about it because I just thought I saw something out of the corner of my eye. It all happened real fast. I told Stephen we should go back and check it out, but he said he saw the match hit the sidewalk."

"It damn well didn't hit the sidewalk, it landed on a table with a bunch of earrings on display. A lady picked one up and got burned by it."

"Was it serious?"

"No, and you better be thankful for that. You idiots could have burned the whole building down."

"It wasn't my fault. I didn't shoot it."

"You were with him, and that was bad enough. First, you are in trouble all the time with Spook James, then there is the whole mess with the Koch Lumber Company and those kids that vandalized it. You were just damn lucky that you didn't have anything to do with that. And now it's this. Maybe Bill and Julie James had the right idea. Maybe you should think about going to school somewhere else where you won't be in so much trouble."

How did he know about the Koch Lumber Company thing? So that's why we didn't hear anything else about it. It wasn't our little band of juvenile delinquents who did it. Whatever "it" was.

"So, here's what you are going to do. First, you are going to apologize to the owner of the Arrow Shop. Then you are forbidden to hang around with Stephen Kellogg or any one of those other kids who are in this little band of idiots. Finally, you are going to come home right after school for the rest of the year. No staying in town. No screwing around town on the weekends until you start work in the summer. In the meantime, I want you to think long and hard about the path you're heading down. I'm not going to tolerate this sort of behavior in this house, mister, so you better get a good grip on yourself."

The lecture goes on for days. Finally he says, "And you may want to start looking into alternatives for high school. This place is not doing you any favors, and you are not doing it any favors. When you've thought about it for a while, we'll talk again. Now get the hell out of my sight."

I go upstairs to my room, fully chastised and depressed. I lie down on my bed and let thoughts wash over me. As they cascade across the mirror of my mind, I watch them. I pull one down and examine it, turn it in my mind, regarding it from all sides, then let it slide away. I lie there all afternoon, through dinner, and late into the night. I know I've let my parents down, even if it wasn't my doing. As an accomplice, I should have had better judgment. I don't like this truth, but there it is.

~ ~ ~

I keep very much to myself for the next week. Then today, Coral Ann catches me in the hall at my locker when I'm getting my books together before getting the bus home.

"What's going on?" she says. "You haven't spoken more than two words to me for a week."

"I'm sorry," I say. "I'm just upset about this whole thing with the Arrow Shop. I'm catching hell for it at home, and it wasn't really my fault. I was just walking down the sidewalk with Stephen. He's the one who shot the match."

"Maybe you shouldn't have been goofing around with him," she says.

"Duh."

Just then, Stephen comes up to us. "Did you get in trouble for the Arrow Shop thing? I don't know why they made such a big deal out of it. Nothing happened. Anyway, I'm not in trouble. My dad is out of town and my mom hasn't heard about it. Besides, it wasn't my fault the match bounced off that window."

I look at him, uncomprehending. He is talking to me like it isn't his fault.

"Darn right I'm in trouble," I say. "I had to apologize to the owner for your stupid-ass move, and I'm grounded for pretty much the rest of my life. And I'm the one who didn't have anything to do with it."

"Too bad," he says. "It wasn't that big a deal."

"I don't want to talk about it. I've gotta catch the bus home."

I stuff the last book in my backpack and slam my locker door.

Stephen walks off, and I say to Coral, "Sorry, but we're not going to be able to see each other after school anymore. I've gotta go home right after school. Bus or bike. My parents are really mad about this stuff. They think I'm turning into a hoodlum."

Coral looks at me and says, "We'll be okay. It's just for a while. I know it wasn't your fault."

"Thanks," I say.

She walks me out to the bus. On the way I say, "I forgot to ask, but would you go to the Senior Prom with me?"

Coral looks at me, and I can tell she is uneasy. She is shuffling her feet and smoothing down her skirt with her hands.

"Terry," she says, "Last fall before we were dating, Nick asked me to the prom. I said 'yes' for some stupid reason. I'd hoped he'd forgotten, but three days ago he reminded me. I think I have to go with him since I committed to it. I'm sorry."

I take in this news. Another punch in the chest.

"Maybe I'll go by myself, and we can have a dance or two," I say. "Or maybe not. I don't know." I'm disappointed. Coral touches my arm.

"See you tomorrow," I say and get on the bus.

Chapter 69

Spring 1961

Two weeks have passed since the episode with the Arrow Shop. Things have normalized at school as much as they ever will. Coral and I are back together again. I've talked my dad into letting me stay in town and study with Coral after school. I'm friends with Tony and Lawren but don't hang around with anyone else.

I spend my spare time with Coral, playing guitar with Edgar Stanton, fooling around with the electronics, and reading up about astronomy.

Mom has announced she is pregnant again and will have a baby in November.

Holy crap! That means there'll be eight of us. Wow! That means she must have gotten pregnant in the hospital, I think.

I've spent some time thinking about my life, the Aspen School system, my jobs, my family, and friends. I've come to the conclusion I have done about all I can do in this environment. I spent most of the eighth grade teaching myself out in the hall, and I have interests few others in school seem to have. I seem to be getting into trouble in spite of the adults in my life trying to help me out. Edgar Stanton has been thoughtful, helping me learn how to read music, and taking his time to play guitar with me. In all fairness Mr. Simons went along with my idea on the telescope and made it happen for me. And of course Spider and John have been very good to me.

~~~

Yesterday I remembered just after the Arrow Shop incident Dad said I should talk to Steve Knowlton. Maybe he would have some suggestions about schools that offer skiing as part of their sports program. I decide to give Steve a call. We talked and set up a meeting for this afternoon after school.

Now, I'm at his house. I'm nervous; not scared, just jittery. Steve answers my knock and says, "Come in, Terry, glad to see you. Have a seat."

I look around and sit on the couch. Steve's house is a 1950s panabode and has a welcome feeling that helps me overcome my nervousness.

"What can I do for you?" Steve says.

"Some time ago my dad mentioned you might know something about other schools that have skiing as an actual school sport."

"Why would you want to leave Aspen?" Steve asks.

"I think I've about done all I can do here for the time being."

Steve sees I'm serious.

"What do you mean?" he says.

"School here isn't challenging. I get bored and make a pain in the ass of myself so the teachers are tired of it, and so am I. I've gotten into some trouble that really wasn't my fault, but I'm blamed because I was along with the other kid."

Steve says quietly, "Yeah, I heard about that. Wrong place at the wrong time."

Steve tells me about his experience attending Holderness School in New Hampshire before the war. It's a challenging place academically, has a great sports program with an emphasis on skiing, and has the goal of creating an environment where students become well-rounded individuals. The school stresses learning how to think, rather than rote memorization of subject matter. He goes on for some time talking about Holderness, about Deerfield,

Andover, Exeter and several other prep schools he knows about. I think he must have done some homework of his own.

We talk about my interests, what's going on at home, and why I'm bored at Aspen High School. Finally, Steve looks at me and says, "It sounds to me like Holderness would be a great fit for you. You should write them and get some information. It's in Plymouth, New Hampshire. It may be too late to apply for this coming year, though. Most of the prep schools require applications to be in by January first."

I'm crestfallen. It's already the first week of May. I was getting excited about the possibility of starting something new, a life I could re-create on my own terms. Nevertheless, I write down the name and address Steve has provided me. We chat a little more before I thank him, say good-bye, and leave.

The next day I cut classes at noon and ride my bike home. It's a good time to do what I'm about to do. Dad is at his office trying to get the real estate business going, and Mom has gone to Glenwood Springs for groceries. Carol and the little kids are home and pay me no mind.

I pick up the telephone and dial information. In a few minutes I have the number for Holderness. It is late in the afternoon in New Hampshire, so I hope someone will answer.

"Holderness School."

"Hello," I say. There is a silence on the line. I don't know what to say next.

"How can I help you?" the woman on the phone asks.

I am tongue-tied for a moment, then I say, "I would like to speak to someone about applying to your school."

"Have you sent in an application?"

"No, I just decided to go there last night."

"You have to send in an application," the voice says.

"I understand. Is there someone I can talk to about all of that?"

"Just a minute please."

I wait for a minute, and a woman comes on the line.

"Hello? This is Pat Henderson."

"Hi, my name is Terry Morse, and I am calling from Aspen Colorado. I would like to go to your school next year."

"That's nice. How did you hear about Holderness?"

I tell Pat about Steve Knowlton; that he graduated from Holderness in 1941, was a really good skier, and recommended Holderness for its athletics and academics.

"So you live in Aspen, Colorado?" Pat says.

"Yes, I've lived here all my life."

"Tell me about your family."

"My parents moved here after the war in early 1947 when I was six months old. We had a ranch."

I continue to tell her about Mom and Dad working on the ranch, selling it, dad's ski accident, my seven brothers and sisters, and the rest of it.

"And what about you? Why do you want to leave Aspen and come to Holderness?"

I talk some more about school being a bore for me, about some of the projects I do on my own, like building the radios and the telescope. We chat a long time.

Finally she says, "I'll tell you what. I'll send an application for you to fill out and send back. You'll have to take some tests that will be given at Colorado Rocky Mountain School in Carbondale, Colorado...let me see..." I hear papers rustling. "Actually, next week. I can give you a number to call to get the testing arranged. When we get your application and your test scores, we can see where things stand. How's that?"

"That would be great!" I say.

We talk a while longer and finally say good-bye. I immediately dial the other number and manage to get myself set up for the testing.

That night when Dad comes home, has had a chance to make a bourbon on the rocks, and relax for a minute, I say, "Can I talk to you a minute?"

"Sure, son, come into the living room and sit down."

I follow him and sit on the couch while he sits in his favorite chair by the fireplace.

"I've decided to apply to Holderness School, and I have arranged to take an entrance exam in Carbondale next week. I'm wondering if maybe Mom can give me a ride so I can take it. They're sending me an application in the mail. I spoke with a woman named Pat Henderson who told me normally it's too late to submit an application for this year, but maybe they'll look at mine if I get it back to them right away."

"That's an interesting development," my dad says.

I can't tell if he is happy about it or not. Then I realize what his concerns are as he continues, "I'm not sure we can afford to send you to school. I'm trying to start the real estate business. It's going well, but all the money I make goes to paying off our bills. Don't forget I haven't been able to work for three full years."

I get a sinking feeling in my stomach. In my mind it's already decided. I'm going, and that's that. I do some quick calculations in my head.

"I have enough saved and am making enough at work so I can pay the plane fare back and forth, buy my clothing and whatever else I need. That leaves the tuition. Fifteen hundred dollars per year. I'm aware that's a lot of money because I know how long it takes me to make it, but I'll just have to figure it out."

My dad looks at me curiously. "Where did this all come from?" he says.

"I talked to Steve Knowlton, like you suggested. He thought Holderness School would be a good match for me because they have a good ski program and are strong in academics. It's not Deerfield, Andover or Exeter, but from the sound of it, those schools are too big, a little stuffy, and don't really have a good skiing program. If I leave Aspen, I want to be somewhere where I can ski on a team like I do here. Also, I'm tired of everyone thinking I'm such a troublemaker. I'm not really that bad. I didn't have anything to do with the Koch Lumber thing, and the thing with the Arrow Shop was not me, it was Stephen. Yet, I'm the one who seems to be getting all the flack from it at school. I'm just tired of it. This whole place is getting on my nerves. It is changing here. After working at the tennis courts this summer, I realized that lots of those people playing tennis don't have anything better to do than to talk about how they dress and who did what at the last cocktail party. There's more to think about than that crap. I had to chase Lefty around town for two days to get my last paycheck. He kept avoiding me. Finally I ran him down at the Meadows eating lunch and told him I needed to be paid right now. He gave me a check, but grudgingly. I didn't trust him after that, so I went and cashed it immediately and put the money in my savings. It's just stuff like that. It bugs me."

"You didn't tell me about the paycheck," Dad says.

I can tell he is miffed about it because he is very honest about everything. He thinks for a while and says, "Maybe you could get a scholarship. You should apply for one when you send in your application. Maybe write a letter and explain your situation so they can understand your wanting to leave Aspen for a more interesting educational experience."

"I guess it would be a smart thing to do if we can't afford to pay for it," I say. "I have to get the money somewhere, and I don't have enough saved to pay for tuition, airfare, and all the rest of the expenses I'll have. I'll only have enough to fly back Christmas and Spring vacations. But I know I can figure it out if I can get the tuition paid for."

"You know your mom and I both support you. If you need us to do anything, you let me know."

I think about this before I answer him. It seems like I'm on my own with this. I know it is a bad time for me to throw this all on them because Dad is just beginning to get his feet back on the ground, so to speak, but I need to move on. I've made up my mind that I'll make it work no matter what.

"Thanks, Dad," I say. "I just wanted you to know what is going on before I ask Mom to take me to Carbondale. Maybe you can fill her in on some of it so I don't have to go through the whole rig-a-ma-role again."

I'm now more determined than ever to hit the road and have a new adventure somewhere other than Aspen. I love it here but realize the truth is that I have gone about as far as I can go with my formal education. I need more of a challenge, and I need classes and books that are more interesting than I am being assigned here. Also I realize I don't want to live in a place where I'm looked on as nothing but a troublemaker.

~ ~ ~

It's the end of May when I hear from Holderness. I took the tests, sent in the application, wrote the essays, and a long letter requesting financial aid. I realized after doing all this it was such a long shot, I might as well resign myself to being in Aspen throughout high school.

I've almost given up when Dad brings me a letter from Holderness. My stomach is churning. On a single sheet of paper held within the monogrammed business envelope is my future. I'm not sure I want to know what it is. For a long time I stare at the envelope, holding it with both hands at chest level, waiting. Waiting for a feeling to come over me that it is going to work out. Waiting for that sinking feeling that all is lost. I wait.

My dad breaks me out of my reverie. "Well, aren't you going to open it?"

I take the letter to the kitchen counter, set it down, and fumble in the silverware drawer for a kitchen knife. I insert the sharp blade beneath the glued flap and begin to draw it across the top of the envelope. As I do, I know what the letter is going to say. I can almost see the words on the page. I know they are there, and a feeling of pride, peacefulness, and relief sweeps over me. It's all going to work out. I read the letter and hand it to my dad.

After taking it in, he says, "Good job, son. Looks like we're not going to be seeing you around here much in the future."

"I'll be here all summer," I say. "I've gotta earn my airfare east."

Chapter 70

Spring 1961

Several days before the Senior Prom, I'm in the hall talking to Coral Ann after school. I've told her that I'll be going to Holderness next year. This is a subject we've decided we just won't think about. It seems like a long time away. Today we are talking about the Prom. Ordinarily we would be headed to her house, but I have a school project I want finish up before term ends out for the summer.

"I hope you'll dance with me some," Coral Ann says. "I'm going with Nick, but that doesn't mean we can't dance."

"Actually, that's what I want to talk to you about. I don't think I'm going to the Prom. It'll be a drag not having a date, and the whole high school is dated up as far as I know. There are a few guys like me without dates. I don't want to be standing up against the wall watching everyone else dancing."

I can see Coral is disappointed and a little mad. "Suit yourself. I hope you change your mind so we can dance some."

"Probably not," I say. "I'll call you on Sunday after the Prom. Maybe we can go for a bike ride or a hike."

"Sure," Coral Ann says. "I've got to go home. I'll see you tomorrow."

We say good-bye, not daring to kiss in the hall, and she walks off.

I'm heading down to the science room, when Sharon Pejack approaches me.

"Terry," she says. "Do you have a date for the Prom?" Of course, she knows I don't. The whole high school knows

I don't have a date for the Prom. That's because I'm not going with Coral.

Sharon says, "Look, I know you don't have a date. Here's the thing. The only girl in the whole high school who doesn't have a date for the Prom is Jill Rowland. It would be a shame if she couldn't go. She's cute, funny, and very nice. Maybe you could call her and ask her to go to the Prom with you. She'd be real happy about it, I'm sure."

I look at Sharon for a minute, weighing the idea of sitting home alone on Prom night or going to the Prom with Jill. Actually it doesn't take much thought. Jill is in a class above me, but she's cute in her own way, and I know she has a good sense of humor.

"Sure, Sharon, I'd be happy to do that. I'll give her a call tonight."

That night, I call Jill, and we arrange a date. She sounds happy to be going.

Chapter 71

Early Summer 1961

Jill and I had loads of fun at the Prom. She got to dance with a bunch of other guys, and I had a few dances with Coral. At the end of the night, Jill thanked me and I could tell she really meant it. I was happy I had invited her.

I've said good-bye to most of my friends, knowing this is the last time I'll see them in school. It feels very natural to me to be leaving Aspen High, these people, and the town of Aspen. I wonder about my feelings, if I should be more sad, or have the feeling that I'll really miss everyone. I decide the way I feel is the way I should feel. Life isn't about standing still. I need to move on, and leaving people is just part of the process.

I'll make an effort to see my close friends, if any of them want to see me, when I return for vacations. The ones who are acquaintances and not close friends probably won't know I'm gone unless someone points it out to them. There are a lot of kids who come and go these days. Their parents live in Aspen for a year or two and then move on to somewhere else. When I leave, Tony and the five girls will be all that's left of our first-grade class.

~ ~ ~

This summer I'm mowing lawns for House Care, a management company that takes care of homes for second-home owners and some permanent residents. I have seventy lawns to mow every week. In addition, I have to water some of the lawns three times a week. It is a huge task because I can't drive legally, so I have to push the friggin' lawn mower all over town carrying a gas can with me. I've got it figured out so I can mow all the lawns on the west end one day, all the lawns on the east end another day, and so on.

Bill Mason runs House Care. When I bring him my hours after the first two weeks, he nearly chokes at how much I have to work to get all the lawns taken care of. He doesn't believe I'm working thirteen and fourteen hours on some days. I don't know who took care of the landscaping in years past, but I imagine there was more than just one person doing it. I don't mind the work because I need the money to pay for my airfare to Holderness.

On the long days, I'm up at five, have had breakfast, and in town by six. I try to mow a vacant second homeowner's lawn first, then, move on to the rest of them. For lunch, I normally have half an hour to eat my sandwich and drink some water, then, it's back to work. I finish the day anywhere between five-thirty and seven depending on how it goes. I'm whipped by the time I get home.

Holderness has sent me a summer reading program of six books I must complete before arrival in the fall. Thus far, I have only read *Lord of the Flies* by William Golding. I enjoyed the book and found it interesting to see how kids can act if they make the rules without any adult supervision. On second thought, that's been my friends and me for years.

Of course in a book like *Lord of the Flies* there's always a bully, a weak guy and one or two guys who stand up to the bully. You have to have the contrasts or it isn't exciting. I also have to read *Catcher in the Rye, To Kill a Mockingbird, The Great Gatsby, The Old Man and the Sea,* and *The Red Badge of Courage.* I'm not sure how I'm going to fit all the reading in, work, have time to myself, and see any of my friends.

When Fred isn't working at the driving range, he and I use every spare moment building the go-kart. We've redesigned Peter's frame, have cut it apart and had it re-welded with lighter tubing, and re-aligned the motor mount so the Mac 20 engine will fit. We've painted the frame a deep metallic red with silver metal flakes that glint in the sunlight. We're waiting for the magnesium wheels and slick tires to arrive, and then we can get her going. It looks as fast as we think it's going to run.

~ ~ ~

Several weeks later, we've received the mag wheels and slicks. I'm still trying to break in the engine. It's been quite a process. To bench drive the engine, it is necessary to stabilize it on a workbench, start it up, and let it run on idle for several hours so the pistons can seat themselves, and the other parts wear in properly without overheating. I've had problems getting the engine stabilized, and have ended up bolting it to the workbench in our garage shop. When I finally did get it stabilized, I couldn't get it started. I pulled on the starter cord for days with no success. I asked Gerry to help me out. He said, "Naw, Terry. I don't really have any experience with two-stroke engines. You'll have to figure it out."

So I went back to pulling the starter until my arm felt like it would fall off. The engine would kick over a few times, then backfire with a loud bang that scared the hell out of me. I'd try a few more licks until my arm was worn out, and I would leave it and do something else. This has been going on all summer and we still don't have the darn kart up and running.

Chapter 72

Summer 1961

I'm upstairs on my bed finishing *High Adventure: The True Story of the First Ascent of Everest* by Sir Edmund Hillary that I have wedged in between my Holderness summer reading books. It's about Hillary's 1953 expedition on Mount Everest, an incredible adventure that stirs the blood.

I think about the times I've been in the high country at or above timberline. Lying here on the bed, my mind takes me to Maroon Lake and higher to Crater Lake and higher yet to West Maroon pass. The high country in the summer is magical. The flowers just blooming as if it were spring, the little water drops coming off the snowfields silently joining together to create small rills that grow into brooks and then bubbling streams. The smell of the pine at timberline - fragile, light. The forest you pass through, gaining altitude to the place where you can see the bones of the earth, stripped of their skin, the different rock formations. Shales, red mudstones, and granite extrusives, each with their own character, their own chemistry, and their own singular beauty. I've yet to go to the high country this summer and know that I must. My mind wanders to work, social life, responsibility, and I wonder when I will find the time.

Gerry walks in and says, "We're headed up to Montezuma Basin tomorrow for some skiing on the ice field. You want to come along?"

That's a big duh!

"Actually," I say, "I would. What time are we leaving?"

We've planned to meet at the Castle Creek turn-off at seven. It takes a good two hours to get up there, and we want to get skiing before the snow warms up too much. Marolt wants to run some gates."

"Sounds great! Thanks for including me," I say.

I hop off the bed to get my equipment ready.

The next morning, we're up on the glacier a little after nine. The snowfield is still in the shade since it's blocked by Castle Peak, a fourteen-thousand-footer peak on the east side. We shoulder our skis, walk the last quarter mile to the snow, and begin the long trek up. At the top, we put our skis on, test the snow with a few tentative turns, then ski down. The hard spring snow makes the skiing great.

After a quick run down, we take our skis off at the bottom. While Bill Marolt, Gerry, and Bob Gorsuch go to one of the Jeeps to get the slalom poles, I stand and look up at Castle Peak. I'm looking at it and thinking of Sir Edmund Hillary. I head back to the Jeep with my skis and change from my ski boots to my hiking boots, still my preferred footwear. I walk past Gerry and say, "I'm going to climb Castle Peak while you guys run gates."

"You sure?" Gerry says, "You got everything you need?"

"Yep, I think so."

I've packed my down parka, a hat, some water, and a sandwich in my LaFuma pack, and I'm ready to rumble. I should be down in a few hours."

I walk up the left side of the snowpack, where I find a small path in the rocks and scree. Since it's easier and faster going on the snowfield, I stay on the snow until the mountain rises above, and I'm forced onto the climbing path. The elevation gain is not great. Montezuma Basin at the bottom of the snowfield is about 11,500 feet. That leaves me 2,700 feet of vertical.

As I climb, the air cools. The sun reflecting off the snow below throws a back light onto the east side of the ridgeline, bathing the rock with a purple alpenglow. My heart picks up, my breathing deepens and steadies. My lungs expand and clear as I take in the cool air; my legs feel strong and light. I feel relaxed and happy. I'm at home in the high country. I realize how much I love being above timberline on top of the world, apart from civilization below and its frenetic pace, ignorant of the stillness surrounding me. A gentle breeze, a cerulean sky, and the solitude of a monastery lightly brush my senses as I look across the tableau of peaks on the horizon. Places to explore, mountains that beckon: discovery and adventure all possible if I but have the courage to take the first step of the journey.

Presently, I gain the summit. There is a cairn of rock with a small box atop it. I open it, take out the stubby pencil, and sign my name and date to the ledger of those who have summited Castle Peak. Admittedly it is an easy peak to climb, a "walk-up" in the vernacular. Yet it is the first 14,000 foot peak I've climbed, and at 14,250 feet is the highest in the Elk Range. I don my parka. It takes the subtle bite off the lightly blowing wind. I sit on the rocks, marveling at the vastness of Colorado. I single out the Maroon Bells and Pyramid Peak to the north-west. Conundrum Peak to the north. It's a stunning view of the Elk Mountain Range. I eat my sandwich and become thankful for my body and my vigor. It occurs to me while sitting that one has to work at it if one is going to be fit. It's easy for me because I'm young and active. I ride my bike all over hell and gone, hike a lot, and ski cross-country in the winter. Breathing the high mountain air is no problem. I think about the millions of people who could not climb this insignificant peak and understand what a gift in life they are missing. I decide I like the feeling of being fit more than the alternative. I make a pact with myself to stay that way.

~ ~ ~

Presently I pack up my things and head down the mountain to the base of the snowfield where everyone is finishing lunch.

"How was the hike, Morse?" Bill Marolt asks.

"Fine. You can see all over Colorado up there. How's the skiing?"

"Skiing's great. We'll take a few more runs before we head down."

I debate with myself whether I should ski another run or two.

"I think I'll sit here and catch a few rays while you guys ski."

I find a comfortable spot in the rocks and sit down to rest in the sun for a few minutes.

~~~

It's the end of the day. I wake up and find everyone piling into the Jeeps getting ready to head down the mountain.

"Wait for me!" I shout. I pick myself up from my resting place and hustle down to the Jeeps.

"Darn," Gerry says. "It's a good thing you spoke up. We probably would have left you."

Rick Deane is driving his Jeep and is headed out first. We go about a quarter of a mile down the rock scree to where the road passes close to the Montezuma mine, one of the hundreds of old silver mines in the area. Rick stops his Jeep and climbs out. We stop behind him and pile out to see what's up.

"I want to take a look in the mine," Rick says.

He heads up the hill about fifty yards, and we all follow him. There's a platform of mine tailings where we stand as we look at the half-caved-in mine entrance. The top beam has dropped, one of the side posts split shaping the entrance into a triangle just big enough for a person to crawl through. We head for the entrance, and Rick says, "Let's go in. I brought a light if it's too dark."

There is general agreement, and we begin moving through the entrance. We're not far into the tunnel, when it opens up enough for us to stand in the tight space. Rick turns on a flashlight and shines it forward into the drift. On the ground about twenty or thirty feet away is a wooden crate. We move forward and see "EXPLOSIVE" stamped on the side.

I have a good view of the box and peer into it as Rick shines his light over the top surface. What I see truly scares me. The surface of the dynamite sticks are crystallized and pitted. I know from my gunpowder days with Robert Rubey, that dynamite can crystallize into almost pure nitro-glycerin if it freezes and thaws enough under the right conditions. It also will crystallize if left in the heat too long. I say to Rick, "We've gotta get out of here, that stuff has crystallized and is really dangerous. It's probably darn near pure nitro."

Rick bends down over the box, looking at it more carefully.

"Don't touch it," I say.

"Aw, its all right. It's more stable than you think."

"Well, you can screw with it, I'm out of here. There's enough dynamite there to blow up half the mountain."

I work my way through the other guys and head for the entrance. The others follow me, and pretty soon everyone is outside except Rick.

I'm really scared now.

If that nut cake even blinks at that stuff wrong, we're going to be plastered all over the snowfield.

Rick comes out of the mine carrying what looks like one of the sticks of dynamite.

"Whoa," I say.

Then, to my horror, I see Rick toss the stick at us. We all scatter. When it hits the ground, nothing happens. We look back at Rick, who is laughing. Then we look at the stick. It is a piece of doweling cut to the same length as the dynamite.

"What the hell are you doing? You crazy idiot!" Rick Henry shouts.

Rick Deane says, "Aw, I've known that dynamite was there for a couple of years. I just thought I'd give you guys a bit of a scare. By the way, Morse, you played right into the whole thing beautifully. Thanks." He is still laughing as he picks up the wooden dowel and gets into his Jeep.

Now everyone is laughing as much from relief that the crazy bugger didn't really blow up half the mountain, as they are at the humor of it all.

We head down the mountain.

It doesn't matter how long he's known that dynamite has been there or how many times he's screwed around with someone's mind playing that joke, the stuff is still dangerous as hell. He keeps doing it, and one of these days we'll find his intestines hanging from a tree in the middle of Paepcke Park.

My thoughts slow down. I imagine I am back on Castle Peak. All is well.

Chapter 73

Late Summer 1961

I've finished my summer reading for Holderness. *The Old Man and the Sea* was by far the best. Hemingway writes in a way that is understandable to me. The battle of Santiago and the marlin in some way relates to the feeling I have about my own life. The struggle of man and nature.

The Great Gatsby was probably my least favorite. All that phoniness of the party scene leaves me cold. It reminded me of the changes I see slowly creeping into the fabric of the Aspen where I have grown up and loved.

I left *Catcher in the Rye* for last because it is about prep school and kids my age. I hope prep school wasn't the cause of Holden Caulfield's neurosis. It'll be a drag if it is. I can see myself going home for Christmas vacation and telling Mom and Dad I need to go to a nut house.

~ ~ ~

Today is the last Saturday I have in Aspen before I leave for Holderness. Fred and I have finished the go-kart, broken in the engine, and completed the assembly of the brake and accelerator systems. Gerry is helping us haul the kart to the Woody Creek racetrack in a borrowed pick-up so we can test it out.

"I'll take the first test drive and see how she handles," Fred says.

Although I don't understand why he is going first without a flip of a coin or some discussion, I don't say anything. I'm just happy we'll get to drive it before we leave for school.

"All right," I say. "But just one lap, then we trade off."

"That's fine." Fred seats himself in the kart.

"How're ya gonna get the thing going?" Gerry says.

"I thought you and I could give Fred a push. The motor should kick right in. It's got a centrifugal clutch, so we'll have to give her a good shove, but I think we'll be able to do it."

"Terry, why don't I just tow it behind the truck with a rope? Fred can hold onto the rope, and when the engine kicks over he can let go of it and go."

"No, I think that's a little risky. The kart accelerates much faster than the truck. Fred may just find himself driving underneath the truck. Besides, I think it'll be too hard for him to hold onto the rope and steer at the same time. No. It's better if we just push him."

Gerry and I get behind the kart and push Fred onto the track. We push him until we're running. Suddenly, the motor turns over, and Fred accelerates away with a high whine. He accelerates down the straightaway and heads into the first corners, moving at a blistering pace. We see him brake, then turn the corners, first right, then a quick left, a straight road, then more curves. The track is a mile-and-a-quarter, so it doesn't take Fred much more than a minute to come whizzing by. He's grinning from ear to ear, going like a bat out of hell. He doesn't even make a pretense of stopping. I run onto the track, shouting at him to stop, but know that there is no way he can hear me. He's blitzing down the straightaway again. We can see he doesn't realize how fast he's going. He heads into the corners, running too hot. I know he's gonna lose it. He brakes, then, hits the first corner, and the kart is halfway into a three-hundred-sixty-degree spin before he knows he's lost it. He does two three-sixties and ends up in the sagebrush.

Gerry and I hot leg it across the track and pull the cart from the sagebrush out onto the blacktop.

"Holy crap!" Fred shouts. "What a ride!" Then he begins to babble. "Did you see how fast that thing goes? The acceleration is huge!"

Gerry takes a minute to look over the kart. It's all in one piece, so we get Fred back into the driver's seat with the agreement he will stop by the truck. We walk back across the sage to meet Fred, who is there well ahead of us.

The kart is a thing of beauty. The red metallic paint glows in the sunlight, each small metal fleck bursting silvery, shimmering rays of reflected light. The sun bounces off the chromed engine, and the highly polished, brushed aluminum gravity-feed gas tank. Fourteen-inch racing slicks mounted on the magnesium-aluminum rims give a slight forward rake to the kart and add to the superb 'badness' of the finely sculpted machine. As go-karts go, it really is a work of art.

"Let me take her for a spin after you finish," Gerry says, now intrigued by the possibility of a speed rush.

"Sure." I settle down in the seat. "Two laps, just like Fred did."

Fred and Gerry give me a running shove, and the engine roars to life. I tentatively step on the gas pedal to gauge the responsiveness of the beast. I feather the gas pedal, the engine roars with a high whine, and the kart streaks forward. Like Fred, I'm headed down the straightaway, eating up the road much faster than I realize. I slow for the curves and barely make it through them, floating on one side of the track and then the other, the smell of sagebrush and exhaust imprinting my mind. Out of the tight curves, another larger sweeping curve and a long straightaway into several more tight ones, and another short straight stretch take me back to the truck. I fly by Gerry and Fred in a blur, going what seems like a hundred- and-fifty miles per hour. It's a major thrill.

When I've completed my second lap, I coast into the pit so Gerry can take a turn.

"Here's my watch," he says. "Try to time my last lap. We'll see what this thing can do." He hands Fred his watch. We know if we're going to time the kart for speed, Gerry should be the one to do it because he's just about the best driver around for a thousand miles. Fred and I give him a push, and he is off and rolling. It looks like he's going into the curves faster than Fred, but seems to have no problem snaking his way through. As he passes by us, Fred looks at the watch and Gerry hits the accelerator. He moves through the turns at a blistering pace, picks up speed around the sweeping curve, streaks across the straightaway, snakes the last curves, and heads for home so fast that neither Fred nor I can believe it.

Fred looks at the watch and does some real quick mental calculations.

"Well, if the track is really a mile-and-a-quarter like they say it is," Fred says, "then he did that lap averaging just around seventy-five miles an hour. That means he had to be going over a hundred on the straight stretches."

"The kart is geared for it, so it shouldn't be a surprise," I say.

"Yeah, but you can never count on the numbers they give you. We just figured that on the specs from the engine and the gear ratios," Fred says.

"I know," I say, "but it's obvious that the numbers don't lie, because he was going faster than a striped-ass ape."

Gerry walks over to us and says, "I'll bet that thing was going over a hundred on the straights. Sheeet does it fly! You guys sure put together a monster with this. It's funner than heck to drive. How fast did I do the lap in?"

Fred says, "I figure you averaged about seventy-five miles an hour. That means you had to be going over a hundred on the straights, like you said. I'd have to time you just on the straights to see how fast it actually was."

"Whatever it was, it seemed like two-hundred miles an hour riding that close to the ground."

We spend the rest of the afternoon taking turns driving until we finally run out of our fuel mixture. I'm pretty proud of what we have done, taking the kart from concept to driving reality. It is a beautiful machine, and now that it's completed I can see we have absolutely no idea what we'll do with it. *Never mind that, it's been a gas making it all happen.*

At the end of the day, we load it up and take it back to Fred's house where we'll leave it for the winter. He has space in his garage.

Chapter 74

Early Fall 1961

I leave for Denver today. Yesterday I had to finish up a last few errands in town. This included stopping by Coral's house and saying good-bye to her. It wasn't as hard as I thought it would be. Coral understands it's time for me to change my life circumstances, which it easier for both of us. We promise to write.

I'll spend the night in Denver before I catch an early flight to New York City. From there, I'll catch a limo bus up to Southport, Connecticut, where I'll spend the night with Popeye and Sylvia. Popeye has agreed to drive me to Holderness the next day. He says he wants to see the school and take a nice ride, so he's happy to do it.

~ ~ ~

I'm standing in the middle of the lane that winds through the Holderness campus. My grandfather has dropped me off. I watch his beige Ford drive around the corner beneath the large maple trees lining the lane in front of Webster House and the Chapel. I have two suitcases, one on each side of me. I turn around and take in everything I can see. I've no idea where I should be going, no idea what I should be doing, no idea who I should be talking to. I'm lost, and I'm not used to that feeling.

I seem to have stood there for a year when I see an older guy walking toward me.

"You a new kid here?"

"Yes," I say.

"Where are you from?"

"Aspen, Colorado."

"Huh," he grunts. "You need to go over to Livermore and check in."

"Uh, okay. Where's Livermore?"

"Over there." He points to a three-story, stately brick building. Brick. There are two faux stone columns at the entrance. Steps up to the door. White trim. Green shutters, or are they black? It is hard to tell with the angle of the sun. My mind feels like a camera. Collecting details. Details of a world that is absolutely unknown.

"Thanks," I say.

He grunts again. I pick up my suitcases and head across the lane, up the sidewalk, up the steps, and through the big white door, entering Livermore Hall and my next three years at prep school. If all goes well.

"Hello. A tall black-haired woman in her thirties greets me. "I'm Mrs. Henderson, Director of Admissions. And you are?"

I the question hangs for a moment, as I wait for her to finish the sentence. I pause after I realize she has finished, and it's my turn to speak.

"Uh, Terry Morse." It is all I can manage.

"Oh, Terry. We're expecting you. So glad to have you at Holderness."

She's a delightful woman. Friendly and not at all condescending. She tells me I'm to be rooming in Upper Niles, that there is a meeting of all the new boys in the Schoolhouse at nine in the morning after a brief breakfast at eight o'clock. "It would be good," she says, "if you get settled before then."

Mrs. Henderson introduces me to a boy who will take me to my room in Upper Niles and make me "feel at home." We trudge down the sidewalk, up the stairs, and down the hall to my room on the corner of the building. The dorm is empty. My pathfinder tells me to get settled and show up for dinner at 6 o'clock in the Dining Hall in Livermore.

My roommate has not yet arrived. There's only one window in the room, north-facing. The room seems dark and very quiet. I stow my clothes in half of the small closet and drawers, taking the least-desirable space in case my roommate is particular. I lie down on the bed to test it and think it's incrementally better than sleeping on the floor would be. I decide to explore my new environment.

This new adventure has begun.

Chapter 75

Fall 1961–Summer 1962

I've been at Holderness for a month and a half. I'm not sure I like it yet. Many of the kids are what I now call "preppy," and at home I would call "snooty and sarcastic." I've learned to banter with the best of them but would rather not. Many times it's insincere and demeaning. The upper class boys don't really bother me much, partly because of my size and partly because they don't understand me. My world is alien to them.

The first week of school, a bunch of upper classmen in the dorm held me down and cut my hair because they thought it was too long. I didn't protest, just told them to get on with it and go about their business. They were disappointed because they were looking for resistance. When they were finished, they'd done a very poor job of it. The headmaster, Mr. Hagerman, saw me the next morning at morning assembly and asked me what happened to my hair.

"I got run over by a lawn mower," I said.

"Well, the lawn mower must have needed tuning."

He reached into his pocket and pulled out a buck and a quarter and said, "Here, go get it cut properly this afternoon."

I didn't know what to do, so I took the money, thanked him, and got my hair re-cut that afternoon. One of the kids overheard our conversation and saw him give me the money for the haircut. Word got around school that I must have some special "in" with the headmaster. This brought on further episodes of some of the students "giving me shit," as they call it.

~ ~ ~

Each evening after dinner we have study hall from 7 to 9 o'clock. Most of the kids can study in their rooms. New kids and kids with poor grades have to study in the study hall at the schoolhouse. After the first six weeks of school have passed, any new kid with good grades can study in his room.

My roommate is a "dink" and a poor student, so he's in evening study hall at the schoolhouse. It works out well for me because I can study hard in the quiet of my own room without distractions.

There's a soft knock on my door. I open it. Three guys come in and sit down, one on my bed and the other two on my roommate's bed. I haven't actually met them, though I know the names of two of them: Art Sleeper and Ned Gillette.

"We hear you're from Aspen," Art Sleeper says.

"Yes." I can see where this is going, and I'm sad that the hazing isn't over yet as I thought it was.

"We hear that you're a skier," the nameless boy says.

"Yes."

"Are you going out for the ski team?" Ned Gillette asks.

"I thought I might."

"You know that the competition is pretty tough in the East. Nothing like skiing in the West."

I wonder how they know what skiing is like in the West, so I say, "Have you ever skied in the West?"

No one answers the question. Their next question comes at me rapid fire. They're covering up that they haven't.

"How big a ski jump have you been off?"

"We have a thirty-meter hill and a fifty-meter hill in Aspen. Mostly we jump on the thirty-meter hill, but we go off the fifty-meter hill when we're training for downhill. The largest jump I have been off is the one in Steamboat Springs, which is a sixty-meter hill."

"That's bullshit," no-name says.

"Maybe you think so, but it's the truth."

I don't bother telling them that the reason I went off was because a bunch of us were standing at the top of the hill after slalom practice looking down the inrun and Bill Marolt had given me a shove. I figured I might as well just dribble off the end and ride down the outrun rather than trying to stop and maybe break a ski in the trees. So I flew off the end, bounced off the knoll, and skied down the landing hill. Seeing me do this, the others followed. At the bottom, Bill had looked at me and shook his head. "You're a crazy sonofabitch," he said.

Then I look at Art Sleeper and Ned Gillette and say, "I'm not really good at ski jumping. I like cross-country and alpine the best."

They ask me a bunch of other questions. I can see they don't believe much of what I say, so I begin to make my answers shorter and shorter until I'm just not answering them anymore. After a while of this, they get up and leave.

I'm sad they don't believe me, confused as to why they are out of their rooms during evening study hall, and why they're doing the third degree on me. We all do have skiing in common, after all. Back home that was a bond. Nevertheless, in the peerless style of true preppies, they become the source of my new name, "The Aspen Kid" - a name that stuck with me through the fall until the first few days after Christmas vacation, when the ski team began serious practice, and I made my statement.

~ ~ ~

My first year at Holderness flashed by. School was hard and structured. There was little or no time to have an adventure, no time to get into trouble, and precious little time to one's self. I studied longer hours, as the homework burden was much greater. My academics were acceptable: not straight As like Aspen High School, but solid Bs.

My interest in the guitar, getting a ham operator's license, electronics, and astronomy faded away, replaced by the strenuous time demands of academics, sports, and learning how to "belong" in my new environment. By the end of the year, I had my confidence, some good friends, and a solid start in the prep school life and I, like many others, had become a "preppy" jock.

Chapter 76

Summer 1962

I'm home for summer vacation. Dad is gaining momentum in his business. Aspen had a good snow year. Excellent ski conditions brought more tourists interested in owning property in Aspen, so Dad had a very successful winter season.

Cullen has been born, and the family is moving from survival to thriving, as we older kids fly the nest, and some of the burden is taken off Mom and Dad.

Coral Ann has dumped me for Nick Garrish, the fellow who took her to the Prom. It takes me about fifteen minutes of sulking to get over it. I realize it's more a blow to my ego than it is to my heart.

Dave Durrance and I have started our own lawn-mowing business. We have about fifty lawns to mow, trim, and water. It is more work than when I was mowing lawns for House Care, but is more lucrative.

I play my guitar once in a while now, but am not practicing two or three hours a day like I did when I was playing with Edgar Stanton. I've become realistic about my talent for music, and know the guitar is something I'll never be great at. It's just for fun.

Fred and I sold the go-kart back to Peter at a good profit. We both decided we didn't have time to fool around with it. I haven't seen Peter use it yet, but I'm sure he will.

Chapter 77

Fall 1962

I'm back at Holderness. Dressed in my school blazer, blue striped tie, khaki pants, and tennis shoes; hair's long, but not blatantly below the ears, and tennis shoes held together by athletic tape. Can't stand it, but it's easier to conform to the simple things, so not conforming to the larger picture goes unnoticed. I'm on the varsity football team, but don't really like it. Too late to go out for soccer.

I stand on the edge of the athletic field located north of Niles and Webster Halls after a game of touch football, but I'm not thinking of football, I'm thinking of skiing. Our ski coach, Don Henderson, is taking a sabbatical in Norway to learn Norwegian and study Scandinavian History. Bill Clough will be coaching in his place. He walks toward me on his way to Livermore Hall.

"Hi, Terry, What are you doing standing out here in the middle of the field by yourself? Homework all finished?"

He's joking. He knows that we never have our homework "all finished."

"No, just thinking about skiing."

"Skiing? It's football season."

"Yeah, I know. I'm not that big on football, so I'm thinking about skiing."

"Hmmm, whatcha thinking?"

"Actually, I've been wondering what it takes to ski in the Olympic Games."

"You think you want to ski on an Olympic team? Alpine or Nordic?"

"I think I'm too tall, not strong enough, and don't have fast enough reflexes to be a world-class alpine skier. That leaves cross-country. I think I could be a competitive cross-country skier, if I train right for it."

"Sounds like you've thought about it. So, what's the problem?"

"It seems like it would be a lot of work, and I'm not sure how to go about it."

"Keep thinking about it. It's a good goal to have. As for the hard work, I've got a piece of news for you, Terry: life's hard work. It's what you have to do if you are going to be excellent at anything. Hard work. You've gotta put in the time. Let me know what you decide," he says. He walks off toward Livermore.

~ ~ ~

It is a week later, we've just finished football practice, and I'm getting ready to hit the showers, when I hear my name called.

"Hey, Morse!"

Bill Clough beckons me over.

"I understand you've got a bunch of younger brothers and sisters."

"Yep."

"Have you taken care of them?"

"I've taken care of three of them since they were babies. Changed dirty diapers, bathed, fed: the whole shooting match. Why?"

"My wife, Ki, and I need a babysitter on Saturday night, and I thought maybe you would be interested in helping us out."

"Sure," I say. "What time do you want me?"

"How about six o'clock? You know where we live?"

"Lower Webster."

"See you at six." Bill says. "Now hit the showers."

I take off to the locker room, thinking that babysitting will be a nice change from the rigorously boring routine of prep school life.

~ ~ ~

I'm standing on the door stoop to the Clough's apartment, my mouth open and my mind numb as Ki Clough opens the front door. *Why haven't I seen her around campus?' I didn't realize she would be so pretty. God, I hope I don't screw up this babysitting job.*

"Hi, you must be Terry. I'm Ki Clough, Bill's wife," she says. Her Swedish accent adds charm to her good looks.

I'm paralyzed in the doorway, fascinated by the accent, the blond hair, the delicate face, the thin, graceful body. I have no feelings of lust like I do when I look at Russ Wood's wife, who is nothing more than a sex-bomb. This is different. I feel as if I have come home. I don't even wonder that a stranger could seem so familiar.

"Are you going to come in?" she says.

"Thanks." I stammer. I follow her into the living room, and she disappears for a minute, coming back with a baby in her arms.

"Where are you from?" I say.

"Sweden. I met Bill in Sweden, and we were married here in New London. We came to Holderness this year and love it. Our baby's name is Wendy."

"Really? That's my dad's name."

"She's six months old and should sleep while we're gone. If she wakes up, just hold her for a little bit, and I'm sure she'll nap again. I've just fed her, so she shouldn't be hungry."

Bill Clough comes into the room.

"Cute little thing, isn't she?"

"She sure is." I'm looking at the baby but thinking of Ki. "I mean, yeah, she is cute. Looks like she's healthy and happy," I stammer.

"We should be back around ten or so."

Bill and Ki leave, and I'm alone with Wendy and my copy of Ralph Waldo Ellison's *Invisible Man*. I hold Wendy for a while, rocking her and talking to her like I did my brothers and sisters. She falls asleep, so I put her in her crib in the other room.

I return to the living room and pick up my book. I think about the author's name and am struck by a coincidence. My great-grandfather was named Waldo Calvin Bryant. My grandfather was named Waldo Gerald Bryant. I think my great uncle was Ralph Waldo Emerson. *While I'm at it, I may as well add William Cullen Bryant on my mom's side as well,* I think.

I read for a half an hour or so, then put the book aside. I look at the living area where I'm seated and notice it is sparsely equipped with furnishings that are beautiful, simple, and elegantly displayed. I wander into the kitchen. I see a plate of cookies on a piece of note paper and walk over to investigate. The note says,

> *Terry,*
>
> *Here are some cookies if you get in the mood for a little snack. There is a soda in the refrigerator. Help yourself. Thanks so much for watching Wendy.*
>
> *Ki and Bill*

I snag a cookie, chocolate chip. My favorite. I grab soda and head back to Ralph. Soon I hear Wendy whimper, and I tiptoe into her room to take a peek. She's fine, just restless in her sleep.

I wander about the apartment. It feels like home, not my real home, but a home that just feels like home even though it's an apartment. I wonder what it takes to make a home feel like a home. Love? Peace? Noise? Children? Struggles? Comedies and tragedies? I ponder all of that and settle back into *Invisible Man*.

Somewhere around nine-thirty, Wendy wakes up and starts to fuss. I hold her and rock her gently as I walk back and forth. She's a cute little thing. Brown eyes, light hair, a little button nose, and rosy cheeks. She looks up at me and is more curious than frightened. She nods off, and I put her back into the crib.

Soon after, Bill and Ki come in laughing.

"How did it go?" Ki asks.

"Great, no problem. She woke up for a short time but went back to sleep quickly after I walked around with her for a few minutes."

"How much do we owe you?" Bill says.

"Nothing. I enjoyed doing it," And I truthfully did. It was nice to be in a home instead of a dorm, and to have company other than teachers and prep school kids.

"Thank you," Ki says.

~ ~ ~

A few days later, I'm going back to my single room in Hoit and see Ki Clough walking toward me. I stop as I see her wave at me. She comes up and holds out a box.

"These are for you. We appreciate your watching Wendy over the weekend."

"I was happy to do it. She's cute. I'd love to babysit for her anytime you need me as long as you don't ask to pay me."

Ki smiles and hands me the box.

"Have a good afternoon," she says.

"Thank you, Ki,"

I stand watching her for a moment as she walks back toward Webster. I open the box and find a fresh batch of chocolate chip cookies. Definitely pay enough.

~ ~ ~

The snow last night is just enough for me to cross-country ski on the football field. Several of us have talked Bill Clough into getting some cross-country skis from the ski room and have packed out a little track around the field. We've skied for an hour. The others have gone, and I'm skiing one more easy lap around the field. Bill is standing by the far goal posts. I ski over to him.

"Getting kind of dark, isn't it?"

"Yep," I say. "But I'm done now. Just wanted to take one more easy lap."

"You better head in for dinner."

"On my way. By the way, I decided I'm going to."

"Going to what?" Bill asks.

"Ski on an Olympic team."

Chapter 78

Winter 1963

I'm back at school after Christmas vacation. Final exams went well, at least as well as I could expect, understanding that I haven't been as diligent a student as last year. School is easier now that I know the ropes and have adjusted to the routine. Although I've taken finals, I still haven't gotten a grade in my theology class because I'm in a big debate with Mr. Payne, our theology teacher, about the existence of God.

In the fall, we had to write a paper defending some Biblical references to God. I wrote my paper from a position outside of the parameters he defined, arguing that because the existence of God cannot be empirically proven, it must be a product of Man's mental construct. This did not go over well. Mr. Payne took the position that God is a "given," and that the Biblical references verify this position.

I told him I thought his position was dogma the Church has put forth to control the masses. Of course, this was going from bad to worse in his mind. Finally I stated my position is-based on my limited experience-God is everywhere, an energy that pervades everything: humans, animals, flora, the very earth we walk on. Nothing is exempt. Eventually we agreed to disagree, and I took a C on the paper, which was a disappointment as it lowered my GPA.

~ ~ ~

Putney, Vermont. It's late January, and I'm skiing in the first try-out race for the Junior National Nordic team. I'm about two kilometers into the ten-kilometer race, working hard and tighter than I would like to be. Tense muscles, ragged breathing.

Relax your fingers. Relax your mouth. Breathe. Gradually the tension leaves my body when, suddenly, *I am no longer in my body. I've popped out, yet my body is moving, floating lightly and smoothly across the snow. I feel unharnessed, free. I'm dancing next to my body. First above, then to the side, then behind, then to the other side. I feel myself floating through my luminescent body, front to back, back to front. Nothing is solid. It's a shadow world of boundless lines, spaces, and free-form thoughts. Weightless, so light that it's impossible to be touching the snow, rather my skis glide above the snow. No effort, no friction, only one smooth, fluid collection of movements propelling me down the track, across the snow, through copses of trees, across snow-covered fields. Snowflakes reflecting light that has broken and shattered so completely that to count the hues and the degrees of brightness is a fool's errand. I see individual light rays become starbursts of rainbows. I must look around them to follow the track winding its way through the Vermont countryside, taking me toward who knows what? Who knows where? Time has broken apart like the rays of light passing through the snow crystals. Has broken into shards of seconds, milli-seconds, sub-atomic seconds, to no-time. No seconds, no minutes. There is only this being, this immeasurable moment in an existence-defying description. I become a part of the breeze gently pushing at my back. Become a part of the snow rolling in waves beneath me. Become part of everything that is passing through me and that I am passing through. And still becoming and becoming until I just am. Everything has stopped. Silence. Not even the sound of my skis on the snow as I float in, out, and beyond a consciousness I can no longer define.*

I'm back in my body and skiing the last kilometer of the race. I cannot find words to describe where I have been during the last seven or eight kilometers. I try not to think about—nor make judgments about—the experience I will not talk to anyone about, probably forever. I cross the finish line, ski past the other competitors and down the track some distance to compose myself. I won't check the results of this race because they do not matter. The race was not a race of winning or losing. It was a race of being. And I am.

~~~

My bear dreams, flying dreams, and raven dreams are back. They are equally as strange as the feeling I had in the Putney race of being completely out of my body watching myself ski. In the dreams, many times the bears or the raven may tell me some small thing that will happen to me or to someone else in some situation I'm in. So far, the events have been small things like, what someone will say, or being in a place and knowing what is going to happen next. I've been reading what little I can find on the subject and find it interesting. I've kept this all to myself. First, I don't really understand it well enough to talk about it. Furthermore, it is not a subject that lends itself to prep school banter. What I do know is some of the dreams I am having are dreams of events that are going to occur in the future. They are similar to déjà vu but clearly are not. Déjà vu is the feeling that you have experienced in the past what you are experiencing in the present. My dreams are clearly not that. From what little I have read about it, I am having what are called pre-cognitive dreams. They are dreams of things that are going to happen. These pre-cognitive dreams are frightening because I have no frame of reference for them. Since I will not tell anyone of these experiences, this is something I must figure out by myself.

~~~

School is going well. Most of the mornings when I have study hall, the period before lunch, I sneak out and ski around the track once to get a little extra training in. Oftentimes I pass Mr. Hagerman skiing on the track on his way to the office. The first time he saw me, he stopped on the track,

"Good morning, Terry," he said. "Fine day for skiing isn't it?"

"Yes, sir," I said guiltily.

"Aren't you supposed to be in class?"

"Actually, I have study hall this period."

"Oh," Mr. Hagerman said. Then he paused, clearly thinking about something. Finally he said, "Well, I guess I didn't see you out here anyway, so make sure you enjoy it."

"Thank you," I said and skied off.

So, the cat is out of the bag, but there has been no word about it. When we cross paths on the trail, Mr. Hagerman simply says "Good morning" as I whiz by.

~~~

It's mid-February, and I'm at the start of the downhill try-out race for the USEASA Junior National Alpine Team. It's been a good year for me. I've been skiing well in both Alpine and Nordic events and hope to make both Junior National Teams.

"Five...four...three...two...one...."

I start, pushing off with my poles to get my speed up as quickly as possible. I ski down the first steep pitch, picking up speed, then head into the fall-away corner to the left. I'm now going fast. Very fast. I accelerate through the corner and realize I'm too low on my line. The course is very narrow with pine and birch trees on both sides. In my peripheral vision, they rush past me. Too fast.

~~~

Am I awake or am I dreaming? In the total blackness, there is a halo of light. Inside the light I see a woman. She is blonde. She is very beautiful.

"Did I win?" I ask her.

"Yes," she answers.

The halo disappears, and the blackness returns.

Am I awake or am I dreaming? A man stands over me. He is wearing a blue shirt. He has something around his neck. His mouth is moving, but I hear no words. He is waving two or maybe three fingers at me. I wonder why he is doing that? The darkness returns.

Am I awake or am I dreaming? A light coming through a window in a place I have never been before. I am in a bed but not my bed. A woman is sitting next to the bed. She looks like my mom. It can't be my mom because mom is somewhere else. Or am I awake? Blackness once again.

I'm dreaming again. I'm awake again. It is night, or maybe it is inky dark out. Everything is dark and black and impenetrable, and I'm awake in my own dream. This is what it is like to be in your own dream awake. Awake in the dream you are dreaming. Dreaming of yourself dreaming in the dream you are dreaming. I'm looking at a small pinpoint of light in the surrounding darkness. I walk through a maze of tubes and needles and beds and men in blue shirts and men in green shirts and women in white dresses. And there is more and more darkness. I'm very tired of dreaming. The darkness is comforting because I don't have to think. Light hurts my eyes. Darkness darker than dark.

I'm awake. How do I know that? I don't know. I just am. I am looking at someone who I do not recognize. She looks at me, turns, and leaves. I am lying in a bed. There are more tubes coming down next to me from a silver hat stand. Tubes and bags of liquids. I move my head to one side to see where she has gone but cannot see her. I turn my head to the other side and see another bed. Someone it in. Beyond that bed is another and another. I turn my head and am looking at the ceiling. Soon a face comes into view. A man says, "So you are awake now?"

I think I am hearing what he is saying, and then think that I am dreaming again and that he is trying to trick me. He is a coyote. The Trickster. I don't answer.

"Can you hear me?"

I look at him and realize he is talking to me.

I make a noise. It sounds like I am speaking, but I am not sure.

"Good," I hear him say.

I fight off the blackness but know I am losing the battle when the light becomes dim and shuts in around me until the darkness has left only a small pinpoint in front of my eye. And it disappears.

Time has passed. Or has it? In the darkness, I cannot tell if one second has gone by, one hour, one month, one year, or if life or death is a lullaby. Song to myself I sing. Death gone by lullaby, Life gone by lullaby. Sing me to sleep, my lullaby.

But no...

Now I am horribly awake, and something is horribly wrong. I am in pain. My head is pounding. My eyelids fluttering against the bright light the sun is bringing into the room. It is not the room of my dreams. Yet it is because there are others here. Men. Only men. All in beds. One, two, three, four, five, six, seven. Seven of them and me. That makes...eight. Eight of us. Eight of us in the same room, all in beds.

I look over to the man next to me. His leg is floating in the air, suspended by a line tied to the ceiling or somewhere up there that I cannot focus on. I see him push a button on the side of his bed. In a moment a woman dressed in white comes in. She walks to his bed.

"He's awake."

She turns and looks at me. I look back at her. She is pleasant, but not beautiful like the blonde woman in my dreams.

"So, now you are finally awake?" she says.

I make a "yes" sound.

"Excellent, I'll get the doctor."

She leaves.

Doctor? I wonder why she needs a doctor? Then it comes to me that maybe she is getting the doctor for me because I'm the one in bed and there are seven...yes, seven men in the same room with me. One with his leg in the air.

"Here you are," the doctor says. "For a while there we thought you weren't ever coming back."

"Where am I?" I croak.

"You are at Mary Hitchcock Hospital in Hanover, New Hampshire."

"What am I doing here?"

"You had a bad fall in the ski race in Vermont. Do you remember?"

"No," I say. "What ski race?"

"You've been here for over a month in…uh…a coma, like sleeping," he explains.

"Oh."

"Now that you are back with us, you can help us with your recovery."

"Uh, huh." But I'm tired. So tired. So I close my eyes and invite in the darkness.

~ ~ ~

More time. More time. Tick-tock. Tick-tock.

~ ~ ~

This time I am awake for real. I now know I will stay awake. I'm looking at the others on the orthopedic ward here at Mary Hitchcock Hospital. They look to be a beat-up bunch. Arms and legs in casts. My arms and legs are intact. It is my head that is broken.

I've learned from the doctor that I was in a ski race at Jay Peak, Vermont, and ran into a tree. The impact of the crash split the motorcycle helmet I was wearing for protection, split it like an egg dropped from a second-story window. The helmet saved my life. I have fractured most of the facial bones on the right side of my head, both front teeth knocked out (again), severest of concussions, hopefully no serious brain damage, in a coma for over a month. My mother was by my bedside for three weeks before having to go home. More medical speak: severe head injury, possible brain damage, dizziness, memory loss, disorientation. I gathered from the explanation that I was lucky to be alive, and all the king's doctors and all the king's nurses were happy to have put Humpty-Dumpty back together again, and it may be some time before I am back to my good old self, if ever.

~ ~ ~

More time passes.

~~~

It has been difficult for me to regain my equilibrium. I notice that things look different. My face is technically the same but somehow different after the surgery. It is hard to tell because I don't remember what I looked like. I've been to the dentist in Hanover, and he's making a bridge for the missing teeth. I'm told I'll leave the hospital sometime this week. Mom is flying east to take me back to Holderness.

~~~

More time, more blackness.

~~~

I'm in the woods. Two bears are chasing me. One is behind me; the other is behind me but off to my left. In my mind's eye, I can see both. They are loping along, not running hard, and keeping up with me. I am running very hard but am going very slow. The bears are gaining on me. The one from the left is now in front of me. I see light filtering down through the trees at the edge of the forest. If only I can make it to the clearing, I know I will be safe. The bears dare not venture out of the woods. I look forward again after a brief look down to confirm my footing. I see the bear in front of me. She is standing in the trail. No way around. Behind me, the other bear is breathing his hot breath on my back. I stop knowing it is time for me to die. The bear in front of me steps forward. She looks at me, tilts her head, and stands on her hind legs. She comes very close to me and whispers, "Everything has changed. Everything has changed. Everything has changed."

Then she goes down on all fours, turns, and disappears into the forest. The bear behind me comes up to my side and says, "I am He, She is She. She is wise. Go into the clearing back to the world, and know your imagination is more important than knowledge. Everything has changed."

~~~

More time. More blackness.

~~~

It is now mid-May, three months since the accident. I've been back at Holderness for a week, although I must admit I don't really remember being here that long. Mr. Hagerman told me it was good to see my mom again while she was here dropping me off. I told him I didn't remember her being here but was glad that he got to see her. He told me to take it one day at a time, I'd get stronger, and my memory would get better. He told me that my body and mind and whole system had had quite a shock.

I am only beginning to feel the magnitude of it.

~ ~ ~

It's finals week. I've taken my math final in Geometry. It was a disaster. I couldn't remember half the stuff I studied. It has completely disappeared. My English final was better, but not much. I had to write an essay about the book we've been reading, comparing it to another book we've been reading, neither of which I can remember at the moment. So now I'm in my French II final. This is a terrible joke. I can recognize most of the French words but am only guessing their meaning. I'm having trouble sorting it all out. It's as if someone has taken all the information in my brain and shaken it up. When it settles back, it settles in random places like autumn leaves falling from a tree. The doctor says it'll get better over time, but that's not helping me in finals week.

~ ~ ~

More time.

Chapter 79

Summer 1963

I'm home in Colorado, working on the trail to Snowmass Lake. There are five of us mending trails for the Forest Service. We're camped two miles below the lake and are on a ten-days-out, four-days-off schedule. Our job is to build water bars, clear downed trees, and open up the trails in the Maroon-Snowmass area.

JC Williams and I have decided we will climb Snowmass Peak, one of the 14ers neither of us has climbed. We set off after work to carry our packs up to the snowfield at the base of the peak where we will leave them, continuing on to the summit with small daypacks. Once taking the summit, we will then descend to the snowfield again, where we will sleep the night, rising early, and walking down to camp a couple miles below in time to begin work at eight.

It's been a beautiful day. The sun is setting behind the ridgeline leading to the summit of Snowmass Mountain, as we break out of the pine forest and climb to the glacial moraine trapping the cold, blue waters of Snowmass Lake. We skirt the lake on the south side and scramble up the scree slope to the base of the snowfield. It's an easy climb. Good rock. Good weather.

As the sun drops lower, the sky begins its post-sunset light show. The witch-tailed clouds turn orange, red, and purple. We climb steadily up, across the snowfield, and onto the upper scree below the ridgeline that will take us to the summit. Once on the ridgeline, we look back to the east for the view of the Bells and Pyramid and to the west for Capitol

Peak. The sun bathes them in purple light it reserves only for those who venture to the heights in the dusk of a clear mountain day. I am walking where I belong, for the first time since my ski accident, along a narrow ridgeline above timberline, to the summit.

I begin to feel faint echoes of myself reverberating inside. They bounce off my innards like hailstones falling from a clear sky. They do not belong. They do belong. My recently acquired protective membrane must molt from my body, melt away so I can once again feel. The unseen trauma from the accident begins burning in me. Burning, burning a stellar explosion of white-hot light exploding outward, burning away the fear, burning away the hurt, burning away the lassitude and stupor that have settled on me in a thick mist since February. The echoes vibrate and become louder, melding with the white-hot light, dancing with it. I sit down to rest a moment while it passes. But it does not pass. I stand and walk to the summit where the light and the echoes and the top of the world come together in one unimaginable collision of feelings, thoughts, senses, knowings, and desires. I look out over the Elk Range to the east, and suddenly, I can see out from the darkness. I can see the bones of the earth.

I walk down from the summit to the snowfield, arriving just at dark, where the light hovers in that space between seeing and not seeing. I unroll my sleeping bag and my ground cloth on the snow and wiggle my way into its mummy-shaped warmth. I look up at the stars in full bloom like blossoms in the spring. I see myself in Ursa Major. I see myself in Hercules and Bootes and Lyra. Vega burns a hole in the blackness just above the western horizon. For the moment I feel alive. For the moment I feel the healing power of the pure mountain air, and the bed of snow upon which I lie, and the brightness of the stars. For a moment... before the darkness settles over me once again.

~~~

I'm in the Quadrant Bookstore. It's a small bookstore Ivan Abrams has opened in town. There is so much to explore, volumes of prose, volumes of poetry, facts and fiction, knowledge and imagination. Ivan and I hit it off the first time we met. He is a short, elfin man with curly, black hair and a ubiquitous pipe sending curlicues of smoke around his smiling visage. He's recommended some books I've found to be rewarding. I wander, looking for a new book.

Ivan sneaks up to my side and says, "Hi, Terry, have you read Dostoyevsky yet?"

"Hi, Ivan," I say. "I read *Brothers Karamazov* this winter in school."

"At the high school here?"

"No, I go to a school in the East now. I thought I mentioned that last fall before I left."

"You may have. Time goes by so fast. What are you looking for?"

"I'm not sure; I'll just browse for a minute, if you don't mind."

My eyes wander the shelves of the little bookstore. It is a comfortable, peaceful environment.

Everyone should live in a bookstore for a few days each week; if they did, it would be a different world.

I keep exploring. Jane Austin, Ernest Hemingway, Kierkegaard, Camus, Nietzsche, Yevtushenko, Dylan Thomas, T.S. Eliot. They're all here, at home on his shelves.

I marvel how a bookstore can hold so many secrets, so many mysteries, so much knowledge in such a small space. I'm in a safe haven for thoughts and ideas to fall on fertile ground and blossom into beautiful manifestations of a mind. It is an extraordinary home for the inquisitive thinker.

I finally settle on a small book of poems by Yevtushenko. I walk over to Ivan and say, "I'll take this."

"Oh, that's a good one," he says. "You'll love his poems. I just got that in."

I know that Ivan has read every book in his bookstore. I hand him the book, and he finds the price. My eyes are wandering. There's a wall to my left where Ivan has posted sayings, coming events in Aspen, business cards, inspirations. I read a scrap of a page, half hidden.

"Imagination is more important than knowledge" – Einstein.

My stomach tumbles. I am dizzy and dislocated. I flash to my current bear dream: I have heard these words before.

I am He, She is She. She is wise. Go into the clearing, back to the world, and know your imagination is more important than knowledge. Everything has changed.

I hear Ivan saying to me, "Terry, are you all right? You look white as a sheet. Is something wrong?"

I collect myself enough to answer him.

"No, I'm fine, I just got dizzy for a minute. It must be coming back up to the altitude."

"You take care of yourself. " He hands me change from the bill I have given him.

"Thanks, Ivan."

Everything has changed.

Chapter 80

Fall 1963

I'm back at Holderness for my senior year. My body has healed from the ski accident, although I am supposed to be careful not to hit my head. The summer passed quickly because I was in *the darkness* much of the time. It seemed as if I was asleep and would wake up to find myself somewhere without knowing why I was there. There was a pervasive feeling of tiredness: deep, unrelenting, bone-wrenching tiredness. Toward the end of the summer I began to feel more alive. The fogs and mists of *the darkness* were lifting, as if blown away by a clear-weather front.

School. *Everything has changed.* I have to work much harder. My memory isn't as good as it was before. It's difficult for me to remember certain kinds of information, like names and facial features, unless I continually repeat them and let them become long-term memory. I'm studying much harder this fall both because of the accident and because last year was a disaster for grades. If I'm going to get into college, my GPA must come up radically. Of course, I do have the accident to thank for my poor marks. Unfortunately, it's doubtful that a college admission office looking at my application, along with four thousand others, will take that into consideration.

I have to expend more effort at just about everything and I'm adjusting to it. I'm not happy about it; however, it's how I must do things in order to return some normalcy to my life.

This year I'm the floor leader in Upper Niles. Full circle. Started in Upper Niles and will matriculate from Upper Niles. I have a single room this year and am glad not to have to deal with a roommate. Mr. Drummy, my English teacher, is the faculty member living in Niles. He's a good teacher and a nice person. He's given me a few outside books to read. At the moment I'm reading *Steppenwolf* by Herman Hesse. I have already read *Siddhartha* and *Magister Ludi*. I enjoy his writing. The extra reading has helped me with my memory, but has detracted from the time I'm spending on some of my other subjects.

I've been going home with Judge Godfrey on weekends. Judge is a nice guy who lives in Concord, New Hampshire. His girlfriend in Concord is Roberta Coughlin. Roberta has a younger sister named Debbie. Whenever we're in Concord, we take them out on a double date. I suppose you could say I'm dating Debbie, because we write back and forth and see each other whenever we can. She's quite attractive and has nice boobs which I don't hesitate to be in touch with whenever possible. It is always nice to have something to look forward to.

Last year the ski team was made up of upper classmen who have all graduated. Dennis Donahue, David Pope, and Skip Bryan are only a few of the great skiers we lost. This year Bill McCollom, Jim McGill, Rat Reed, Tom Allen, and several other hot-shot younger guys will keep our team very strong. Most of the older guys were my friends, and I miss them. This year it is more difficult for me to focus on more than just a few friends, so I hang out with just a few: Judge Godfrey, Dan Redmond, Ron Hall, Jeff Hinman, Bill McCollom, who is probably my best friend, and a handful of others.

Football has ended, and we are doing dry-land training for ski team. I actually did play football, which I probably shouldn't have, but I played defensive end, so all I had to do was to box in the offensive end and block passes. It required very little contact.

Ski Team is more difficult this year. Don Henderson is back from his sabbatical but will be away coaching the US Olympic Team, so Bill Clough is our coach while Don Henderson is with the US Ski Team. I'm hoping to have a good year so I can ski on the Junior National Team and maybe get an edge up on getting into a college with a good ski team.

~~~

I'm walking across campus heading to my room, when I see Ki Clough coming out of Livermore. Mr. Hagerman has retired, and Bill Clough is the acting Headmaster. He and Ki have moved to Livermore. As Ki comes near me she says, "Hi, Terry. I'm wondering if you can babysit Wendy tonight?"

"Sure, I'd love to," I say.

Ki looks at me and sees that I have a substantial rip in the pocket of my pants caused by catching them on a small nail on the windowsill of Bill McCollom's room in Marshall.

~~~

Last night I had gone over to Bill's room during evening study hall to talk and hack around a bit since my homework was mostly done and wholly boring. Bill had a hunting knife that we somehow got into throwing at the molding on the door to his room. Admittedly not smart, but fun. The door was cracked about five or six inches, so we could hear what was going on in the hall. We had been successfully planting the Bowie Beauty in the molding at will, when we heard a ruckus in Jim McGill's room next door. Whatever was going on was loud enough to bring Mr. Backe, the faculty dorm leader, out of his quarters at the end of the hall to quell the noise. With the ruckus next door, Bill and I did not hear him walking down the hall. It was Bill's turn to throw the knife and, just as he released the blade and sent on its way, we heard Mr. Backe say in his best angry voice, "What the hell is going on down here?"

Now you have to understand that Mr. Backe is about six-foot-four and weighs about two-fifty, probably only six or seven percent of that is body fat. I headed for the window. Bill watched in horror as the knife shot through the crack between the door and the door jam, across the hallway, and embedded itself in the door molding of Rick Eberhardt's room. I was head first out the window and on my feet before I heard the thud of the knife hit the wood, then went stealthily on to my room in Upper Niles.

This morning Bill told me there was some confusion surrounding the whole series of events, but apparently Mr. Backe was so intent on the noise from McGill's room, where Jim was in a wrestling match with Rat Reed, that he merely grabbed the knife out of the door molding as he walked by, stuck his head in McCollom's door, and asked, "This belong to you?" He handed the knife to Bill and continued on to Jim's room to reprimand Jim and Rat for wrestling during study hall.

Ripping my pants on a nail on the windowsill was a small price to pay for a clean escape.

~ ~ ~

Ki says, "When you come, bring your pants, and I'll wash and mend them for you. It looks like they need some attention."

"You don't have to do that," I say.

Ki looks at me and says, "I am aware of that. Just bring them along. I've made a fresh batch of chocolate chip cookies."

November 22, 1963

I'm walking from Upper Niles over to Rathburn to see if I can find Jeff Hinman. I'm thinking of hacking around a bit, maybe heading into town. It is about quarter to three and we have a couple of hours to kill before dinner. I'm between Hoit and Rathburn when I see the very person I'm looking for coming out of Rathburn. He is walking toward me in a very disconcerting manner.

As I approach him, Jeff says to me, his voice catching, "Have you heard?"

"No, what's the latest?" I say light-heartedly.

"President Kennedy was just shot in Dallas. They think he's dead."

"Holy shit!" This is all I can say.

I stand on the sidewalk dumfounded. Jeff walks past me and off to who knows where. I'm thinking of JFK. Only a year and a half ago it was the Cuban Missile crisis and then the rumblings and rumors and half-truths of military advisors or green berets in Vietnam. Now this. For what reason? No one will say. Things in the country are changing, I can tell. Life is different than the era of the 1950s when I was growing up on the ranch. I don't understand enough to realize how different it will become. I'm sad that the innocence of my ranch years and growing up in the Roaring Fork Valley seem so far behind me. I'm just barely seventeen years old and had been optimistic about life. Without knowing why, I feel a shift in my inner being. The world seems to be experiencing small, seismic social tremors, which are intensifying each month, each year. Tremors leading to upheavals, deformational movements which will cause current realities to fold back on themselves in great anticlines. Faults rending generations, and societies, and political promises. I can feel this, but I can't explain it. It is bigger than me, bigger than Holderness School, and bigger than life as I know it. As I stand here on the sidewalk between Hoit and Rathburn dormitories in the protected environment of Holderness School, I wonder just how fragile life is. I sound the depths of my naiveté of life in the real world, far from the comfort of the privileged environment I find myself in. I realize I can no longer live in an age of innocence. I feel a great loss.

~~~

I'm at Bill McCollom's house for Thanksgiving. We've had a good time hacking around Woodstock, Vermont, and the surrounding area. Bill has a girl he's been dating named Pam, I think. I'm still not great with names. She has a cute friend named Elizabeth, and we are on our way in Bill's Covair to get some ice cream after having seen a movie. Bill is in the back seat necking with Pam. Elizabeth and I are in the front. We are headed over to South Pomfret. Elizabeth gives me directions. I'm driving pretty fast on the hilly, winding back road but within several percentage points of the speed limit. Close enough. But not for what happens next.

The car travels up over a hill. I look down to the bottom of the hill and lose sight of the road. I see only trees in front of me. In the next instant, I see that the road turns to the left at ninety degrees and over a narrow bridge. The car is travelling much, much too fast. There is no way we will make it around the corner. I brake, hoping the car will not go into a skid and that its wheels will not lock up. But it's too little. It's too late.

Suddenly I'm no longer in the car, perhaps in the car but not in the car. I am above the car looking at myself driving the car. I can see Elizabeth in the seat next to me laughing about something I cannot hear. She is unaware she is about to die unless the car can somehow make it around the corner without hitting the bridge abutment. I'm watching her through the window. Above her. In front of her.

Time is no longer. Seconds may be hours, or they may be centuries. They have no meaning. I'm confused. Why am I here, out of the car, floating in the ethers? My body feels as if it is suspended in space by some invisible cloud, witnessing the scene below me through a gauzy veil, the edges of my vision are soft and insubstantial. When I focus on the car, on her face, my vision has absolute clarity; details more pronounced and my senses more acute. I can feel Elizabeth more as an energy field than as a person. She feels good. Bill and Pam are a pulsing energy bubble behind her. I know we are all going to die if I don't do something. I must do something. DO SOMETHING! By force of will, I make myself look down at the car as it approaches the bridge abutment. By force of will I coax, entreat, DEMAND that the steel missile change course ever so slightly, just a couple of feet, just a handful of inches, just enough. Just enough. Just enough to miss the concrete structure and pass unnoticed and unscathed through the few yards it must travel to the other side and safety.

Yes. But no. I am unable to do anything. I know in that instant that I am no longer. That Elizabeth is no longer. Gone. Car, flesh, concrete have become a mix of elements fused into a sculpture of meaningless inorganic and organic matter overlooking some small stream bubbling along some small road in rural Vermont. Yet, what is this? I am. I think therefore I am? I feel therefore I am? I am here sitting in a car.

I'm here, holding onto the steering wheel. I'm here where we are parked at an ice cream shop perhaps a hundred yards from the bridge. The people who are with me are getting out of the car. I'm shaking in abject terror, my body in micro-convulsions, skin crawling, mind reeling. I'm both mortally afraid and infinitely relieved at the same time. Slowly I get control of my body, my senses, my mind, and memory. I open the door, step out of the car, and walk unsteadily, only slightly behind the others, into the small shop to order an ice cream.

It is Thanksgiving. Silently I do just that.

Winter / Spring 1964

The winter and spring were a blur of college applications, studying hard to maintain my GPA, and hoping for the best when the acceptance and rejection letters arrived, and sports. I took a second in the cross-country and a second in the Nordic combined at the Junior Nationals in Squaw

Valley. The results helped make up for my memory-muddled poor-academic performance last year.

I was accepted at all the schools I applied to—Middlebury, Universities of Colorado, Wyoming, and Montana—with a "free ride" to all of them except Middlebury. I have decided to go to Middlebury even though it means I'll have to continue working hard to pay the tuition and expenses. It's a smaller, more academically challenging school than the others. And the ski team is superb.

I walked away from the graduation ceremonies knowing I really learned only one life-changing thing of real value from Holderness that will serve me for the rest of my life. I learned how to think critically. And if that's all I took away from the three years in a boys' prep school...it is enough.

Chapter 81

Summer 1964

Early this morning, Fred and I drove to the trailhead at Maroon Lake. We decided last week that we would climb Pyramid Peak today and have just begun the initial scramble up the scree slope on the north face of the mountain. Pyramid Peak is one of the seven 14,000-foot peaks in our area. It's time for me to bag another 14er.

It's still dark. The ambient light from the setting half moon and few visible bright stars is sufficient for us to manage the hike up to the first serious rock faces above the scree slope.

The broken shale and sandstone on the scree slope move under our feet as we balance first on this rock and then on another, trying to gain altitude and purchase on the mountain, as the fading darkness gives way to the grayness of a dawn that promises a clear day. By now my steps upward have become a mantra. Focus on the placement of the feet. Breathe in, breathe out. Step, pause, step.

As I climb higher, the larger rocks give way to smaller rubble and talus packed hard by the now-melted winter snows. Easier climbing but somehow more treacherous. We move on to a spot on the mountain that holds deceit. Looks easier, smoother, more inviting. Yet these qualities are fraudulent, enticing. The rock is traitorous, a harlot. We look to our climbing boots for purchase. It is slippery. Dangerously slippery. I scramble from one miniscule outcropping to the next.

We've kept a steady pace since leaving our vehicle at the trailhead already almost two full miles and two-thousand vertical feet below us. I'm reaching the borders of tree line when I step onto one of the remaining tufts of mountain grass. I take stock. The smell of pine is not so redolent as below.

I reach down, pick up a sandstone pebble, and put it in my mouth. I want to taste the earth upon which I am standing. I want to taste it, to own it in a way that will imprint itself on my DNA. The mountain wild. Timberline. Snowline. Lifeline. Touched and tasted through the glacier-ground sediments upon which I stand. Felt through the cool, pure air. Knife slice of wind forming vortices in small couloirs. Seen in the sunrise as a prism of rays radiates up an unseen east face to ignite little light splinters through the tangle of chimneys, and winding them around each small arête. Heard through the gentle whispering of a glacial wind, or the moaning of an afternoon blow that is saying you have been on the mountain too long. Go down. Go down. Go down. Known through the innate connection at the cores of us both, earth and human. It will tell me when and where and why and how if I listen, if I feel, if I know.

I want to know this treeline as surely as I want to know every tree line in my life. When I am passing from one ecosystem to another, from one heady altitude to another. It is something I must know. Soon I will pass onto the world of rock, which holds somewhere in its depths the possibility of organic life; but here, on the tree line, I can have both. The promise and the reality.

I pause once again at the top of the scree slope to take in the dawn drifting up in the east, eat a handful of dried fruit and nuts, take a drink of water, and listen to the gentle breeze whispering around the north-facing cliffs above us. From here we begin the climb on seriously rotten sandstone and shale. Our route takes us up a narrow ridgeline to a small saddle only ten feet wide that looks three-hundred feet down into the glacial pan of the north face.

We make our way slowly and very carefully up to the saddle. I look into the abyss below, and then at the nearly vertical section of rock I must climb to hit the ridgeline that gives way to the continuing route and the summit. I pause only for enough time to take a breath or two, look at my first two or three moves, and feel the adrenaline beginning to course through me. I can do this. First zig to the left. Now I have full exposure. Nothing between me and the rocks three-hundred feet below. It is only a twenty- or thirty-foot scramble, but a dangerous one. Focus. Control the adrenaline rush. Don't look down.

Three points of contact on the rock. Always. Free-climb up. Now zag to the right. Three, no four steps. Now if there is a fall, it will be broken at fifteen or twenty feet instead of three hundred. Heart rate slows. Up three or four more steps onto and over the ridgeline that takes me into the west bowl of the upper mountain. Fred follows. The worst section is now history. I feel my adrenaline ebb.

We take another short break before traversing a large amphitheater at an upward angle, to the final chimney that spits us out onto the summit. As I look up at this part of the ascent, I see that there are some spines and outcroppings to be negotiated on the route to the top. These have minimal exposure because they are close to the base of the amphitheater. Still, they will need careful attention.

We move on. Skirting the amphitheater proves to be a minor challenge nonetheless. A few minutes later, I find myself at the bottom of the crack that will take me to the summit, a jagged wound. I see that it could separate the peak into two massive earth slides, toppling the whole mountain to the valley below in one tremendous explosion of stone, silt, and rising grey dust.

I scramble up the crack and find myself standing on the top of the world. I look west at the red layers of sandstone dipping gently to the north and forming the Maroon Bells against the blue, cloudless sky. To the east rises the snow-capped Sawatch Range. I see the bones of Mother Earth. I see the layers of Her skin in each formation of sandstone in the ridgelines and peaks that surround me. I sense the age, the indefinable eons of time She has lived without Man walking on her surface despoiling, raping, and exploiting her. I am pleased She will be here long after my species has become a fossiliferous memory. Even the seemingly inert sediments upon which I stand energize me. We take our sustenance from the symbiotic relationship we have with Mother Earth in indefinable ways. There is no need for definition. There is a need for awareness, for sensing. Standing here on the top of this peak, I can feel Her energy coursing through my body, and I am thankful.

I know in my heart that the mountains are my heart song.

65794315R00275

Made in the USA
Charleston, SC
04 January 2017